... OF HOUSING

... gree in Philosophy, Politics,
and Economics at Oxford University in 1950, then
taught at the Universities of Manchester and Toronto
until he went to the London School of Economics in
1956. He has been Professor of Social Administration
there since 1961.

Professor Donnison's interest in housing led him
into membership of the Central Housing Advisory
Committee, and the Milner Holland Committee which
reported on London's housing problems in 1965. He is
also a Vice-President of the London Rent Assessment
Committee. He recently worked as a consultant for the
U.N. Economic Commission for Europe, making a
study of housing policies in European countries. His
other particular interest is in education, and he is a
member of the Central Advisory Council for Education
and Vice-Chairman of the Public Schools Commission.

Professor Donnison lives in London with his wife and
four children.

D. V. DONNISON

THE GOVERNMENT OF HOUSING

PENGUIN BOOKS

Penguin Books Ltd, Harmondsworth, Middlesex, England
Penguin Books Inc., 3300 Clipper Mill Road, Baltimore, Md 21211, U.S.A.
Penguin Books Australia Ltd, Ringwood, Victoria, Australia

—

First published 1967

—

Copyright © D. V. Donnison, 1967

—

Made and printed in Great Britain
by Cox & Wyman Ltd,
London, Reading and Fakenham
Set in Monotype Imprint

HD 7287.5 D6
719703
UC

CONTENTS

LIST OF TABLES AND FIGURES

TABLES

European Countries

England, Britain or United Kingdom

FIGURES

ACKNOWLEDGEMENTS

SINCE a study of housing policy must range over so extensive a field, the author of a book on this subject is compelled to draw on the help of his friends and colleagues, and apply or reject their advice in ways of his own choosing. This book could not have been written without constant discussion and professional collaboration proceeding over the years in several overlapping circles to which the author has been privileged to belong. These groupings should be briefly explained because they illustrate the diverse contributions that must be combined and brought to bear in every field of social policy. To restrict the list to manageable proportions, the individuals mentioned are those who have given the author detailed comments upon one or more chapters of this book, but many others have helped him.

Staff of four universities have worked on a succession of inquiries, known collectively as the Rowntree Trust Housing Study. Among those who particularly helped with this book are Barry Cullingworth, John Greve and Miss A. A. Nevitt. They and the author have throughout had the help of an advisory committee, under the chairmanship of Professor R. M. Titmuss. Among its members, Sir John Wrigley gave special attention to this book. Drafts were discussed with other academic colleagues – particularly Dr Peter Hall, Dr Ian Byatt and Professor John Griffith of the London School of Economics and Political Science, Professor Duccio Turin of University College, London, and Mrs Ruth Glass, Director of that College's Centre for Urban Studies.

A major contribution to the book was made by those with whom the author collaborated in the course of a study carried out for the United Nations Economic Commission for Europe* – particularly by Professor Adam Andzrejewski and Professor Wanda Litterer-Marwege (of the University of Warsaw) and Dr Jiří Musil (of the Research Institute of Building and

* United Nations Economic Commission for Europe, *Major Long-term Problems of Government Housing and Related Policies*, New York 1966. (Referred to subsequently as U.N. 'Major Problems' Study.)

Architecture, Prague). That study would never have been completed without the constant support and help of Dr B. F. Reiner and his colleagues on the staff of the E.C.E. in Geneva.

Meanwhile the author's participation in studies of various kinds sponsored by government (including particularly the work of the Central Housing Advisory Committee, and the Milner Holland Committee on Housing in Greater London) gave repeated opportunities of seeking the help of officials, particularly in the Ministry of Housing and Local Government, and the Building Research Station. Mr Roger Walters (of the Ministry of Public Building and Works) and Mr Louis Moss (Director of the Social Survey) also gave valuable advice.

During the closing stages of the study Miss Clare Ungerson, the author's research assistant, checked, revised, and added many points in this book, and helped with proof reading and the preparation of an index. Miss Jean Charman did the bulk of the typing and gave general secretarial help.

The whole series of studies, of which this forms one of the closing products, would never have been initiated or carried through without the support of the Joseph Rowntree Memorial Trust and the constant advice and encouragement of its Director, Mr Lewis Waddilove. The comment made upon the Trust in Professor David Owen's monumental survey of English Philanthropy does no more than justice to this remarkable body.

Among all of the assorted institutions and organizations that go to make up the British charitable world, none has shown a livelier awareness of 'the new occasions' which 'teach new duties', or a more imaginative understanding of the uses of private philanthropy in semi-collectivist Britain.*

D.V.D.
London School of Economics and
Political Science. February 1966.

*English Philanthropy, 1660–1960, p. 453. Harvard University Press, 1964.

INTRODUCTION

HOUSE and home stand at the centre of people's lives, providing a shelter for sleep and for half their waking activities, a shield against the elements and the world – which yet admits both in controlled and selective fashion – and a storage place and show-case for most of their possessions. To study 'housing' is to explore a cross section of a whole society and its affairs. To study 'housing policy' is to examine, from a particular standpoint, the functions, capacities and responsibilities of government, and its relations with the governed. And to study these things in Britain today is to study the social, economic and political changes now at work in this country, the impact these changes are making upon the housing situation, and the repercussions that changes in housing conditions and housing aspirations have upon our economy, our way of life and our government. This country is once more at a critical stage of its political evolution – a potential turning point that may have profound effects upon the role and character of government. Housing policies are playing a central part in this story, and there has never been a more interesting or perplexing point at which to study them.

No one can claim to be expert in all the branches of knowledge that must contribute to such a study – knowledge about the processes of economic and social change, the management of the economy, the planning of investment, the layout of cities and neighbourhoods, the design of houses, the technology and resources of the building industry, and the administrative tradi-tions and structure of the central and local authorities respon-sible for formulating housing policies and putting them into practice. Moreover the making of policy in so central a sphere of the nation's development calls for political judgement and decision, a sense of history and a vision of the future – qualities that cannot be derived even from a library of books. Therefore there can be no compendium of knowledge in this field, and this book cannot take the place of more intensive studies of the problems it touches on. Neither can there be any comprehensive and conclusive prescription for housing policies, and those advocated here claim no authority beyond that which well-informed and critical readers are prepared to grant them. But this book may offer an introduction to the problems of housing policy and to some of the more specialized studies which throw light upon them; it may clarify the alternatives open to those responsible for resolving these problems and provide some understanding of the scope and limits of their endeavours; and it may help to explain the character of the whole enterprise in which policy-makers are engaged and suggest directions in which this enterprise should lead.

Authors seeking to convey an understanding of the policies of government adopt a variety of approaches to their task. The history of their chosen field often furnishes their point of departure, but this approach too readily presents existing ways of doing things as a culmination of past progress rather than a preparation for a different future. Alternatively, the task may be approached through the methods and concepts of a particular discipline – by studying the economics of the subject, for example, or the administrative structure and legal powers of the authorities concerned. But although each discipline is commendably rigorous in analysing the problems it was created to deal with, the price of this efficiency is a tendency to resort to simplified and lazy-minded assumptions when confronted with problems which fall outside that territory. This book therefore adopts another approach, which likewise has its characteristic drawbacks.

Part One discusses the sphere and scope of housing policy. If a government says its country has housing problems, then of what do these 'problems' consist? Are they perceived mainly as a scarcity of dwellings and building capacity, or as a difficulty in determining the levels of rents, loan charges and other housing payments, or as a question of social justice, or as some combination of these and other problems? If a government claims to have a housing policy, then what is this 'policy' about? Is it a policy for stimulating or for controlling house building, for increasing the quantity or for altering the distribution of housing, for promoting economic growth or for counteracting its ill-effects, or for some potentially conflicting combination of these and other objectives? What determines the character and interpretation of housing problems and policies, and the priorities accorded to them? These questions are explored in four chapters dealing with the nature of housing problems, the scope for solutions, and the roles adopted by governments in western and eastern Europe.

The danger of this approach lies in the inevitable superficiality of any international comparison that is not rooted in a thorough understanding of the differing social, economic and political systems concerned. For that, a separate and lengthy study would be required for each country. This book does not provide a comprehensive account of the different 'housing systems' to be seen in Europe; it only offers an essay on the role of government in one field, illustrated and documented from the experience of countries with differing traditions and cultures and at differing stages of economic and social development. Its purpose is to clarify the principal questions and decisions calling for more sustained examination within each country. Despite its drawbacks, this approach may prove fruitful – particularly in an insular society accustomed to regard the experience of other countries as irrelevant to its own needs.

Those whose interest is confined to this country and to the practical and more urgent aspects of the subject may prefer to start with Part Two of the book which deals with the case of the United Kingdom – though the vagaries of the data available often restrict its coverage to Britain, to England and Wales, or to England alone. Part Two begins, in Chapter 5, with an account of our housing situation and the housing responsibilities assumed by our government, identifying the distinctive features of this system and the problems it poses, and briefly tracing the main phases of its development since the Second World War. This chapter links the two parts of the book, summarizing for this country the main conclusions of the European survey, and outlining the approach to housing policy adopted by our own government. The next chapter examines the various housing 'markets' operating in this country, showing the types of people served by each and the needs these markets meet and fail to meet. This should make it clear that some of the problems to be discussed are unlikely to be resolved by the existing system or by government action conducted through the local housing

authorities – the instruments traditionally identified with housing policy. Attention must be given to the distribution and redistribution of incomes and housing costs and the flow of
investment into different sectors of the market, to the resources
and productivity of the construction industry and the management and allocation of new building, improvement and replacement, and to the complex processes linking the growth of
population, employment, earnings and households, and the
problems of regional and local planning posed by these processes.
Chapters 7, 8 and 9 deal briefly with these questions. The
questions themselves are so intertwined that they reappear in
different guise in different chapters. These chapters should be
read together: their common theme is the analysis of the present
situation – the existing stock of housing and the manner in
which households are distributed within it – followed by an
examination of the changes working upon this situation. This
approach may correct the tendency, too common in discussions
of housing policy, to become mesmerized by new building, new
towns and new administrative and technical devices – the new
frontier of development which only affects a tiny fraction of the
population at a given point in time.

The next two chapters differ from the previous ones. Chapter
10 presents a brief but comprehensive account of London's
housing problems; it amounts to a case study, showing how the
developments examined in previous chapters impinge upon one
area, and gives warning of stresses and hardships that may become more widespread if present trends are allowed to continue.
Chapter 11 deals with the research and information services
required by government. It is not an appeal for more research –
if a book based largely on past research cannot demonstrate the
value of doing more, such exhortation is pointless – but a
discussion of the contribution that various forms of inquiry can
make to policy, practice and innovation in this field, suggesting
steps which should be taken to make that contribution more
effective.

The whole book is itself a case study of the functions and
responsibilities of government and the manner in which these
evolve, posing many of the questions that would have to be
considered in a similar study of health services, education,

pensions, or any other field of social policy. How and why are the government's responsibilities being extended? How can the validity or 'rightness' of its policies be tested? How are these policies likely to evolve in future, and what scope for choice and change will they permit? What are their implications for policies in other fields? These are among the questions considered in a more speculative concluding chapter which draws again on the experience of other countries.

PART ONE

THE POLITICAL ECONOMY
OF HOUSING

CHAPTER I

THE HOUSING PROBLEM

THE struggle to find a home and the desire for the shelter, privacy, comfort and independence that a house can provide are familiar the world over. William Cobbett caught the essentials of our needs 140 years ago, commenting upon a preacher who was telling his flock that those among them who were 'saved' would be awarded houses in the heavens.

Some girls whom I saw in the room, plump and rosy as could be, did not seem at all daunted by these menaces; and indeed, they appeared to me to be thinking much more about getting houses for themselves *in this world first*; . . . houses with pig-styes and little snug gardens attached to them, together with all the other domestic and conjugal circumstances, these girls seemed to me to be preparing themselves for.*

The squalor, degradation and anxiety which people suffer when these needs are frustrated are likewise part of the common currency of human experience, transcending time and place. The hero of a recent novel from Russia works in the Moscow housing administration:

Every day we were besieged by thousands of people. They wanted only one thing – the chance to live in human conditions. . . . A family of five usually had seven or eight square metres of living space; they could claim twenty, but for this they had to keep on calling at our office for eight or ten years, begging, imploring, cursing, throwing fainting fits, going into hysterics . . . Some of them, mostly women, came every day as if to work. Their living conditions were horrible beyond description, and our clients described them with the zest of beggars showing off their sores.†

The tones and colours of the picture may be distinctive, but the

*William Cobbett, *Rural Rides*, p. 227. J. M. Dent. Everyman Edition, Volume 1.

†Ivan Valeriy, *The Bluebottle*, pp. 88–100. Trans. David Alger, Collins & Harvill, 1962.

needs and emotions it portrays will be equally familiar in London, New York or Tokyo. William Cobbett and his predecessors, though they might have been bewildered by the demands we make for education, transport, entertainment and many other things, would have had no difficulty in understanding these needs.

Thus there is no mystery about the *symptoms* of housing problems. Indeed, it is the very familiarity of these problems – their 'obviousness' – which constitutes the first obstacle to be surmounted by those trying to grapple with them. Public concern may be so concentrated upon the most immediate and urgent hardships that scant attention can be spared for their causes. Or the contemplation of hardships for which there appears to be no ready solution may encourage people to turn away from them in despair, to assert that nothing *can* be done about them, or to solace themselves with the thought that the victims of housing shortage accept or even deserve their lot. (The belief that many people prefer to put coals in the bath has been succeeded by another, equally unverified, that many prefer television sets to decent housing.) Thus before embarking on a discussion of housing needs and the means for meeting them we must penetrate beyond the symptoms of stress to identify and disentangle the principal elements to be considered in any analysis of the housing problem and clarify the nature and meaning of this problem.

The changing character of the problem must be constantly borne in mind, for the housing situation and the criteria by which it is judged are continuously developing. The stock of housing does not change fast. Britain, like most industrialized countries, normally adds about 2 per cent to its stock of housing in a year; thus most of our houses are many years old, a product of the expectations and capacities of our ancestors. But the size and geographical distribution of the population, our style and standard of life and the kind of housing people want, change more quickly. So do the functions of government and the part that people expect their government to play in resolving housing problems. The continually evolving character of this situation is too easily forgotten.

When looking ahead, people naturally fix their eyes on finite goals not too far beyond their reach, for to look further would invite despair; it is only as these goals are approached that more ambitious targets are substituted for them. The job of clearing the slums, for example, has always been presented as a once-for-all task.

In the opinion of the Minister, to make sure that the evil should be remedied, it is necessary to fix a limited time for the work, and to prepare a time-table for its progress and completion within the time limited. The time-table must, of course, be based upon a complete appreciation of the whole problem in the area concerned ... The programme should, so far as practicable, be drawn up on the basis of clearing all areas that require clearance not later than 1938.

This kind of statement, drawn from a Ministry of Health circular of 1933, has been repeated many times since – in a 1961 White Paper, for example: '*Slum Clearance*. This has been a priority task of housing authorities since 1955, and will remain so until it is complete. With the exception of a few areas, unfit houses should have practically disappeared within the next ten years ...' Four years later, and long before the task was complete, a new Minister invited his Central Housing Advisory Committee to reappraise present procedures and criteria for determining the 'fitness' of housing for human habitation, and to propose new standards for the future.

Thus any analysis of housing problems is a study of a nation's attempt to adapt its inheritance to new needs and to add to this inheritance in ways that accord with a changing economic and social structure and rising human aspirations. It is not a study of one branch of the economy or of the elimination of a particular social problem or of the implementation of specific government programmes, but a chapter in the continuing story of social change. Housing targets, programmes and policies are always provisional and always superseded before long. The more determined a nation is to resolve its problems, the faster will be the tempo of social change and the sooner will new aspirations take the place of the old.

The principal elements that must be explored and related to each other in the course of appraising a country's housing problems will emerge from the answers to four questions, each of which calls for the prediction of complex social changes. During the next decade or two: (1) How many people must be housed? (2) How many separate households will they form? (3) How many houses will these households require? (4) How much building must be done? Many of the steps in this analysis must be based on guesswork, but they are worth spelling out in some detail because the importance of each element to be considered, and hence the character of the country's housing problem, varies from time to time and from one country to another – and even to identify the extent and implications of our ignorance may be helpful. Regional and local problems arising within this national context can be considered later.

HOW MANY PEOPLE?

The first steps towards finding the number of people to be housed are to estimate the size of the population, and its rate of natural increase – that is, the surplus (for deficits are very rare) of births over deaths during the period in question. Provided wars and other cataclysms are avoided, demographers can furnish reasonably accurate predictions of future death rates, for normal mortality depends heavily on living conditions experienced throughout the lifetime of the population concerned and past experience cannot be changed. Birth rates are much harder to predict because they depend on future conditions – not least on future housing conditions – and because too little is known about the factors determining the size and growth of families. The estimates of future births made by the Registrar General for England and Wales in his annual reports have been revised upwards year by year over the past decade, and the total number of live births now expected in the United Kingdom during the year 2000 (1,527,000) is 50 per cent greater than the numbers actually born in 1964 (1,012,000).* This forecast is likely to be as unreliable as its predecessors. Since very few people set up home on their own before the age of twenty these uncertainties do not seriously affect the numbers of households to be catered for during the next twenty years, but they do

* Central Statistical Office, 'Projecting the Population of the United Kingdom', *Economic Trends*, No. 139. H.M.S.O. May 1965.

affect the size of these households and the kind of houses they will want. The annual rate of natural increase in the United Kingdom (now running at about seven per thousand) has for a decade been one of the lowest in western Europe and only half the rates experienced in Holland, the U.S.S.R., and the U.S.A., which have in turn been surpassed by those of most Asian, African and South American countries. Thus although the errors likely to arise from such calculations may be appreciable, they are unlikely in this country to prove disastrous.

Migration between countries is the remaining element to be considered when predicting the numbers of people to be housed. This, too, can present serious difficulties for the forecaster. In Western Germany, for example, the surplus of immigrants over emigrants between 1952 and 1959 was as large as the natural increase in population, while in Italy the net losses from migration between 1951 and 1958 were equivalent to 42 per cent of the country's natural increase and more than twice the figure forecast at the beginning of this period. Austria and Portugal lost approximately the same proportions of their natural increase, and net emigration from Ireland was equivalent to about 150 per cent of natural increase.* Amongst the younger workers and parents who provide the bulk of these migrants the proportionate effects of these population movements are much greater, presenting serious difficulties for any attempt to forecast the rates at which new households will form.

These trends can be quickly altered by political changes such as those that led to the building of the Berlin wall, and by economic changes such as the growth of industry in Northern Italy – which, if continued at its recent rate, will draw in as many workers as those previously lost to other countries from Southern Italy. Moreover such trends cannot be forecast in isolation from each other: as West German industry is deprived of recruits from East Germany and Italy – its principal sources hitherto – growing numbers of Greeks, Turks and North Africans are being drawn in to replace them. But the only appreciable change in the United Kingdom's migration pattern – usually producing a steady but small net loss – appears to have been largely

*Organization for European Economic Cooperation, *Demographic Trends*, 1956–1976 *in Western Europe and the United States*, Paris, 1961.

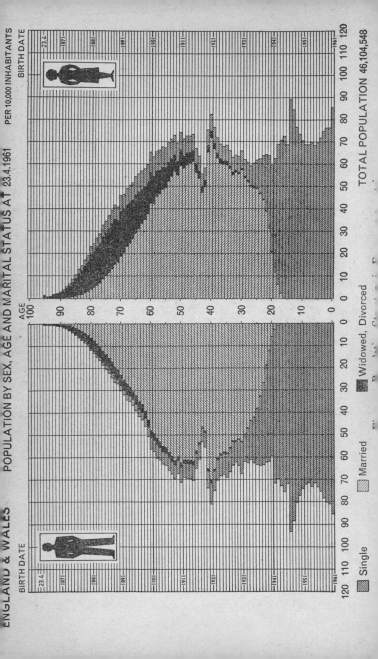

ENGLAND & WALES   POPULATION BY SEX, AGE AND MARITAL STATUS AT 23.4.1961   PER 10,000 INHABITANTS

BIRTH DATE   BIRTH DATE

TOTAL POPULATION 46,104,548

AGE

Single   Married   Widowed, Divorced

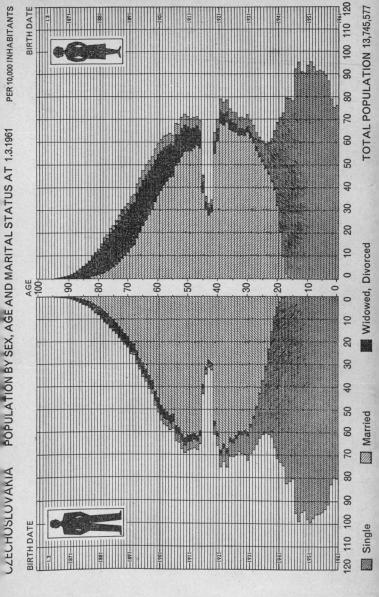

CZECHOSLOVAKIA   POPULATION BY SEX, AGE AND MARITAL STATUS AT 1.3.1961   PER 10,000 INHABITANTS

BIRTH DATE

BIRTH DATE

AGE

TOTAL POPULATION 13,745,577

■ Single   ▨ Married   ■ Widowed, Divorced

FRANCE ▶ POPULATION BY SEX, AGE AND MARITAL STATUS AT 1.1.1962 PER 10,000 INHABITANTS

BIRTH DATE

AGE

TOTAL POPULATION 46,422,000

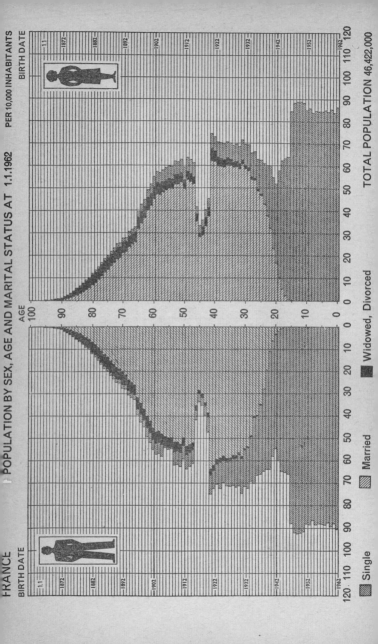

■ Single   ▨ Married   ■ Widowed, Divorced

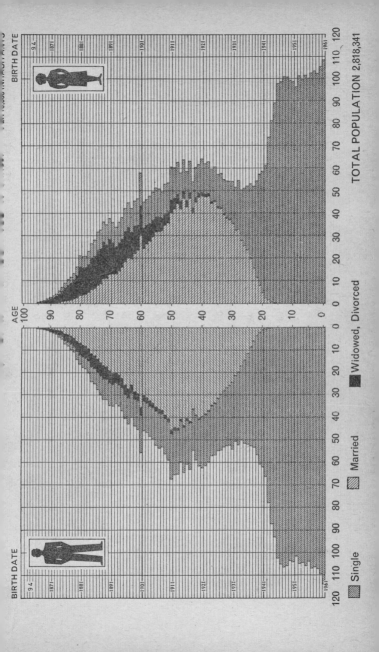

BIRTH DATE

TOTAL POPULATION 2,818,341

AGE

Single   Married   Widowed, Divorced

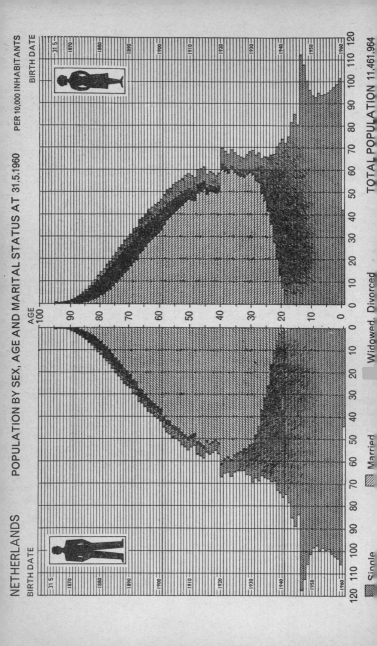

NETHERLANDS   POPULATION BY SEX, AGE AND MARITAL STATUS AT 31.5.1960   PER 10,000 INHABITANTS

BIRTH DATE

BIRTH DATE

AGE 100

TOTAL POPULATION 11,461,964

Single   Married   Widowed, Divorced

PORTUGAL   POPULATION BY SEX, AGE AND MARITAL STATUS AT 15.12.1960   PER 10,000 INHABITANTS

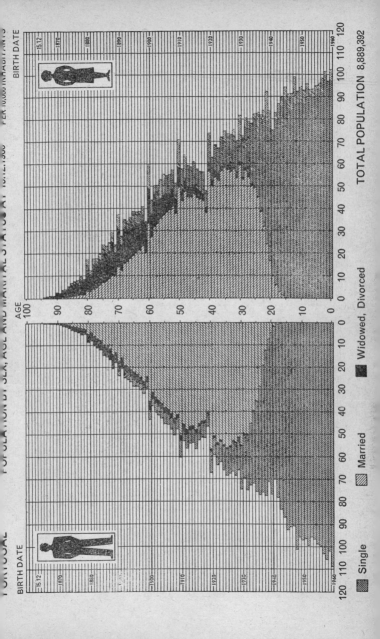

BIRTH DATE

AGE

TOTAL POPULATION 8,889,392

■ Single   ▨ Married   ■ Widowed, Divorced

SWEDEN — POPULATION BY SEX, AGE AND MARITAL STATUS AT 1.11.1960 — PER 10,000 INHABITANTS

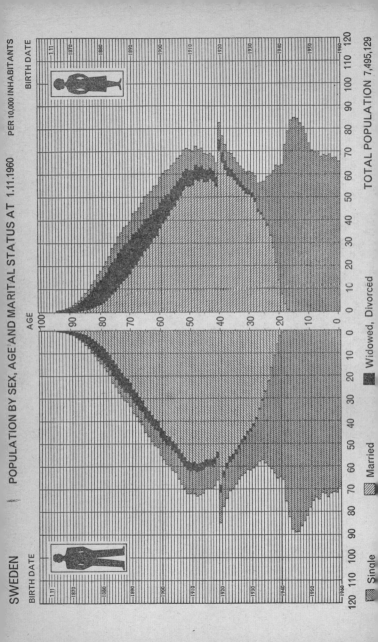

Single · Married · Widowed, Divorced

TOTAL POPULATION 7,495,129

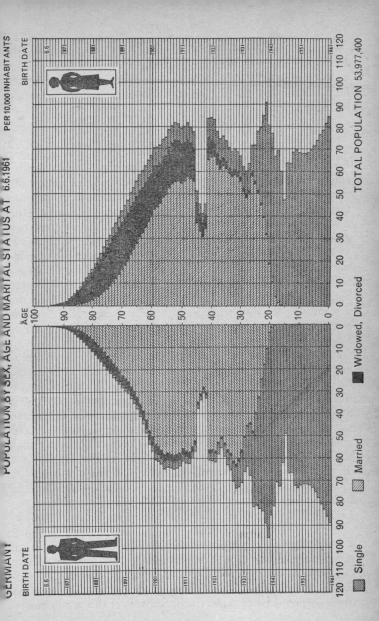

TOTAL POPULATION 53,977,400

BIRTH DATE

AGE

BIRTH DATE

▨ Single   ▩ Married   ▪ Widowed, Divorced

provoked and then firmly eliminated by the Commonwealth Immigrants Act of 1962, and for the next few years this element in the sum is unlikely to present serious difficulties in national forecasts for this country (though it may present more serious local problems).

HOW MANY HOUSEHOLDS?

Estimates of the numbers of people to be housed must next be converted into estimates of the numbers and types of households they will form. The first step in this process is to prepare forecasts of the 'structure' of the population, showing the numbers of men and women, the numbers in different age groups, and the numbers of each who are single, married, widowed or divorced. A good deal is known about the proportions of people in each of these groups who form separate households, and these proportions have remained fairly stable over long periods since they reflect fundamental social patterns determining the opportunities and family responsibilities that people have at different stages of their lives. But the quantity of housing available and the manner in which it is distributed go far to shape these patterns, and houses built to meet demographic requirements may create new and unforeseen demands.

Although changes in marriage rates and birth rates cannot be predicted with certainty, the principal demographic tendencies in western Europe – for more people to get married, for people to marry younger and have their children sooner, and for more people to survive to old age – have not altered radically in recent years and reasoned forecasts can be made, at least for the next decade. In industrial, urban societies such as our own, the great majority of married men have separate households, the widowed and divorced are more likely to form separate households than the single; single women are somewhat more likely to establish their own households than are single men, and in all these groups older people – other than the very oldest – are more likely to be heads of households than the young. These observations can be quantified and compared with the aid of a simple statistic known as a 'headship rate' which shows, often in the form of a percentage, the proportion of the population or of any group within it who are heads of households. If assumptions can be made about future headship rates, these assumptions provide a convenient means of showing the implications of changes in the structure of the population, provided it is remembered that such figures are no more than a statistical device – there is nothing unchangeable or magical about them.

In most European countries – and Britain is no exception – the proportions of older people and of married people are increasing. Since both these groups tend to have relatively high headship rates, these demographic changes mean that the population would divide into more households even if there were no increase in its total numbers. But that trend may be partly offset by others. In France, for example, the growth in the proportion of married people has arisen not only from the growing popularity of marriage but also from the fall in the numbers of widows, as the generation bereaved during the First World War begins to pass out of the population. Since more than half the widows in the higher age groups are heads of households, their replacement by married men and women (only half of whom can be heads, if they are living together) reduces the numbers of households among the older age groups. In Sweden the growth in the married proportion of the population is thought to have accounted for 27 per cent of the increase in households between 1945 and 1960,* but headship rates among younger single people are now rising so high that further increases in the married proportion of the population may begin to work the other way, reducing the numbers of households in the younger age groups.

Between the censuses of 1931 and 1951, the population of England and Wales increased by 9·5 per cent while the number of households increased by 28·2 per cent – three times as fast. The headship rates for 1931 are not known because heads of households were not distinguished in the census, but an examination of the country's demographic structure at these two dates shows that nearly all the increase in households could have been brought about by changes in this structure, without people of any given sex, age and marital status having a better

*U.N. Economic Commission for Europe, *Studies of Effective Demand for Housing*, Geneva, 1963.

opportunity of forming separate households than was available to similar people twenty years earlier.* The demographic development of this country will be examined in greater detail in a later chapter; our purpose here is only to show why the evolution of demographic structure is an important element among the social changes which may contribute to the housing problem.

In some countries headship rates appear to have continued unaltered over long periods of time. This happened in the United States between 1890 and 1950 for nine age groups in which small changes in the rates could probably be accounted for by changes in the proportion of people who were married. But such stability – though sustained through sixty years in which standards of living changed beyond recognition – cannot be relied upon to continue. Indeed it arises partly from features of the housing market which government is perfectly capable of altering. Coupled with economic and social changes, a more plentiful stock of houses and new procedures for allocating them are now raising the headship rates in many European countries. In Holland the number of households increased by 8·9 per cent between the censuses of 1956 and 1960; of this increase, 5·4 per cent could be accounted for by changes in the size of the population, 1·3 per cent by changes in demographic structure (mainly increases in the proportions of older people and married people) and 2·2 per cent by increased headship rates (appearing in all groups, but showing the greatest proportionate changes among single women and the divorced).† Thus a quarter of the increase in households during these four years was devoted to raising the headship rates – devoted, that is, to providing greater opportunities for people to secure privacy and independence by setting up home on their own.

Similar changes have been occurring in Sweden where the movement of people coming to the towns from the countryside has encouraged the break-up of large three-generation households into smaller units of one and two generations. There, in 1960, the proportion of young married men (aged twenty to twenty-four) who were heads of households was only 9 per cent

*See J. B. Cullingworth, *Housing Needs and Planning Policy*, Chapter 2. Routledge & Kegan Paul, 1960.

† U.N. 'Major Problems' Study, Volume 1, p. 36.

in rural districts but over 20 per cent in the towns. Among the age group ten years older (between thirty and thirty-four) more people had established separate households, but the urban advantage remained; less than 60 per cent of those in rural districts were heads, while nearly 80 per cent of those in urban areas were heads.* If all married couples want a home of their own or if those in the country want the same independence and privacy as those in the towns, then Swedish headship rates can be expected to rise a great deal further – and this has in fact been happening. In Britain too, the number of households has in recent years begun increasing a good deal faster than changes in the size and structure of the population can account for, and variations in headship rates between one area and another suggest there is plenty of scope for further growth.

But an estimate of the number of households to be sheltered does not show the number of houses that will be required, and it is to this next stage of the analysis that we must now turn.

HOW MANY HOUSES?

Estimates of the numbers of people to be housed and the numbers of households they will form are derived from assumptions about social change expressed in demographic statistics. However hedged about with qualifications and uncertainties, these forecasts are based on precisely defined concepts and well tried statistical techniques. But the next moves in the analysis are more complicated and far less rigorous. Once the present number of houses is known, forecasts of three types of change are needed before future requirements can be predicted: changes in the number of shared houses, changes in the number of households occupying two or more houses, and changes in the number of empty houses.

Even if reliable forecasts could be made, none of these concepts has a clear or unique meaning. Houses, or 'dwellings', are readily definable when most families consist of married couples, living, with their dependant children, in blocks of purpose-built flats or in suburbs where each household owns or rents its own home, and no one shares, subdivides or sublets his

*U.N. 'Major Problems' Study.

accommodation. But where the typical family includes several generations, with uncles, cousins and grandparents living in associated but semi-independent sets of rooms, or where large houses have been subdivided with varying efficiency, and let and sublet in rooms, floors and 'flatlets', it becomes very difficult to interpret the census definition of a 'dwelling' in a consistent and meaningful fashion. The brief definition given in our own census – 'a building or part of a building which provides structurally separate living quarters' – is amplified by a further five hundred words, dealing with difficult cases, which are laced with phrases such as 'generally if . . .', 'normally there would be . . .', 'usually counted as . . .', and so on.

If dwellings and households are hard to define and vary greatly in character, then the 'sharing' of dwellings is bound to mean many different things. Spacious, well-equipped and well-managed houses may be used to accommodate single people who have rooms of their own while sharing lavatories, bathrooms or kitchens – students and other young people, perhaps, who value the social contacts and low costs of this housing, and have no wish to buy or rent self-contained accommodation. Or cramped, ill-equipped, ill-managed and decaying houses may be crowded with large families who fight a running battle for living space and survival against neighbours, landlords and the public health authorities. Both situations constitute 'shared housing', but their implications are very different. Likewise a family may use two houses, having besides their normal home a holiday cottage in the highlands which would otherwise be abandoned, or a room in the city which enables the breadwinner to work in town and travel twice a week instead of commuting for two or three hours every day. Or an unemployed man in Londonderry may be compelled to leave his family there and take a room in London, where he can find work but cannot afford to rent a house. He, too, is occupying two dwellings. Once again the statistics – if there were any* – would look the same, but the situation they would represent may be voluntary or involuntary, constructive or destructive. A proportion of empty houses is required to permit movement, and the conversion and improvement of older property. But the statistics of

* No information on this important question is available for Britain.

vacant dwellings have a different meaning if growing numbers
of houses are left empty, prior to abandonment or demolition,
because they are not needed in the places where they stand, or if
city houses are left empty by owners who deliberately encourage
decay to prise people out of neighbouring property in the hope
of a profitable sale.

Those attempting to measure and forecast these changes must
employ some of the least reliable concepts in the social statisticians' armoury: the definitions of a 'dwelling', of a 'household'
and of 'occupied' and 'vacant' accommodation all defy
precision. Thus it is difficult to forecast changes of this kind or
to be sure of the implications of those known to have occurred.
In Britain, however, there are relatively few shared, 'secondary'
or empty houses, except in particular districts, and *changes* in
these numbers will be smaller still. Thus although such changes
can make a big impact in some neighbourhoods – in parts of
central London or in the highlands of Scotland, for example –
they are not too serious a hazard for the forecaster concerned
with the country as a whole.

HOW MUCH BUILDING?

When estimates of housing requirements have been made, much
further work has still to be done in order to arrive at a forecast
of the building actually needed. Some allowance must be made
for the replacement of houses demolished in officially sponsored
schemes of slum clearance, road widening, school building and
general improvement. Demolitions brought about by private
redevelopment and commercial building operations, the amalgamation of separate dwellings brought about by conversion
and modernization (or simply by householders who decide not
to relet previously sublet and self-contained parts of their
homes), and the abandonment of housing that is left empty or
converted to warehouses, barns, offices and other uses – all
these processes are harder to record or forecast with accuracy.
These losses may be offset by the subdivision of larger dwellings
into several smaller units, and in areas with many large old
houses such conversions often outweigh losses from other
causes, producing a net increase in dwellings.

Allowances must be made for all these factors – and also for errors and omissions in official reports dealing with such statistically intractable data – before any estimate of building requirements can be attempted. Calculations made for England and Wales by the Ministry of Housing and Local Government show a net loss of about 9,600 dwellings a year between 1961 and 1964, arising from all causes other than new building, slum clearance and the demolition of temporary houses and former service camps. The principal features of these changes were a net gain from conversions (7,400 a year, nearly half of which occurred in the London and South Eastern regions) offset by heavier losses due to road widening, commercial building, the provision of new schools, open spaces and other developments (11,500 a year, half of which occurred in London and the Midlands). This net loss of some 10,000 dwellings a year is very small. It amounts to only 4 per cent of the increase achieved during the same four years through the combined effects of new building and slum clearance.

In some places unplanned or 'spontaneous' gains and losses assume much larger proportions than they do in this country. In France, for example, 2 million new houses were built between the censuses of 1954 and 1962, and 160,000 were demolished in officially recorded schemes. But the number of houses in the country increased by only 1·3 million during this period. There was thus a 'spontaneous loss' of 640,000 houses, averaging 80,000 a year (a good deal more than the United Kingdom slum clearance programme) and amounting to no less than 35 per cent of the 'planned' increase (i.e. new building, less officially sponsored demolitions).* In Sweden the building of 820,000 houses between 1945 and 1960 produced a net increase of only 520,000; thus losses from all causes (very few of them due to slum clearance and planned redevelopment) amounted to 37 per cent of the numbers built. In Norway net losses from all causes amounted to 35 per cent of gross output over the decade between 1950 and 1960, and in Holland they amounted to about 15 per cent of gross output, yet these countries, too, had very small slum clearance programmes. The

* G. Calot, *Les Besoins en Logements, Colloque sur la politique des logements sociaux*, European Economic Community, Brussels, 1963.

amalgamation of previously separate dwellings, the conversion of city housing to commercial uses (peculiarly difficult to keep track of since it is often prohibited by law) and the abandonment of rural housing in depopulated areas appear to account for most of these losses.

In West Germany, on the other hand, the increase in the number of houses achieved between the censuses of 1956 and 1961 was 370,000 *greater* than gross ouput less recorded demolitions – a 'spontaneous *gain* amounting to 16 per cent of the planned increase'.* The difference may be due in part to differences in census definitions and enumerating techniques, but West Germany's heavy wartime losses of older urban housing (most easily amalgamated or converted to commercial uses) and the massive influx of refugees from the east who have been distributed throughout the country, compelling widespread improvement and subdivision of existing houses, probably go far to explain this unusual situation.

Comparisons between these figures should not be pressed too far since the census definitions employed by different countries are not precisely the same, but they serve to show that powerful forces are at work, producing large, unplanned and widely varying changes in the stock of housing. Subdivision, amalgamation and abandonment of housing, conversion of housing to other uses, demolitions, and improvements which postpone demolition – these and other factors must all be allowed for in any attempt to forecast the amount and types of building required. It is clear, too, that the countries with the largest slum clearance programmes are not always those in which the largest numbers of houses are lost from the existing stock.

The previous paragraphs have dealt with 'building' without troubling to define the term. A more rigorous analysis would distinguish between 'construction' (including civil engineering), 'building', and 'house building' – progressively more restricted concepts, within each of which 'new work' should be distinguished from 'repair and maintenance'. United Nations studies of industrial countries show that roughly a third of their expenditure on housing work is normally devoted to repair and

*U.N. 'Major Problems' Study, pp. 87–9.

maintenance, and two thirds to new building and major improvements.* Thus if houses typically last a hundred years and the new ones built each year amount to 2 per cent of the existing stock, expenditure on repair and maintenance will average approximately 1 per cent of capital costs each year. It follows that a country like the United Kingdom – with a relatively slow rate of new building and a relatively elderly housing stock – should devote a larger than average share of building resources to repair and maintenance. But a country like the Soviet Union – with a much faster rate of new building and a newer stock of houses – should devote a smaller proportion of its building resources to repair and maintenance. The efforts now being made in many countries to improve building productivity may upset these relationships: the productivity of new building is easier to improve than that of repair and maintenance operations, and the new buildings erected by industrialized methods may actually need more repairs. Thus the share of building resources devoted to repair and maintenance may rise, unless the rates of new building and replacement are considerably increased.

The amount of new building to be done will depend on the rates of replacement and conversion, the amount of subdivision and improvement, and on many other factors. Meanwhile a large volume of resources, often amounting to about half those devoted to new building, will be required to maintain the existing stock of houses. But such statements are only a means of expressing – not of explaining – the changes which underlie the housing problem. These changes must be explored further to show *why* headship rates rise or houses are replaced, and *when* such things are likely to happen.

SOCIAL CHANGE AND HOUSING NEEDS

The growth of the economy, and the population movements and the changes in living standards associated with this growth, are the central processes to be considered. Economic development is never spread evenly across the country; it is concentra-

* U.N. Economic Commission for Europe, *Cost Repetition Maintenance. Related Aspects of Building Prices*, Geneva, 1963.

ted in the expanding industries and regions, and it often confers its greatest benefits on those employed in these industries and regions, on those commanding the most urgently needed skills and holding the strongest bargaining positions, and on the working population generally (rather than children and the retired). Thus, in a geographically and socially uneven fashion, economic growth enables people to marry and to have children sooner, to buy or rent more or better housing, and to give up sharing or subletting parts of their homes. The worst housing may be abandoned and some people may secure two or more houses; people move to the expanding regions and, since they cannot take their homes with them, more houses tend to be built on the fringes of the growing centres. The migrants often leave their older relatives behind, and headship rates may rise both in the growing centres and in the static or declining areas. Thus migration, whether internal or international, tends to break up families into smaller units and changes their style of life, increasing the numbers of separate households and the demand for separate dwellings. Increases in incomes may bring about changes in cultural patterns, leading people to devote slightly larger proportions of larger incomes to housing.

To these more or less spontaneous economic and social changes there are added the interventions of government, directed to housing young families or old people, creating new suburbs and towns, redeveloping cities and replacing slums. Subsidies, rent restrictions and tax privileges enable some groups to secure more or better housing than others. Insurance and pension schemes – public and private – national assistance, and better health and welfare services enable people to live longer, to maintain separate households until later in their lives, and to keep their homes together despite misfortunes such as sickness, injury, widowhood and unemployment. Meanwhile more general trends in social policy may be deliberately designed to enable old people, deprived children, the physically and mentally ill and others previously cared for in institutions, to go on living in their own homes.

These economic, social and political changes, and their housing implications, cannot be clearly distinguished from each other; they are all part of the same general process of development. Moreover economic development and government policies, which form the central strands of the story, cannot be treated as independent factors, for they too are closely related.

The British tend to assume that government interventions typically follow in the train of economic change, for that has been the normal pattern, historically speaking, in a country whose industrial revolution came at a time when the role of government was restricted. But even in this country the sequence is now frequently reversed. The scope for government intervention depends to a great extent upon the wealth of the country concerned and the stage of economic and demographic development it has attained. With growing wealth and greater understanding of the scope for deliberate planning, governments are taking increasing responsibility for shaping the growth of the economy. Interventions in housing and in other fields, which frequently began as an attempt to control or correct the effects of economic growth, are increasingly designed to stimulate and direct growth itself. Thus housing policy – most obviously in the centrally planned economies of eastern Europe – may be designed to initiate, rather than to follow, changes in production, consumption and the growth of the population.

The factors included in this brief summary take the analysis of the housing problem a stage further, but they are far too complex and variable to form the basis for any precise and authoritative forecast of housing needs.

Even if we disregard the contribution made to such forecasts by political judgement, the impact of the processes we have discussed varies greatly from one country to another. Holland contains about the same number of people as Norway and Sweden together, but a growth of manufacturing industry which brings about wholesale migration and widespread rural depopulation in Scandinavia may produce relatively little movement in the crowded Netherlands where many workers who move from farm to factory can remain in the same house – simply cycling to work in the opposite direction. The growth of motor transport makes it easier still to combine industrial mobility and residential stability. Even when migration does take place its housing implications vary greatly. The expanding industries of West Germany and Switzerland have drawn in vast numbers of workers in the past dozen years – the 'stokers' of central Europe's 'overheated' economies, as they have been called. But most of the migrants to West Germany have been Germans, of all age groups, who come to stay, while most of those drawn to Switzerland have been younger workers from foreign countries who are not entitled to bring their dependants or settle permanently. Likewise there is no uniform relationship between industrial and demographic growth and the demand for housing, even in countries such as Norway and Sweden which appear superficially similar: the Norwegians have relatively large families and live mainly in owner-occupied houses; Swedish families are small and live mainly in rented flats. Recent industrialization has been associated in Czechoslovakia with a reduction in family size, in France with an increase in family size – possibly because the supply of homes and dwellings is more plentiful in France,* and the growth in personal incomes has probably been greater.

The complexity of the factors underlying and generating a country's housing problems is such that no precisely articulated and generally valid 'working model' can be devised for the measurement and prediction of housing requirements in different countries. It will usually be more fruitful to examine the operation of these factors on a local and regional scale than to pursue analytical refinements to extreme lengths on a national scale. At local and regional levels the relationships between changes in employment, population, incomes, and the formation, movement and disappearance of households are more easily comprehended and have a more direct bearing on policy decisions. Examination of these local factors may show, for example, that the growth of new commercial or technical industries alongside older industries can produce an increasingly unequal local distribution of incomes which weakens the relative bargaining strength of households with the lowest incomes and results in an improvement of average housing standards coupled with a deterioration in the standards of those in the worst housing – unless special steps are taken to prevent

*See Tables 1 and 2, pages 49, 50.

this. Examination of demographic changes occurring in municipal property may show that the building of a few really large
houses and many more small houses (rather than continued
building of middle-sized houses) would more effectively meet
both the needs of ageing municipal tenants and the needs of
those still on the waiting list. Likewise, at certain levels of
income and rent, it may be found that the demand for good
housing depends more heavily upon the relative prices of new
and old housing than upon the absolute price of the new; thus an
increase in price that is concentrated on the lower grades of the
market may result in greater demand for good housing. In these
and many other ways the factors explored in this discussion of
national requirements may be applied in local contexts. Indeed,
when national housing programmes are not securely based on a
groundwork of reconcilable regional analyses they amount to
little more than a political gesture.

But the persistence of population pressures, migrations,
obsolete housing, overcrowding and other factors that may
appear to present housing problems does not of itself compel
governments or citizens to take action or even to accept the
need for action. The experience of many countries – and notably
of Russia – shows that it is politically and economically feasible,
under a sufficiently ruthless and firmly established régime, for
industrial production and the population of towns to grow for
decades without an equivalent increase in urban housing.*
France, which has the oldest stock of housing in Europe, has
only recently begun to plan major slum clearance programmes.

*Timothy Sosnovy (*The Housing Problem in the Soviet Union*.
Research Program on the U.S.S.R., New York, 1954) calculates that
the urban population of the U.S.S.R. increased from 21·6 millions in
1923 to 74·5 millions in 1950. Over the same period urban dwelling
space rose from 139 to 297 million square metres and space per head
fell from 6·4 to 4·0 square metres. The war must have contributed to
this trend, but the decline continued throughout this period with no
intervals of improvement. Gregory Grossman, in a foreword to this
study, estimates that the government must in effect have purchased
two years of industrial investment by permitting a reduction of some
40 per cent in the housing standards of urban workers. A radical
change in policy took place after 1952, when the first public recognition
was given to this problem, and since then the Soviet Union has been
rapidly making up for lost time.

George Orwell, 'talking once with a miner ... asked him when the housing shortage first became acute in his district; he answered, "when we were told about it"', meaning that till recently people's standards were so low that they took almost any degree of overcrowding for granted.* Thus our analysis of the housing problem must end, as it began, with the changing political climate of the country concerned. The 'problem' cannot be explained or measured by an objective summary of housing conditions; it is a problem *as perceived by someone*, and thus its meaning depends on the understanding, the interpretation and the perceived implications of housing conditions to be found in the minds of those concerned. Government is conducted by people, drawn from particular political movements and responsive to particular political pressures. The housing demands of some groups – young families in marginal constituencies for example – will be communicated more effectively by these pressures than the demands of other groups – old people or immigrants, for example. Moreover housing policy can never be given absolute priority over other needs; the defence of the country, the prevention of unemployment, and the maintenance of national solvency and minimum standards of public health are among the responsibilities that will normally be accorded a higher priority by government. Changes in the scope for manoeuvre permitted by other responsibilities and changes in the political perceptions of government bring about changes in the definition and interpretation of the housing problem. This study of housing policies must therefore be an essay on the role of government, concerned as much with government's response to housing conditions and the factors determining this response, as with the conditions themselves.

BRITAIN

Nevertheless an understanding of the economic and social changes underlying the development of the housing situation helps to clarify the needs confronting governments. How varied these can be may be illustrated from a glance at our own history.

* *Road to Wigan Pier*, p. 65. Secker & Warburg (Uniform Edition), 1959.

At the height of Britain's first industrial revolution the provision of shelter for migrants coming to the growing industrial centres from all over the British Isles, and the struggle to establish minimum standards of hygiene through the provision of clean water and efficient drains and the paving and cleansing of streets, were the principal features of the 'housing problem'. Sharing of dwellings probably increased during this period, and much 'replacement' occurred spontaneously through the abandonment of shacks and cottages in Aberdeenshire, County Kerry and other places deserted by those seeking work in the towns, and later through the demolition of slum courts and 'rookeries' that were cleared to make way for railway stations and the growing commercial and administrative centres of the big cities. By the end of the nineteenth century the size of families was declining, the expectation of life was rising, improved transport was creating a growing ring of suburbs round the towns, and second- and third-generation city dwellers (no longer so exposed to the demands of country cousins following them to the towns) were seeking separate, self-contained homes. Changes in demographic structure, an increase in the space and equipment expected of a dwelling, a reduction in sharing, and possibly an increase in headship rates were now playing bigger parts amongst the pressures which together constituted the 'housing problem'. These trends continued through the first half of the twentieth century; changes in demographic structure were then proceeding apace as the proportion of people marrying rose and the age at marriage fell, and as the numbers of old people increased. The demand for new houses and the obsolescence of the old were hastened by a great expansion in the provision of domestic gas, water and electricity supplies. A national replacement programme began during the 1930s, attaining a considerable scale at the end of the inter-war period, and political pressures made it increasingly difficult for government to abandon housing responsibilities first assumed on a temporary basis.

Recent trends in this country and the experience of other countries suggest the character of our housing problems is now changing again. Increasing wealth and improvements in transport are leading to the creation of much larger economic regions within which there is a growing diversity of demographic and social structure, just as there used to be in the more restricted neighbourhoods of one town – whole towns or urban areas attracting a growing proportion of young workers or of growing families or of retired people. Headship rates will continue to push upwards, but henceforth mainly among the youngest and oldest, and among single or previously married people of all ages; the central age-groups among married couples nearly all have separate homes of some kind. Dissatisfaction with old housing and the rising rate of obsolescence (due to increasing wealth and the large numbers of houses built in the last quarter of the nineteenth century) will soon call for replacement on a vastly greater scale than hitherto. Regional inequalities, particularly affecting Scotland, Northern Ireland and the older industrial cities, will become increasingly intolerable. A growing demand for country cottages and city flats as secondary housing will undoubtedly make itself felt particularly among those who work in the vast city regions which are becoming the urban form most characteristic of the latter part of the twentieth century.

Yet despite these changes in the character of Britain's housing problems the most urgent and harrowing housing needs have remained much the same over the last two centuries, appearing in the form of overcrowding, sharing, ill-equipped and insanitary housing, and homelessness. But to attend to these hardships without an understanding of the changing economic and social pressures that underlie them will not effectively resolve our difficulties, and may even exacerbate them. Thus the attempt to find further means for enabling families with children to buy or rent housing, without pausing to note that the growth in demand will henceforth be concentrated among smaller households of younger and older people, may be self-defeating. The attempt to pursue slum clearance with the aid of medical criteria and public health procedures at a point when rising living standards and improved medical care have gone far to transform the problems of squalor from a question of health to a question of management, economic obsolescence and simple social justice, may likewise be ill-judged. And to draw up a plan for the South Eastern region of England on the basis of population projections which are not converted by any reliable computation into an estimate of the numbers and types of households this population will form is to conceal essential features of the region's needs and produce a dangerous underestimate of the numbers of households to be catered for in the central parts of the metropolis where housing pressures are most severe.

But before considering policies we must proceed from this general analysis of the housing problem to a more concrete survey of the housing situation and the resources available for improving it, in this and other countries. We can then examine in greater detail the different roles assumed by governments in their approach to the housing problem.

CHAPTER 2

THE SCOPE FOR SOLUTIONS

HAVING gone some way towards clarifying the meaning and character of housing problems, we can now examine the scope for solving them. The first point to note is a very simple one: the total stock of houses grows very slowly. In the countries of Europe, the new houses completed during the latest census year averaged less than 2·4 per cent of the stock of houses existing at that time. Since large numbers of houses were being demolished, abandoned and turned over to other uses, their numbers were growing at net rates of less than 2 per cent a year in the majority of these countries.* For the United Kingdom the net rate of increase in dwellings has been about 1·5 per cent a year for nearly a decade. Thus, in the short run, the scope for meeting a country's housing needs depends largely on the houses already in existence and on the way in which they can be distributed amongst households. This chapter therefore begins with an analysis of the stock of housing and the housing conditions achieved in European countries. In time the stock can be increased and improved, but the housing standards attained depend partly on the rate at which needs are growing. Only after considering the evolution of needs in these countries can we turn to the resources available for investment in housing and draw some general conclusions about the scope for progress.

The international comparisons presented here may be read as 'league tables' of housing progress, but that is not their purpose. Each country's policies reflect its own needs, resources and aspirations, and some of those at the head of the league are so dissatisfied with their housing conditions that they are now redoubling their efforts to improve them. The main purpose of

* U.N. Economic Commission for Europe. *A Statistical Survey of the Housing Situation in European Countries Around 1960*, Geneva, 1965; and *Annual Bulletin of Housing and Building Statistics for Europe*, Geneva, 1964.

these comparisons is to show how a country's housing situation evolves, to identify strengths and weaknesses in this situation which are typical of particular phases of economic and social development, and to explore the opportunities available for improving housing conditions, thus setting the scene for the discussion of housing policies which follows in the next two chapters.

THE HOUSING SITUATION

A country's housing situation can be clarified by asking four questions about it. (1) How many separate houses are there in relation to the population to be housed? (This is an attempt to assess the opportunities potentially available to people for establishing separate households and finding a home to live in – an approximate measure of the family's independence and privacy.) (2) How large are these houses? (An attempt to assess the opportunities for personal independence and privacy these houses afford to the individual.) (3) How much living space do people have in practice? (An attempt to measure the living space people actually secure from the distribution of houses amongst households.) (4) How good is this housing? (An attempt to assess the quality of housing and the convenience and comfort it provides.) These questions will be considered in turn.

Houses, or 'dwellings', are not defined in the same way in all European countries. Most, including the United Kingdom, define them as structurally separate units built for people to live in, with an entrance opening onto the street or onto a space within the building to which the public has access. But some countries define a 'dwelling' as a unit of accommodation occupied by a household, and others define a 'household' as one or more people occupying a structurally separate dwelling. In these cases (distinguished with an asterisk in Table 1) the numbers of households and dwellings are the same and no household is recorded as sharing a dwelling with another. This makes comparisons difficult. The table provides estimates of the numbers of houses and rooms available in these countries. It shows that the more industrialized countries, concentrated in north-western Europe, have the most plentiful supply of dwellings in relation to their population. Sweden and Belgium

TABLE I

The Quantity of Housing Available, Around 1960

Country	Census date	Population in millions	Number of dwellings per 1,000 inhabitants	Number of rooms per 1,000 inhabitants
United Kingdom	1961	52·7	315	1423
Austria	1961	7·1	304	1060
Belgium*	1961	9·2	328	1572
Bulgaria	1956	7·6	228	545
Czechoslovakia	1961	13·7	278	762
Denmark	1960	4·6	323	1420
East Germany	1961[1]	17·1	321	832
Finland	1960	4·4	272	747
France*	1962	46·5	313	955
Greece	1961[2]	8·4	229	647
Hungary	1960	10·0	272	666
Ireland*	1961	2·8	240	1062
Italy*	1961	50·6	257	858
Netherlands	1960	11·5	244	1260
Norway	1960	3·6	299	1268
Poland	1960	29·8	236	580
Portugal*	1960	8·8	267	882
Spain	1960	30·6	240	1025
Sweden*	1960	7·5	344	1181
Switzerland*	1960	5·4	291	1387
U.S.S.R.	1960[2]	214·4	244	685
Western Germany	1961	54·0	288	1007[3]
Yugoslavia	1961	18·6	220	613

SOURCE: U.N. 'Major Problems' Study.

NOTES: Except where otherwise indicated, dwellings include occupied and vacant conventional or permanent housing, and houses for secondary or seasonal use, but exclude residential institutions and improvised housing not intended for human habitation. Population figures are for total population, including people living in institutions and improvised housing.

*The countries marked with an asterisk define households and dwellings in ways which assimilate one to the other, giving equal numbers of each.

1. Occupied dwellings only, including improvised and temporary housing.
2. Estimates or preliminary data.
3. Including kitchens and all rooms of at least six square metres' area other than those used for business purposes only.

TABLE 2

Occupied Conventional Dwellings, by Size and Density of Occupation

Country	Census date	Percentage of dwellings with the following numbers of						Average persons per room
		Rooms			Persons per room			
		1–2	3–4	5 or more	Less than 1	1 but less than 2	2 or more	
		%	%	%	%	%	%	
United Kingdom[1]	1961	6	40	54	71	25[8]	4[10]	0·68
Austria	1961	26	54	20	23	46	31	1·20
Belgium[2]	1961	10	38	52	66	32	2	0·62
Bulgaria	1956	61	36	4	—	—	—	1·83
Czechoslovakia	1961	44	51	5	19	59	22	1·30
Denmark	1960	5	55	39	72	28	1	0·69
East Germany[3]	1961	52	43	5	—	—	—	1·19
Finland	1960	49	42	10	21	51	27	1·31
France	1962	39	46	15	38	47	16	1·01
Greece	1961	51	38	9	62		37	1·45
Hungary	1960	63	36	1	—	—	—	1·42
Ireland[2]	1961	9	51	39	53	37	9	0·90
Italy[2]	1951	42	38	19	42	37	22	1·31
Netherlands	1956	5	28	66	64	32	4	0·76
Norway	1960	13	49	38	60	36	4	0·77
Poland	1960	58	38	4	30[7]	44[9]	27[11]	1·66
Portugal[2]	1960	30	46	23	22	68	10	1·11[12]
Spain	1960	15	44	41	44	41	15	0.93
Sweden[4]	1960	25	55	19	52	44	4	0·83
Switzerland[2]	1960	7	45	49	73	26	1	0·69
U.S.S.R.[5]	1960	—	—	—	—	—	—	1·5
West Germany[4, 6]	1960	10	61	29	53	44	3	0·88
Yugoslavia	1961	47	45	9	10	53	37	1·59

Percentages have been rounded to the nearest unit and hence do not always add up to 100.

SOURCES: U.N. *A Statistical Survey of the Housing Situation in European Countries Around 1960*, and U.N. 'Major Problems' Study.
Footnotes: see p. 51.

show the highest figures, but Belgium defines 'dwellings' in a way that may slightly inflate their numbers in comparison with the figures recorded for other countries. The numbers of rooms available (also subject to minor differences in definition) are shown in the final column of this table and in Table 2; these figures produce a slightly different 'league table' of rooms per person – Belgium, Denmark and the United Kingdom heading the rank order in this respect.

But a simple comparison between the numbers of people and the numbers of houses or rooms takes no account of differences in need, of which those arising from differences in the structure of the population are among the most important. A country with many widows and old people, for example, will need more and smaller houses than a country with a younger population, because the old form smaller and more numerous households than the young. There are striking differences in the age distributions of European countries owing to long-term divergences in the pace and pattern of their demographic growth and the devastating effects of war on the death rates and (particularly) the birth rates of the generations affected. These differences emerge vividly in the population 'pyramids' shown in Figure 1. More revealing, therefore, than the number of dwellings available for the total population would be figures showing the numbers available for particular groups within the population and the proportions in each group who had been able to establish separate households. Unfortunately few countries have such figures. Table 8, at the beginning of Chapter 5, presents some comparisons which show that the smaller and richer countries – Switzerland and the Scandinavians – have done better than their neighbours in this respect.

Some measure of the adequacy of the housing stock and of the living conditions it actually provides can be seen in the 'density

---

1. Persons per room based on households, not dwellings.

2. All statistics of dwellings based on households.

3. Including improvised dwellings but excluding those in non-residential construction.

4. Excluding rooms of less than six square metres area.

5. Estimates made by U.N. Secretariat.

6. Sample survey, excluding dwellings in basements and those without kitchens.

7. Including 1 person per room.

8. Up to and including 1·5 persons per room.

9. Including 2 persons per room.

10. Over 1·5 persons per room.

11. Over 2 persons per room.

12. Preliminary results.

of occupation' – the numbers of households living at varying levels of crowding. These figures reflect not only the amount of housing available but also the geographical distribution of housing and population (for if the houses do not stand in the areas where they are most needed there are bound to be local shortages and overcrowding). They also show the extent to which the distribution of house sizes in the total stock 'fits' the distribution of sizes among the households using it, and the 'fairness' or 'efficiency' with which houses have been distributed amongst households by market forces and by various forms of government regulation and allocation. Table 2 shows once again that it is the countries of north-western Europe which have the most rooms, per head and per dwelling – Belgium, Switzerland, the United Kingdom and Denmark standing out among them. But the extent of overcrowding depends on the way in which these houses are used. Austria, for example, has more dwellings and more rooms per person than her neighbour Czechoslovakia, and she has fewer small dwellings of one or two rooms; yet the proportion of her houses with two or more persons per room (31 per cent) is appreciably worse than Czechoslovakia's (22 per cent) while she also has slightly more dwellings with less than one person per room. By subdividing and converting larger old houses, by concentrating new building in the areas where needs are greatest, and by rationing housing space and redistributing households amongst the houses available, Czechoslovakia appears to have made better use of her housing stock, minimizing both overcrowding and 'underoccupation'. Poland may likewise have been rather more successful than Greece in eliminating overcrowding, though both countries have a similar stock of houses. But in this case the comparison is uncertain because a slightly more rigorous standard has been employed to distinguish the most crowded dwellings in Poland ('over two persons per room' instead of 'two or more'). For the United Kingdom the numbers of dwellings with two or more persons per room are not available, so precise comparisons cannot be made. (Recent changes in the definitions and tabulations used in our census have repeatedly frustrated comparisons, not only with other countries but also with our own previous records.)

Reliable assessments of the equipment and quality of housing are harder to devise, and their meaning – for people living different lives in widely varying climates – is even less clear. Table 3 provides some comparisons which show that baths and a built-in water supply are more plentiful in England, Switzerland and Sweden than elsewhere. While these indicators of housing quality may distinguish the bad from the adequate, they are too crude to distinguish between the adequate and the good. For that a more sophisticated assessment would be required, covering such things as the design and 'finish' of buildings, insulation against sound and temperature, heating systems, electricity and waste disposal services, built-in storage and other equipment, and – outside the dwelling itself – the provision of lifts, garages, laundries, nurseries, play space and other common services. If statistics about such things were available they would show that new building in this country falls below that of some European countries (in Scandinavia, Switzerland and parts of eastern Europe, for example) in certain of these respects – particularly in the scale and efficiency of heating systems and insulation, and the provision of nurseries, play space and built-in storage. This is due partly to traditions fostered by our climate (or by illusions about our climate) and partly to the large proportion of our dwellings built in the form of houses and the small proportion of flats. Whatever the reasons for such differences, they can have profound implications: if most of the rooms in the United Kingdom are too cold to sit in for several months of the year, and if many children have nowhere safe to play outside their homes, then this country may have less *usable* living space than other countries with fewer rooms per head.

The general impressions of a foreign expert searching for the best in Europe's modern architecture deal only with new building, but they nevertheless provide some revealing comparisons. Discussing housing, he says:

. . . few countries can match the achievements of this branch of English architecture. The London County Council . . . has done splendid work in creating economical new neighbourhoods throughout the city . . . British speculative housing, now that financial controls are off, is universally ghastly: among Europe's worst.

By far the largest statements of housing and planning in England can be seen in the New Towns. These – along with several large-scale Swedish experiments – are the most important architectural and urban developments in Europe.

TABLE 3

Equipment and Age of Housing

Country	Date	Percentage of dwellings:			
		With piped water within dwelling	With fixed bath or shower	Built or thoroughly rebuilt	
				Before 1919	After 1945
		%	%	%	%
United Kingdom[1]	1961	96	73	46	23[12]
Austria	1961	64	30	60	22[12]
Belgium	1960	77[5]	24	—	—
Bulgaria	1956	9[5]	—	—	30
Czechoslovakia	1961	49	33[7]	45[9]	20
Denmark	1960	93	48	—	24[13]
East Germany[3]	1961	66	22	65	11
Finland	1960	47	44[8]	23	46
France	1960	78	28	62[10]	17[14]
Greece	1961	29	10	—	—
Hungary	1960	23	18	—	13
Ireland	1961	51[5]	33[7]	58	19
Italy	1961	35	10	—	—
Netherlands	1956	90	27	42	20
Norway[3]	1960	90	45	35	42
Poland[2]	1960	56	26	40[11]	14
Portugal	1960	29	19	—	—
Spain[2]	1960	65	23	—	—
Sweden[3]	1960	90	61	35	34[15]
Switzerland	1960	98[6]	69	—	27[16]
U.S.S.R.	1960	—	—	19[2]	—
West Germany[4]	1960	97	49	41	38[14]
Yugoslavia[2]	1961	42	23	33	36

SOURCE: U.N. 'Major Problems' Study.
Footnotes: see p. 55.

Central heating and hot water, particularly in houses, is . . . still suspiciously regarded . . . Moreover kitchens, even in luxury flats, consist of a sink and perhaps a stove. No effort is made to integrate all fixtures, to build in suitable cupboards, to organize the house-wife's most important workshop into an efficient and delightful whole. And in the bathrooms one almost always finds the hot-water tap in its little corner and the cold in its. Never the twain shall meet. Flagellating!*

Approximate comparisons can be made of the equipment of housing and the living standards this housing supports from recent surveys of Britain (not the U.K. or England and Wales) and the Common Market countries, made for the Reader's Digest Association. These findings, presented in Table 4, may not be as reliable as those in other Tables since they deal with households, not dwellings, and are derived from interviews with housewives and household heads carried out in the course of sample surveys of the adult population. They cannot all be reconciled with census data and should therefore be treated with caution. Nevertheless they suggest that among these countries Luxembourg had the highest living standards, and British houses, when compared with their neighbours in the Common Market, were better supplied with baths and television sets (the latter likely to be a temporary advantage only) but were equalled or surpassed by one or more countries in all the other items listed. The last items in this list are 'consumer durables'

*G. E. Kidder Smith, *The New Architecture of Europe*, pp. 36–9. Penguin Books, 1962. Since this book was written there have been a few enterprising developments in speculative housing. Though gener-ally undistinguished, it can no longer be described as '*universally ghastly*'.

---

1. First two percentages based on households, not dwellings. Last two percentages derived from 1960 survey and refer to England and Wales only. Houses in remainder of U.K. are older.
2. Urban areas only.
3. Including housing other than occu-pied conventional dwellings.
4 Sample survey, excluding basements and dwellings without kitchen.
5. Including piped water outside the dwelling but inside the building.

6. Percentage of dwellings having a kitchen or kitchenette.
7. Bath only.
8. Including Finnish baths in separ-ate buildings.
9. Before 1920.
10. Before 1915.
11. Before 1918.
12. After 1944.
13. After 1940.
14. After 1948.
15. Before 1921.
16. After 1946.

rather than 'housing equipment', but since the demand for these things depends partly on the character of the housing that shelters them and the main services it affords, it is useful to include them.

TABLE 4

Housing and Electrical Equipment, 1963

Percentages

	Britain	Belgium	France	Italy	Luxem-bourg	Nether-lands	West Germany
Percentage of households having one or more:	%	%	%	%	%	%	%
Running water supply	98	81	80	76	100	98	94
Separate bathroom	68	26	33	35	59	55	56
Private garden	72	64	52	16	79	64	48
Telephone	20	22	14	21	55	37	18
Electric or gas refrigerator	30	21	41	30	57	23	52
Electric vacuum cleaner	72	40	37	7	60	95	66
Electric food-mixer	5	31	24	14	39	22	23
Television set	82	37	27	29	21	50	41

SOURCE: *Reader's Digest European Surveys 1963*, Reader's Digest Association Ltd. Based on interviews with heads of households and housewives in the course of sample surveys carried out in January and February 1963.

EVOLUTION OF THE HOUSING SITUATION

Thanks to studies made by the United Nations, the foregoing comparisons are already familiar to the few who know where to find them, but the origins and evolution of the housing situations they portray are less clear. A country's housing conditions go far to determine the current standard of living its people can attain, but they are the outcome of a much longer history.

The quantity of housing in comparison with the numbers to be housed – and hence the opportunities potentially available to people for setting up home on their own – depends mainly on the comparative rates at which the population and the housing stock have grown over the past fifty years or so. In the poorer and less industrialized countries of Europe, populations have grown fairly rapidly, investment has been restricted and concentrated – until, recently at least – on the expansion of productive resources rather than on the improvement of urban housing, and there has been no widespread easing of rural shortages through depopulation of the countryside. Starting from low standards, the rate of building in these countries has not greatly outpaced the growth in their needs. Meanwhile in countries with high living standards, a long industrial history and slow rates of population increase, the stock of dwellings is correspondingly plentiful.

The living space available depends on the sizes as well as the numbers of houses. In most European countries, rural housing tends to be slightly larger than urban housing, though less well equipped. But the largest houses are not found in the least urbanized countries – such as Greece and Yugoslavia – because it is in those that the average size of the whole stock tends to be smallest. It would be nearer the truth to say that the largest houses are found in countries in which wealth (e.g. in England), large families (e.g. in Ireland and Holland) and other features of the cultural pattern established an early tradition of spacious building that was carried over into the towns and adapted to urban life – usually in the form of houses rather than flats. Norwegians, for example, have until recently built larger houses than the wealthier Swedes, who have smaller families and appear to prefer living in flats. The space standards actually achieved and the extent of overcrowding depend on the location of houses, their distribution amongst households and many other factors.

The quality and equipment of the housing stock follow a somewhat different pattern, reflecting different aspects of a country's history. They naturally depend on the living standards the economy permits and the aspirations it encourages. Industrial revolutions creating the major industrial centres, followed by transport revolutions creating the suburbs surrounding these centres, produced the great housing inheritance of the wealthier countries. But the quality of this inheritance depends largely on the date at which these social changes took place, the living standards considered acceptable at that time, and the willingness of governments to enforce these standards. Thus the quality of housing tends to be best in countries where industrial revolutions created or expanded the cities at a point when wealth permitted, and government imposed, the most rigorous standards for new building. Long industrialized and wealthy countries, like Belgium and France, therefore have housing of poorer quality than the Scandinavian countries where cities have been created more recently, or western Germany where wartime devastation was followed by the most extensive rebuilding programme in Europe.

These observations may be summarized by saying that the *quantity* of housing depends mainly on the relationship between the rates at which housing and population have grown in the past fifty years, and therefore tends to be most plentiful in countries which are economically and demographically 'mature'; the *quality* of housing depends mainly on the age of the housing stock, and therefore tends to be best in countries which have built and replaced most housing since the point in their history at which adequate water, main drainage, gas and electricity services became available, and modern building standards were effectively enforced.

FUTURE NEEDS

The concepts we have used to explain the character of a country's present housing situation can now be brought to bear on its future needs. Many of the trends already noted will continue. The rates at which populations can be expected to grow in European countries depend heavily on the patterns of migration assumed, but among the market economies it is clear that Belgium and the United Kingdom are likely to be among the most slowly growing. In Ireland the outward flow of population seems likely to be checked, and the outlook for West Germany, Portugal and Austria also depends heavily on migration. Holland and (if immigration is permitted to continue) Switzerland are likely to grow fastest. In eastern Europe migration across frontiers has been tightly controlled and – unless tentative relaxations of these controls are greatly extended – it is unlikely to exert a major influence. The

U.S.S.R., Yugoslavia and Poland show the most rapid rates of natural increase, while the populations of Hungary, Czechoslovakia and East Germany are growing relatively slowly.

Meanwhile changes in demographic structure will also add to housing needs: the principal changes to be considered are the growing numbers reaching marriageable age owing to past increases in birth rates, the continued increase in the proportion of the population getting married at some stage of their lives, the continued fall in the age at which they do this and in the age at which they have their first children, and – for most European countries – the continued increase in the proportion of elderly people. These changes will operate in divergent ways and their implications cannot be precisely foreseen. Forecasts for western Europe covering the period 1966–76 suggest that the proportion of people aged sixty-five and over among the total population aged fifteen and over will rise most steeply in West Germany, Holland and Switzerland. The numbers attaining marriageable age during the period 1961–81 will rise most steeply in Finland, France, Norway and Holland. In the United Kingdom the combined effects of these changes in demographic structure, though considerable, will be much less dramatic than elsewhere.*

It was shown in the previous chapter that movements of population associated with economic growth exert a major influence on housing needs. The United Kingdom has a slow rate of economic growth and a negligible rate of international migration; she already has a much smaller proportion of her labour force in agriculture and a larger proportion in areas classified as 'urban' than any other European country, and the proportion in areas classified as 'urban' has not changed in the past thirty years (though this is partly explained by the inadequate classifications we use for such areas). In this country, therefore – and in Belgium and Holland which have similar characteristics – there is much less scope for future population movements which have an impact on housing needs than there is in other countries. In Portugal and the Mediterranean countries, in Yugoslavia, Poland and other east European countries, and even in France and West Germany, there remain

*U.N. 'Major Problems' Study.

large numbers of farm workers who will leave the land and seek work in the towns. In West Germany – the most industrialized country in this list – the government intends to eliminate 300,000 small farms in the next decade, compensating their owners for the readjustments this will impose on them. In France the 1961 census shows that the number of agricultural workers fell by 25 per cent in the previous eight years – a loss of 160,000 a year.*

Economic growth, the natural increase of population, international migration, changes in demographic structure, and internal movements of population brought about by industrial development are factors which together constitute the 'housing climate' within which policy makers have to operate. The policy makers must take careful account of this climate but they can exert very little control over it. Ireland, the United Kingdom and Belgium are among the countries with the 'mildest' housing climates in western Europe, and it is at the eastern end of the continent that some of the most 'rigorous' climates are to be found. The post-war bulge in birth rates is the factor that will often make the biggest impact on the housing needs of these countries during the next decade. Its influence can be roughly forecast by showing the numbers of children aged between ten and fourteen in 1961 as percentages of those in the two older age groups. In this country the generation aged ten to fourteen in 1961 was 14 per cent larger than those aged fifteen to nineteen and 25 per cent larger than those aged twenty to twenty-four. To the British that may seem a considerable rate of increase, but in France the youngest of these generations was 31 per cent larger than the second and 46 per cent larger than the third – suggesting an increase in households, from this cause alone, about twice as large as our own. Meanwhile in Poland the first of these age groups was 74 per cent larger than the second and 64 per cent larger than the third.† Thus, by comparison with the storms blowing up elsewhere, the future 'climate' for which policies must be designed in this country is a mild one.

*For an analysis of changes in the economic structure of European countries see U.N. Economic Commission for Europe, *Some Factors in Economic Growth in Europe during the 1950s*, Geneva, 1964.
†U.N. 'Major Problems' Study.

Figure 1 illustrates some of these differences in demographic structure.

Although policy makers cannot completely control the remaining factors affecting their countries' housing needs, they can exercise much greater influence over them. The principal factors involved are the rates of demolition, conversion, sub-division and replacement, changes in the proportion of shared, empty or secondary dwellings, and changes in headship rates. All reflect the progress of fundamental economic and social changes, but all depend heavily on the numbers and types of houses built, replaced and improved, the geographical distribution of building, the money people spend on housing, the minimum standards permitted, and the terms and prices at which houses change hands – factors which fall at least partly within the control of government. It is these factors which will largely determine the needs to be met during the next twenty years in the countries with the mildest demographic and social 'climates', and the housing conditions that will be achieved in those countries at the end of that time. And among these elements it is the rate of replacement, followed by the increase in headship rates, which will generally prove most important, numerically speaking.

The same conclusion can be stated in plainer terms for our own country. In Britain it is not the living space available which poses the principal housing problems; although that needs to be expanded, we already have a high standard in this respect and our needs for additional living space will not increase as rapidly as those of most European countries. But the quality of our housing is not improving as rapidly as that of other countries because we are building more slowly than most, and the growth of our economy does not automatically replace housing by bringing about widespread depopulation of rural areas – and in any case it is not in rural areas that the bulk of our worst housing stands. In the mature urban economies the replacement of old housing no longer takes care of itself, as to a great extent it did in the course of population movements brought about by earlier industrial development. Replacement becomes a matter of deliberate choice and decision to be carried out, not as a by-product of rural depopulation, but in towns where people must

continue to work and live. Meanwhile the growing proportion
of old people and the break-up of multi-generation households
into smaller units of one and two generations mean that
special measures will be required in these countries if the wide
variety of households to be catered for – including old people,
young people and single people – are to secure the independence and privacy they want within a stock of housing much
of which was built long ago to meet quite different needs.

RESOURCES

No housing policy can be formulated without considering the
resources available to carry it out. A brief examination of three
questions about resources may clarify the situation confronting
the policy makers. (1) How much does it cost to build a house?
(2) How much can those who live in the house be expected to
pay for it? (3) What contribution can the community at large
make to these costs through its government?

The cost of a house, like the length of a piece of string, depends
on the unit in question. Despite repeated attempts, no one has
been able to produce a completely satisfactory definition of the
basic 'housing unit' to be measured in international comparisons; standard 'social dwellings', the average floor areas of
dwellings and habitable rooms, square metres and cubic metres
of 'usable space' – these are the concepts most often used.
Further difficulties arise in choosing means for comparing the
costs of such units: the media employed for this purpose include
national currencies converted into dollars, man-hours of
building labour, and house prices expressed as multiples of
average earnings or of gross national product per head.

It is simplest to start with the standard type of family housing
provided, approved or subsidized by government in the country
concerned, and compare the costs of building such units – whatever their size, equipment and quality. These units range from
Swedish flats – centrally heated, well insulated, double-glazed,
and equipped with lifts, refrigerators and parking spaces – to the
relatively simple structures built for the different climate and
living standards of Greece or Portugal. In Sweden and other
Scandinavian countries, housing of this kind is available to the

majority of the population; elsewhere it may be provided for working class families or for skilled urban workers only. The average earnings of men doing manual work provide a readily available unit for comparing the costs of this housing. The question to be answered thus becomes: 'How many years' earnings of a manual worker does it take to buy a new house that is regarded as adequate, though not luxurious, in the country concerned?'

Differences between the economic systems of centrally planned and market economies render comparisons between them hazardous. Statistics of housing costs and incomes are prepared for east European countries in ways that differ from those applied in the west. In the east a large proportion of government revenue is raised through taxes levied on goods sold to the public, and building materials and components sold to state building enterprises are often priced at rates that differ from those charged when the same goods are sold to individuals. Rents are kept very low – often at a level which does not even cover the costs of maintenance and management – but wages can therefore be kept correspondingly low too. Thus comparisons between incomes and house prices in east and west are likely to prove misleading.

The latest comprehensive attempt to answer this question for western Europe * is now ten years out of date, providing figures for the years 1955–7 which show that in thirteen of the seventeen countries examined houses cost between 2·7 and 4·9 times the average annual earnings of male workers. In the remaining four countries (Turkey, Greece, Spain and Portugal) the figure depended entirely on the type of housing used for the comparison – ranging in Greece, for example, from 2·9 for a 'minimum type social dwelling for earthquake victims' to 7·5 for a 'working class urban dwelling'. The United Kingdom's figure of 2·7 was lower than that for any other country in western Europe, despite the fact that the size of the U.K. dwellings selected for the comparison was appreciably larger than the sizes of new dwellings in other countries. (In the U.S.A. the figure was lower still.) More recent figures of housing costs for six east

* U.N. Economic Commission for Europe, *The Financing of Housing in Europe*, pp. 40–41. Geneva, 1958.

European countries are slightly higher than those for the west, but most of them fall within a similar range.* The exception – Yugoslavia – is still at an early stage of industrialization and has a standard of living well below that of the other countries examined, like the exceptions among the market economies. These comparisons should not be pressed too far. While it might be expected that housing would cost more in poorer countries, this finding may be largely due to the fact that each country selected modern, urban dwellings for the purposes of the comparison and then related their costs to average incomes of manual workers which in poorer countries are largely derived from low-paid rural occupations.

More recent studies of building costs in Britain made by the Building Research Station suggest that the cost of building a new house has remained close to three times the average annual earnings of male industrial workers for the past forty years, apart from intervals of higher costs after each world war. Figures for the U.S.A. covering the period between 1948 and 1960 show a similar pattern, although American earnings are much higher.† Thus when comparisons are made for one country over considerable periods of time or for different countries at similar stages of economic development, the cost of a house in man-years remains much the same, despite considerable differences in living standards.

This suggests that the size and quality of housing built in the more industrialized countries depends on the standard of living the economy will support and the expectations of those living at that standard. Unlike saucepans, stockings, bread or ball-point pens, 'housing' is not a single commodity whose price can be expected to fall as productive techniques improve. Housing is a whole complex of commodities and services, forming a central feature of a nation's living standards and largely determining the demands for many other goods. The demand for books, television sets, record players, frozen foods, cutlery, kitchen equipment, furniture and furnishings depends heavily on the kind of house that must accommodate them, the number

---

*U.N. 'Major Problems' Study.

†Building Research Station, *International Comparisons of the Cost of House Building*, Note No. C918. October 1962.

of people it houses, the opportunities it affords and the aspirations it encourages. Thus while the price of doors, electrical wiring, toilet fittings, and many other components of a house may fall, the price of an 'adequate house' is likely to keep pace with average incomes, although temporary fluctuations in supply and demand, government interventions imposing higher standards of building and layout and other special factors will produce occasional departures from this pattern. This does not imply that attempts to reduce building costs must be fruitless, but suggests that the fruit they bear will generally be harvested in the form of better housing rather than cheaper housing.

This conclusion may be rephrased in economic terms. If the preference people give to housing when making decisions about their spending remains unchanged, then the amount of money they are prepared to devote to this part of their consumption will only change as their incomes rise or fall. Any reduction in building costs will be swallowed up by other elements in the total price paid for housing – by an increase in the cost of land or the profits of developers, by an improvement in the quality and quantity of housing people buy, or by an increase in the taxes levied on house property, for example. Unless they operate on a sufficiently massive scale to alter these basic preferences, government interventions in the market are more likely to alter the distribution of resources within these subheads of the total cost of shelter than to change the proportion of income devoted to the total. Likewise, unless a government succeeds in achieving a widely distributed increase in the real incomes of its citizens it is unlikely in the long run to raise their housing standards. But it should not be concluded that economic development can proceed regardless of housing standards, any more than housing can be improved regardless of the economic resources available.

What determines the proportion of their incomes that people are prepared to spend on housing? The problems posed by interpersonal, let alone international, comparisons of housing expenditures defy precision. A student paying one third of his grant to share a bedsitter that overlooks Regent's Park, his landlady whose rent is more than covered by her tenants' payments, a father of three children who buys a 'desirable residence' in the suburbs in the knowledge that his expenditure will eventually give him a capital asset that may be worth more than he paid for it, a large family with several earners renting a similar house on a Council estate, a man living rent-free on an upper floor of the public house he manages – in each of these cases the housing and the legal rights secured, the payments made and their relation to the incomes from which they are derived have different meanings. Any averaging of these figures presents almost insoluble technical problems and is liable to conceal the most important features of the situation. In western European countries, where the numbers of owner-occupiers are steadily rising, comparisons of private expenditure devoted to housing depend heavily on the varied (and often dubious) methods employed for estimating the owner-occupier's housing costs.

Nevertheless, certain general conclusions emerge from comparisons of this kind. During and immediately after the Second World War, rent restrictions greatly reduced the proportions of income spent on housing in western Europe. There was also a sharp fall in housing standards owing to war-time destruction, migration and the postponement of repairs. Since then, the proportion of income devoted to housing has risen considerably but in some countries in the west may not have returned to the levels at which it stood before the war. (In this as in other respects, there is no reason to assume that the 1930s provide authoritative and permanent norms.) In the eastern countries, other than Yugoslavia, housing expenditures have until recently remained very low but are now beginning to rise quite rapidly. Among the market economies of Europe it is among the richer countries – including Belgium, Sweden and probably Switzerland and the United Kingdom – that the largest *proportions* of personal incomes, and hence by far the largest sums of money, are devoted to housing costs. These patterns will be explained again in Chapter 7.

Thus the difficulties of the poorer, less developed countries arise from their poverty, or (to put it another way) from their attempt to build housing at standards similar to those of their richer neighbours. But the difficulties of the richer countries arise not from an absolute shortage of the personal income required to meet housing costs, but from an unequal distribution of incomes amongst households, and from a relationship

between incomes and housing needs which is ill-matched, both
in terms of income groups and in terms of the lifetime of
individual households. This is to restate the problem rather
than to resolve it, but the point is worth clarifying further.

The builders of houses, private and public alike, have generally catered principally for the family with young children or for
young married couples about to start having children. Single
people and older people have generally been housed in older
property, originally built for young families, which may or may
not have been adequately converted for different uses. Young
couples starting a family are generally entering a phase in their
history in which their income per head falls as wives give up
work and the numbers of dependants to be supported on
the husband's income increase. Their rent-paying capacity is
strictly limited. Thus the scope for meeting their needs and
the needs of subsequent generations who will live in their house
depends on the builder's ability to reduce costs (and standards)
to a level they can afford, and on the government's willingness to
assist with subsidies, tax reliefs and other measures.

But the previous generation of young families, whose children
are starting to earn and leaving home while wives often return
to work, is now capable of paying greatly increased housing
costs – often at the point where inflation, the repayment of
housing loans and the arbitrary effects of rent control and
decontrol actually reduce the real cost of their housing well
below the levels imposed on their younger successors. Later still
as people attain the age of retirement the household's income
falls again, often catastrophically. We shall return to these
problems and the means for solving them in later chapters. Here
it need only be noted that the question 'What is a fair rent?' so
beloved in housing debates, is virtually meaningless in urban,
industrial societies characterized by a poverty cycle which
afflicts people in childhood, early parenthood and old age –
characterized, that is, by big changes in the income per head
available to the household at different stages of its history. The
student who is willing to spend a third of his income on the rent
of a room, and later to rent a flat for a quarter of the income he
and his wife earn together, may be unable to afford more than
a tenth of his income for the larger house they require to shelter

a growing family. Later their rent-paying capacity may rise again for fifteen or twenty years, to fall once more in old age. The problem is complicated still further in most European countries by the fact that the people who have the larger families generally have the lowest incomes. But, in the richer countries at least, the problem of rent-paying capacity can be largely resolved by a government capable of redistributing incomes in a fashion that matches households' resources more closely to their changing housing needs.

Any redistribution of the nation's income that is to help poorer households and larger families pay for the housing they need will call for the participation of government, and the government will have to devote considerable resources to this task, even if most of the funds required are collected and disbursed through voluntary savings schemes of various kinds, rather than through taxation, tax relief and subsidies. Thus the resources of government are an essential part of the means to a solution of housing problems. The provision of finance for private housing and the building, management and allocation of public housing require a network of local services capable of operating efficiently in every area to which the programme is to be extended. Meanwhile the planning and execution of a national housing policy call for skilled and experienced central direction. It may seem self-evident that well organized public services staffed at central and local levels by experienced administrators of undoubted integrity are the first requirements for effective government intervention in this field, but housing programmes have so often furnished opportunities for corruption, speculation and administrative chaos that these requirements must be constantly borne in mind.

The financial resources the government commands or controls set limits to the scope of its interventions, as do the other commitments it has to meet from these resources. Table 5 provides some indication of the proportion of their countries' gross national product directly controlled by governments in western Europe. The degree of control exercised by governments over other sectors of the economy lying outside their own immediate authority can be equally important, as will be shown in the next chapter, but this influence cannot be measured with

the statistics available. It is clear from this table that governments of the wealthier and more industrialized market economies spend proportions of their gross national products that
are both larger than those found in the poorer southern
European countries, and remarkably uniform. All, however,
have increased the share of their gross national products which
they command since the post-war low point occurring about
1955, and the plans of many suggest that these increases are
likely to continue. The position in 1955 was summed up in a
study dealing with eighteen countries of western Europe:

> In general, high-income countries spend larger amounts of
> money per person for current government operations than do low-
> income countries. The ranking of the countries by per capita
> income and current government spending is nearly perfectly
> related, with only Switzerland and France diverging (in opposite
> directions) from the otherwise consistent pattern. Most countries
> . . . show an income elasticity coefficient of 1·5, which means that
> the government of a country with a per capita income double that
> of another country spends three times as much as the government
> of the other country.*

But governments have many claims upon their resources
besides the claims of their housing programmes. Education,
health, social insurance and public assistance programmes make
heavy but broadly similar demands. Two items of government
expenditure call for special attention because they are potentially
large yet extremely variable commitments. These are defence
expenditure and the payment of interest on the national debt.
Estimates of these two items can be seen in Table 5. The former
should be treated with special caution since published figures of
defence expenditure are notoriously unreliable. Nevertheless
the pattern that emerges is fairly clear. Greece (still extricating
herself from a civil war), the United Kingdom (coping with the
aftermath of imperialism) and Portugal (still being disen-
cumbered of her empire) devoted the largest proportions of
government expenditure to defence. These commitments must
restrict the scope for government investment in other fields. In

*J. Frederic Dewhurst and others, *Europe's Needs and Resources.
Trends and Prospects in Eighteen Countries*, p. 406. New York, Twentieth Century Fund; London, Macmillan, 1961.

a United Nations study dealing with the years 1957–9, military expenditure was compared with gross domestic fixed capital formation and was found to be equivalent, in Belgium, to 18 per cent of investment, in France to 35 per cent of investment and

TABLE 5

Current Expenditure by Governments

	Gross national product per head in 1963 U.S. dollars	Government current expenditure as percentage of gross national product		Percentage of 1963 government current expenditure devoted to:	
		1955 %	1963 %	Interest on public debt %	Current spending on defence %
United Kingdom	1,497	25	27	15	23
Austria	936	23	28	3	4
Belgium	1,324	21	25	12	13
Denmark	1,560	20	24	4	12
Finland	812	21	27	2	—
France	1,493	29	33	4	14
Greece	412	18	20	2	20
Ireland	793	21	21	13	5
Italy	980	24	28	6	12
Netherlands	1,295	22	28	9	—[2]
Norway	1,723	23	30	4	12
Portugal	381	15	14	4	35
Spain	444	9	9[1]	8[1]	—
Sweden	1,890	25	30	5	16
Switzerland	1,951	—	19	6	1
West Germany	1,879	27	30	2	15

SOURCE: U.N. *Yearbook of National Accounts Statistics 1962*, New York, 1963.
1. 1962.   2. 1958, 17%.

in the United Kingdom to 42 per cent of investment. During this period defence expenditure recorded in the United Kingdom was larger, both in relation to gross national product and in relation to gross domestic fixed capital formation, than in any of the other twelve western European countries for which figures were provided.*

Variations in the cost of servicing the national debt arise partly from differences in fiscal traditions, but also from the effects of the drastic inflations which obliterated debts in several European countries after the Second World War. Thus the governments of Greece, West Germany, Finland, Austria and France – countries which all suffered severe inflations or currency reforms – spend very little on their national debt, and are now in a stronger position to borrow without incurring crippling burdens than are governments which were fortunate or virtuous enough to 'save' their currencies.† In the United Kingdom the proportion of government expenditure devoted to servicing the national debt is approached only by Ireland and Belgium. Payments of interest or principal on the national debt are no more than a transfer of income, constituting no drain on the nation's resources if the lenders to whom these payments go are not foreigners. (As a result of recent balance-of-payments crises, much of our own government's debt *is* held by foreigners.) Such payments must nevertheless begin with taxation of some kind, and in peacetime there are limits – political if not economic – to a government's capacity to tax its population. Hence any commitment that pre-empts (in our own case) nearly a sixth of government's current expenditure inevitably imposes severe restrictions on the scope for public expenditure elsewhere.

It would be a mistake to assume, however, that the opportunities of the policy maker in this field depend only on the amount of money his country appears capable of spending on its housing. The confines within which he operates are physical, though they may be expressed in monetary terms. Just as housing constitutes a central feature of a nation's consumption, closely related to

---

*U.N. Department of Economic and Social Affairs, *Economic and Social Consequences of Disarmament*, New York, 1962.

† See J. Frederic Dewhurst, op. cit., for a fuller analysis of government expenditures in western Europe.

the consumption of many other goods and services, so also do the building, maintenance and replacement of housing play a central part in production.

A few figures will show the scale of this sector of the economy. Most of the countries of western Europe devote between 15 and 30 per cent of their gross national product to investment in fixed capital. Approximately half of this investment goes into construction of various kinds, including the building of roads, factories, hospitals and so on. Housing usually takes between 35 and 50 per cent of investment in construction. Meanwhile expenditure on the maintenance and repair of housing – treated in various ways in statistics of national accounts – typically amounts to about one third of the expenditure on new building, although this depends on the age and character of the housing stock and the standards of maintenance expected. The resources devoted to building new housing – shown in Table 6 to amount to between 3 and 5 per cent of gross national product in most of western Europe – make heavy demands on labour, and are the outcome of a complicated network of relationships, including the operations of many industries supplying components for building whose operations depend on the volume and flows of saving and investment elsewhere in the economy. Any change in the housing programme therefore requires responses in many other sectors of the economy which compete for resources that may be used in housing. It must be related not only to the supply of building land, labour and materials, but also to their location. For most of the productive work in building – unlike other industries – still has to take place on the site where the finished product is to be used. Moreover houses generally take a year or more to build (much longer if land acquisition and planning procedures are included in the process) and unlike ships and aircraft they often have to be built before they are sold. Risk and uncertainty can therefore play havoc with investors' decisions.

Thus although the proportions of the national income invested in housing and in other forms of fixed capital vary considerably from one country to another, these proportions cannot be altered quickly. In peacetime, among countries with fully employed economies, these relationships often continue with little change for many years. During the decade from 1953 to 1962 the proportion of the United Kingdom's gross national product that was devoted to gross domestic fixed capital formation rose slowly from about 14 to about $16\frac{1}{2}$ per cent. The proportion of gross national product devoted to house building

TABLE 6

Investment, Construction and House Building, 1958–61

	As percentages of gross national product, during the years 1958–61		
	Gross domestic fixed capital formation %	Construction works %	Residential buildings %
United Kingdom	16·2	7·8	3·0
Austria[1]	22·2	10·3	3·9
Belgium[1]	16·5	8·7	4·3
Denmark	19·5	8·7	3·0
Finland	27·8	17·6	5·8
France	18·5	9·6	4·4
Greece	25·2	12·8	5·4
Ireland	13·5	7·2	1·7
Italy	22·3	12·5	5·6
Netherlands	24·1	12·1	4·6
Norway	29·2	13·3	4·0
Portugal	18·1	10·7	3·4
Spain[2]	18·0	9·4	—
Sweden	22·0	14·4	5·4
Switzerland	22·8[3]	14·1	4·6
West Germany	23·4	10·9	4·9

SOURCE: U.N. *Yearbook of National Accounts Statistics, 1962*, New York, 1963.
1. 1958–60.　　2. 1958–9.　　3. Including increase in stocks.

fell steadily from 3·7 per cent at the start of this period to 2·6 per cent in 1958, and then rose slowly to 3·1 per cent in 1961 and 1962. The rate of building achieved by this investment and the corresponding rates in other parts of Europe during the past decade are shown in Table 9.* Any attempt to raise these

*See page 156.

(exceedingly low) figures to levels typical of western Europe will call for a profound adjustment of the country's whole pattern of savings and investment. The task is a manageable one – similar adjustments have taken place elsewhere in Europe – but it cannot be achieved in a hurry without danger of inflation and deterioration in the balance of payments. Before it can be taken seriously, any proposal for increasing the output of housing in such an economy must show how and where the concomitant savings are to be made, and where the physical resources for a bigger building programme are to come from.

CONCLUSION

The purpose of this chapter has been to explain the environment within which housing policies evolve, and to explore the scope and limits of the impact that governments can make upon the housing conditions of their people. Some of the conclusions of this exploration can be briefly summarized. Countries heavily dependent on the simpler forms of agriculture and primary production usually have a poor and rapidly growing population; the revenues of government are correspondingly low, trained administrators are scarce and the techniques of administration unsophisticated. Housing conditions may or may not be adequate to support the standard of living commonly expected in the country, but in any case government cannot rapidly improve them. Its slender resources may be better deployed in educating people for the work that must be done to increase productivity, in providing them with the capital equipment appropriate for this task, and in preparing the groundwork of roads, drainage, water supplies, town plans and the supporting administrative structure that will be required to sustain and control the growth of cities. It should beware of endeavouring to follow too quickly *or* too slowly in the footsteps of wealthier nations. Rapid industrialization conducted without regard to housing needs may endanger public health and social and political order.* In the extreme situations of Africa there are regions where labour is embarrassingly plentiful and totally

*See Charles Abrams, *Housing in the Modern World*, Faber & Faber, 1966.

unskilled: the purchase of wheelbarrows, where men previously moved building materials by hand, may there be more productive than the gift of a bulldozer. But within the same country it may be necessary to build in the desert or the jungle where labour is non-existent, and there the most advanced forms of construction may be best – involving airlifted prefabricated dwellings and the like. Thus primitive and sophisticated building techniques may for a long time operate side by side, and expert advice will be needed to select the best forms of investment.

In the early stages of industrialization, population often continues to increase so rapidly that the growth of cities is liable to create serious urban housing shortages without greatly easing scarcities in the countryside. Meanwhile, though housing conditions may not be much improved, the stock of housing grows fast, and the fate of future generations will be determined for years to come by the standards of building, planning and urban equipment achieved at this stage. Government may still be compelled to give first priority to education, industrial investment, health and defence, but it can impose minimum standards of town planning without much cost to the community and it can direct building resources to the most rapidly growing centres and to the most urgent needs within these centres. It must make heroic and frequently unpopular decisions, choosing between a restricted, high-quality building programme – always popular with the rising urban middle class – and a numerically larger housing programme built at lower standards. Likewise the acquisition of land in advance of development and the imposition of wise controls on its use, though never popular with landowners, will pay handsome dividends for future generations. In major cities throughout Europe the point at which effective controls over building and layout were first imposed is still clearly visible to anyone walking outwards from the town centre. During this stage of rapid urban growth, ten years' delay in taking control may condemn thousands to live in slums from which the more fortunate or enterprising are still fleeing sixty or a hundred years later.

At the next stage in their development, many countries have a less mobile and more slowly growing population. They grow much richer. This is the point at which fundamental changes occur in the conditions under which housing policies are made. The policy makers have hitherto been responding with scanty resources to major increases in population, major flows of migration and major changes in industrial structure – factors they can do little to control. Henceforth the needs generated by these forces considerable though they may be, no longer exceed the capacity of a properly organized building industry. Improvements in the quality of housing, greater opportunities for the establishment of separate households, the elimination of shared housing, and other advances in standards, then play an increasingly important part in the schedule of requirements to be met. These are factors over which the policy maker can exercise considerable control. Meanwhile the resources that can be devoted to housing, by government and private households alike, grow much larger; in market economies the payments people make for housing and the revenues of government both take a larger proportion of the growing national income. But the wage system of an industrial economy is not adjusted to the needs of households at different phases of their development. Hence the nation's capacity to pay for better housing will not be realized unless government takes steps to achieve that. This is the point that the countries of north western Europe have reached. Similar distinctions appear in eastern Europe too; the housing problems of Czechoslovakia and East Germany are very different from those of Poland and Yugoslavia. Holland stands out among the western European countries as having the most rapid rate of population growth, a sharply growing proportion of older people and a falling age of marriage – combining the characteristics of a mature and wealthy economy with those of an earlier stage of demographic expansion. But even in Holland the rate of building, which is no more than the average for north western Europe, has been sufficient to cope with these developments and an appreciable volume of 'spontaneous losses' through demolitions and conversions, and still achieve a considerable improvement in standards – as shown in the previous chapter.

The next phase of development, into which the United Kingdom and other countries are now moving, cannot be so clearly foreseen, but some of its characteristics are already apparent. The drive to establish more, and smaller, separate households has reached no ceiling. But the rise in headship rates has to be concentrated increasingly among the single, the young and the old, since nearly everyone else by now has a home of some kind. Greater attention may have to be given to the needs of smaller groups hitherto neglected – large families, the elderly and the physically handicapped, students and foreign immigrants, for example. Under the impact of transport revolutions big cities give way to vast urban regions; Manchester, Liverpool and their surrounding towns are gradually being welded into such a region, and similar developments are to be seen elsewhere – most dramatically in the urban complexes of the Rhine-Ruhr and Randstad Holland.* Severe housing stresses may result as households redistribute themselves into increasingly specialized districts each of which houses distinctive social classes, age groups and household types. But of greater numerical importance than these problems is the need to initiate a wholesale replacement of the first generation of urban housing and to maintain a continuing and permanent programme of replacement thereafter.

Governments and political movements which may have taken half a century to mobilize and deploy resources for the construction of new houses of standard design to meet the urgent needs of successive generations of young households are often caught on the wrong foot – psychologically, technologically and administratively – by this turn of events. They cling to the assumption that replacement is not a major and permanent problem but a matter of 'slum clearance' to be resolved by a once-for-all effort. House designs and procedures for borrowing and subsidy which were well suited to meet the needs of young families prove difficult to amend, inappropriate though they may be for the needs of old people, single people and the other types of household to be catered for.

Given time and determination there is no longer any question that the resources of the economy are capable of resolving these new problems. It is equally clear that only government *can* resolve such problems – though how much of the financial

*See Peter Hall, *The World Cities*, Weidenfeld & Nicolson, 1966.

resources it must itself provide and how these resources should be secured and distributed remain open questions. Thus in the next phase of development the pressures compelling governments to assume responsibility for the solution of housing problems are likely to increase rather than diminish. Similar phases of development can be seen in other branches of the public services – in those responsible for education, health and the maintenance of incomes, for example – which explains the paradox that the extent and cost of government 'interventions' in the economy are increasing, both absolutely and as a proportion of the national product, as wealth increases and as needs become, in a world context, less urgent.

But it does not follow from this analysis that governments are compelled by irresistible or impersonal forces to embark on more comprehensive attempts to improve housing standards. The decision to assume or decline responsibility, to develop or preserve existing structures and methods, has still to be made by each government, again and again, through the usual processes of controversy, experiment and improvisation. It is to these processes that we must now turn.

CHAPTER 3

THE ROLE OF GOVERNMENTS IN WESTERN EUROPE

THE growth of population, industry, cities and wealth – these underlie the major currents of social change which determine the needs to be met and the resources for meeting them, in the field of housing as in every sphere of government. But the aims of government and the extent and character of its responsibilities must be determined by governments themselves. This chapter deals with these responsibilities, identifying and comparing different 'roles' that governments assume, and discussing the origins and implications of each. Three contrasting patterns of responsibility will be discussed, typical of those to be seen in many parts of western and southern Europe, but it is not suggested that every country in this area has adopted one or other of these patterns. These three roles are not intended to represent 'good' or 'bad' housing policies, for different objectives are pursued, with varying success, within each of the groups of countries compared. Neither are they distinguished by their success in getting houses built, for large and small building programmes are to be found in each group. Moreover a 'successful' policy and a large building programme are not necessarily the same thing. Governments are not principally concerned with maximizing the output of houses; all of them have other responsibilities that are even more important. This chapter explores the evolution of different approaches to the housing problem and the scope that each affords for progress in various directions. The reader must decide for himself what is 'good' and 'bad', and whether he wants more houses built, and what sacrifices should be made to achieve that end.

ADMINISTRATIVE STRUCTURE AND TRADITION

It may be felt that so ambitious an attempt to generalize about the work of many different governments in an exceedingly complex field, conducted without any historical preamble, must forfeit any real understanding of the policies to be discussed. But while such histories remain unwritten a comparison of current practice in European countries may still yield insights that will be useful to those interested in the housing policies of predominantly industrial urban societies of the kind found on this continent.

Nevertheless the origins of the institutions which form the instruments of housing policy clearly go far to determine their potentialities, and we should pause to consider the influence of this institutional structure before embarking on a more general survey of the responsibilities it bears. This can be done by examining the setting within which our own housing policy has developed, paying particular attention to those features of our society and its 'administrative culture' which we normally take for granted as part of the natural order of things.

The British are aware that parts of Scotland, South Wales and the North appear older and dirtier than the rest of their country, but the differences between the living standards of different regions are not very large, and the great majority of their countrymen live an urban or suburban life, reading the same newspapers, watching the same television programmes and aspiring to – if not achieving – similar comforts and opportunities. They expect to be able to borrow 80 or 90 per cent of the price of a recently built house of standard type at an interest rate of about 6 per cent and repay this over twenty or twenty-five years, provided their income and age clearly demonstrate that they will be capable of honouring their obligations. Every part of the country has its elected local authority with similar powers for the provision of housing, depending in similar ways on subsidies from the central government; and despite an infinite local variety in minor matters these authorities are treated by the Ministry of Housing and Local Government as independent and theoretically equal bodies. Each is expected to meet the most urgent housing needs and clear the slums, so far as its resources permit. Although growing numbers of people from all social classes are buying their own homes, the renting of unfurnished accommodation was until fifty years ago the normal method of securing a home

among all classes and is still regarded as the natural procedure
to adopt when government provides for those who cannot afford
to meet their own needs unaided. The uses to which land can
be put are now controlled, but the land itself is normally owned
by private individuals or by companies; the state buys land
from time to time but its operations, though conducted through
special procedures for purchase, valuation and appeal, are not
regarded as being in principle very different from those of any
other body that buys and sells in this market. Taxation is now
used as an instrument for restraining inflation and regulating
the general development of the economy, and is manipulated
to confer benefits upon particular industries or classes of the
population, but its principal function is still assumed to be the
raising of revenue to pay for public services. This picture of
the Englishman's world is grossly over-simplified and misleading
at many points. It is nevertheless a reasonably accurate summary
of his assumptions about that world – indeed, many will
wonder why so platitudinous a statement of the obvious should
be made – and these assumptions exercise a profound influence
on his rulers, whether in Whitehall or town hall. Yet in countries
not far away this picture would seem incomprehensibly
exotic.

Even in Norway and Italy, where living standards do not
diverge greatly from our own, there are major economic,
cultural, climatic and linguistic differences between regions.
North Italians are accustomed to say that 'Africa begins in
Sicily' – if not a good deal closer. Such differences, coupled with
a sparsely scattered population and great distances (Oslo is
further from the North Cape than London is from Belgrade)
make it impossible to establish a uniform system of independent
local authorities or to treat each authority on the same footing.
Altogether different institutions may have to be created to build
and manage housing. In many countries it is only the rich who
can borrow money in the 'open market' and the rate of interest
charged in that market may commonly stand, as in France, at 10
or 12 per cent. In many countries it is normal to raise three
separate loans from different sources to buy a house; the periods
of repayment expected may be ten years, forty years or sixty
years, or the bulk of the money – as in Switzerland – may not

have to be repaid at all. The credit-worthiness of the first household to occupy the house, crucial to our own system, may be of little or no importance in determining the size and terms of such loans. In Britain, voluntary bodies early abandoned the attempt to build working class housing on a massive scale, leaving a handful of housing associations and a tradition of housing management followed by a minority of the profession as their principal contributions to progress in this field. Henceforth they and the labour movement relied increasingly on local government to provide for those who could not secure loans from the growing array of building societies. But in Austria, Germany, Scandinavia and Holland, industrial, political and religious movements developed various patterns of voluntary and cooperative association which were later adopted by government as its principal instrument for the provision of housing – just as our own Friendly Societies were called upon to administer national health insurance between 1911 and 1948. Many countries – particularly those closer to an independent, yeoman farming tradition – do not assume that weekly tenancies provide the natural system of housing rights and tenures; some have adopted other patterns that combine features of owner occupation and tenancy. In Sweden and Norway – and, much earlier, in Germany too – it was more readily assumed that government had a duty to acquire land well in advance of development and itself to shape, rather than regulate, the growth of cities. Where much of the land was literally created by government, as in Holland, it was natural for the state to adopt rather different attitudes to its ownership and use. Taxation, too, often performs different functions from those assumed in this country: it may be the principal instrument for the collection and deployment of the country's savings, as in Norway, or a deliberate means for redistributing the burden of debts – as in West Germany, where the experience of two runaway inflations within a generation has gone far to clarify the meaning of debt.

Government's first interventions in the housing field are not necessarily prompted by the need to protect public health and provide homes for heroes. The story may have begun, or been carried forward, by attempts to bring about agricultural reforms and assist poverty stricken regions (as in Italy), to combat depression and mop up unemployment in the building trades (as in Sweden), to rebuild a war-shattered economy and erect a defence against Communism (as in West Germany), or to attract key workers to growing industries (as in several east European countries), and several such motives are usually to be found embedded somewhere in a housing policy.

The function and status of civil servants and of government itself vary from country to country. Where a British administrator speaks with the tact and reticence that befit a secretary of his Minister, his French counterpart has the authority and directness of a spokesman of the Republic – however misleading both guises may be. Where a foreign visitor pursuing his researches in a British provincial town may be received by aldermen and chief officers in the town hall, he would in France be received by the prefect and his staff in the local offices of the central government. If he endeavours to trace the sinews of power to their source he will eventually come to the politicians, but his route will lead, in some countries through the Treasury or the Ministry of Finance, in others through the Central Planning Commission. The officials he meets on the way may be aware of the world beyond their departments and national frontiers, quoting the findings of research in several disciplines and three languages, or they may only be able to tell him about their own department's work – the next budget or the next election forming the outermost horizons of thought. When they talk about 'housing needs' they may be referring to the requirements of a whole nation over the next decade, or to the current waiting lists for restricted types of accommodation. When they talk of 'short-term' programmes and 'the immediate future' they may be referring to the next five years or the next five months.

It is obvious that each country is different, and to multiply illustrations of this platitude is of little value unless it demonstrates the impact such differences make upon policy. The rest of this chapter is devoted to that task, but some of the immediate implications of the administrative framework which forms the vehicle for housing policies can be illustrated from British experience.

Though our own 'housing system' is now in a phase of rapid development, it still owes a great deal to its reliance on a well established network of lending institutions specializing in serving private borrowers at an early stage in the growth of their households, and an equally well established network of local authorities whose principal achievement has been to serve two generations of working class ex-servicemen in similar age groups. This system is peculiarly well suited to meet the needs of the young family. To that contribution our local authorities have added their slum clearance programmes, which constitute a greater achievement than anything else of this kind in the world – inadequate though it may be. It was natural that the work of clearing the slums and providing for young families in the greatest need should be taken on by bodies whose origins lie in the nineteenth-century sanitary and poor law authorities, and whose presiding Ministry has descended in direct line through the Ministry of Health from the Poor Law Board. But this system tends to harden the social distinctions of a class-ridden society by perpetuating them in bricks and mortar and street plans – council estates of tenanted houses being clearly distinguished from the speculative builders' owner-occupied estates, despite the basic uniformity of the houses in both. Few communities have gone to the lengths of the Oxford suburb in which seven-foot walls surmounted by revolving spikes were built across two roads and maintained there for twenty-five years to divide the social classes,* but the distinctions symbolized so dramatically there have been repeated all over the country. Our housing system – including the terms on which money can be borrowed – makes it increasing difficult for people as they grow older to cross these boundaries or move from one kind of housing to the other. Countries with a greater variety of institutions building houses with the aid of more varied and widely distributed forms of subsidy have been more successful in avoiding this social polarization, though in some cases they have been less successful in housing or re-housing those in greatest need.

A pattern of independent local authorities, each in principle equal, presided over by a Ministry that must be continually

*Peter Collison, *The Cutteslowe Walls. A Study in Social Class*, Faber & Faber, 1963. Similar cases occurred in Cardiff in 1955, and in Dartford, Kent, in 1958.

prepared to arbitrate between these authorities or between them and the public, is peculiarly unfitted to cope with problems that call for strong leadership from the centre or a deliberate concentration of resources on particular regions at the cost of neglecting others. Countries that recognize regional differences more frankly and have a stronger regional and central administration – often exercised through Ministries of Construction or through Central and Regional Planning Commissions, rather than Ministries of Health, Welfare or Local Government – may be better equipped to relate the growth of housing to the changing regional distribution of employment, and to stimulate and guide the development of the building industry.

This country's tax system exercises a growing influence over the types and numbers of houses built and their distribution amongst households, as rising incomes and the spread of owner occupation give greater play to the effect of various forms of tax relief. Taxation plays an important part in the housing systems of many other countries, but its influence may be deliberately planned and need not be an accidental outcome of a revenue-raising process. Rent controls in this country have until recently taken a virtually unique pattern. Elsewhere in western Europe the private landlord has generally been regulated *and* subsidized; restrictions on his rents have been repeatedly modified and relaxed, and concentrated most heavily upon selected areas of shortage. In this way he has been employed, unwillingly maybe, as an instrument of housing policy, and in return has often been prepared to sustain or extend the contribution he makes to the housing market. In this country he has been treated in an altogether different way, sometimes as a parasite to be ruthlessly suppressed, sometimes as a paragon of free enterprise to be unleashed in haphazard and unselective fashion. Not surprisingly, he has extricated himself from the market whenever he gets the chance to escape with profit.

This glimpse of the legal, financial and administrative framework, and its implications for the housing policies of one country should be sufficient to show the importance of the setting within which these policies develop. But the framework and the traditions it enshrines do not dictate the objectives a government adopts. The rapid evolution of housing policies in Europe over the past decade clearly demonstrates the enormous scope for change that even the most firmly established structures permit. The structure and its traditions determine the means for implementing new policies and the people who must be convinced in the process. They do not determine the objectives and achievements of policy itself.

The adaptability of administrative structures and traditions springs not only from the inventive leadership that men of vision can infuse into them, but also from the diverse origins and objectives to be found in every housing system. The potential conflicts within a housing system must be constantly remembered, for contradictions between the varied necessities which compel governments to intervene in the housing field can be constructive as well as destructive. A policy of housing those in most urgent need may conflict with a policy of replacing the worst houses, and both may conflict with a policy for stimulating demand through subsidies directed to those who are most likely to be persuaded by such help to build or buy homes for themselves: different people will benefit from the pursuit of each of these objectives. An attempt to keep pace with the housing needs of expanding industrial centres may conflict with an attempt to revive poverty stricken regions. A policy designed to improve productivity in the building industry may not be best suited for eliminating unemployment in the building trades. A policy designed to eliminate rent controls and create a 'free market' in housing may conflict with the need to avoid inflation of living costs and wages. Every country's housing policies contain the seeds of several such conflicts, for housing is so central a feature of the economy and the way of life it supports that many of the competing aspirations at work in society gain some expression in this field. By seizing opportunities to adjust the balance between these contending claims the policy maker can adapt the administrative framework to the pursuit of new objectives. Thus the history and structure of a country's institutions exercise an influence on its housing policies that is always important, but never all-important.

The outline to be given here of the roles which governments adopt omits a great deal that would be looked for by anyone seeking a systematic description of European housing policies and procedures. What follows is a sketch of three different roles, or patterns of responsibility, to be seen amongst the governments of western and southern Europe, stressing and contrasting the distinctive features of each, attempting no comprehensive survey, and abstracting from the rapidly changing complexities of real life a simplified picture that may come uncomfortably close to being an outdated caricature – but at least, it is to be hoped, a revealing caricature. It must be stressed again that this essay explores the responsibilities assumed by governments, but does not evaluate their policies. Each of the roles outlined is capable of accommodating different objectives and exhibiting different virtues and vices, as will be shown. The chapter concludes with a discussion of the circumstances bringing about transitions from one system to another, and the prospects for the future.

FIRST INTENTIONS AND SECOND THOUGHTS

Examples of the first pattern of housing responsibilities to be outlined are to be seen amongst the countries of southern Europe, stretching from Turkey to Portugal. In Turkey, the poorest of these countries, the population doubled its size between 1927 and 1960, and the yearly rate of increase grew steadily throughout this period, reaching 3 per cent by the end of it. By then the population of the cities was growing more than twice as fast as that of the rural areas, and that of rural areas was growing nearly four times as fast as the population of the United Kingdom. Turkey's situation was summarized in her first development plan with a frankness unusual in official documents:

Of the population of school age and above, 60 per cent is illiterate. 53 per cent of the villages and 55 per cent of the small towns have either no drinking water or not enough, 69 per cent of the population is without electricity. Out of every 1,000 babies born, 165 die in the first year. 2·5 per cent of the population has tuberculosis. There is one medical doctor for every 4,000 inhabitants, and in the hospitals 1 nurse for every 111 beds. There are 60 students for every school teacher and 25–30 villages to every agricultural expert. On the average, there are 2·7 persons per residential room in the cities and 2·1 in the villages. 30 per cent of the city dwellings are in very poor condition and not fit for habitation. In the three biggest cities, 30 per cent of the population live in single-room dwellings. The number of people living in *gecekondus* (shacks) is 1·2 million . . . It is calculated that even at the most active season, there are about one million unemployed in the agricultural sector . . . The expansion of cultivated land which started in 1950 has now reached its limit.*

It is a long step from this state of affairs to Italy, whose northern towns have attained a standard of living and a level of industrialization comparable with the rest of western Europe. Between the standards of these two countries lie Portugal, with a poor economy that is growing almost as slowly as the United Kingdom's, and the rapidly growing economies of Greece and Spain. The countries in this group are entering a period of rapid industrialization, or already in the throes of one. In recent years Italy and Spain have probably achieved a faster rate of economic growth than any other country in western Europe† and Greece may follow their example before long.

Housing policies in this region are likewise in a state of rapid development, and only their salient features can be indicated. Much of the population has living standards and life expectations similar to those experienced in Britain a hundred years ago, but the educated and prosperous naturally expect the best standards of the day, and frequently attain them – with the aid of technically advanced branches of the building industry, and the financial and administrative resources of governments over which they exercise great influence. Thus housing loans and subsidies similar to those in north-western Europe are available but often directed to the urban middle-class – helping, in Spain and Turkey for example, to build houses which are larger than those provided for council tenants in Britain (which, in turn, are nearly twice the size of those built by the state in several east European countries). Such policies confer scant benefit on the 1·2 million people living in '*gecekondus*'. Meanwhile governments have embarked on various programmes of agricultural reform, regional development, unemployment relief and urban improvement which include house building or aid for builders – often provided in one country under many

*The Union of Chambers of Commerce, Industry and Commodity Exchanges of Turkey, *First Five Year Development Plan, 1963–67*, p. 24. Ankara, 1963.

†U.N. Economic Commission for Europe, *Economic Survey of Europe in 1962. Part 1: the European Economy in 1962*, Geneva, 1963.

different laws and through many different procedures. Tax reliefs of various kinds have been devised to promote the building or letting of housing, to encourage employers to provide housing for their workers, and to assist particular regions or classes of the population. To these schemes some governments have added further building programmes to house their own officials.

Spanish housing policies of the mid 1950s illustrate this kind of situation. Their subsequent development will be outlined later, but at that time about 60 per cent of house building was assisted by direct grants to builders and by government loans to buyers which covered up to 40 per cent of capital cost and were repaid over twenty years. Since no special steps were taken to select the people who were given this help, most of these houses appear to have gone to families with incomes well above the average. Another 15 per cent of the houses built were wholly financed by the government and let at controlled rents under a system designed to confer ownership on some future tenant after fifty years – rent being treated as a form of long-term hire purchase. These houses were let to people selected by the official trade unions, civil servants' cooperatives, savings associations and other bodies that sponsored their construction, and most of them went to skilled industrial workers and the urban lower middle class. About another 7 per cent of the houses built were assisted by tax reliefs only, but in a country with many small taxes these took a bewildering variety of forms. They included reductions in stamp duties of various kinds, reductions in tax levied on capital gains from the sale of land, and reductions in taxes on the portion of private or corporate incomes invested in housing, on income derived from controlled rents, and on income devoted to the payment of interest on loans for housing. Meanwhile further building was done by three separate government agencies providing houses for people in the Army, Navy and the public works department, and houses or housing allowances were provided for teachers; two more government agencies bought and sold land for housing purposes and another was responsible for housing loans.*

* *The Economic Development of Spain.* Report of a Mission Organized by the International Bank for Reconstruction and Development, Baltimore, Johns Hopkins Press, 1963.

Rational and progressive people are no scarcer in southern Europe than elsewhere (though, as elsewhere, their access to power may be restricted) and the problems presented by such patterns of housing administration are keenly appreciated in the countries concerned. The inadequate resources available to these governments are often wastefully dispersed on a large number of small programmes and on projects which may confer their greatest benefits upon those best able to solve their own housing problems; thus building may continue for years at an impressive rate without appreciably reducing the hardships of those in greatest need. Policies for building, lending, town planning and economic development may be ill coordinated; and lacking the means to reconcile policies in these different fields, governments may run into damaging contradictions of the kind that produced drastic inflations in the price of building materials in Spain and Turkey during the 1950s and in Italy more recently. Houses may be started and left unfinished for long periods: Spain was reported to have 450,000 houses under construction during 1961 but completed only 135,000 that year, whereas many of the north-western countries average less than a year for the completion of a house. Bold attempts to tackle such difficulties may run into insuperable obstacles. In Portugal, for example, a recent attempt by government to build good, low-priced housing appears to have been halted by contractors who have refused to tender for the work and have succeeded in dissuading competitors across the border from taking their places. Overshadowing all these countries are the problems of unemployment and under-employment, particularly in rural areas, and these lead to potentially conflicting attempts to increase production and relieve poverty, to develop industrial centres and assist depressed regions. Political pressures and a sense of social justice compel governments to invest in rural areas, but there are good reasons for arguing that such areas benefit most from investment designed to promote the growth of industrial centres.* An illustration of the impact such conflicts make upon the housing field can be seen in Italy where the government endeavours to improve building techniques

* See, for example, Vera Lutz, *Italy. A Study in Economic Development*, Oxford University Press, 1962.

while the principal publicly sponsored building agency, INACASA, lists amongst its annual achievements the 'numbers of man-days of employment' it has provided. Frequently the development of good town plans, the provision of adequate water, drainage and other services, the use of local materials and the improvement of traditional construction methods – based on the high standard of craft skills often available in these countries – deserve more encouragement (but get less) than the building of large and costly blocks of flats. Criticisms of this kind are often heard in the countries concerned, and are now leading to reappraisals of housing policies in several of them.

The housing responsibilities assumed by governments in these countries consist of a variety of interventions, prompted by equally varied intentions. Each of these projects and devices had its own validity at the outset, but although they have since grown and proliferated within separate branches of central and local bureaucracies they were never intended to form a comprehensive policy for housing. At the point when such interventions began, several of these countries were suffering the effects and after-effects of war and civil war, the resources of government were limited, the techniques of economic planning were not understood, and political support for any serious attempt at planning was lacking. Since then, people and their governments have grown richer, and planning has become fashionable and increasingly effective. As the scope and confidence of government expand and people look beyond their current crises to the long-term development of their country, so the separate programmes that play a part in the housing field are seen to fall short of a rational or effective housing policy. It will never be possible to perfect a completely single-minded and universally agreed policy in this field; indeed, the housing systems of these countries are often revealing to others because they pose in more obvious forms the contradictions that have been concealed, rather than resolved, elsewhere. But the clarification and reconciliation of objectives and the formulation of more comprehensive national policies are now the principal tasks confronting those concerned with housing in countries at this stage of economic and social development.

It is in Spain that the most impressive attack has been made on these problems.* A Ministry of Housing was established in 1957, combining many functions previously exercised by different agencies, and a long-term projection of housing needs and the resources required to meet them was drawn up for the period 1961–76. In three years after 1961 the annual output of dwellings rose from 135,000 to 240,000; there has been a steady growth in the proportion of the capital required for this programme which has come from private sources, and government funds have been increasingly used to ensure continuity of demand by reducing fluctuations in output and to provide help for households in greater need of it. Building has been concentrated in the major industrial centres where population is now growing very fast, and it is intended that a start should soon be made on the major programme of replacement that will be required and on the provision of housing for the elderly (whose expectation of life is rising rapidly). These developments called for careful planning and extensive administrative reorganization; but they were rendered possible by the pace of economic growth and the rising trend of saving and investment achieved in Spain during recent years, and carried forward by general political pressures for an improvement in living standards. The government's housing responsibilities are taking an increasingly comprehensive form which can no longer be classed among the first group discussed here since they are assuming patterns more akin to those that will be described later in this chapter.

'SOCIAL' HOUSING POLICIES

The next countries to be considered have a longer industrial history and this, in conjunction with other characteristics, goes far to explain the different pattern of housing responsibilities assumed by their governments. Switzerland and the United Kingdom, though dissimilar in many respects, may be described as following 'social' housing policies and other north European countries – Norway and Sweden, for example – once had the

* See Paul F. Wendt and Eric Carlson, 'Spain's Housing Policy: an Evaluation of the National Housing Plan, 1961–76', *Land Economics*, XXXIX, 1 February 1963.

same sort of system. Ireland* and Belgium exhibit some of the same characteristics. Governments adopting this pattern may build or subsidize a large or small proportion of the houses produced (40 per cent in the United Kingdom and 10 per cent in Switzerland, for example) and the total produced each year may be large or small in number (9·7 houses per thousand population in Switzerland and 3·2 per thousand in Ireland).† It is not the scale but the character of their governments' operations which distinguish them. The United Kingdom's pattern is now changing, and its current development will be considered in the second part of this book. Here, where our purpose is to identify and describe particular phases of development, it is the pattern of 1960–64 that is discussed.

In these countries government's principal role is to come to the aid of selected groups in the population and help those who cannot secure housing for themselves in the 'open market'. Its operations are designed to meet particular needs and solve particular problems; and, whether they consist of building, lending, subsidy, rent controls or other measures, these operations are regarded as exceptional 'interventions' – often temporary interventions – within an otherwise 'normal' system. Thus government is not assumed to be responsible for the housing conditions of the whole population, except in the negative sense of enforcing certain minimum standards for the protection of public health, and it is not expected to prepare and implement a long-term national housing programme. These generalizations are too crude to do justice to the complex and changing policies of the countries named. The United Kingdom, for example, adopted a rather different pattern during the years immediately after the war – when the government controlled all building and was responsible, through the local authorities, for 80 per cent of the housing programme – and she now appears to be moving again towards a more comprehensive system. Nevertheless, the scope and time-scale of our government's responsibilities for housing have always been more restricted

*Paul A. Pfretzscher, *The Dynamics of Irish Housing*, Dublin, Institute of Public Administration, 1965.

†U.N. *Annual Bulletin of Housing and Building Statistics for Europe, 1964*, Geneva, 1965.

than those of the policies it has adopted for the health services and for education. A 'local housing authority' is not responsible for preparing long-term forecasts of requirements in the manner that is expected of local education authorities and (more recently) of the health services, it is not required by law to have a chief housing officer, and the central government does not have a nationwide inspectorate responsible for maintaining nationwide standards of service as it does in other fields.

The setting within which the United Kingdom's policies have developed has already been briefly sketched, but common features distinguishing the countries in this group deserve further examination. For various reasons their shortage of houses is not as severe as that afflicting most of the rest of Europe. The population to be housed in Ireland has been falling for many years, and the United Kingdom's rates of population growth and internal migration are well below the average for western Europe. Their major centres of population were established long ago, at a time when the state was not expected to play a part in providing housing. These countries have a well developed system of local government with a strong poor law and public health tradition, making it natural for the state to employ local authorities as the principal instrument of its housing policies, and for their efforts to be concentrated mainly upon problems of squalor and over-crowding. To these characteristics the Swiss add a distrust of government itself (reflected in the salary scales of officials) that springs from a long republican tradition, and an administrative system that is more completely decentralized than that of any other industrial country; the cantons – often minute in size – still constitute the principal unit for citizenship and administration.

The restricted and specialized role of governments in these countries is sustained and rendered viable by well organized and long established private capital markets that enable the credit-worthy to borrow money for the building and purchase of houses. London, Brussels and Zurich are three of the world's principal financial centres, and the scope for lending and borrowing they provide has major implications for housing, as for other forms of capital investment. The Swiss situation is unique: private borrowers could in 1963 raise 60–65 per cent of the purchase price of housing through open market loans, which under normal conditions need never be repaid, at an interest rate of $3\frac{3}{4}$ per cent. Second mortgages, at $4\frac{1}{4}$ per cent interest, repaid over twenty or twenty-five years, left the borrower to find from his own savings and the banks about 20 per cent of the capital he required. If he wishes to get rid of his property later he can usually transfer his obligations to subsequent purchasers without difficulty. Since 1963 there has been a considerable tightening of the terms on which credit can be secured, but there remains an effective 'open market' which a large proportion of the population can rely on – more often as tenants of the companies building flats than as owner-occupiers of separate houses – and any major addition to these resources contributed by government would add to the dangers of inflation already threatened by scarcities of building capacity and the continuing inflow of funds seeking refuge in the fiscal and political haven that Switzerland offers to the rich throughout the world. This situation largely explains why Switzerland has been able to go on building at about twice the rate of the United Kingdom (in relation to her population) although only 2 per cent of her houses are built by the state and the federal government's contribution to the housing programme amounted, in 1963, to only 4 million francs in a total budget of 4,598 million. To these factors restricting the scope of the government's housing responsibilities there has in recent years been added a crucial social factor: Switzerland now employs some 650,000 migrant workers, including much of the manpower for agriculture and service trades and no less than 34 per cent of the total labour force in factories. Though hostels and housing of various kinds are provided for some of these workers, they are not permitted to bring their relatives to Switzerland (unless they work too) and they cannot remain in the country if they lose their jobs.

The situation in the other countries mentioned is very different. Interest rates and the terms on which loans must be repaid are far less favourable to the borrower, and the role of government is therefore a much bigger one – particularly in the United Kingdom. But here, too, the existence of a long established nationwide system for lending money to the house buyer through building societies and insurance companies, and the provision of generous support for this system through tax reliefs on payments of mortgage interest, have permitted government to restrict its contribution in a manner that would have been intolerable to countries in which housing shortages were more severe, capital was more scarce, regional disparities in resources were greater, and there was greater wartime devastation – whether of the housing stock or of the institutions available to finance building operations. Another factor enabling our own government to restrict its responsibilities has been the low cost of building in relation to the average wage. Partly, perhaps, because private builders and lenders have had to cater for large numbers of people who would elsewhere be entitled to participate in publicly supported housing schemes, the quality of new building has been held down to a level that is modest – if not mean – by comparison with other countries that have a similar general standard of living.

A number of countries have tax systems which enable borrowers to deduct interest payments on housing loans from their taxable incomes, and it will be shown later that this practice has important implications for housing policy. But the contribution to housing costs made in this way by governments adopting a 'social' system is not employed as a deliberate instrument of housing policy; it is an accidental outcome of fiscal tradition that is not designed to discriminate in any systematic fashion between the housing needs of borrowers or between the types of houses built and bought.

The United Kingdom lies at one extreme within this group. The government financed and organized the bulk of the housing programme during the years immediately after the war, and in 1949 it removed the restrictive phrase 'working classes' from the housing Acts; but its contribution to the programme was still designed to help those in greatest need – virtually the same people it had served hitherto – and this contribution was cut back in the mid 1950s when most of these needs were thought to have been met and attention was turned to reviving a 'free market' in housing. The endeavours to promote publicly subsidized improvements in older houses and to encourage the development of housing associations were forerunners of new extensions of the role of government which are now giving the state more comprehensive responsibilities in this field. At the other extreme lies Switzerland where the government's housing powers are severely restricted, being based on short-term legislation, typically authorizing no more than a four-year programme, with the intention – so far unrealized – that these powers be terminated at the end of that time. But despite the diversity of their policies and procedures, the limited and essentially residual roles assumed by these governments can be distinguished from the patterns found in the next group of countries to be considered.

TOWARDS A COMPREHENSIVE COMMITMENT

Most of the countries with long industrial histories and high living standards have followed a 'social' housing policy at some stage of their development. But since the Second World War several of them have extended their commitments to a point at which they can no longer be regarded as 'interventions' within an otherwise 'normal' market; governments now shape and control this market to such an extent that their housing responsibilities have assumed a national or 'comprehensive' form.

This phase arises when industrialization and the growth of cities have reached a point at which considerable savings can be mobilized for house building, good urban living standards are in demand throughout the country, labour is fully employed and additional resources cannot be diverted to the housing programme without compensating cuts in other sectors, and government itself has a well trained and reliable body of administrative and technical staff at central, regional and local levels. Since the countries with 'social' housing systems have attained this level of organization, these conditions alone are insufficient to account for the pattern of reponsibilities to be discussed. To these conditions must be added a constructive sense of crisis, derived from severe housing problems and a determination to solve them. In Sweden this sense of crisis appears to have been provoked by the collapse of the building industry during the early years of the Second World War, and a constructive response was fostered by the political climate of

T – G.O.H. – D

the country at that time. In France the shock of defeat was followed after the war by a determination to shake off the years of stagnation and to fashion a more dynamic and deliberately planned society, and this development wrought changes which had their effect – a belated one – on housing as on other sectors of the economy. Similar developments appear to have been provoked in Holland by wartime devastation, a rapid growth in population and the loss of empire; in Norway by wartime devastation – particularly of the northern territories – and rapid post-war growth of population and cities, coupled with the paucity of this small nation's capital resources; and in West Germany by the obliteration of most of her principal cities, the collapse of the currency, the threat of Communism and the flood of refugees from the east. Austria, Denmark and Finland shared many of these experiences, but their housing systems differ in various ways and to varying degrees from those of the countries to be discussed.

The development of more comprehensive housing responsibilities sprang from urgent needs, the capacity to meet these needs – given time – and the determination to do so. But when they embarked upon more comprehensive commitments none of these governments envisaged their future pattern with any precision; the immediate tasks of providing food, shelter, work and the essential services were too pressing to leave much time for contemplating the future, and in most of the belligerent countries housing programmes did not get going on a big scale until the 1950s – though building in north western Europe recovered much faster than in the south and east. Thus the systems to be discussed emerged from successive adaptations and improvisations; they were not foreseen and planned as a whole.

Shortages of building materials often presented the first problem to be surmounted. Sites had to be acquired, and equipped with the services needed for housing – and, despite the unpopularity he sometimes attracts, it must be remembered that the skills of the 'developer' are scarce and play a crucial part in the provision of housing. Then labour became increasingly scarce. As building costs rose in response to these shortages, the size, standards and design of housing had to be reappraised – and were frequently reduced to secure more houses from the resources available. When the sites that had been blitzed or left in the 'pipelines' of abandoned prewar building schemes were exhausted, the shortage of land and the rise in land prices presented increasing anxieties and the continuing – and largely unforeseen – growth of the major cities still poses urgent problems of land scarcity. The order and severity of these bottlenecks varied from one country to another but each government has had to contend with successive 'crises' on most of these fronts – crises which were the price of success in the principal task of getting houses built. The success of a housing policy is not to be judged by the absence of crises but by the successful confrontation of the right crises in the right order. The absence of crises suggests a timid housing programme; their persistence over many years suggests incompetent government.

It was the determined attempt to resolve these problems which led governments step by step into increasingly comprehensive housing commitments. The process is by no means complete; no western country claims to have a solution for the problem of land pricing, for example. New problems have still to be confronted; the countries facing the worst housing shortages have scarcely begun to organize effective replacement programmes. But the crucial elements in the pattern are already clear. Nine of them can be listed.

1. Estimates and projections of housing requirements are prepared for the *whole* country, and revised from time to time, contrasting the implications of different assumptions, and showing the programmes envisaged for the next five or ten years: thus the needs to be met are defined and discussed in a comprehensive fashion.

2. The government may itself commission a large or small proportion of the houses in the programme or it may (as in West Germany) build no houses at all. But it draws up a long-term programme, which includes *all* forms of house building, and its own contribution is regarded as an integral part of that total. Policy will be revised and modified from time to time, sometimes at short notice, but builders, lenders, town planners and the public at large have confidence that building will

continue in a reasonably predictable fashion. Thus the housing programme is comprehensively defined and, subject to marginal variations, virtually guaranteed by government. The government's own contribution to this programme is not regarded as a 'marginal' intervention designed only to meet residual needs which cannot be met by other investors.

3. By whatever means prove appropriate – and we shall see that many are available – government secures control of a sufficient volume of savings to ensure that money is available to sustain the level of building it requires.

4. Government does not merely predict but actively controls the total output of housing – often with great precision – and it relates this programme to other sectors of the economy. Therefore it is responsible both for expanding and for restricting output when either appears to be called for, and for ensuring that appropriate numbers of households prove capable of buying or renting the houses built.

5. The government has means for relating the output and geographical distribution of new houses to the general development of the whole economy and of particular industries and regions within it. This is a peculiarly difficult task that cannot be performed with precision in a changing society – even in centrally planned economies where government owns all the principal means of production – but systematic and increasingly effective attempts are made to forecast the growth and distribution of employment, population and households, and to show the relationships between these trends and the demands for housing and transport, and the pattern of land uses.

6. In addition to its responsibilities for new building, the government also has some control over the distribution of existing housing, particularly in the areas of greatest shortage, or has at least the right to exercise such controls, usually through municipal authorities. Thus housing policy deals with the use to be made of the whole stock of housing, not only with the distribution of new houses. To be effective such policies call for fairly extensive regulation of rents in areas of shortage.

7. The government also finds it has to assume considerable control over the standards, types and sizes of the new houses built, in order to ensure that the existing stock is increased in

ways that match the needs to be met, and that resources are used in an economical fashion to produce a sufficient quantity of houses that can be let or sold at prices appropriate for the households who are to go into them.

8. The development of the building industry that is to fulfil these programmes cannot be left to chance without jeopardizing the rest of the system, and the government therefore assumes increasing responsibility for improving the technology, organization and general efficiency of the industry, through research, education, practical demonstrations, development projects and other means.

9. These responsibilities cannot be fulfilled unless government is constantly informed about the development of relevant features of the economy, armed with long-term forecasts of future needs and resources, and briefed by officials familiar with current research in a variety of technical and social fields. Thus government conducts, promotes and uses research on a considerable scale.

Governments of the countries mentioned vary in the extent to which they abide by these requirements and it should not be assumed that each precisely fulfils the conditions listed. Moreover the list does not exhaust the characteristics of a genuinely 'comprehensive' housing system; nothing has been said, for example, about the replacement of existing houses or the regulation of the prices of land, though obligations under both these headings will soon become a crucial part of the pattern. But the validity of these criteria does not depend simply on the observed performance of governments. It could be predicted from the nature of the first two responsibilities that any government committed to meeting housing needs in a comprehensive and sufficiently ambitious fashion would in time be led, as a matter of logical necessity, to assume most of the remaining commitments. Those that have gone much further find themselves applying, in the sphere of housing, a new philosophy of government. They are no longer regulating, supplementing, stimulating or restraining the operations of an independent market. They have assumed responsibility for determining the objectives to be attained, and hence for mobilizing the resources and creating the conditions required for that purpose. The

distinctions between the 'public' and 'private' sectors of
housing – distinctions which are central to the thinking of
those accustomed to a 'social' pattern of housing policies –
have lost most of their significance. Private enterprise
usually has as large a part to play as ever; often a larger one.
But it operates within the context of a plan determined by
government.

A particular conjunction of needs, resources and ambitions
has been stressed in explaining the origins of this pattern of
responsibilities. But government cannot realize its ambitions
until it secures sufficient control over the resources required to
support the housing programme – and in market economies this
means financial resources. The techniques employed for this
purpose vary from one country to another but have certain
common characteristics.

In France, where building societies of the British type scarcely exist, the government has close control over the principal
agencies handling small savings, although most of them retain
a private form: the *Crédit Foncier*, a mortgage bank lending
money on the security of completed building, the *Sous-Comptoir*
lending to builders during the course of building operations,
the *Caisse des Dépôts et Consignations* through which deposits
from local savings banks are channelled, and the *Banque du
Trésor* are among the most important, and much of their
resources are invested in housing on terms which include, or
are supported by, a considerable subsidy. Every enterprise
employing ten or more people is required by law to set aside
1 per cent of its wage bill each year for housing schemes
serving its workers. All building is controlled through a
licensing system and the allocation of credits for building
purposes is supervised by a central authority presided over by
the Minister of Finance. Tax privileges of various kinds help
people to repay loans on housing, and are used with some
discrimination to direct private investment into channels
favoured by government policy: for example, additional taxes
are paid on vacant houses (whereas in the United Kingdom
until very recently no rates were levied on an empty house) and
the owner of a new house is relieved of property taxes for the
first years after it is built.

In West Germany the capital market was entirely destroyed by the collapse of the currency and could not be re-established until the currency reform of 1948. During the next few years the government provided half the capital for a huge building programme. Since then the contribution made by loans and grants from the federal government has fallen to one fifth of the total cost of house building, but the steeply progressive tax system bequeathed to it by the occupying powers enabled the government to give away extensive tax reliefs which have been heavily concentrated upon those who save money to buy houses. Regular premiums are added to the savings of those who commit themselves to long-term saving schemes which (with restricted exceptions) can only be used for house purchase. Tax payers buying new houses are entitled to generous tax reliefs for ten years. With typical wages and house prices, a skilled worker with a wife and child is practically exempted from income tax and church taxes for these ten years and can claim additional direct subsidies as well; a businessman supporting a wife and two children on an income about three times as large would be relieved of 20 per cent of his tax payments, amounting to 15 per cent of the cost of his house.* A special tax is levied on the owners of property which survived the war undamaged and the proceeds are used to compensate others. This, too, provides resources for investment in housing.

In Norway the government provides well over half the funds for house building from its own resources, a small but crucial proportion of which come in the form of interest-free loans which call, as yet, for no repayment. The resources for this lending are mainly derived from a high rate of taxation: the Norwegian government's net lending is probably higher, in comparison with its revenue, than that of any other country in western Europe, and much of this money is channelled through a state bank specializing in loans for housing. In Sweden the government again uses the budget to provide a large share of the resources for housing. It also has a rapidly growing pension fund accumulated from heavy contributions that will outweigh the payments drawn from the fund for many years to come, and

*Federal Ministry of Housing, *Housing and Urban Development in the Federal Republic of Germany*, Bad Godesberg.

nearly half the investments made by this fund are directed to housing. In 1962 these credits covered 20 per cent of the costs of house building and if they continue to increase at their recent rate this fund will in a few years be capable of financing the bulk of the housing programme. The Norwegian pension fund, more recently established, is also expected to play a major part in financing house building.

Each of these systems reflects the needs and traditions of the countries concerned: in France the large and widely dispersed population of small savers and the pervasive authority of government, in West Germany the imaginative use of taxation and the determination to foster owner occupation as a protection against Communism, in Norway the use of severe tax policies and generous credit policies to maintain the very high level of investment needed by a country whose economic survival depends on industries (such as shipbuilding, mining, electrical generation and the merchant marine) in which there are thousands of pounds' worth of capital behind every man employed. Such are the factors which dictate the diverse patterns of housing finance. But these patterns have a number of common features.

The development of a comprehensive national housing programme depends upon government's ability to secure control over a continuing flow of small savings contributed by many people throughout the population and to direct these savings into investment in housing. Control may be exercised in a variety of ways, and it is not necessary for the funds to pass through the hands of public authorities. In each country these savings are garnered from several different sources; there is no single device or institution which provides all that is required. Although the people currently rehoused pay quite heavily for the privilege, it is not principally from their savings that the capital resources for the programme are derived, nor does the scale of the housing programme depend directly on their income expectations. It depends on the growth and resources of the whole economy and on government decisions about the allocation of those resources.

The capital controlled by government is invested by different means in different types of housing and is not concentrated upon one sector of the programme. By offering money on different terms to a wide selection of investors – owner-occupiers, municipal housing authorities, private landlords, housing associations and cooperatives, for example – and by direct control of bank lending and the final, comparatively small, 'top loans' which actually determine whether particular building schemes proceed, governments can spread their influence through every sector of the programme. Thus they can secure more extensive and sensitive control of the pro-gramme than our own government achieves, and provide a greater variety of housing for a wider variety of households, although the capital they invest in the programme may be no greater than the contribution made by British public authorities to the financing of council houses.

The Swedish system illustrates this pattern particularly well. There has never been an extensive private capital market in Sweden, and the costs of building are high, owing to the ex-cellent quality of Swedish housing and the rigours of the climate and much of the terrain. Government has therefore provided three types of loan for house-builders: first loans, at a rate of interest slightly below the market level, covering 60 per cent of the valuation and calling for no repayment until other loans have been repaid, and second and third loans, at similar privileged rates of interest, repaid over thirty to forty years. All three types of loan are available to all the principal types of investor, but their size varies: municipal authorities can borrow 100 per cent of the capital cost of their building, non-profit-making cooperatives can borrow 95 per cent of the government's (realistic) valuation of their schemes, owner-occupiers can borrow 90 per cent, and private landlords 85 per cent. The distribution of these credits among the different investors and the different geographical regions of the country is planned with care, in the light of up-to-date reports on building capacity furnished by local Labour Market Boards, and the short-term credits covering the remaining margins of capital cost are provided by the banks which work in close collaboration with government. The cost and quality of housing financed in this way are subject, repectively, to upper and lower limits. Since the war, more than 90 per cent of Sweden's large housing programme has depended on government lending and controls of this kind.

'Comprehensive' housing systems have many other characteristics, some of which we shall return to in later chapters dealing with the planning of land uses, the organization of the building industry, research and other matters. But their financial characteristics are the starting point of these systems, providing the foundation for their subsequent development in other directions.

CONCLUSIONS

The first pattern of responsibilities discussed in this chapter arises during the period between a government's initial interventions in the housing field and the development of more coherent national policies – a phase that is transitional and liable to become increasingly confused, though it may continue for a long time. The second pattern can be more legitimately identified as a distinctive governmental 'role' or policy, and under favourable conditions it can continue more or less indefinitely. If the responsibilities of government remain specialized and restricted and the 'open market' for housing proves reasonably effective and survives unscathed by economic or political upheavals, then the continual modification of priorities and procedures (to be expected in housing as in any other sphere of government) can be confined within the stable liberal-democratic framework of 'social' housing policies. The third pattern discussed is again a transitional phase – at least in its present form. Government assumes increasingly comprehensive responsibilities for housing its population, but the directions of development are easier to discern than their ultimate outcome. Before discussing these patterns further, a number of potential misconceptions should be cleared away.

It is not suggested that every market economy in Europe can be fitted into one of these categories. Some of these countries show a mixture of these patterns and others cannot fairly be classified in this way at all. There is no inevitable progression from one pattern of responsibilities to another. Countries in an early stage of economic development may adopt systematically planned housing policies of some sort, but for a while they do not have the resources to assume the comprehensive commitments to be seen in some of the wealthier urban societies of north western Europe. As their technical and material resources grow, however, and as the scope for economic planning is realized, poorer countries seem more likely to adopt these comprehensive patterns than the 'social' housing policies to be seen in some of the long-industrialized democracies. Spain is now moving towards an increasingly comprehensive system and her example may be followed by others. Meanwhile governments which assume more comprehensive commitments are not compelled to sustain these for ever. In West Germany it is the government's declared intention to recreate a 'free market' and reduce its commitments during the next few years; steps are now being taken to extricate government from its dominant place in the market and to revert to something more closely resembling a 'social' policy. The French claim similar intentions, but have no immediate prospect of achieving a disengagement since France is much further from satisfying her housing needs and her government is permanently committed to a more decisive and pervasive system of economic planning.

The three roles outlined should not be regarded as three different 'policies', for each can accommodate a wide variety of objectives. Large and small housing programmes are found in all three: in their output of houses (per thousand population) Switzerland and West Germany have long been close to the head of the European league tables, and Greece also appears to maintain a remarkably high rate of building (though in her case the statistics, being based on houses started rather than completed, are less reliable). In some countries – and until recently France appears to have been one of them – the machinery of a comprehensive system has been used not to maximize house building but to restrain it in the interests of other sectors of the economy.

Neither should it be assumed that one pattern is necessarily more 'progressive' or equalitarian than others. Governments adopting 'social' systems endeavour to meet specific needs which are regarded as the most urgent, and achieve this to varying degrees. The extent to which their efforts correct or reverse the inequalities of an unregulated market depends on the proportion of building that is devoted to social objectives and on other features of their policy – on the forms of rent restriction employed and on the way in which subsidies are distributed, for example. Governments adopting comprehensive systems tend to be more concerned with the development of the whole housing programme than with the needs of particular types of household. This is partly because they make use of a wider variety of semi-independent institutions – housing associations and voluntary bodies of various kinds – whose allocations of houses cannot be strictly controlled, and partly because their policies were originally designed in crisis situations to recreate building and lending industries and a supply of housing, not to modify and supplement a going concern. In these countries controls over building often restrict the types of dwelling produced to a narrow range, squeezed from above by maximum costs and from below by minimum standards. In this sense, comprehensive systems may be described as 'equalitarian': everyone gets much the same kind of house or flat. But the programme may lack variety and the poorest families may fail to secure a place in the queue. In France the government's aim has been to break out of a pre-war tradition of particularly severe rent restriction and to secure a larger contribution to housing costs from personal incomes; inevitably, therefore, the bulk of the building programme has gone to households able to make an appreciable contribution from their own incomes, though steps are now being taken to extend the benefits of this building to lower income groups. In Scandinavia the aim of housing policies has been to promote the output of good housing for ordinary families, and the poorest still tend to search several years longer for this privilege, even if they usually secure it in the end. The lack of large slum clearance programmes also condemns poorer families, in those countries that still have slums, to live in bad housing for long periods if not for their whole lives.

The description of these housing systems may suggest that policies under each proceed smoothly within a framework of general agreement, only running into controversy when the possibility of changing from one system to another is considered.

But in fact controversy about housing policies continues unceasingly in all countries. Indeed, it takes certain classical forms. Politicians and officials attached to Finance Ministries, responsible for the orderly growth of the economy and the stability of the currency, often regard housing as an 'unproductive' investment that is liable to reduce saving and generate inflationary demands for consumption goods; some therefore prefer to treat house building as an economic 'regulator' to be increased only when there is a threat of deflation and unemployment. In Ministries of Construction or Housing and in organizations responsible for building houses or concerned with the technical development of the building industry, people tend to seek long-term, rising programmes, sustained by high savings and high rents, that will enable them to put up as many houses as possible, increase productivity, and perfect new building methods and materials. If the economy requires adjustment they look for cuts elsewhere, and if some people cannot afford the new houses produced, their needs, it is assumed, must be disregarded or met in other ways. Others, primarily concerned with the development of backward regions or the needs of the poverty stricken and the badly housed, are more interested in the distribution of the housing programme than its total size, and call for low rents, generous subsidies and a fairer distribution of existing houses. They are also more likely to be interested in the improvement or replacement of older property – always a costly process.

The growing influence of economic planning commissions and the industrial and administrative bodies attached to them has in many countries strengthened the second group of contenders at the expense of the first. The third group often finds it hardest to secure a hearing, unless the people they are concerned about live in marginal constituencies and politically sensitive regions. Their aims are expensive and unlikely, on the face of them, to increase the national product. Conflicts of this kind cannot be eliminated since they reflect the fundamental issues that policy-makers must deal with in every field of government.

Some final questions should be posed before this survey of western Europe is concluded. If a growing range of decisions about housing and the economic framework within which it develops are to be taken by government, and if the time-scale of decision is to stretch ten years or more into the future, how can the decisions that have to be taken be reconciled with each other and with the human needs and aspirations they are designed to satisfy? Parliamentary democracy is not well suited for the taking of decisions whose impact may not become fully apparent before the election after next. New procedures may be needed, both for expressing and for educating public opinion, on a national and a regional scale.

While comprehensive long-term plans furnish the only means for achieving certain things, they also provide opportunities for monumental error. Careful thought and research and frank public discussion will be required to avoid such errors. The standardized, mass-produced housing units now being hoisted into position at an impressive pace in some European countries – with kitchens, baths, electric wiring and other fittings cast into place in a manner that defies subsequent modification or replacement – will preserve the household equipment and living patterns of mid-twentieth-century low-cost housing for generations to come, like flies in amber. The building rate goes up, but the replacement problems of the future may prove devastating. This is not an argument for abandoning planning, but an argument for planning that leaves scope for second thoughts and for our successors' reactions to situations we cannot foresee. It has urgent implications for the density at which towns, town centres and new estates are built: highly sophisticated multi-level designs, stacked like aircraft carriers into compact spaces, may attain the heart's immediate desires – and a big spread in the Sunday papers – but they are exceedingly difficult to modify and extend in ways that will accommodate the unpredictable future. Likewise, when designing individual dwellings, it should be remembered that our successors may be more grateful for ample space, well insulated against heat, cold and sound, than for the rapidly obsolescent equipment we build into it.

However large the contribution that governments may make to the programme, much of the resources required for a major attack on housing problems has to come, and come voluntarily, from private pockets. The need to recruit private capital for investment in housing, both from the owner-occupiers' and cooperators' small savings and from the development companies' millions, has led many countries to buy the participation of the private investor with generous subsidies and tax reliefs which confer growing privileges upon the fortunate at the expense of the general body of tax payers – sometimes without giving much help to those who need it most. The distribution of public funds may too readily confirm and reinforce the inequalities already dividing society. Governments must learn to make constructive use of private initiative and private resources without becoming imprisoned in the embrace of those who furnish this help. This can only be achieved by a building programme large enough, and a stock of housing plentiful enough, to eliminate the severer scarcities and weaken the more powerful monopolies.

It has been pointed out that governments are not compelled to maintain comprehensive commitments in this field indefinitely, but a country (such as the United Kingdom) which appears to be embarking on more comprehensive commitments should be aware that they may prove exceedingly difficult to shed. The Danish case illustrates the problem. In 1958 Denmark abandoned many of the controls previously operating in this field and redistributed its subsidies in an increasingly selective fashion. In the years that followed there was a rapid and unforeseen increase in house building (due partly to reasons unconnected with the change in housing policy) and the balance of payments deteriorated, compelling the government to reimpose controls on building. No longer possessing the more pervasive and sensitive means of control hitherto available, it had to use cruder financial and licensing restrictions which cut back the most readily controlled parts of the programme – particularly public building, for people in greatest need, in areas of greatest shortage, employing the more advanced building methods – while private building for owner occupation in suburban and rural areas continued unchecked. Thus an economic crisis compelled government to reassert its control on house building, but the reins had passed from the hands of those concerned primarily with housing to those concerned primarily with inflation and the balance of payments; and Finance Ministries are always less averse to expensive building that attracts the savings of its occupiers than to building that calls for subsidy or the additional costs of slum clearance and urban redevelopment.

Some of these problems will be discussed later in this book. But before pursuing them further, it may be helpful to take a look at the other half of Europe to see whether the centrally planned countries have found solutions to these dilemmas.

CHAPTER 4

HOUSING IN EASTERN EUROPE*

IN western Europe many governments are assuming increasingly comprehensive responsibilities for the housing of their people.
The mechanisms of the market remain important, but these
mechanisms work within a framework of controls, subsidies,
credit policies and publicly sponsored building operations which
produces an outcome very different from that to be expected of a
'free' market. Governments' activities can no longer be regarded
as marginal interventions within the market; they go far to
determine the supply of housing and the demand for it, the
structure of the market and its regional development. Meanwhile the governments of eastern Europe are beginning to use
market mechanisms to improve the efficiency of their systems
and extend the range of choices they offer. Private saving and
spending are being drawn in to bear an increasing share of the
burden of housing investment which would otherwise fall on
state budgets. There is a convergence of policies and procedures
between east and west which is likely to prove increasingly
interesting to both sides. As the dogmas of capitalism and
Communism recede, the fundamental problems of housing
policy emerge more clearly.

The housing systems of eastern Europe's centrally planned
economies differ from those of the west in fundamental ways;
little has been written about them in English and comparisons
are liable to be misleading if these systems are not first explained
in some detail. Housing programmes in the east are regarded as
an integral part of the whole economy; the scale of house
building and many features of its distribution among regions and
households are determined by the requirements of a broader
economic strategy. At the local level, house building is carried
out in close conjunction with other forms of construction

*An earlier version of this chapter appeared in the *Transactions of the
Bartlett Society*, Volume 3, 1964–5. Bartlett School of Architecture,
University College, London, 1966.

– factories, roads, shops, hospitals, schools and housing being planned and erected together, often by the same building enterprises. Thus in one sense the scope and ramifications of 'housing policy' are more extensive and its objectives less easy to define than in the market economies. For the same reasons, however, the most important decisions about housing are not taken within organizations principally responsible for this field but at higher levels of the political and administrative hierarchy. In another sense, therefore, 'housing policy' may be interpreted as dealing only with a restricted range of problems – particularly the technical problems arising from the industrialization of building methods, and the problems of repairing, maintaining, replacing and managing existing property. This restricted, technocratic, interpretation of the term is more often found in the Soviet Union than in Poland, Yugoslavia and other countries where public discussion of the fundamental issues of economic and social policies has been more freely permitted. Nevertheless, the meaning of the term 'housing policy' is liable to be ambiguous in any comparison between east and west.

Viewed from a thousand miles away, through a curtain of foreign languages from which debates about current developments seldom emerge in English translation, the housing systems of eastern Europe all appear very similar. Housing programmes form an integral part of successive economic plans, prepared in central planning commissions in accordance with the general directives of those in power. The state can readily acquire and redistribute such land and housing as it does not already own, and the rights of property owners have been so circumscribed that virtually no commercial profit can be derived from them. The building and distribution of houses in the programme is largely organized by regional and local units of government, and (until very recently) rents have been so low that they do not cover the full costs of repair and maintenance. In and around the bigger towns the building of houses – or more often flats – usually proceeds in the form of large projects on a scale resembling our new towns and largest estates. The Moscow housing authority, for example, is now building over 100,000 dwellings a year – half as many, each year, as the London County Council built throughout its history – and the standard neighbourhood units employed in the planning of Russian housing developments provide for between six and ten thousand people, several units being grouped to make up 'micro-regions' of 30,000–50,000 people. Housing conditions in eastern Europe are cramped and new flats are by our standards small, poorly finished, but fairly well equipped – centrally heated, averaging between $2\frac{1}{2}$ and 3 rooms per dwelling, with 400–550 square feet of 'useful floor space'. Housing privileges and hardships are reasonably equitably distributed through rationing systems of various kinds which give priority to families with children and to the most urgently needed workers and industries. Meanwhile the pace of economic development is rapid, productivity in building is rising and long term perspectives reach ahead to a dawn of abundance that is expected to break some time after 1980. This, in broad and fairly accurate outline, is the picture that reaches us. But despite these similarities, there are major differences in needs and policies that distinguish these countries from each other.

NEEDS AND RESOURCES

As in the west, the countries with the longest industrial history and the most slowly growing populations have more old housing, larger houses, the most plentiful stock of houses, and the greatest opportunities for improving their situation. Although the populations of these more fully industrialized countries are increasing slowly, the growing proportion of old people amongst them means that the numbers of households are growing a good deal faster than their rate of natural increase would suggest. Meanwhile, though shortages are less severe than elsewhere, much of the housing stock will have to be replaced before long. East Germany and Czechoslovakia are in this position. Hungary's situation is more complicated, combining a slow rate of population increase with a low but rapidly increasing degree of industrialization. At the other extreme lie the predominantly rural countries. Data are scarce for Yugoslavia, Bulgaria, Romania and Albania, but all appear to have more rapidly growing populations and severe housing shortages. Between these two groups stand Poland and the U.S.S.R. with an intermediate

PLANS OF FLATS BUILT IN

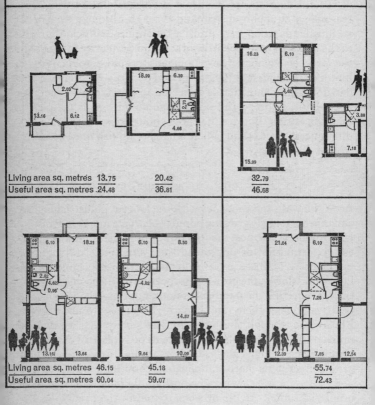

Living area sq. metres 13.75	20.42
Useful area sq. metres 24.48	36.81

32.79
46.68

Living area sq. metres 46.15	45.18
Useful area sq. metres 60.04	59.07

55.74
72.43

Figure 2.

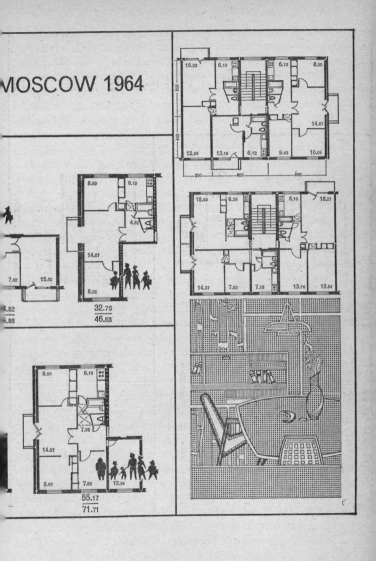

MOSCOW 1964

standard of housing but even faster rates of population increase. Russia* neglected her housing needs for many years, but having established the heavy industrial foundations of her economy and repaired the ravages of war, she turned in the mid fifties to deal with her housing problems and has for some years been building about half the dwellings going up throughout the whole of Europe – 14,234,000 out of a total of 27,370,000 during the peak period between 1958 and 1962, and slightly less since then. But Poland, with a less advanced building industry, and other investment priorities dictated by a frighteningly large generation of young people for whom to find work in the coming years, has one of the smallest housing programmes in Europe – building 4·6 houses per thousand inhabitants in 1962, compared with averages of 7·5 for north western Europe, 6·4 for southern Europe, 11·7 for the Soviet Union, and 5·6 for the rest of eastern Europe. (See Table 9 in the next chapter. The United Kingdom's rate was 6·0.)

The ownership and management of housing in the eastern countries varies widely too. Owner occupation is most common in rural areas, though this depends partly on the extent to which agriculture has been reorganized into state farms, cooperative or collective units, and on the types of housing provided for such units. In 1960–61 the proportions of housing that were owner-occupied in Czechoslovakia (50 per cent), Poland (over 50 per cent), Hungary (62 per cent) and Yugoslavia (78 per cent) – and probably in other eastern countries, too – were appreciably greater than in the United Kingdom (about 40 per cent). Russia (39 per cent in urban areas) must also have a proportion of owner-occupiers larger than our own. In the west, owner-occupation is sometimes regarded as a symbol of the bourgeois virtues; in the east it more often distinguishes the rural population, living in separate houses, from urban flat-dwellers. In the more rural economies new building is largely initiated and owned by private households – often with help from the state. In 1964, building for owner-occupation accounted for over half the output in Yugoslavia (58 per cent), Romania (60 per cent) and

*Strictly speaking, the term 'Russia' refers only to one of the Republics of the U.S.S.R., but it will be used here to refer to the whole country.

Bulgaria (77 per cent), and a large though declining proportion of Russia's (about 25 per cent in 1963). Building by the state and its industrial enterprises accounted for the largest proportions of output in East Germany (51 per cent), Poland (53 per cent) and Russia (about 60 per cent, including urban cooperatives). Building by cooperatives, though still accounting for only a small proportion of the total stock of housing, is now the most rapidly growing sector in the eastern countries – particularly in Poland (where it formed 18 per cent of total output), Czechoslovakia (33 per cent) and East Germany (41 per cent). In Czechoslovakia the building of houses by industrial enterprises has now been stopped, and a new form of cooperative housing is taking its place. The growth of these cooperative forms of ownership is likely to have a major impact on the development of housing policies in the centrally planned economies, as will be shown.

Even if the vast contrasts of Russia are disregarded, it must be remembered that there are great economic and social differences between the different regions within many of these countries, and hence between their housing conditions too – for example, between predominantly rural Slovakia with its rapidly growing population, and Bohemia where families are small and the landscape is dotted with industrial towns; and between the three regions of Poland which still bear distinctive traces of their long period under German, Austrian and Russian rule (the housing stock being generally best in the ex-German territories and worst in the ex-Russian). Thus attempts to compare these countries or to generalize about any one of them are bound to be oversimplified.

THE EVOLUTION OF POLICIES

The founding fathers of Marxist thought did not devote their most prolonged and rigorous analyses to housing questions, which they tended to regard as a problem created by capitalism and readily, but only, capable of solution once that system was overthrown. In his book on 'The Housing Question' Engels assumed the housing 'problem' was simply a product of this system.

. . . one thing is certain; there are already in existence sufficient buildings for dwellings in the big towns to remedy immediately any real 'housing *shortage*', given rational utilization of them. This can naturally only take place by the expropriation of the present owners and by quartering in their houses the homeless or those workers excessively overcrowded in their former houses. Immediately the proletariat has conquered political power such a measure dictated in the public interests will be just as easy to carry out as other expropriations and billetings are by the existing state.

He attacked proposals for the provision of owner-occupied cottages and a plot of land for working men as a reactionary attempt to defeat the inevitable progress of economic and political evolution:

... the ownership of house, garden and field, and security of tenure in the dwelling place, is becoming today, under the rule of large-scale industry, not only the worst hindrance to the worker, but the greatest misfortune for the whole working class, the basis for an unexampled depression of wages below their normal level ...

He was equally caustic about socialist proposals for the abolition of rent, lecturing his opponents in a paragraph that our Association of Land and Property Owners might well quote in its next submission to a government committee inquiring into this question:

Firstly, it is forgotten that the rent must not only pay the interests on the building costs but must also cover repairs and the average sum of bad debts, unpaid rents, as well as the occasional periods when the house is untenanted, and finally pay off in annual sums the building capital which has been invested in a house which is perishable and which in time becomes uninhabitable and worthless. Secondly, it is forgotten that the rent must also pay interest on the increased value of the land upon which the building is erected and that therefore a part of it consists of ground rent.

As for speculation about the housing policies of a Communist society:

... it does not occur to me to try to solve the so-called housing *question* any more than I can occupy myself with the details of the still more important *food question*. I am satisfied if I can prove ... that there are houses enough in existence to provide the working

masses for the time being with roomy and healthy living accommodation. To speculate as to how a future society would organize the
distribution .. of dwellings leads directly to *Utopia*.*

In effect, Engels treats housing as a peg upon which to hang his
indictments of capitalism and reformist socialism. Yet this was
the principal Marxist text on its subject, and Lenin read and
annotated a copy during the months before he assumed power.

The private landlord and his rents have long been symbols of
the exploitation of man by man, and it might have seemed natural for revolutionaries to abolish both of them together. But the
first systematic attempt to legislate for rents in the Soviet Union,
made in 1927 just before the first Five Year Plan, imposed standard levels of payment that were reasonably high in relation to
income and not very different from those to be found in capitalist
countries at the time, although there were deductions to help
families with low incomes. It was the freezing of these rents,
coupled with the serious inflations that took place during the
next twenty-five years – a period of slow building with an inter-
val of catastrophic destruction – which reduced rents to a sum
that became negligible. The basic law on rents today is still that
of 1927. Low rents, leading eventually to the provision of free
housing, were espoused as a principle of Russian social policy in
1961; but this principle was not derived direct from the gospels,
it emerged from the slow erosion of economic change under
political pressures in a fashion not unfamiliar in regulated
capitalist economies. Nevertheless, housing has clearly been
accepted as the responsibility of the state, to be provided as a
form of social service.

Table 7 shows how small a proportion of household spending
is devoted to rent and related housing costs in the east European
countries. Further inquiries made between 1959 and 1961 in
five of these countries showed that the average annual rents of
new dwellings ranged from 0·4 per cent of the total cost of the
dwelling in Poland, to 3·0 per cent of total cost in East Germany.
(The Ministry of Labour's survey of United Kingdom households, made in 1963, records 9 per cent of the average U.K.

* Frederick Engels, *The Housing Question*, pp. 32, 13, 21 and 98.
Lawrence & Wishart, 1936.

household's expenditure as devoted to 'housing costs'.)*
Governments of the other eastern countries generally began by following the Russian example. In many of them wartime devastation had been appalling, wholesale migrations and frontier changes had taken place, and equally drastic redistributions of housing were required to provide shelter for the

TABLE 7

Average Annual Expenditure of Manual Workers' Families on Housing and Related Items, Around 1960

Country	Year of inquiry	Percentage of expenditure devoted to:			
		Rent	Fuel and light	Furniture, upkeep and equipment	Total
		%	%	%	%
Bulgaria	1957	1·2	3·2	10·7	15·1
Czechoslovakia	1963	1·4[1]	2·9	6·2	10·5
East Germany	1957	6·7[2]	3·5	—	—
Hungary	1962	1·6	4·5	10·6	16·7
Poland	1962	1·2[1]	3·0	5·6	9·8
U.S.S.R.	1958	3·7[3]		—	—
Yugoslavia	1961	4·9	5·7	6·7	17·3

SOURCE: U.N. 'Major Problems' Study.

1. Raised considerably in subsequent years.
2. In 1962, 4·1 per cent.

3. Inquiry in Leningrad only; very similar results were obtained from an inquiry in Moscow. It is estimated that rent is approximately 2 per cent of expenditure.

homeless and to eliminate the social injustices of earlier years. The state took over houses that had belonged to municipalities, the larger landlords, and the dead and dispossessed – property that had belonged to Jews in Poland, and to Germans expelled from the Sudetenland, for example. In rural areas much of this housing was given or sold cheaply to individuals; in towns it was let by the state at low rents. The smaller landlords were in most places left with a formal title to their property, but their tenants

*Ministry of Labour, *Family Expenditure Survey, Report for 1963*, H.M.S.O., 1965. Note that 'housing' costs included rent, rates, insurance, less the proceeds of subletting, and for owner-occupiers, the rateable value of dwellings – i.e. a sum, for owner-occupiers, well below the payments actually made to secure a home.

were selected by municipal authorities, their rents were frozen and mostly paid into special funds used for meeting mainten-ance costs, and the principal advantage conferred by their title to property was the opportunity of getting a flat for themselves somewhere within it. House building revived slowly. As in the western countries, the first estimates of housing requirements made after the war tended to be too low; the effects of changes in the size and structure of the population and the pace of migra-tion to the towns were not fully foreseen, and a few – like Engels – may have thought that most needs could be met by the redis-tribution of housing space. The first official housing programmes often produced large houses, but far too few of them. As in Britain and other western countries, standards were gradually reduced and the quantity of dwellings built was increased. Under Stalin the Soviet Union built large and ornate flats worthy of the millennium to come, and placed two or three families in each of them. Thereafter, smaller flats were built, and since 1960 each new flat has been allotted to one family only. As a simple ratio of new dwellings to total population, Russian output rose to the levels of western Europe by the mid fifties, and then beyond, but among the other eastern countries only Romania has attained the average quantitative output of the west. Very high levels of saving and investment have been maintained in the east (though comparisons with the west are difficult owing to differences in pricing and accounting procedures) but until recently priority has been given not to housing but to the more 'productive' sectors of the economy.

The U.S.S.R. is a vast country which defies generalization. But the policies adopted in Czechoslovakia and Poland may be contrasted. Next to East Germany, Czechoslovakia* is the wealthiest of the centrally planned economies. Her industry continued to develop during the war and suffered little damage, her population is falling slowly in Bohemia but growing in

*See Jan M. Michal, *Central Planning in Czechoslovakia*, Stanford University Press, 1960, and Jiří Musil, *Housing Needs and Policy in Great Britain and Czechoslovakia*, University of Glasgow, Department of Social and Economic Studies, Occasional Papers No. 2; Oliver & Boyd, 1966. For a more general and theoretical analysis of the deve-lopment of the centrally planned economies see Peter Wiles, *The Political Economy of Marxism*, Blackwell, 1962.

Slovakia, and labour is very scarce. In recent years her economy has run into stagnation and disorganization: the rigid and centralized forms of control which continued here after other eastern countries had adopted more decentralized and flexible methods of administration appear to be peculiarly ill-suited to a complex and relatively wealthy economy. The growing independence of other countries in the eastern bloc is depriving Czechoslovakia of her role as industrial arsenal to her neighbours, and a new economic role has yet to be worked out. Agriculture has been extensively reorganized but the results have so far been disappointing. The current five-year plan was abandoned in 1963 and a more modest and realistic set of targets was adopted in its place. That year production and national income fell below the levels of the previous year. The government now appears to be engaged in a major overhaul of the economic system the outcome of which is still unsure; economies have been made in the welfare services, greater use is being made of the price mechanism as a means of raising productivity, and increasingly public criticism of the objectives and methods of economic planning is permitted. Housing policy is undergoing corresponding changes.

Poland emerged from the war as the charnel house of Europe: a fifth of her population – and much larger proportions among trained men in the prime of life – had been killed or lost; Warsaw had been systematically obliterated; more than 20 per cent of the housing stock, amounting to fifteen years' production at the prewar rate, had been destroyed. Today, half the Poles still live in rural areas and more than a third of them depend on agriculture for their living. Since the war Poland's birth rate has been the highest among the eastern countries, and though unemployment has not become an overt problem it remains a threatening possibility. Cities are growing fast, and priority has had to be given to building up an industrial structure capable of keeping a rapidly growing population fed and working. No major reorganization of the country's rather primitive farming methods has been attempted, and none will be possible until means can be found for employing and housing the large exodus from rural areas such a reform would bring about.*

*See John Michael Montias, *Central Planning in Poland*, Yale University Press, 1962.

CZECHOSLOVAKIA

In Czechoslovakia national plans are prepared by the State
Planning Commission, which is assisted by a newly established
Investment Commission that organizes and coordinates capital
investment of all kinds. Major decisions about the application or
modification of such plans are taken by the political bodies to
which these commissions are responsible. Programmes for
each sector are worked out, and subsequently implemented, by
a large number of Ministries – the Ministry of Construction
being the department principally responsible for the enterprises
that build housing, though not for the preparation and implementation of the programme itself. This Ministry's local building enterprises also construct factories, schools and other
buildings to designs prepared in the Ministries responsible for
the sectors and services concerned. Allocations of housing are
distributed to the twelve regional administrations, each averaging a little over a million in population, which work in turn
through districts of about 100,000 population, and through
smaller units of local government and special authorities established for major projects such as new towns. These allocations
are expressed in terms of money, with close control on the
varying maximum costs of housing permitted in each region.
Money for the programme is found through the state budget
from revenue raised largely from taxes on productive enterprises. The state does not finance its operations by borrowing
– which is not surprising since there have been three major currency reforms in the last thirty years, and the present régime
repudiated the national debt. The distribution of the housing
programme among particular towns and regions is based on
estimates of shortage, population growth and the growth of
employment, and the process of allocation calls for a good deal
of discussion and bargaining, of a kind familiar in this country,
between central and local authorities.

The state's building, which used to account for the bulk of
the housing programme, was designed until 1963 to meet three
types of need: 1) the housing of key workers – miners, metal
workers and farmers, for example – and workers in growing
industries, 2) the housing of the poorer and larger families, and

3) the rehousing of people whose homes were demolished in the course of slum clearance. Replacement accounted for 18 per cent of the annual building programme and between 0·3 and 0·4 per cent of the housing stock was demolished each year – one of the largest official clearance programmes in Europe. Of these three requirements met by the state, it was the needs of industry which were given highest priority, both in the total allocations made to different areas and in the distribution of housing at the local level. The large number of small towns closely spaced throughout Bohemia gives workers a considerable range of jobs to choose from, and in a country whose government has been reluctant to use wage rates or any other price mechanism to distribute resources, housing privileges have provided an alternative means of attracting and retaining labour for the industries to which highest priority is given. The state could not afford to organize and finance the whole housing programme, and building for owner occupation in rural areas and small towns was at first permitted and then encouraged – through loans, grants, sales of land and the provision of public services and house designs.

Cooperatives, which form the third and most rapidly growing sector of housing building, were set up for groups of workers – for the employees of an enterprise or the members of a trade union – and (with municipal help) for any individual who chose to apply for membership. They build flats of the same kind as those provided by the state, but they cater for people who can afford a considerable down-payment and larger subsequent payments. Unlike the state's tenants, cooperative members are responsible for the full costs of repairs and maintenance. All sorts of enterprises – from factories to research institutes – collaborate with the trade unions and professional associations representing their workers to set up cooperatives, and they can provide loans and technical resources to help these cooperatives build. Thus in addition to the priority it may secure within the state's programme, a growing industrial organization can attract and retain workers by devoting part of its surplus or 'profit' to housing them. From the state's point of view the cooperatives provide a welcome addition to the housing programme without a heavy drain on the budget; they also mop up a good deal of purchasing power that would otherwise add to the awkward problem of controlling demands for consumer goods. (A Czech who wants a car – the down-payment on which costs about as much as the down-payment on a cooperative flat – must put down half the purchase price and then wait three or four years for his turn in the queue, paying the rest as soon as his car is available. Yet despite these deterrents, and the high price of petrol, many are joining this queue.)

Further modifications were made to this system in 1963 and 1964. Rents were raised and reorganized to eliminate unjustifiable differences between the payments made for similar housing and to make the management and maintenance of housing more nearly self-supporting. Workers who got new housing by taking jobs in priority industries had shown a regrettable tendency to change their jobs again a few years later. The provision of housing for these workers by the state and the employing enterprises was therefore brought to an end, and its place taken by new cooperative schemes for which the enterprises provided the fairly large down-payments required. If the worker stays sufficiently long in his job (ten years in the mines, twelve years in the chemical industry and fifteen years elsewhere) he will only be asked to repay 10 per cent of this loan. Those leaving sooner will only be entitled to stay in their homes if they repay the whole loan. Meanwhile more help is being given to people building their own houses provided they work in priority industries (including agriculture) for prescribed periods, and build on sites sufficiently close to their place of work. Thus housing policy is being deliberately and increasingly employed as an instrument of economic policy.

The existing stock of housing is rationed by allocation procedures determining the numbers of rooms which each type and size of household is entitled to, and by a system of rents which calls for increased payments from households occupying more space than their numbers justify. By taking in lodgers and subtenants (whose rents cannot in practice be effectively controlled) a household may maintain the required 'density norms' and keep their flat, but they still pay an increase in rent. The state provides a repair and maintenance service for its own housing. Private landlords – who usually own the oldest and poorest property – are expected to repair and maintain their houses, but the rigid restriction of rents renders it difficult to enforce their obligations and the decay that results in some neighbourhoods is frightening to behold. The property of landlords can be taken from them in default of repairs, but the state is in practice reluctant to do this since it would find it difficult to assume the burden itself.

Great efforts have been made to standardize and improve house designs, and to industrialize building so that an increasing proportion of the work is carried out under factory supervision. Brick is giving way to concrete panels of larger and larger dimensions, and steel frames are likely to play a growing part in the next phase of development. The preparation of these designs is carried out by research teams in central institutes whose architects are often moved out subsequently to the regions to help in applying the house designs and building methods they have devised. Between 1956 and 1961 this development work achieved a reduction of 33 per cent in the current costs of state and cooperative housing; meanwhile the flats being built, though still small by British standards, are now slightly larger in size, and there has been an increase in earnings. The cost of dwellings expressed as a multiple of average annual earnings fell from 6·5 to 3·9 over this period. Owing to the poor insulation provided by cross-wall construction in concrete panels, most tenants still prefer the older flats, built in brick, but growing numbers of people can now be rehoused with a given volume of resources. It would be a mistake to compare the ratios of house prices and wages in eastern and western countries, since the elements entering into calculations of costs differ, and wages in the east can be kept 'artificially' low owing to the very low level of rents, the absence of income taxes, and a system of social insurance which is largely financed from levies on productive enterprises. But in Czechoslovakia, the Soviet Union and elsewhere there have clearly been great increases in the quantitative productivity of the building industry. In this industry, as in others, the demand for annual production increases and cost reductions, backed by substantial cash bonuses for successful managers and the demotion of the unsuccessful, has undoubtedly borne fruit in quantitative terms, though in qualitative terms the results tend to be less satisfactory. The quantity of dwellings can be counted and the producers rewarded, but the convenience of house plans and the quality of finish are harder to measure and control.

The planning of land uses and the location of housing within regional plans are based on forecasts of industrial growth, converted through successive approximations to estimates of employment, population and the expected increase in households. The layout of towns and sites is prepared by regional offices and their local branches, staffed mainly by architect-planners whose resources are concentrated on the growing towns and on urban redevelopment. Land prices, though determined by complicated scales reflecting current ownership (state or private), current use, and prewar price, are so low that they provide neither an obstacle to purchase nor an effective guide to economic use. Rents are determined by the size and equipment of the dwelling, with reductions for families with children, but they take no account of the location of the property, a new flat in Prague being let at the same rent as a similar flat in a distant village. Negotiations for building sites proceed according to general planning principles, and final decisions depend not on prices but on the administrative and political influence of the organizations concerned.

POLAND

Housing policies and procedures in Poland are broadly similar to Czechoslovakia's. Differences arise from the fact that Poland is a larger country (with 31 million people, while Czechoslovakia has 14 million) and is less fully industrialized. Her more rapidly growing population is still heavily dependent upon small, primitive and widely scattered farms. Over larger areas in the eastern and southern parts of the country there are few villages – only a continuing straggle of small wooden houses, interspersed with more recent brick building and linked by lanes, dusty or muddy according to the season. The housing needs of such regions, and their lack of electricity, main drainage and piped water supplies, are not so much a housing problem as a reflection of the underlying and greater agricultural problem. The population in rural areas is not yet falling, but the increase is concentrated entirely in the towns. The country's industrial structure and the communications serving it grew up, before 1918, as offshoots of neighbouring economies; thus in 1945 Poland's industrial resources were still heavily concentrated around the fringes of her territory. This patchwork is being knit together by developing new industrial centres with better communications between them. Regional disparities in housing conditions are also being corrected. Immediately after the war large numbers of younger people moved from the territories lost to Russia and settled in those gained from Germany. The housing stock in the western and northern parts of Poland tends to be better and less crowded, while that in the eastern and southern parts of the country tends to be poorer and more crowded, but these differences have been appreciably narrowed in recent years, partly owing to the high rate of natural increase among the young migrants who went to the ex-German areas.

As in Czechoslovakia, the preparation of housing programmes forms an integral part of the national economic plans drawn up by the Central Planning Commission and approved by government. A clear distinction is drawn, as in Czechoslovakia again, between the two divisions of the Commission concerned respectively with 'perspective planning' and 'operational planning'. The former furnishes 'perspectives' – the most important of which deal with the plan starting in 1980 – derived from the analysis of social, economic and technical trends and assumptions. The operational division prepares the next five-year plan and implements planning decisions. The research findings of the former division and the policy intentions of the latter are regarded as attempts to answer different kinds of question, and they do not have to coincide.

The starting point for housing plans is the proportion of investment to be allocated to house building. This proportion, despite public dispute on the question, has been declining as the big post-war generation of children comes onto the labour market. Increases in productivity and further reductions in the already severe standards of new building should nevertheless permit a rising output of dwellings. Priorities for the allocation of this investment are determined largely by targets expressing the number of dwellings per hundred households, the square metres of living space per person, and the numbers of houses to be provided with a bath, a central heating system and other equipment. In the course of formulating such estimates, assumptions have to be made about the future rates of natural increase, migration and household formation, the replacement of dwellings, the size and quality of houses to be built, and so on. Errors inevitably arise in such projections and annual adjustments are made to the housing programme in the light of changing needs and resources. The quantitative output of dwellings designed to reduce sharing in the growing industrial centres is given first priority when such adjustments are made; the general increase in living space comes next in importance, and it is the replacement, improvement and maintenance of the existing stock of houses that are most likely to suffer cuts and restrictions. Plans and programmes deal mainly with the towns, and development in the rural areas – which means for half the population – is left largely to private initiative.

Once the broad totals of the plan and their regional distribution have been approved, responsibility for the administration of the programme is delegated – to a greater extent than in Czechoslovakia – to an extensive system of regional, county and district authorities. Most of the building is organized by a network of development agencies, set up by the Ministry of Local Government (or 'Communal Affairs') but responsible to local authorities. These agencies act as 'developers', arranging and coordinating building operations for local authorities, for enterprises seeking housing for their workers, and for cooperatives – though the last two of these also carry out much of their own development work. Through its local agencies the Ministry is also responsible for the management and repair of existing state housing.

In 1964, nearly 160,000 houses were built: 53 per cent by the state (about two thirds by local authorities and the rest by enterprises) and 18 per cent by cooperatives (all at 'wholesale prices'); the remaining 29 per cent were built for owner-occupiers (at prices about 9 per cent higher) about half of them with the aid of government credits. In Czechoslovakia, where 83,000 houses were built during the same year, 42 per cent were built directly for the state, 1 per cent for enterprises, 33 per cent for cooperatives, and 24 per cent for owner occupation.

In both countries it is the cooperatives that have been gaining ground most rapidly, mainly at the expense of enterprise housing and owner occupation. But the enterprises' needs play a large part in this allocation : local authorities with expanding industries get the biggest allocations, 10–15 per cent of the municipal programme is reserved for enterprises too small to build their own houses, and many enterprises make loans or grants to cooperatives housing their workers. The allocation of enterprise housing now rests largely in the hands of workers' organizations, not with management, but workers who leave their jobs with a good record cannot be evicted from enterprise housing when they change their jobs (unless the enterprise finds them another house, which in practice it cannot do). Enterprises appear to have no difficulty in raising funds for housing from their surpluses and the scale of their building therefore depends on the numbers of houses allocated to them in the building programmes and – more generally – on the building resources available locally. As in Czechoslovakia, the system is largely designed to serve the needs of economic growth without creating a mass of 'tied cottages'. As in Czechoslovakia, too, the municipal authorities are responsible for housing larger and poorer families. But in Poland the maximum incomes per head which entitle people to get on to the municipal waiting lists had been reduced by the early 1960s to a level that excluded most of the single and childless and compelled all who could afford it to seek cooperative housing. Similar developments appear to have followed later in Czechoslovakia.

Although the state has done some building for people on the farms, most rural housing is built by people who start by getting help from local tradesmen and then complete the rest of their home with the aid of relatives and neighbours. Vast numbers of fairly spacious but exceedingly ill-finished and poorly equipped houses are built in this way, often far from schools, water supply and other public services.

The costs of building a house in Poland, expressed as a multiple

of average earnings, have fallen (from 6·3 to 5·2 between 1956
and 1961) but not so dramatically as in Czechoslovakia, although there were price changes for building materials during
this time which render comparisons hazardous. About half this
reduction appears to be explained by cuts in the living space
provided. Industrialization and technical development in
building have been held back by scarcities of steel and capital
equipment, and by a fairly plentiful supply of unskilled labour –
often following the classical route of migration to factory work in
the towns via temporary jobs on building sites.

The Poles make greater use of the price mechanism in their
town planning procedures than do the Czechs, partly because
of the scarcity of properly equipped sites and the need to ration
building land. Draft legislation proposing a general system of
graduated taxes designed to discriminate between urban land
of differing values has been defeated (state enterprises being no
less determined to defend their property rights than capitalist
landowners) but sites leased to cooperatives and owner-
occupiers pay a rent which reflects their scarcity value and the
cost of public services provided for them. The shape of new and
rebuilt towns is noticeably different from that dictated by
competition for sites in a 'free' market. Densities and building
heights tend to be lower in central areas and more uniform
throughout a town, because they reflect the cost of the buildings
rather than the land, and industrialized building methods are
most economical if heights are standardized. Public open
spaces, district heating plants serving very large areas, community centres and other amenities are more readily incorporated, and historic buildings are preserved and restored
with a passion that seems peculiar to revolutionary governments.
Meanwhile the location of a steel works may have been selected
with the intention of breaking up a concentration of potentially
bourgeois households, and housing cooperatives appear to
secure some of the finest sites and also some of the worst –
depending on the political and administrative influence they
wield.

While such procedures for determining land uses may
appear untidy to a western economist, their outcome seems no
more arbitrary, the mechanisms employed seem no less clearly

understood and the living conditions achieved seem no less satisfying than those to be seen in market economies with similar living standards. More determined steps are now being taken to control development in rural areas, but the shortage of planners, the need to concentrate all available resources on the towns, and uncertainty about future agriculture policy have combined to produce one of the most completely unregulated rural landscapes to be seen anywhere in the world. In East Germany and Czechoslovakia there is a long tradition of solid and attractive rural building. But in Poland, as in Russia and other eastern countries, rural housing has traditionally been of poor quality, and the new methods developed for the construction of mass-produced blocks of flats have not yet been adapted to the building of satisfactory and attractive small-scale housing projects in the countryside.

ACHIEVEMENTS AND DILEMMAS

The foregoing sketch of two centrally planned economies provides a fuller account of their housing systems than has been attempted for other nations, and in a book designed for English readers it may seem odd to devote so much space to countries in which most of the problems that fill the housing debates of English-speaking countries have been abolished or transformed beyond recognition. If the regulation of rents, the eviction of tenants, the rate of interest, the price of land, and the grievances and misdoings of the private landlord were virtually eliminated from public discussion, would there be any 'housing problems' left for us to debate? From the experience of countries which have stripped away these issues the fundamental dilemmas of housing policy may emerge more clearly.

Determining the size of the housing programme in a centrally planned economy is a major political decision, made by the government with the aid of its economic 'high command' in the course of working out long-term plans for the whole economy. It is only under the more liberal Communist régimes that such decisions can be publicly debated, and the criteria on which they are based can never be clear-cut. In the short run the programme depends largely on the level of output attained in the previous year or two. Over longer periods, housing forms a residual element within a general strategy that normally gives higher priority to other sectors of the economy – heavy industry, agriculture, mining, defence and education, for example. Estimates of population growth and the rate of household formation play a part in discussions of the housing programme but do not determine its size in any direct fashion. Indeed a country with a rapidly growing population, such as Poland, must invest so much in schools and in the factories that will employ the growing labour force that it is compelled to devote less resources to housing than a country like Czechoslovakia with a slow rate of natural increase. Thus the scope for improving the housing situation depends, as in the west, largely on the economic and demographic 'climate' confronting the planners, and on the size and efficiency of the building industry – a complex and widely scattered industry which cannot be quickly changed. Although the colossal scale of Russian house building is now widely known, it is often forgotten that the industrialized methods which made this achievement possible took many years to organize, starting from experiments with prefabrication begun during the 1930s.

Once the volume of resources available for housing has been determined, decisions have to be taken about the proportions of these resources that are to be devoted to increasing the stock of houses, to repair and maintenance work, and to the replacement of obsolete property. These three elements of a housing programme are closely related and should be planned in close conjunction with each other. Any increase in the stock of houses will in time produce predictable increases in the burden of maintenance and replacement; but that burden will depend on the quality and cost of past building – the better the building, the longer its life should be and the lower the costs of maintaining it. Meanwhile the rate of replacement should depend on the housing standards required and the comparative costs of achieving these standards through improvement and rebuilding.

It used to be believed that the price mechanism could automatically weigh and relate the elements in these equations, and bring about an economically 'efficient' distribution of resources between new buildings, repair, improvement and replacement.

In practice a free market never worked as smoothly as that. Moreover government interventions (such as the imposition of legal minimum standards that are well above those that many households can afford, the regulation of rents and land uses, and the provision of grants, subsidies and tax reliefs) long ago destroyed genuinely 'free' markets for housing in western countries. In the west, decisions about repairs and improvement depend to a great extent on the patterns of rent restriction and the loans and grants provided by government; decisions about slum clearance depend on the interpretation of public health regulations and the subsidies offered by government; replacement by private developers also depends heavily on government policies and procedures – on the alternative uses permitted by town planning authorities for the site in question, for example. The rate of interest on borrowed money should in theory measure the scarcity of capital and hence determine the volume, distribution and timing of investment – showing, for instance, where a higher initial cost of building is likely to be recovered in lower maintenance costs and postponed replacement. But the *effective* rates of interest on money employed for housing purposes in the market economies now depend heavily on government lending conducted at special rates, and on the various forms and rates of tax relief attached to the repayments made on such loans. Thus the rate of interest no longer constitutes a generally valid instrument for the solution of these problems.

Meanwhile in the centrally planned economies of eastern Europe the state has assumed control of the housing stock, it provides most of the capital for new building, and it has reduced rents to a level which lays most of the costs of maintenance upon government and gives administrators the principal responsibility – in urban areas at least – for allocating new or vacant housing. With the aid of their central planning commissions, equipped with economic analysts and electronic computers, the Communist countries should therefore be able to achieve deliberately what the 'free market' was once supposed to achieve automatically. But although there has been some discussion of these problems in eastern Europe, their solution has not so far been more deliberately or efficiently planned than it is in the west. The situation is confused by the side effects of major economic and social readjustments proceeding in these countries. Small-scale craft industries of many kinds have been discouraged or obliterated altogether, and such trades play an essential part in the repair and improvement of housing. The profit motive, so often the basis for these trades, has been outlawed. Meanwhile great efforts are being made to increase the productivity of building by the introduction of large-scale factory methods of construction. These developments reduce the costs of building a new house but increase – relatively at least – the costs of repairing and improving existing property. The building of new housing is also a more attractive proposition – politically, professionally and aesthetically – than repairing or improving old property, and the latter activities are therefore less favoured and more likely to suffer cuts when adjustments have to be made to the programme. Moreover, although the state has greater resources for repairs and improvements than the private owner, it tends, by historical accident, to own the *better* old property. (Houses belonging to the large and efficient landlords were more likely to be nationalized than those belonging to small landlords and owner-occupiers.) Thus repairs and improvements proceed rather haphazardly, and are often concentrated on the property in which they are less urgently needed, and replacement programmes tend to be less ambitious and less promptly achieved than programmes that add to the existing stock. All these problems are only too familiar in the west.

The geographical distribution of house building presents further problems of choice. In the short run it depends heavily upon the distribution of building labour, equipment and materials, and on the vigour and efficiency of municipal authorities and local building enterprises. But in the longer run the natural increase and migration of population are the principal factors to be considered. For a while it seems to have been thought that a government which employs and houses most of the population, and regulates people's movements by a system of passes and permits surpassed only in South Africa, should be able to determine the population of each area by administrative decree. Attempts were in fact made to regulate the growth of Moscow, Leningrad, Belgrade and Warsaw in this way, and to restrict their populations to predetermined figures. But although this seems to have been achieved fairly successfully in Prague, experience elsewhere has shown that the population of an area depends on the regional distribution and growth of industry – and that can only be controlled or predicted in an approximate fashion. 'Temporary' residence permits are given and extended for successive years, and, although the holders of these permits have no right to housing provided by the authorities, they – and many others – find living space in the homes of friends and relatives who moved to the city ahead of them. It is only in the well-housed countries, where the bulk of the population has already moved to the towns and few city dwellers have country cousins to whom they cannot refuse shelter, that housing short-ages begin to impose effective barriers to the growth of urban employment and population – which may explain why the size of Prague has been more successfully controlled.

Thus plans for industry in each region provide the key factors determining the geographical distribution of the housing pro-gramme. The numbers of houses to be built in each area depend largely on the growth of employment in the area and the econo-mic importance of the industries concerned, and when selecting the people to be housed first priorities go to key workers and to the industries currently judged to be in most urgent need of expansion.

In parts of eastern Europe, and particularly in Russia, it would seem odd to leave the problems of building technology to so late a stage of this discussion, for to many in the east these technical questions constitute the most important features of a 'housing policy'. Other aspects of housing are either too impor-tant or too trivial to figure among the preoccupations of a Con-struction Ministry and its associated institutes and committees. This whole-hearted concentration upon building technology has undoubtedly produced remarkable progress in several of the centrally planned economies. The simplification and standardi-zation of the dimensions and technical requirements of every building component (their load-bearing and insulating capaci-ties, and their junction systems, for example) form the starting point of these developments. Considerable diversity of materials and methods is permitted within these standards, so that each region can use and adapt the building materials and labour available to it. The development of factory prefabrication is gradually reducing the man-hours required for building a house, substituting factory work for labour on the site, and concrete panels for other materials.

But the building technology appropriate for each country depends on local resources and traditions, and such methods cannot be exported indiscriminately. None of the other eastern countries has concentrated as single-mindedly as the Soviet Union on the room-sized load-bearing concrete panel, and although Russia is now beginning to export plants for the construction of housing components the other eastern countries do not appear to be among her customers. By 1964 concrete panel construction accounted for 32 per cent of Russian urban building and this proportion should rise to 60 per cent by 1970; it plays a large part in rural building too. This method seems peculiarly appropriate to a centrally planned economy (where the demand for building and its location can be closely controlled), in which craft skills are very scarce (plumbing, carpentry, glazing and the finish of buildings are still of very poor quality), where the land is generally flat and stoneless (prefabricated foundations and basement panels can be dropped straight into holes scooped out of the earth), and where towns tend to be large and isolated (one factory can turn out components in large and predictable numbers for a whole city, one enterprise builds the houses, and vast suburbs can be extended indefinitely into the surrounding steppe or forest). It produces less dramatic results in other settings.

It must also be remembered that in house building, as in other industries, a 'classical' communist economy is free to concentrate on production with the assurance that output will be taken up by an urgent and docile demand, uncomplicated by fashion, class distinctions, personal or municipal idiosyncrasies, or the prejudices of money lenders. This does not mean that building proceeds regardless of needs. Immense trouble is taken to provide dwellings of the prescribed size for each type of household. The standards applied vary from one country to another according to the wealth and the degree of shortage in each. Three and four people are the most common household sizes in these countries (they constituted 52 per cent of all house-holds in the Soviet Union in 1960) and for such households the 'useful floor space' provided in new flats during the early 1960s ranged from 47 to 50 square metres in Russia, from 54 to 67 square metres in Czechoslovakia, and from 33 to 48 square metres in Poland. Figure 2, based on plans prepared in Moscow, shows the types of flat being built in 1964 and the types of house-hold to which each was allocated in order to provide them with the square metres of 'living space' and 'useful space'* prescribed by the norms. These flats are small and their layout is cramped; bathrooms and lavatories are windowless internal cabins, and the living room often serves as a passage between them and the bedrooms; refrigerators and washing machines could not easily be accommodated in the space available. But every flat has hot and cold water, a balcony, and adequate built-in cupboards, and every block is centrally heated and supplied with sheltered and well planted outdoor play-space for children. The 'norms' to be adhered to by developers include a maximum distance from the front door to bus-stop or railway station (with rent reductions where this is exceeded) and prescribed ratios of shops, schools, day nurseries and other public services for each neighbourhood.

Thus although the demand for housing is 'docile', this does not mean that 'anything goes' or that builders and developers are undisciplined. It means that while money and prices play a 'passive' part in determining the demand for housing, they play an 'active' part in the supply of housing – being used by accoun-tants, banks and state inspectors as a means of measuring, con-trolling and rewarding the performance of builders. Rents in housing provided by the state or its industrial enterprises have until recently been negligible – but are now rising quite rapidly in Poland and Czechoslovakia. The distribution of this housing among tenants and the quality of the houses they get depend scarcely at all upon what the tenants can pay; their chances of

---

*'Useful floor space' includes the whole area within the walls of a self-contained flat – i.e. including kitchen, bathroom, passages, etc., but excluding common hallways and staircases. 'Living space' is the total area of habitable rooms of at least 4 square metres in area with a ceiling height of at least 2 metres over the major part of the room.

securing a new flat depend mainly on their contribution to the economic system, and next on the number of children they have; the size of the family then determines the size and type of flat the tenant gets. Once rehoused, most people appear to stay put for long periods and seldom move again unless their households change sufficiently in size. Much of the larger old property of pre-revolutionary times has been converted and subdivided into smaller units, all new flats are built to similar designs, varying only in size, and as obsolete property is gradually cleared away the urban housing stock is assuming an increasingly standardized form. Thus while some neighbourhoods will remain more attractive than others, dwelling units themselves may become an increasingly homogeneous, interchangeable commodity – like pints of milk or packets of cigarettes. The standardization of housing is expected to be an asset later on when people will be required to move about more freely in order to attain the rising norms of density projected in long-term plans. In the U.S.S.R. these norms now provide eight square metres of living space per head when new flats are allocated; by 1980 the norm should have risen to twelve square metres – which will still be appreciably less than council tenants in England have today.

The Soviet Union is the only country which has clearly declared its intention of providing free housing, but other eastern countries have sometimes appeared to endorse this policy – if only as a distant objective. The proposed abolition of rents often shocks westerners. To understand this policy it is essential to appreciate the character of the housing situation – particularly in Russia – and to be realistic about the meaning of the objective. When housing is desperately scarce after a devastating war and a long period in which few houses have been built, when whole families count themselves lucky to rent one room and sublet the corner behind the wardrobe to a lodger, then no one can hope for much and the immediate needs of every household are very similar. A small flat which they do not have to share with anyone else is every family's hope and the outermost limit to their aspirations; anything more would be unimaginable. People need privacy and a little living space – the range of consumer goods available to put in a flat is very restricted – and once they have secured a decent home most of them do not expect to move again. When everyone wants the same thing and wants it very badly, it is natural to regard housing as a basic and standard necessity that should be provided free. Somewhat similar situations have occurred in Scotland, with similar results.

But what does 'free housing' mean? Rents are already so low – frequently amounting (as shown in Table 7) to less than 2 per cent of total consumption expenditure – that governments could easily abolish them altogether if they wanted to. It would make very little difference if they did. Housing would be 'free', not in the sense that the air we breathe or the sea we swim in is free, but in the sense that a schoolboy's books or a soldier's uniform are free. It would be more accurate to describe it as 'rationed'. Housing, in urban areas at least, is allocated in prescribed amounts to people who qualify for it owing to their needs and owing to their place in the productive system: it is a ration, provided along with wages. This is very different from a system in which housing is distributed according to the tenant's capacity to pay, but it does not matter greatly whether the tenant pays very little for it or nothing at all.

As the housing situation and the general standard of living improve, however, and as the Soviet example loses its unquestioned authority among neighbouring countries, the conditions that gave rise to this system are beginning to disintegrate. Although the long-term objective of 'free housing' is seldom openly rejected, practice is leading in other directions. Cooperative housing is now the most rapidly growing sector of new building in most of these countries. In Poland in 1964 it was provided, under various systems, for households who paid 15 per cent of the capital cost, borrowing 45–52 per cent from the state (interest free) and repaying these loans over forty years. The rest of the capital was provided by the state as an outright grant. In Czechoslovakia, in 1963, the members of cooperatives paid 20–40 per cent of the capital cost, borrowing 30–50 per cent from the state (at 1 per cent interest) and repaying this over thirty years. Further extensions of this system took place the following year. In the Soviet Union, in 1964, cooperative members paid no less than 40 per cent of the capital cost, and were entitled to borrow all the remainder (at 1 per cent interest) repaying this over the short period of ten or fifteen years. Similar procedures operate in other eastern countries. Meanwhile houses are built for owner occupation on terms that usually call for a still larger contribution from the household. A cooperative member's payments – before he gets his house, and year by year after he moves into it – are often bigger in relation to the average wage than the payments made by a typical house buyer in Britain, though the large number of working wives in the eastern countries reduces the proportion of the *household's* income devoted to these payments. In return he gains the opportunity of buying his way out of the queue for state housing – a particularly valuable privilege for smaller, childless households who are given low priority in these queues – and his relatives, if he was previously sharing their flat, at last get a home to themselves by giving or lending him the down-payment he needs. His flat may be rather better equipped than the state tenant's, it may stand on a more desirable site, and the density norms will be less rigidly enforced. Cooperative households that shrink in size are not compelled to move to smaller flats, as the state's tenants may be. In some forms of cooperative the members can sell or bequeath their property, or select their successors. To these incentives for cooperative membership some countries have added more compelling pressures by excluding households with more than a certain level of income per head from the waiting lists for state housing. The tenant of state housing is also being asked to pay more, first through sizeable down-payments at the point of rehousing and through charges that cover the full cost of heating and other services, and more recently through higher rents; and it is already clear that a determined campaign to develop cooperatives soon leads to strong pressure for rent increases in the (almost exactly similar) state and enterprise housing with which the cooperatives are competing.

Meanwhile, after concentrating for many years on producing a larger quantity of housing, often at the expense of reductions in the size and quality of dwellings, there is growing pressure in the wealthier eastern countries for *better* housing. In Poland the standards of new housing are still falling, but in Czechoslovakia they are rising. In the Soviet Union it is being argued that further improvements in building productivity should be used to raise standards rather than increase output. That would make a decisive break with previous traditions. As consumer goods grow more plentiful in the centrally planned economies some increase in the size of dwellings will be needed to accommodate the greater range of possessions people own. This development will bring growing pressure for an increase in the contribution people make from their incomes to the cost of their housing. As new flats are built to more generous dimensions, housing will become a much less uniform commodity, and those fortunate enough to get a new flat are likely to be asked for a higher rent. It would be absurd if low rents enabled people to buy television sets, record players, refrigerators and furniture which could not be fitted into flats built to the restricted standards dictated by the attempt to provide free housing for all.

The 'principle' of free housing is not deeply rooted in Communist theory, but arose from a transient combination of political and social conditions, and is likely to be abandoned as these conditions change. In Yugoslavia, which has set an example of decentralization and cautious use of price mechanisms that other eastern countries have often followed, the government intends to rely increasingly on a system of publicly subsidized owner occupation which will call for a fairly heavy contribution from personal incomes. It will probably penalize poorer households, but it may give others greater security and independence, and greater opportunities for choosing the sort of home they want.

CONCLUSIONS

Does the experience of the centrally planned economies offer any guidance to a country like Britain – a relatively wealthy, liberal democracy in which government is now tentatively embarking upon a bolder and more comprehensive interpretation of its responsibilities in the housing field?

A policy for raising housing standards throughout the country, for improving productivity in the building of houses and for eliminating overcrowding and slum conditions must be prepared as a part of a more general plan for the development of the whole economy. To be successful it will call for a high level of savings and investment, and careful coordination between the regional distributions of industry, employment and house building. Any attempt to raise productivity in the building industry and to control its costs must deal with the construction industry as a whole – not merely with that part of it which happens to be currently employed on housing. The resources devoted to the housing sector of construction cannot be deployed to the best advantage unless plans for adding to the stock of dwellings are closely related to plans for maintaining, improving and replacing this stock.

Simple though they are, these conclusions have complex administrative and political implications. They mean that a more comprehensive and effective housing programme is likely to remove many of the principal decisions on housing policy from the departments of government now frequently responsible for them in the west – the ministries concerned with housing and local government – and give these powers to departments responsible for economic planning, regional development, the construction industry and the labour force. Once the broad outlines of policy have been established, the implementation of the programme depends largely on smaller units of government, but these authorities must deal with areas that form an appropriate basis for coordinating the growth of employment, population, households and housing, for assuring continuity of demand for building, and for linking up the production of building components, the location of housing projects and the deployment of building labour. Thus the local authorities traditionally responsible for government housing programmes in many western countries – the municipalities – may lose power to new and larger units of government created to meet the needs of a more comprehensive policy.

Given time and extensive preparation, it is clear that radical improvements can be achieved in the performance of the building industry. The standardization of dimensions and components, and the assurance of a predictable volume and geographical distribution of demand – now widely recognized as necessary – are no more than a starting point for such progress. Effective links must be forged between the whole network of industries involved. The finishing trades of the building industry and the various branches of the chemical industry which play a vital part in providing materials for joining and sealing large components are both more highly developed in western Europe than in the east; if properly organized they could surmount many of the difficulties that have held up the industrialization of building in the east and coarsened the quality of its products.

But it must be remembered that the British construction industry already builds houses very cheaply by eastern standards (tricky though such comparisons must be) and it is particularly efficient when using traditional methods and materials. Further advances in productivity are therefore likely to be achieved by methods that differ from those which have proved successful in the altogether different circumstances of eastern Europe.

It must also be remembered that the building industry exists to meet human needs, not merely to produce statistical triumphs of quantitative production. Without systematic and imaginative studies of household routines, domestic equipment, and the standards and patterns of living to be expected in future, it may produce houses that soon become obsolete. Several governments in eastern Europe are building on the assumption that people will make increasing use of public restaurants and public laundries, that wives will always leave their children in nurseries and go to work and their sons will continue to do two years' military service, and that travel will be confined almost entirely to public transport. Some of these assumptions may prove valid. But most of the industries now flourishing in the west – those producing prepared and frozen foods, washing machines, refrigerators and private cars, for example – are likely in time to develop equally extensively in the east. If Communist societies are to be permanently deprived of these things, then what is the purpose of their all-consuming drive for economic growth? Present shortages and hardships may compel these countries to disregard such possibilities for the time being, but if their house designs are based on these assumptions for much longer then an unnecessarily high rate of obsolescence and a slum problem of frightening dimensions are being prepared for the next generation.

Extreme injustices and hardship can be eliminated provided the building programme is closely geared to changes in the regional distribution of employment and there is a determined policy for regulating the distribution of housing amongst households, for adapting and converting property built for earlier generations and for redistributing the households living in it. Poland has gone far to achieve a fair distribution of housing space, as was shown in a previous chapter,* despite a poor stock of housing, a low rate of building, a rapid increase in population and massive migration to the towns from the countryside. During the decade between 1950 and 1960 the population of Polish towns increased from 9·6 millions to 14·1 millions while the rural population remained virtually unchanged, rising from 15.0 to 15.2 millions. By concentrating the country's relatively small building programme in the growing towns this radical change in the distribution of the population was absorbed and a fractional increase in rooms per dwelling and rooms per person was achieved in the towns. This is an outstanding achievement.

But the general improvement of a nation's housing standards, as opposed to the elimination of the worst hardships, calls for a major change in the relationship between the quantity of housing and the population to be housed, and this depends on long-term economic and demographic trends that determine the social 'climate' within which policy makers must operate. Central planning may influence these trends but it cannot work miracles. If population generally, and the cities in particular, are growing fast, and if steel is scarce and labour is plentiful, the improvement of building productivity and housing conditions is bound to be slow. Thus the Poles will face a tougher housing situation than the Czechs for at least another generation. But the countries of north western Europe have passed through this stage of economic development, and the social 'climate' confronting their governments is a much more favourable one, affording greater opportunities for progress.

There will always be considerable differences in housing conditions within a developing economy where aspirations and living standards are rising: houses last a long time, and once the

*See page 52.

most urgent needs have been met there will always be pressure to build new houses to a higher standard than the old. Thus the distribution and pricing of houses will always present problems of social justice and political decision. The eastern countries' contribution to the solution of these problems lies in their determined attempt to relate housing space to household size, and to prevent the development of one-class neighbourhoods; but there are signs that those who are willing and able to pay most for their housing – often with the help of several earners within one household – are beginning to secure additional benefits within this general framework of priorities. Something rather like a class distinction in housing standards may be re-emerging.

The extensive use of owner occupation by Communist régimes contrasts oddly with the prejudice against this form of tenure often expressed by the left wing in capitalist countries, and suggests that a more searching analysis of the strengths and weaknesses of individual home ownership is called for. The spread of owner occupation may be objectionable if it leads to an unduly wasteful use of land and housing space, if it creates or reinforces class divisions and the educational and social handicaps typical of socially segregated neighbourhoods, if it leads to a wasteful or unfair distribution of public funds through the provision of tax reliefs, grants and subsidies that are concentrated on wealthier sections of the population, and if it distracts attention and resources from the needs of the old, the young and the transient for whom this form of tenure may not be appropriate. But these are not inevitable features of a housing market in which a large proportion of people own their homes and it is difficult to conceive of any valid objection to home ownership in itself and for its own sake.

We have examined the social, technical and administrative environment confronting governments in the centrally planned economies and the housing policies that have evolved within this framework, but little attention has been paid to the political character of these régimes. Are these policies tied to an authoritarian form of government and the suppression of political rights? If so, is the tie inevitable or accidental? Some will be tempted to dismiss this problem, asserting that the style of government is unrelated to the content of its housing policies – such policies will be tyrannical if administered by tyrants, liberal if administered by liberals. But it must be admitted that a government can act with greater authority if the nation's objectives can be clearly and simply defined; the east European countries often remind the westerner of war economies in which the expansion of a limited range of industries has become the 'victory' to be attained. Wholesale reorganization of the building industry can be more easily carried out in the absence of independent and strongly entrenched federations of employers and workers, a regional distribution of house building that matches the distribution of employment is easier to achieve if elected local authorities are administratively and politically subservient to central government, the elimination of overcrowding is easier if the state regulates the distribution of housing space, and if immigration and the private landlord are virtually abolished. Civilized and convenient town plans are easier to create where the government owns all the land or can readily acquire it at negligible prices without resort to time consuming appeals.

Most people in the west hold that some of these conditions constitute an infringement of human rights, though they would not agree precisely which of them offend or how far the injustice is outweighed by opportunities for achieving greater justice in other directions. They would more readily agree, however, that a government which drastically restricts the operation of price mechanisms and the rights of property owners needs to be peculiarly well equipped with alternative criteria for determining what people want and how the stock of housing should be used; its decisions should be publicly discussed in the light of accurate information prepared by technically competent critics whose jobs are not in the gift of the policy makers; and the households whose privacy and independence depend upon the decisions of such a government must be represented by spokesmen entitled to speak plainly on their behalf, and must be protected by clearly formulated and generally accepted rules specifying the strictly limited circumstances in which they can be compelled to relinquish their homes. If they adopt policies pursued in the east – and some of them are already doing so – the countries of western Europe must bear these warnings in mind.

Britain and her neighbours should be better equipped than most countries, both by political tradition and by professional training, to provide the safeguards that make such policies tolerable to democrats.

PART TWO

HOUSING POLICY IN BRITAIN

CHAPTER 5

CONTEXT FOR A HOUSING POLICY

To compare our own country with its neighbours can provide a general understanding of our housing situation, the opportunities it presents and the constraints it imposes. But such comparisons will not furnish us with a housing policy. The needs, resources and aspirations of the countries of Europe are much too varied to derive any compelling prescription from that source. This chapter summarizes the main lessons Britain can learn from the European survey presented in the first part of the book, and provides a starting point and context for the discussion of our own policies which follows in the second part. It deals, first with the distinctive features of our housing situation, next with the principal social and economic changes to be taken into account when formulating plans for the future, then with the resources available to those who must put these plans into practice, and finally with the evolution of our housing policies since the Second World War.

THE HOUSING SITUATION

In comparison with our neighbours, we have a fairly plentiful stock of reasonably large houses providing almost as many rooms per person and as many dwellings per thousand people as can be found anywhere in Europe, although the Belgians, Swedes and Swiss do as well or better. Since our families are not large by European standards, and our population includes a relatively high proportion of older people, this country has smaller households than most other countries. But opportunities for people to establish separate households in this country are appreciably poorer – i.e. headship rates are lower – than those in countries which have built houses at a faster rate during the last twenty years. Serious overcrowding is rare, but it remains a problem in parts of Britain and its incidence is not appreciably less than in one or two countries with a less plentiful stock of housing. That may be partly due to the fact that we have a large proportion of old housing, built to suit the needs of an earlier pattern of household structure and an earlier geographical distribution of the population.

Table 8 shows, for selected countries, the numbers of households recorded at the time of the last census, and the numbers of households these countries would have had if their headship rates had been the same as those found in England and Wales at the time of our own 1951 census. (If rates for the

TABLE 8

Numbers of Households in Selected European Countries

Country and census date	Numbers of households (Thousands)		Column (1) as percentage of Column (2)
	Actual (1)	At England and Wales 1951 headship rates[1] (2)	(3)
England and Wales, 1961	14,890	14,002	106
Denmark, 1960	1,544	1,303	119
France, 1954	13,418	12,739	105
Netherlands, 1960	3,130	2,881	108
Norway, 1960	1,139	1,010	113
Romania, 1956	4,346	4,729	92
Sweden, 1960	2,582	2,207	117
Switzerland, 1960	1,580	1,405	112
West Germany, 1961	18,370	17,152	107

SOURCES: U.N. *Demographic Yearbooks* and national censuses.

1. i.e., the number of houses there would have been if the headship rates found in England and Wales in 1951 had been applied to the population found at the census date shown.

United Kingdom had been available they would have made very little difference to the figures.) In the final column of the table the numbers of households at the time of the latest census are expressed as a percentage of the hypothetical numbers presented in the second column. Minor differences in the figures should be disregarded because the data do not permit great precision. The definitions of a household used in the censuses of different countries are not precisely the same; and there are differences in the age distributions of the people within the broad age-groups used for this comparison which may have some effect on the results. But the table suggests that Denmark, Sweden, Norway and Switzerland have all gone ahead of this country in the numbers of households they have formed. West Germany (despite wartime destruction), France (in 1954, before her building programme really began to grow) and the Netherlands were at about the same stage that England and Wales had reached in 1961. Romania (in 1956) was at a somewhat earlier stage in the subdivision of households – by now they may have caught us up.

Our houses are as well supplied with the basic plumbing and water-using equipment as any in Europe, but many of them are ill-equipped in other ways, particularly with heating systems and internal storage space. This is often true of the newest houses as well as the oldest:

... over a third of Liverpool's council houses do not have a reasonable number of power points. They do not, therefore, permit the use of heating and other modern utilities. Most of these dwellings are less than thirty years old and will be occupied for some time. Yet installing the power points would be a major undertaking, interfering seriously with new building. One decade's compromise is the next decade's vexing problem.*

The comparisons presented in previous chapters would be less complacent if countries such as the United States, Canada and Australia had been included in the league tables. But their outcome is of the kind to be expected in a long-industrialized country with a slow rate of economic and demographic growth, and a preference for houses rather than flats; a country in which civic planning, public health legislation and building by-laws were originally fashioned by a militant generation of sanitary engineers and medical officers who were ignorant of the germ theory of disease and of much that has since been learnt about nutrition, and therefore believed that cleanliness was the surest route to health. We have reason to be grateful for their

*Alvin L. Schorr, *Slums and Social Insecurity*, p. 120. Nelson, 1964.

error, but that it was an error – or at least an oversimplification –
can be seen from the experience of Denmark, Finland, Holland,
Norway and Sweden which have all achieved lower infant
mortality rates and longer life expectations than our own,
despite having fewer baths and taps and less water-borne
sanitation in their houses.

TABLE 9

*Dwellings Completed per Thousand Inhabitants in the United
Kingdom and the Regions of Europe, 1953–64*

	Region					
	United Kingdom	Western Europe[1]	Southern Europe[2]	U.S.S.R.	Remainder of Eastern Europe[3]	Total Europe
1953	6·5	6·6	3·1	6·6	2·8	5·3
1954	7·0	7·2	3·6	7·0	2·9	5·8
1955	6·4	7·2	4·4	7·7	3·2	6·2
1956	6·1	7·3	4·7	8·2	3·5	6·5
1957	6·0	7·4	4·8	10·8	4·5	7·6
1958	5·4	7·0	5·8	13·0	4·9	8·3
1959	5·5	7·5	5·2	14·5	5·2	9·0
1960	5·9	7·5	5·3	13·6	5·3	8·8
1961	5·9	7·6	5·7	12·4	5·8	8·6
1962	6·0	7·5	6·4	11·7	5·6	8·4
1963	5·9	7·5	6·3	11·0	5·5	7·6
1964	7·2	7·9	7·2	10·2	5·7	8·3

SOURCE: U.N. *Annual Bulletins of Housing and Building Statistics for Europe.*

1. Austria, Belgium, Denmark, Finland, France, Ireland, Netherlands, Norway, Sweden, Switzerland, U.K., West Germany.

2. Greece (dwellings begun), Italy, Portugal, Spain.

3. Bulgaria, Czechoslovakia, East Germany, Hungary, Poland, Romania, Yugoslavia.

The mild demographic 'climate' which gives us a relatively
plentiful supply of housing has also permitted a leisurely pace
of house-building. Hence, as can be seen in Tables 3 and 9, our
housing stock is older and grows more slowly than that of other
countries which build to similar standards. Houses built since
the Second World War now amount to between a third and
a half of the total stock in Finland, Norway, Sweden and West

Germany, while only a quarter of the houses in England and Wales were built during this period.

Changes in the quality of a country's housing arise not only from new building and improvements to existing property but also from the loss of obsolete housing. West Germany's big-city slums were eliminated by the housing policies of the R.A.F. and the U.S.A.A.F. and her remaining obsolete houses are scattered in small towns and villages which escaped destruction. In the Scandinavian countries the older houses without baths, water supply and flush toilets are mostly concentrated in rural areas where large numbers are abandoned or converted to city dwellers' country cottages each year. In several of these countries the annual loss of dwellings is greater, in proportion to the total stock, than our own slum clearance programme.* Most of the slums in this country stand in the cities, where they will not be automatically and painlessly replaced in the normal course of economic development and migration.

A nation's housing is a central feature of its living standards and style of life, going far to determine the pattern of demand for consumer goods of many kinds. More important still, perhaps, are the patterns of opportunity arising from the social composition of cities and city neighbourhoods as they are shaped and reshaped by their builders and rebuilders. Much of the Newsom Report on the education of children aged thirteen to sixteen 'of average or less than average ability', and even more of the Plowden Report on primary education was addressed to the Minister of Housing and Local Government rather than the Secretary of State for Education and Science. If Britain is to maintain the same pace of economic and social change that is now at work amongst her neighbours, then the foregoing summary of our situation shows the most urgent needs to be met in future.

In the longer run the most urgent need is a big increase in the rate at which old houses are replaced. Meanwhile the type, character and quality of new building must be reappraised: in future more of it will have to cater for old people, single people and others for whom new housing has seldom been provided in the past; and the government will soon have to decide whether

*See pages 36–7.

the recommendations of the Parker Morris Committee* – which called for more generous living space, better heating, better planning for the conflicting needs of children and motor traffic, and a general improvement in house design – are to be taken seriously or relegated indefinitely to the category of 'important suggestions'† that need not be regarded as binding upon local authorities and private developers. At the same time, steps must be taken to eliminate the extremes of hardship and overcrowding typically found amongst the larger and poorer families. This will call for the building of some houses appreciably bigger than those hitherto provided by the local authorities: between 1961 and 1965 only 2 per cent of the houses and flats they built had more than three bedrooms. But in a country where houses are relatively large and the average size of households is still falling, serious overcrowding could be eliminated by a fairer and more efficient distribution of the space already available – and to achieve that some redistribution of incomes will be necessary. 'We do not greatly help if we are generous with the funds that build houses and niggardly with the funds that poor people use to pay for them.'‡ To list the country's most urgent housing needs is easy enough: to choose which should be given priority is harder, but many other problems must be considered before we return to that question.

SOCIAL AND ECONOMIC CHANGE

To judge from public debates of the last few years, the United Kingdom might be thought to be in the throes of a population explosion, an immigrant invasion, a crippling increase in the proportion of elderly people and a headlong rush from the north to the south east. The reality is less dramatic. In comparison with her neighbours, the most striking feature of this country's demographic patterns is the *slow* rate at which they change. Our rate of natural increase is one of the lowest in

*Central Housing Advisory Committee, *Homes for Today and Tomorrow*, H.M.S.O., 1961.

†Ministry of Housing and Local Government, Circular 13/62, 12 February 1962.

‡*Slums and Social Insecurity*, p. 142.

Europe. The average age at which people marry is still falling, but it already lies below the averages found in many other parts of Europe and the scope for a further reduction must be correspondingly limited.* The post-war bulge in the birth rate will bring growing numbers into the household-forming age groups during the next few years, but this bulge was not a large one by European standards – as was shown in a previous chapter.† For a dozen years after the war there was a small net outflow of migrants from the United Kingdom; but between 1958 and 1960 this changed to a modest inflow that rose steeply during the two years before the Commonwealth Immigrants Act was brought into force – an increase that may have been largely brought about by the impending Act itself. But by 1964 the net movement of migrants was again an outward one. Further restrictions imposed since then and the recent increase in emigration from Britain will ensure that this loss continues. Even during the brief years of inflow the rate of immigration was well below the rates experienced over most of the past decade in Switzerland, West Germany and France. The proportion of old people in our population is rising, but again the pace at which this change is proceeding is slower than that experienced in most European countries.‡ Movement within the country to the most rapidly developing regions is undoubtedly exerting pressure on the supply of housing in certain areas, but the pace of change is again a modest one by European standards. By 1961 even the much discussed 'drift' to the south east had only raised the proportion of the population living in this corner of England and Wales from 35 to 39 per cent in the course of the previous hundred years – a change which brought us back to the proportion living in this region when the first census was taken in 1801. In the London area itself, where the shortage of housing has been most severe, the population has actually been falling – by 2·7 per cent between 1951 and 1961.

* U.N. *Demographic Yearbooks.*
† See Figure 1, pages 22–9.
‡ See Commonwealth Relations Office, *Oversea Migration Board Statistics for 1964*, Cmd 2861, and Organization for European Economic Cooperation, *Demographic Trends 1956–76 in Western Europe and the United States*, Paris, 1961.

Hardships and scarcities in this area have been due to altogether different causes – to changes in the age structure of the population and the number of households, to an unequal distribution of income, to mismanagement and inequitable distribution of the existing stock of houses and other factors, as will be shown in Chapter 10.

Thus we have one of the mildest demographic 'climates' in Europe, and with it goes one of Europe's slowest rates of economic growth and change. Our economy has long been organized mainly for the production of manufactured goods and commercial and public services. In 1931 six per cent of our labour force was employed in agriculture and the remainder were divided equally between industry and construction (47 per cent), services and other work (47 per cent). A quarter of a century later, these proportions were practically unaltered (5 per cent, 50 per cent and 45 per cent respectively). Elsewhere in Europe there had been dramatic changes during this period: the proportion of Sweden's labour force employed in agriculture had fallen from 36 per cent to 16 per cent and the proportion of Holland's from 21 to 11 per cent, for example. Between 1931 and 1961 the proportion of people in England and Wales living in areas classified as 'urban' remained unchanged at 80 per cent. Meanwhile the proportion of Swedes living in urban areas rose from 38 to 73 per cent, and of Dutch from 49 to 55 per cent.* These figures should be treated with caution because they depend so heavily on arbitrary definitions of 'urban areas'.

Whenever such comparisons are made they reveal again the basic stability of Britain's economic structure. This stability has many advantages – industrial revolutions and the migrations and social adjustments associated with them are inflationary, and pose severe economic and human strains. But in the housing field, as in other spheres of investment, stability places a specially heavy responsibility upon government to bring about the modernization and replacement which elsewhere occur as a by-product of more rapid and widespread economic development.

*U.N. *Demographic Yearbooks*, and F. Dewhurst, J. Coppock and P. Lamartine Yates, *Europe's Needs and Resources*, Twentieth Century Fund, New York, 1961.

THE SCOPE FOR PROGRESS

The same stability has important implications for the resources likely to be available in future for building houses. The United Kingdom is, by European standards, a wealthy country; its housing needs are growing slowly and – like other wealthy countries – its people devote a relatively large proportion of their expenditure to housing and its government controls and spends a relatively large proportion of the national income. At first sight this would appear to give us exceptional opportunities for improving our housing conditions.

But this country has long been heavily committed to branches of industry which show, on the world stage, a relatively slow rate of expansion. A growing proportion of old people, coupled with a birth rate which has been rising for a decade, will bring about a temporary fall in the proportion of the population in the working age groups. On the assumption that existing trends continue, the Government Actuary's Department expects that the proportion of the United Kingdom's population between the age of fifteen and the age of retirement (sixty-five for men, sixty for women) will fall from 62 per cent in 1964 to 60 per cent in 1970 and 58 per cent in 1980.* The growing proportion of women who get married and the younger age at which they marry also produce a loss in the working population which will be roughly counterbalanced by the growing number of married women who go to work; the proportion of women in the labour force will probably remain the same but they will be less mobile and more of them will be part-timers. A fear of the immigrant that is in danger of assuming pathological proportions has severely restricted the recruitment of labour from overseas and is likely to ensure a continuing loss, through emigration, from the younger working population. Meanwhile there is no large reserve of agricultural labour waiting to join the industries most urgently seeking recruits. For all these reasons we are deprived of the reserves of mobile manpower which give adaptability and dynamism to the economies of West Germany, France, Italy, Spain and many other countries.

* Central Statistical Office, 'Projecting the Population of the United Kingdom', *Economic Trends*, No. 139 H.M.S.O., May 1965.

T – G.O.H. – F

The resources of government in this country, though large, are more heavily committed to defence and the service of the national debt than those of any other country in western Europe. Hence the 'leverage' that government can itself exert in housing, as in other fields that call for heavy expenditure, is correspondingly restricted. Underlying these restrictions are the United Kingdom's extensive international commitments, both in the military sphere where the shedding of an empire is proving more expensive than the winning of it, and in the monetary sphere where we are obliged to defend the world's principal trading currency and cannot risk serious inflation or a prolonged deficit on our balance of payments. While these patterns continue, governments in this country will find it exceedingly difficult to bring about a major increase in our low rate of investment without cutting down on consumption to a degree that would imperil their parliamentary majorities. And it is this low rate of investment – not the proportions of investment devoted to construction and house building, both of which are typical of western Europe – that distinguishes the United Kingdom from its neighbours. Once a higher rate of saving and investment have been achieved, this country will have greater freedom to redeploy its resources and make real progress in housing, or in other sectors of the economy to which priority may be accorded, without reducing current consumption. Therefore, to justify arguments for a major improvement in this country's housing conditions, it is not enough to show that this improvement can bring about desirable social changes. (It can indeed, but it may also cause inflation.) Neither is it enough to show that the building industry is capable of increasing its productivity and sustaining a much higher rate of output. (It is, but more houses, and the provision of schools, roads and other public services that must go with them – not to mention the mass of furniture and equipment their occupants must buy to render them comfortably habitable – call for a great increase in capital and current expenditure, by public authorities and private households alike.) It must also be shown that housing policies, along with other measures, can help bring about an economic change of gear which will increase savings, and do that in a manner sufficiently acceptable to give the government of the day a reasonable chance of staying in power.

POLICIES SINCE THE WAR

Certain features of the British housing system were briefly touched upon in Chapter 3 to show how an administrative structure and the assumptions it expresses help to determine the role and responsibilities of government in this field. A fuller account must now be given of the evolution of British housing policies since the Second World War. This will be no more than a sketch – a selective commentary on twenty years of highly controversial history.*

Britain emerged from the war with 200,000 houses destroyed, another 250,000 so badly knocked about that they could not be lived in and a similar number severely damaged. Millions of men and women were about to come home, and the marriage and birth rates were rising fast. The prewar construction labour force of a million men had fallen to a third of this number, mainly concentrated in south-east England, in the path of the flying bomb and rocket attacks. The rents of privately owned houses had been frozen at their 1939 levels, and in England and Wales 71,000 houses had been requisitioned by local authorities.

But amidst the confusion there was determination and high confidence, fortified by an underestimate of long-term needs and a war-won capacity for bold decisions. Procedures for compulsory purchase were temporarily simplified to enable the Minister to confirm orders 'without public local inquiry or hearing'. Prewar slum-clearance subsidies were extended to cover housing built to meet 'general needs', and were later increased, three fourths of the subsidy (instead of the prewar two thirds) being paid by the central government. Orders were issued for the production of prefabricated temporary houses, and local authorities were empowered to erect them on public open spaces where no other land was available. 'The Minister'

* Much of this account is taken from D. V. Donnison, *Housing Policy Since the War* (Occasional Papers on Social Administration No. 1, Codicote Press, 1961) where references to its sources can be found. For a summary of much of the legislation affecting England and Wales, see *Report of the Committee on Housing in Greater London*, Cmnd 2605, Appendix 1.

explained one of his supporters in the Commons, 'is not going to negotiate separate agreements with every local authority. They have got to take what he gives them. . . . What it needs will not be determined by the local authority; it has been determined by the enemy.' 'Housing' said Mr Tomlinson, introducing the first postwar housing Bill, 'should be tackled as one would tackle a military operation. . . . Let there be no misunderstanding; it is the intention of His Majesty's Government to go into business both in the manufacture and in the distribution of building components in a big way. . . .' The caretaker government had estimated that 750,000 new houses would be required 'to afford a separate dwelling for every family desiring to have one,' and expected that between three and four million houses would be built in the next ten or twelve years. (It took seven years for the first million, three more for the second.)

The dimensions of the standard three-bedroom council house were enlarged from the prewar 750 square feet to 900 square feet, plus a 50 square-foot outhouse. Local authorities were given still wider powers to requisition property 'to ensure as far as possible that all houses are reasonably fully occupied' and 'for the purpose of preventing a situation where people become or are likely to become homeless' (i.e. to prevent evictions). They built most of the houses, and were responsible for controlling and rationing work on repairs and the small amount of new private building permitted. But their designs, layouts, methods and materials were tightly controlled by the central government, and the Ministry directed a continuous flow of instruction and exhortation at them – an average of five circulars a week in 1946. Their status was tersely explained by the Minister, Aneurin Bevan: 'If we are to plan we have to plan with plannable instruments, and the speculative builder, by his very nature, is not a plannable instrument. . . . We rest the full weight of the housing programme upon the local authorities, because their programmes can be planned, and because in fact we can check them if we desire to. . . .' Builders could be forced into less profitable areas by restricting building quotas in the most profitable centres. Meanwhile, town planning powers were transferred from the smaller authorities to the Counties and County Boroughs, and greatly enlarged; any change of land use was subject to control and to a development charge designed to secure for the community the profits arising from permission to develop.

Although the 'housing drive' was mounted quickly and successfully in this way, it did not call for any fundamental reappraisal of prewar thinking. The 1947 Town and Country Planning Act (crucial parts of it later abandoned) and the new towns (which did not make an appreciable contribution until a decade had passed) were the only major innovations in this field. The twin pillars of the whole programme – rent control and subsidized council housing – were devices that had been employed since the First World War. The 'prefabs', Europe's first post-war experiment in industrialized building, were designed to produce rapid results during the inevitable delay while men were released from the forces and conventional building resources were mobilized. They were produced by workers employed in defence industries caught over-extended by the unexpectedly sudden defeat of Japan; they proved very expensive, gave prefabrication a bad name, and were dropped as soon as possible. Requisitioning was an avowedly temporary procedure, cut down after 1948 and brought to a close in 1960, provoking no fresh thought about government's responsibility for acquiring or assisting privately rented housing. Proposals for municipalizing private property, advanced in the debate on the 1949 Housing Bill, were dismissed by Aneurin Bevan in characteristically forceful fashion: 'It cannot and would not be done at the present time . . . if we tried to do that through the 1,700 odd local authorities, it would be an operation compared with which the Italian campaign was one of the most simple ever carried out.'

Taken as a whole, the provisions made were bold and expensive, by prewar standards; but they bore the marks of a 'crash' programme, being designed to meet essentially temporary needs (for housing requirements were gravely underestimated) with instruments (such as rent control, requisitioning and the 'prefabs') many of which were also avowedly temporary. Little more could be expected in the critical and chaotic months between V.E. Day and the economic crisis of 1947, when this system was being created. But much further thought would have to be given to housing needs and housing policies before the system could be rendered as comprehensive and constructive as those being created at the same time by reforms of the health services, the national insurance and pensions schemes, the child care service and the education system. In the housing field there had been no equivalent to the Beveridge Report, the Curtis Report and other studies made in neighbouring fields of social policy during and immediately after the war. Unfortunately, many thought the mixture of wartime controls and postwar improvisations hastily assembled as a housing policy, was a form of Socialism: necessary perhaps, in the opinion of Conservatives, but to be dispensed with as soon as possible; necessary without question, in the opinion of the Labour Party, and to be defended without serious modification.

By the end of 1946 the United Kingdom was well ahead of the field in getting her housing programme going, and the government announced a further increase that would take output to 240,000 during the following year. But the building industry was already running short of materials; and then came a hard winter and the fuel crisis, followed by a first class crisis in the balance of payments. The export drive became the government's all-consuming concern and, with it, the restraint of inflation, the control of imports, the rationing of building materials and the restriction of building. Despite occasional increases in the programme, notably in 1953 and 1964, house building has been overshadowed by anxieties about the balance of payments and employed as one of the principal regulators of the economy ever since. For the next five years after the crisis of 1947 – while most local authorities, regardless of Party colouring, were determined to build as many houses as possible – the main task of central government was to restrict the building programme to the level permitted by those responsible for the balance of payments.

The imposition of a rigid numerical ceiling on output sustained for so long a time had a chilling effect on the outlook and morale of all concerned. Ambitious schemes devised at the end of the war to recruit and train more building workers were thrown out of gear; the recruitment of apprentices fell off sharply and the training scheme for adults was abandoned.

(Twenty years later an attempt is again being made to recruit and train adults for the industry.) As building costs continued to rise, the standards of council housing were gradually pared down. In 1951 local authorities were encouraged to abandon the minimum requirement of 900 square feet for a three bedroom house, 'provided that the sizes of the individual rooms and the total amount of living space do not fall . . .' (passage ways, larders, store-rooms and coal bunkers were not classed as 'living space'). Next year they were asked to economize '. . . not merely in the design of the house but also in the services and equipment to be installed in them . . .' The circular pointed out that 'a significant reduction in the cost of the house – and consequently in the rent at which it can be let – can be made if the essential is distinguished from the unessential. The authority . . . should have due regard to the requirements of those to whom the house will be let', but it was not told how to discover what their tenants regarded as 'essential' and 'unessential'. The average floor area of three-bedroom council houses in England and Wales fell from 1,050 square feet in 1951 to a low point of 897 square feet in 1959 and 1960. (See Figure 4 on page 252.)

As resources gradually grew more plentiful and the most urgent needs were met, controls on building materials and prices were relaxed: hardwood was freed from licensing control in 1949, general controls over the distribution of steel ended in 1950, price controls on softwood ended in 1951, and in 1952 a new and less negative form of discipline was introduced – the 'Economy Bulletins' on steel, cement and bricks, which prescribed methods of using these materials that the Ministry expected to see adopted before approving new building. Building for private ownership was also permitted more freely: local authorities were allowed to devote up to a fifth of their allocations to private building in 1948, up to a half in 1951; in 1952 the 'free limit' below which building licences were not required was raised to £500 and licenses for houses up to 1,000 square feet were given 'without question', and in 1954 the licensing of house building came to an end. The proportion of houses built for private owners – almost entirely for owner-occupiers – rose from 15 per cent in 1952 to 63 per cent in 1961. Authorizations and controls imposed by central government on the detail of local authorities' building procedures were simplified, and greater reliance was placed on the judgement of professionally qualified surveyors, architects and accountants. Interest rates were increased; local authorities were gradually forced into the open market for their borrowing, and cut off from the Public Works Loan Board which had previously been the main source of their loans. Development charges and the attempt to 'nationalize' the profits accruing to land owners from development were abolished in 1953.

The government was gradually restricting its commitments in the housing field and creating the framework for a return to something resembling a free market. But this process was held up for a while by the determination to build 300,000 houses a year which formed one of the most publicized promises of the Conservative government returned to power in 1951. To increase the building programme by 50 per cent in a fashion that would meet some of the more urgent needs called for a major increase in the local authorities' output and an even larger increase in subsidies to cover the rising interest rates they had to pay. Exchequer subsidies on post-war housing in England and Wales quadrupled between 1950 and 1956. Thanks partly to a reduction in housing standards and the building of more small houses, the higher building target was achieved and surpassed. The threat to the balance of payments was averted by a fortunate change in the terms of trade which began in 1951 and has continued since then (apart from a small setback in 1955) benefiting all the industrial countries at the expense of the primary producers. In the peak year of 1954, 357,000 houses were completed in the United Kingdom, placing this country high in the European 'league' (building seven houses per thousand inhabitants) though still below some of her neighbours (West Germany, for example, then building eleven per thousand and Norway building ten per thousand). Housing conditions were improving.

The stage was now set for a major change of direction. The freeing of the private builder, whose output had hitherto been squeezed when economic crises demanded cuts in investment, meant that the local authorities had henceforth to furnish the variable element in the programme and bear the brunt of any cut-back. The general rise in the cost of borrowing and the refusal to give local authorities a reduced rate of interest – most unusual among European countries – imposed a heavy burden of housing subsidies on government. These subsidies were confined to one sector of the market, and gave government less pervasive and sensitive means of assisting and controlling the market than those available to governments in other countries. Sooner or later there was bound to be an attack on these subsidies which were a cumulative commitment, continuing for sixty years on each new house built by the local authorities. They had risen to 104 millions a year for the United Kingdom by 1954 (including both central and local government contributions). This was only one third as much as the subsidies then paid for food and agriculture, but it was a large sum nevertheless, and one that had been rising by nearly 10 per cent a year. Meanwhile there was growing concern about the decay of older property, most of which was still subject to rent control; and as the bombed sites were exhausted many authorities were finding it increasingly difficult to secure land for new building. There was also a growing demand, pent up since 1939, for commercial buildings and private houses – a demand the building industry was anxious to meet. The original prescription, first formulated in 1919, of subsidized council housing and rent control could not last much longer as the basis of housing policy. And once the local authority building programme lost its central position among the instruments of housing policy, the tide of opinion could rapidly turn against it. Council housing, by now sheltering a fifth of this country's households, would no longer offer a hope of escape for the many from overcrowding and squalor; it would increasingly be regarded as a privilege confined to the fortunate few.

The new order took shape between 1954 and 1957. Its principal objectives were first explained in a White Paper, 'Houses – the Next Step', and implemented through a succession of measures, the most important of which were the Housing Repairs and Rents Act of 1954, the Housing Subsidies Act of 1956, and the Rent Act of 1957. The local authorities' building programmes were reduced, and switched to slum clearance and – to a lesser extent – to the housing of old people and the expansion of smaller towns taking population from the most rapidly growing centres. Local authorities, said the Minister, 'should subsidize only those tenants who require subsidizing, and only to the extent of their need', using the money thus saved to build new houses 'with appreciably less Exchequer assistance than hitherto'. Requisitioned houses were to be purchased outright or returned to their owners by 1960. Subject to the restraints imposed by rising interest rates, higher land prices and building costs and the withdrawal of the 'general needs' subsidies, local authorities were given greater freedom to determine their own building policies and no longer obliged to contribute a subsidy from the rates before claiming subsidies from the Exchequer. The central government would henceforth assist and advise rather than exhort or direct them.

Rent restrictions were removed from a few of the most expensive houses, while the rents of the remainder were raised to higher levels; wherever existing tenants moved or died rents were freed from all control. Simultaneously, the local authorities were empowered to lend more generously to people buying their own homes and encouraged to sell council houses to their tenants, and the government offered guarantees to building societies lending to people buying old houses. More generous grants and more intensive propaganda were directed to the improvement of private property, and here the local authorities were given less freedom than hitherto – some of them had previously been reluctant to make grants to private owners who were therefore to have henceforth a statutory right to various grants financed by the central government. Taken together, these steps greatly increased the opportunities and incentives for landlords to sell their houses to owner-occupiers. Meanwhile, as building licences were abandoned and planning restrictions were relaxed, the office building boom began to get under way – starting in London and then spreading to the major provincial centres.

The pattern took shape gradually, and for a while it looked as if the government was extricating itself from its extensive, though never comprehensively planned, involvement in the housing market. The local authorities would clear the slums –

still regarded as a finite, public health problem for which a final solution would soon be found – and thereafter they would administer their inheritance of some three and a half million houses as a form of social service, adding a few to bring about the expansion of selected towns and to meet the special needs of selected groups in the population. The 'free market' for lending, borrowing, renting and building would meet all normal requirements.

But government was not to be let off the hook so easily. Economic and social changes were already at work, increasing needs and demands, distorting and restricting the capacity of the market to meet these demands, and sharpening the political tensions that would in due course drag government back into a deeper involvement in this field. The principal factors making it difficult for government to restrict itself to a residual, 'social' housing policy can be briefly outlined.

The relatively slow growth of the United Kingdom's population had throughout the century distracted attention from underlying changes in demographic structure. These changes called for an increase in housing which had to proceed much faster than the increase in population if headship rates were not to fall – that is to say, if people of any given age, sex and marital status were to have as good a chance of finding a home as their predecessors had. Between 1931 and 1951 the population of England and Wales had increased by less than 10 per cent, but households had increased by over 28 per cent. Although it was three times as large as the increase in population, this increase in households probably occurred without any appreciable rise in the headship rates for particular groups within the population: single men aged twenty, married couples aged forty, or widows aged sixty, for example, probably had about the same chance of forming separate households as their predecessors in the same demographic groups had twenty years earlier. (If some had a better chance, then others had worse: census data do not permit a more precise conclusion.) The fall in family size, the growing numbers of old people and the increasing popularity of marriage meant that one- and two-person households had increased from 29 to 39 per cent of all those in the country, while households of six or more people fell from 16 to 8 per cent of the total, and there were 300 instead of 256 households for every thousand people. But these changes occurred without any improvement in the privacy and independence actually afforded to individuals by the housing available. The dynamics of these changes in demographic structure – which are still continuing, though now at a slower rate – were not widely understood in this country until the publication of J. B. Cullingworth's book, *Housing Needs and Planning Policy*, in 1960. This partly explains why housing needs were continually underestimated, even by radical prophets, from the time when Sidney Webb, Ramsay MacDonald, J. R. Clynes and others published a pamphlet in 1917 estimating that when a million houses had been built, only 100,000 a year would be required for replacement and further growth of the population,* to the time when the Economics Committee of the Royal Commission on Population predicted there would be so sharp a fall in household formation during the 1950s that a major programme of slum clearance would be required to prevent a slump in the building industry.†

In 1951, national income per head scarcely surpassed the level attained in 1939; but in the years that followed it began to rise – at a modest rate by European standards, but more rapidly than ever before in living memory. One of the first things to which the British devoted their extra wealth was the bearing and raising of children. From the mid fifties the birth rate began to rise, steadily and quite unexpectedly. It would be another twenty years before this change could affect the numbers of households to be sheltered. But many people on modest incomes now depended on rent control and council housing to enable them to secure living space for their growing families, and they would be seriously threatened by a reduction in council building, a reorientation of municipal priorities that restricted or abolished the rehousing of families from the waiting lists, or by the elimination of rent controls.

The new households endeavouring to set up home for the first time were not scattered evenly over the country at large, but concentrated in the more central parts of towns (where

*Joint Committee on Labour Problems After the War, *A Million New Houses After the War*, 1917.

†See pages 315–16.

there are also many old people who add to the growing numbers of small households) and in the expanding industrial and commercial centres generally. An increase in wealth and personal incomes, tending likewise to be concentrated in areas of shortage, does not automatically resolve this problem; indeed, it may render it worse if those who are growing richer compete for housing with pensioners and low paid workers in the same areas, thus producing a more unequal distribution of incomes in districts where housing scarcities are most severe.

The young, the old and the single, poorer households generally, and the many groups whom local authorities and building societies are unable or unwilling to serve, had in the past depended mainly upon the private landlord for shelter. But private rented property, as will be shown in a later chapter, had been dwindling for years. The growing slum clearance programme, the encouragement of owner occupation through more generous loans and improvement grants and the workings of a tax system which favoured the owner-occupier and penalized the private landlord, all hastened this process – demolishing private rented property or converting it to owner occupation, while ensuring that new investment was concentrated in other sectors of the market. Those who could not gain a foothold in the expanding sectors of the market were thus compelled to compete for a dwindling supply of poor quality housing.

Meanwhile more forceful and comprehensive controls on land uses and housing densities imposed since 1947 had produced a set of town plans most of which were based on serious underestimates of the rate at which urban populations would increase. Too many development plans, and the densities, green belts, road improvements and other land-consuming elements incorporated in them, had been drawn up on the basis of over-cautious forecasts which underestimated the regional and local growth of employment, population and incomes. Thus as employment and incomes grew, particularly in the region within commuting distance of London, severe shortages of the cheaper accommodation began to appear.

The Rent Act of 1957 did nothing to ease or clarify the situation. Based on a statistical error that led to a gross overestimate of the number of tenancies to be immediately decontrolled, on no preliminary study of rented housing or its owners, and no understanding of the scope and effects of 'creeping decontrol', this measure provoked a longer and more acrimonious debate than any other Bill introduced since the war. Some of the passion aroused was generated by politicians seeking issues that would unite their followers – exceptionally divided at that time. ('We have been talking about rents, but our minds have been more on Suez' said one candid member.) But supporters of the measure were in fact concerned mainly with rents and their economic implications for the management and improvement of housing, while its opponents were concerned mainly with security of tenure and its human implications. Each had justice on their side, but the two issues were inextricably confused. Tenants, said one of them, 'have no right, however long they have lived in it to think that . . . the property belongs to them'. 'A landlord and a tenant each has a legal interest in the house; it belongs to both of them' replied a member of the opposition. The continuation of various forms of rent restriction since 1915 made it impossible to distinguish the two issues at stake. Farmers, shopkeepers, and tenants of factories, offices and virtually every other form of property except housing, were already protected by legislation giving them security of tenure, together with sane legal procedures for fixing fair rents. The residential tenant had presumably been forgotten because the owner-occupier and the council tenant both have security of tenure, for practical purposes, and most private tenants could rely on the security that automatically went with rent control. If effective means of rent regulation had been devised for areas of shortage, permitting flexible and regular reappraisal, it would have been possible to eliminate the negative and destructive rent freeze while retaining a large measure of security of tenure.

But such solutions were not considered, and the Act was passed to the applause of politicians rallying to the colours of 'free enterprise' and economists in search of a problem to which their ready-made academic solutions could be applied. Both were unaware of the massive and permanent shortages building up as the uncontrolled growth of employment sharpened competition for housing space in areas where town

planning controls and slum clearance restricted the supply.
Neither understood the long history of government policies
(in which rent controls played a relatively small part) that had
weighted the scales against the private landlord.* The economic
opportunity conferred on landlords by the 1957 Act was largely
illusory; its full effects were postponed by an amending Act the
following year, and massively counterbalanced shortly after by
other measures which strengthened the trend towards owner
occupation in the very property which was intended to be
retained for renting. No other country in western Europe had
so consistently discouraged private investment in rented property. No other country had abandoned its rent controls in a
manner that neither distinguished between the extent of the
shortage in particular areas, nor offered allowances or subsidies
to the families least capable of paying increased rents.

It took several years for the stresses resulting from these
developments to break surface. But after a time problems arising
at the opposite ends of the social processes now at work
demanded growing attention. Newspaper readers were repeatedly reminded of the decaying and under-employed cities of
Scotland, the north of England and (more faintly) Ulster, and
of the increasingly ruthless battle for space going on in the
booming inner areas of London. In the summer of 1961
homeless London families, who had been growing in numbers
since the last quarter of 1957, began to appear on the television
screens; thereafter every editor made a regular feature of
'human stories' about housing. The London County Council
commissioned a study of the problem and reorganized its
procedures for coping with the homeless,† but over a thousand
children remained in its care simply because their parents
could not find a home, and over a thousand families – amounting
to 4,700 people – were housed in the Council's welfare accommodation. Then in 1963 a public scandal blew up, involving
two girls, an osteopath, the Secretary of State for War and a
notorious London landlord who had disposed of most of his
residential property in 1960 and died in 1962. The uproar that

*See Chapter 7.
†John Greve, *London's Homeless*, Occasional Papers on Social
Administration, No. 10, Bell, 1964.

followed succeeded – where researchers, social workers, local government officials and council members had failed – in securing action on London's housing problems. A Committee of Inquiry was appointed which proceeded to make a more thorough investigation than may have been expected.

Meanwhile, there was rising concern about the deprived northern regions of the country and the general stagnation of the economy. The National Economic Development Council had been established, and its officials began to study the scope for hastening Britain's rate of economic development. Their first report,* dealing with the period from 1961 to 1966, included a figure never before produced for this country: an estimate of the potential output of the construction industry, incorporating explicit and economically reasoned assumptions about the number of houses that might be built. At the same time the Town and Country Planning Division of the Ministry of Housing and Local Government had begun making regional studies and the first of these to be published – the South East Study – discussed housing requirements and made proposals about the size and distribution of the future house building programme within this region.

Besides researching and prognosticating, the government had taken a number of practical steps to cope with particular features of the continuing housing shortage. As it became clearer that council housing and owner occupation could not between them provide new housing for all those in need of it, an attempt was made in 1961 to promote housing associations of new kinds with the aid of government lending, and in 1964 a national Housing Corporation was established to provide technical advice for them, backed by Exchequer loans of £50 millions (which may be increased to £100 millions) and an assurance of additional support from the building societies. It was recognized too, that many of the hardships in private rented housing were due to irresponsible subdivision and mismanagement of this property: the 1961 Act gave local authorities greater powers of compulsion in dealing with these problems, and the 1964 Act extended these powers much further, enabling authorities to

* National Economic Development Council, *Growth of the United Kingdom Economy, 1961–1966*, H.M.S.O., 1963.

compel owners in designated areas to improve their housing, to offer more generous improvement grants, and to take over the property of recalcitrant landlords under 'control orders' for a period of up to five years, paying minimal compensation to the owner and recouping from him the costs of necessary improvements that were not covered by rents.

The Ministry of Public Building and Works was meanwhile centralizing a number of government building responsibilities outside the housing field and embarking on a systematic programme of architectural research and development work, one offshoot of which was the establishment of the National Building Agency whose task it was to promote more efficient industrialized building methods throughout the country, particularly in the housing sphere. Encouraged by this leadership, local authorities in many parts of the country were beginning to organize themselves into 'consortia' and other groupings, some of them employing the same development and design teams, building methods and contractors, in an attempt to realize the advantages of operating on a larger scale. Comparisons were frequently made with the success achieved by similar methods, years before, in improving the design and reducing the cost of schools. But the revolution in school building began at a point when costs were high and existing designs were often wasteful. The attempt to reorganize the house building industry began after a decade of continuous economies and dwindling standards when more generous dimensions and equipment were urgently needed. This was bound to be a harder row to hoe.

During the general election that followed in 1964, much of the debate centred on housing, rents, the rights of tenants, the rising price of land, the building of offices – many of them still standing embarrassingly empty– the needs of the homeless, and the plight of decaying and depressed areas. The outcome of the election was widely attributed to public disquiet about these issues. Government was being drawn ineluctably back into deeper involvement in the housing field. The evidence of stress was now plain, and the political penalties of neglecting these stresses were equally clear. A great deal of information had been assembled from three Regional Studies, and from the Milner Holland Report (on Housing in Greater London), the Buchanan

Report (on Traffic in Towns), the Banwell Report (on the
Placing and Management of Contracts for Building and Civil
Engineering Work) and other official inquiries. But the first
steps taken after the election, dealing with the prevention of
evictions and abuses in private property, the control of office
building, the provision of additional help for housing associations and the establishment of a system of rent regulation, were
dictated by the immediate crises confronting the government
and did not amount to a systematically planned housing policy.
Since then a more comprehensive programme has begun to
take shape, which will be discussed in later chapters of this
book.

How far the government will proceed from these tentative
beginnings must depend on its capacity to resolve peculiarly
intractable problems whose ramifications extend well beyond
the housing field and deep into the structure of our society.
Some of the principal problems on the agenda can be briefly
posed.

Any major programme for the rebuilding of Britain will
founder in a welter of political rhetoric at the first unfavourable
turn in the balance of payments unless we first build a more
robust domestic economy. That will call for a higher rate of
saving, permitting a higher rate of investment. This is not a
country in which government can compel an abrupt reduction
in consumption by taxation, rationing or inflation, followed by
the imprisonment of those who lead the resulting disturbances.
(Spain, too, has found its working class must be permitted an
appreciable share of the country's increasing wealth; and the
Hungarian revolution of 1956 was not unconnected with the
rate of investment sustained during the preceding years – an
exceptionally high one, even for Communist countries.) Neither
will the change be brought about by waiting for economic
planners to invent a technical solution for our economic problems. A higher rate of saving calls for a fundamental change in
national 'time preferences' – in the relative values people accord
to present and future consumption. But since the acquisition,
equipment and improvement of a home to which the family has
a secure and continuing right is one of the principal future
objectives for which people are prepared to sacrifice current

satisfactions, the provision of housing need not be regarded as a purely inflationary 'overhead' in such an economy; it can also contribute to a solution of these problems.

Increasing wealth is not spread evenly, like jam, across the country. It accumulates most rapidly in the economically growing centres through a combination of relatively modest wage differentials and varying levels of employment, particularly among women. If left to accrue without any deliberate plan it can render housing scarcities in these regions worse and also produce a general impoverishment of the stagnant regions as they continue to lose their more enterprising, skilled and mobile citizens. Can we create new centres of industrial growth in these stagnant areas, and distribute more deliberately the opportunities that growth confers? (This is being achieved in hitherto decaying areas of South Wales, but Scotland and Ulster have far to go before they secure their share of expansion.) Much of the expansion will continue to be concentrated in the Midlands and the South East and it must be distributed in a way that enables us to meet housing needs.

Government regulation of land uses, through development plans, density regulations, green belts and the like, was intended to render cities delightful, not intolerable. They must form a vehicle within which the growth of employment, population and housing can be carried forward together – not a constricting shell that paralyses change.

The replacement of obsolete housing will demand heavy investment, continuing and growing for the foreseeable future. The medical criteria and the administrative structures and procedures appropriate for dealing with the older concept of a limited 'slum' problem will no longer be appropriate for a period when housing, like lathes, presses and other machinery, must be continuously depreciated and replaced. The scale of the effort required will call for more technically trained staff in and around government than has yet been realized.

Table 8 indicates that the growth of households in this country still has a long way to go. But young married couples – the people for whom most of our housing has till now been built – will form a declining proportion of the extra households to be formed. If the needs of other kinds of households are to be met there will have to be fresh thinking about the design, layout, financing and ownership of housing.

In this country, government tends to draw clear distinctions between private and public enterprise and to treat the profit motive with a suspicion equally chilling, whether derived from socialist hostility to capitalism or aristocratic contempt for those 'in trade'. Whether dealing with builders, landlords or developers, government has traditionally tended to assume the role of policeman, directing the traffic and reprimanding the minority of delinquents. In an age when the policies and decisions of government increasingly determine the flow and volume of the traffic itself, these patterns are no longer adequate. How to foster private enterprise and incorporate it as a deliberate instrument of government policies is a question that will recur in many spheres of housing policy.

The solution of these problems will call for a reappraisal of many long-established features of the structure of British government: the preparation of national plans, the endeavour to shape and invigorate the economic framework of regions, the industrialization and redeployment of the building industry, the building and rebuilding of whole towns, the provision of housing for groups of the population not hitherto catered for by municipal authorities – such developments cannot leave the structure of administration and the distribution of power within it unchanged, whether at central, regional or local levels.

But the fundamental dilemma underlying most of our housing problems arises from a willing acceptance of great inequalities in the distribution of personal incomes, coupled with a rejection of similar inequalities in the distribution of housing. Britain appears to be gradually incorporating a concern about bad housing conditions into its collective social conscience, alongside the concerns for unemployment and medical care incorporated there a generation earlier. But a determination to provide decent housing for people now deprived of it cannot bear fruit unless they are enabled to pay for what they need. The present 'system' of government contributions to housing, if it can be called that, includes housing subsidies, improvement grants, tax reliefs, and Social Security rent allowances. It is quite inadequate for this purpose, though it brings about redistributions of income that are large enough, if effectively deployed, to go a long way towards achieving it.

This is a familiar problem: in our health services and in our system of education we are beginning slowly and painfully to ensure that an exceedingly unequal society provides reasonably equal opportunities for all its members in these important fields. We may now be embarking on a similar endeavour in the field of housing. The remainder of this book will explore the problems confronting a government that sets its hand to that task.

CHAPTER 6

THE ENGLISH HOUSING MARKET

THE market for housing is exceedingly complex, and differs in crucial ways from the markets for other things. Houses remain rooted to the spot where they are first placed and it is their occupiers who must move when they change hands. The materials and components of which they are made are bulky, heavy and costly to transport, and most of the work that goes into assembling these materials must be done at or near the place where the finished product is to be sold. The demand for houses is closely tied to the demands for many other goods and services, from furniture and kitchen equipment to transport and schools, and cannot be understood in isolation from these related markets. Housing is exceedingly expensive by comparison with other goods and services retailed to the public, and very few people build or buy a house for cash down; the volume and character of the demands for housing which are actually met therefore depend not only on the level and distribution of incomes but particularly on the supply of credit and the operation of the channels through which loans for housing flow. Since houses last a very long time, the great majority of those changing hands are 'second-hand', and people's opportunities of getting one depend greatly on the supply of alternative housing available to other people now occupying the accommodation they want and partly on the demand for their own present homes. Therefore the movement of households and the 'effective demand' for housing must not be thought of as a mass of unrelated impulses like the mass of individual purchases that constitutes the demand for a consumer good; since most movers go to a house previously occupied by someone else and most of them relinquish a house that others move into, these moves form a continuing flow, each one depending in part on previous and subsequent moves. But the process depends on many other factors, too. Houses, even when they look exactly the same, are infinitely varied in character and quality; their occupiers buy not only bricks and mortar but a location and all that goes with it – security of tenure perhaps, a fashionable address, proximity to work and schools, the neighbours next door, and a view of the park or the gas works. Even within one income group, the urgency of buyers' needs – affecting their 'elasticities of demand' – varies greatly, depending particularly on the stage they have reached in their life cycle: when people get married or start a family or change their jobs they are prepared to make sacrifices to secure a home which would be intolerable at other times. Thus the housing market cannot be understood in isolation from its social and demographic environment. Finally – as has been argued throughout this book – the impact made on the market by government, whether it be deliberate (as in the case of housing subsidies and rent controls) or an accidental by-product of other operations (as with many forms of tax relief), now goes far to determine the way in which this market works and the needs it is capable of meeting.

Conventional forms of economic analysis, employing various elaborations of the concepts of supply, demand and price, provide useful techniques for reasoning about this market. But its complexity, and the pervasive influences exerted upon it by demographic and political factors and by the institutional framework within which it operates, make it impossible to explain the workings of this market in economic terms alone. At the same time, the complexity of the system makes it essential to attempt some general explanation of its operations: for lack of any general understanding of its workings, government interventions designed to solve particular housing problems have too often produced unforeseen damage at other points in the system.

The initial concepts for the analysis that follows will therefore be kept as simple and concrete as possible. The procedures and opportunities for getting a house, the legal rights and the character of the housing secured, all depend heavily on the household's 'tenure' of its accommodation. Much of the analysis will therefore be based on comparisons between the principal 'tenure groups': owner-occupiers, private tenants of various kinds, and council tenants. More conventional forms of economic analysis will be brought to bear in the next chapter, when the fundamental structure of the system grows clearer.

The whole chapter adopts one major simplification which should be constantly borne in mind: '*houses*' *are defined not as structurally separate dwellings but as* '*household spaces*' – *the accommodation occupied by one person living alone or a group of people who share a dwelling and are catered for by the same person.* Empty houses have therefore been excluded from the analysis, and dwellings shared by several households bulk slightly larger than they would in a study conducted in terms of the 'dwellings' defined in the census.

The chapter begins with a description of the housing currently in use, followed by a description of the households occupying it and the housing conditions they secure, contrasting the different tenure groups. These paragraphs present a brief summary of the housing situation at one point in time. Next comes an analysis of the principal changes now taking place in this system, dealing with changes in the stock of houses (new building, conversions, demolitions and changes in tenure), the formation of new households, the movement of existing households, and the dissolution and amalgamation of hitherto separate households. The amount of information available about these changes varies, but all must be incorporated in the analysis, even if some stages of the discussion contribute little more than unanswered questions.

An attempt will then be made to draw the analysis together and present a 'moving picture' or 'working model' of the whole system. The chapter concludes with a discussion of some of the more important conclusions to be derived from this model, comparing the housing opportunities of different groups in the population, and identifying the longer-term changes now at work within the system and the hardships these changes are likely to produce. The next chapter goes further in explaining why the system works as it does and in discussing what should be done about it. It is at that stage that rents, prices, subsidies and other more conventional economic concepts must be brought into play. In economic terms, this chapter describes the distribution of housing and discusses the generation of demands for it; the next deals with supply, and the factors that determine which of the potential demands are met or 'made effective'.

Ideally this analysis should deal with the United Kingdom, or at least with England and Wales. But the most relevant material from the 1961 census was still unavailable at the time of writing, and in any case such data has serious limitations, being designed to describe the situation at one point in time rather than to record the changes which form so important a part of the analysis. Therefore the main sources used are the sample surveys of England carried out for the Rowntree Trust Housing Study by the British Market Research Bureau in 1958 and 1962. The character and value of this data has been discussed elsewhere,* and here it has been checked and supplemented wherever possible from census data and other official sources. A brief postscript to this chapter draws attention to the principal differences between the English situation and the situation elsewhere in the United Kingdom; but little attempt has been made to contrast the situation in different regions of England, and readers will often find that their own part of the country differs from the broad averages derived from a national survey.

HOUSES

Table 10 shows how the numbers of households in this country have increased in recent years and how they are distributed amongst the different sectors of the market. Although the estimates – like the other figures in this chapter – can be no better than an approximation, the spread of owner occupation and the decline of privately rented housing can be clearly seen, showing that the situation to be discussed is a rapidly changing one for which any description will soon be out of date. Tables 11 and 12 summarize the main characteristics of the houses in each sector of the market.

Rather more than half the owner-occupiers live in detached or semi-detached houses, but two-fifths live in terraced housing, much of which consists of older property previously rented from private landlords. The great majority of owner-occupied houses

* See J. B. Cullingworth, *English Housing Trends*, and D. V. Donnison, Christine Cockborn and T. Corlett, *Housing Since the Rent Act*, Occasional Papers on Social Administration, Nos. 13 (1965) and 3 (1961).

have two or (more often) three bedrooms; virtually none of the smallest houses are found in this sector (only 1 per cent of the sample had less than three rooms) and the few really large owner-occupied houses are mostly found in older property. The majority of owner-occupied houses are well equipped but an appreciable minority are old and ill equipped; a tenth of them had (pre-1963) rateable values of £10 or less, a tenth had no hot water supply, and nearly a fifth had no bath or a bath shared with another household.

Council housing, despite the growing numbers of one-bedroom flats and bungalows now being built for this sector, is a highly standardized product: nine out of ten of these dwellings have two or three bedrooms; a fifth consist of flats or maisonettes, but nearly all the rest are semi-detached or terraced houses. The essential plumbing and kitchen equipment is available in virtually all these houses, the few exceptions being found mainly among older houses purchased for improvement or demolition. Of the amenities included in this study, it is only the garage that is still generally reserved as a privilege for owner-occupiers. Single and elderly people who live by themselves and need the smallest dwellings have a slightly better

TABLE 10

Estimates of the Tenure of Households, 1947–64

| Tenure | Households | | | |
	Great Britain 1947	England 1958	England 1962	England and Wales 1964
	%	%	%	%
Owner-occupiers	26	39	43	46
Council tenants	13	20	21	26
Other tenants	61	40	36	28
Total (millions)	—	13·6	14·2	—

SOURCES: Column 1, P.G.Gray, *The British Household*, The Social Survey, 1949 (total unknown); Columns 2 and 3, Rowntree Trust Housing Study. Column 4, The Social Survey.
In this and subsequent tables the rounding of percentages occasionally produces totals which do not add up to exactly 100.

TABLE 11

Tenure, Rateable Value, Type and Size of House, 1962

	Household's Tenure of Accommodation					All house-holds
	Owns / is buy-ing	Rents from coun-cil	Rents priv-ately unfur-nished	Rents furn-ished	Rent-free, etc.	
Number of households in sample	1,398	673	1,018	73	69	3,231
Type of Accommodation	%	%	%	%	%	%
Whole house, detached	19	3	7	8	26	12
Whole house, semi-detached	35	41	11	12	25	28
Whole house, terraced	38	36	52	7	16	41
Flat or maisonette	7	19	27	48	30	17
Part house /rooms	*	2	4	25	3	2
Average number of rooms	5·0	4·3	4·2	3·1	4·5	4·55
Number of bedrooms	%	%	%	%	%	%
1	3	7	16	56	9	9
2	32	32	47	22	36	36
3	54	58	32	22	43	47
4	8	4	5	0	7	6
5 or more	3	0	*	0	4	2
Median rateable value[1]	£25	£21	£15	£15	£17	£21

*Less than 0·5 per cent.
1. These are the 'old' rateable values in force before the 1963 revaluation. The 'median' value is the point at which half the houses have a larger and half have a smaller value.

This and many of the subsequent tables in this chapter are taken from J. B. Culling-worth, *English Housing Trends*, 1965, where fuller information can be found.

TABLE 12

Tenure and Housing Amenities, 1962

		Household's Tenure of Accommodation					All house-holds
		Owns / is buy-ing	Rents from coun-cil	Rents priv-ately unfur-nished	Rents furni-shed	Rent-free, etc.	
Number of households in sample		1,398	673	1,018	73	69	3,231
Households having use of (E=exclusive use; S=shared; N=entirely without)		%	%	%	%	%	%
Cooker with oven	E	99	98	94	78	94	97
	S	*	2	3	16	3	2
	N	1	1	3	5	3	2
Kitchen sink	E	99	98	94	74	94	97
	S	*	2	3	25	3	2
	N	1	0	3	1	3	1
Fixed bath	E	82	96	41	42	75	71
	S	4	2	6	40	7	5
	N	14	3	53	18	17	24
Flush toilet	E	93	97	79	51	84	89
	S	3	2	14	47	6	7
	N	3	1	7	3	10	4
Hot water from tap	With	89	95	58	70	83	80
	Without	11	5	42	30	17	20
Garden	E	81	85	45	33	71	69
	S	3	3	11	51	7	7
	N	16	12	44	16	22	24
Garage	With	34	7	5	16	13	19
	Without	65	93	94	84	87	81

*Less than 0·5 per cent.

chance of finding one in council housing than in owner-occupied housing, but the needs of the large family, looking for six or more rooms, are unlikely to be met unless they can buy a home of their own – 9 per cent of council houses and 30 per cent of owner-occupied houses being of this size.

Private houses that are rented unfurnished present an entirely different picture. They are old and a great many are obsolete: half have no bath, two fifths have no hot water supply (accounting for over two thirds of all the houses in England without bath and hot water supply); one fifth have no flush toilet or share one with another household, and scarcely any of them have a garage. Half of these dwellings are built in terraces, and most of the rest are flats, maisonettes or parts of houses. This is the picture typified by Coronation Street, and by once grander neighbourhoods whose houses have been subdivided into separate rooms and 'flatlets'. Nevertheless, this dwindling sector of the market has assets that the country can ill afford to lose: it offers a wide variety of house types and sizes, and it is the only sector where a large number of small dwellings can be found: 10 per cent have one or two rooms, and 16 per cent have only one bedroom – well over a half of the country's stock of one-bedroom dwellings. If properly equipped and distributed to the people who need them, these smaller units can be of great value to a country whose population is dividing each year into more and smaller households. And despite the scandals caused by a tiny minority of landlords, the bulk of this property is still let at low rents to tenants many of whom would have difficulty in paying more for their homes.

Very little accommodation is rented furnished and it shelters only 2 per cent of the country's households. Thus the numbers of furnished tenancies appearing in sample surveys is correspondingly small and conclusions derived from such figures should be treated with caution. Most of this property is found in London and in bigger cities in the southern half of the country – generally the centres which have attracted migrants from other parts of Britain, visitors from overseas, students and other temporary residents. Most of these units consist of flats and 'rooms', and half of them have only one bedroom. Table 12 shows that these furnished lettings are less likely to provide exclusive use of the essential equipment than any other group of dwellings, but so many tenants share this equipment with other households that the proportion totally deprived of bath, hot water, gardens and so on is smaller than that found among the unfurnished tenancies. Clearly the adequacy of such accommodation depends a great deal on the needs of the households living in it; a couple of rooms whose tenants have to share a bathroom and lavatory with several neighbours may inflict severe hardship on families with children – and on the neighbours – but the same accommodation may be tolerable or welcome to nomadic young workers and students, and to long-range commuters seeking a week-day *pied-à-terre* – people looking for temporary shelter rather than a permanent family home. For such people the high mobility such tenancies permit is a real asset: half these tenancies change hands every year.

The remaining tenants, classified as 'Rent-free, etc.', are a residual group including all those who cannot be fitted into other tenures – farm workers in tied cottages, resident porters in blocks of flats, parsons, publicans and the Prime Minister. The heterogeneity of these people and their accommodation is clearly visible in the tables and a separate analysis cannot usefully be made of this small group.

The principal features of each sector of the housing market can be briefly summarized. The two growing sectors are the owner-occupied houses (many of them large, and scarcely any of them really small; mostly well equipped but with an appreciable fringe of poor quality) and council houses (a uniform group well equipped, with few really small units and even fewer large ones). The shrinking sector consists of private houses, rented unfurnished; most of them are old and obsolete, but they offer a greater variety of types and sizes, including most of the country's smaller and cheaper dwellings. Furnished accommodation appears to be retaining its very small place in the market; concentrated in the south and in the cities, it consists of small units, and its tenants share much essential equipment with their neighbours.

HOUSEHOLDS

We can now turn to consider the people who live in each sector of this market. The next tables – numbered 13, 14 and 15 –

show some of the principal characteristics of households in each tenure group. The owner-occupiers, as might be expected, include the richer households and the great majority of more senior managerial, professional and administrative workers. But they are by no means a uniformly prosperous group: two fifths of them are manual workers and a tenth are clerical workers; nearly a quarter are retired or unoccupied. Many – particularly among the latter groups – have very low incomes. (The income distribution shown in Table 14, though confirmed by similar results published by the Government Social Survey, can be no more than an approximation, chiefly valuable as a means of comparing the relative positions of different groups.) The age-groups, and the types and sizes of households living in owner-occupied housing, are broadly typical of households throughout the population. Since their houses are larger than most and their household size fractionally smaller, they have more space than any other group, one fifth of them having at least three rooms per person.

Council tenants form a more distinctive group. The great majority are manual workers; there are children under sixteen in more than half these households, while for the country as a whole only 40 per cent of households include children. Their families are also larger than most. The numbers of earners in council houses, full-time and part-time, are appreciably higher than elsewhere, but the *proportion* of household members who are earning is slightly lower than elsewhere, owing to the larger numbers of dependant children they support. Since their households are larger than others they are also more crowded. A large proportion of these tenants are in the middle-aged groups, and they include relatively few people under twenty-five and over sixty-five.

Surveys carried out for the Rowntree Study, the Ministry of Labour, the Ministry of Housing and Local Government and other bodies* during the early 1960s all show that council tenants, often having several earners in the family, achieved

---

* See *Family Expenditure Surveys* of the Ministry of Labour, 1958–63; Report of the Committee of *Inquiry into the Impact of Rates on Households*, Cmd 2582, 1965; *Report of the Committee on Housing in Greater London*, Cmd 2605, 1965; and the Social Survey's report on *The Housing Situation in 1960*.

household incomes that were not very different from the average
for all households in the country, falling between the owner-
occupiers, above, and the private tenants, below, and excluding
only the highest incomes – more than £40 a week being exceedingly rare. But the larger numbers of dependants they have to

TABLE 13

Tenure and the Sizes and Types of Households, 1962

	Household's Tenure of Accommodation					All households
	Owns / is buying	Rents from council	Rents privately unfurnished	Rents furnished	Rent-free, etc.	
Number of households in sample	1,398	673	1,018	73	69	3,231
Average number of persons per household	2·9	3·8	2·7	2·6	3·0	3·05
Average number of children under 16	0·7	1·3	0·6	0·7	0·8	0·78
Household type[1]	%	%	%	%	%	%
Individuals under 60	3	2	4	16	1	3
Small adult households	17	7	18	28	13	15
Small families	23	22	18	30	30	21
Larger families	9	24	9	7	10	12
Larger adult households	24	29	21	7	19	23
Older small households	25	16	30	11	26	24
Age of housewife[2]	%	%	%	%	%	%
Under 25	4	2	7	29	3	5
25–44	36	47	28	49	41	36
45–59	33	30	31	14	28	31
60 or over	27	20	33	8	29	27

Footnotes: see p. 193.

support, coupled with the absence of really large earnings, gave them *incomes per head* that fell below those of the other tenure groups. Council rents have been rising rather faster than private rents over the past decade, and the growing numbers of earners in these households should not be viewed too complacently: to pay the rent and support the younger members of the family, some children may be encouraged to leave school too soon and some housewives may be returning too quickly to work. Stories of Jaguar-owning council tenants may be true in freak cases, but for the vast majority of these tenants the car could only be a very ancient model.

Households in property that is rented privately, unfurnished, include larger than average proportions of the youngest and oldest people, and of unskilled workers and the retired, though appreciable numbers of all groups in the population are found among them. One third of their housewives are at least sixty years old. Hence they include large numbers of the smallest and poorest households. Half the households appearing in the Rowntree Survey with 'take home pay' (usually a pension) of £5 a week or less were in this group, as were nearly half the people who lived alone.

The small group with furnished tenancies consisted mainly of younger childless people, many of them in the middle and upper income groups. But an appreciable and disturbing minority living in these crowded conditions – about a third – were families with children, the fathers generally being manual workers.

---

1. *Household types* are based on the size and age-structure of the household, as follows:—

	Number of persons aged	
	Under 16	16 and over
Individuals under 60	Nil	1 ⎫ None aged 60 or over
Small adult households	Nil	2 ⎭
Small families	1 or 2	1 or 2
Larger families	3 or more or 2	any number 3 or more
Larger adult households	0 or 1	3 or more
Older small households	Nil	1 or 2 (at least one aged 60 or over)

2. The *housewife* is defined as the member of the household principally responsible for domestic duties: 4 per cent of them were men.

T – G.O.H. – G

This sketch of the people living in each sector of the housing market in 1962 is no more than a snapshot of a continuously changing situation. Comparisons with the findings of a similar survey made in 1958* show the main changes between those dates. During the four years separating these surveys, owner occupation had been spreading rapidly among manual workers, including by 1962 39 per cent of the heads of households in skilled manual jobs (33 per cent in 1958) and 26 per cent of the heads in less skilled jobs (20 per cent in 1958). At least 300,000 private unfurnished tenancies had been lost, roughly half by demolitions and half by sales to owner-occupiers (some of them sitting tenants buying their own homes). Old people formed a growing proportion of the private tenants left behind by this continuing flight from the private rented sector.

The most typical council tenant was still the ex-serviceman of 1945, doing a manual job and supporting a family of several children on a modest wage. But as these people and their predecessors rehoused before the war grow older, and as council building for old people continues, the number of elderly people in council houses is slowly rising to produce a more balanced age distribution. Likewise the number of households with several earners is increasing as teenage children leave school and wives return to work: in 1958 there were two or more earners (full-time or part-time) in 48 per cent of council households, and by 1962 55 per cent of them had two or more earners. By now this trend may have gone a good deal further. But the continuing growth of the younger families prevented any easement of their comparatively crowded living conditions; already having more persons per room than any other group in 1958, they were the only group to achieve no improvement in rooms per head during the period. Both surveys – like every other study that has dealt with the question – discredited another item of housing folklore: the assumption that a great deal of space is wasted in council houses. Despite the restricted range of house sizes available in this sector, there were fewer households in it (5 per cent) with three or more rooms per person than were found in any other sector (for owner-occupiers the figure

*See D. V. Donnison *Housing Since the Rent Act*, and *Essays on Housing*, Occasional Papers on Social Administration, Nos. 3 (1961) and 9 (1964).

TABLE 14

Tenure, Jobs and Incomes, 1962

	Household's Tenure of Accommodation					
	Owns / is buying	Rents from council	Rents privately unfurnished	Rents furnished	Rent-free, etc.	All households
Number of households in sample	1,398	673	1,018	73	69	3,231
Occupation of head of household	%	%	%	%	%	%
Administrative, professional and managerial	18	3	6	18	16	11
Farmers, shop-keepers and small employers	8	1	4	1	4	5
Clerical workers and shop assistants	9	7	6	19	6	8
Foremen and skilled workers	31	44	34	38	17	35
Other manual and personal service workers	10	24	21	15	35	17
Retired and unoccupied	23	19	26	7	21	23
Unclassified	1	2	3	1	0	2
Number in household with full-time job[1]	%	%	%	%	%	%
No persons	19	13	22	10	22	18
1 person	53	45	45	60	55	49
2 persons	22	25	24	25	19	23
3 or more persons	6	17	9	5	4	9

Continued overleaf

TABLE 14 – *contd*

	Household's Tenure of Accommodation					
	Owns/ is buying	Rents from council	Rents privately unfurnished	Rents furnished	Rent-free, etc.	All households
Weekly take-home pay of chief earner[2]						
Number in sample giving information	1,014	548	826	60	60	2,508
	%	%	%	%	%	%
Up to £5	11	12	22	5	18	15
Over £5 to £7 10s.	7	6	9	3	17	8
Over £7 10s. to £10	15	24	24	22	28	20
Over £10 to £12 10s	18	29	21	20	13	21
Over £12 10s to £15	19	21	13	27	12	17
Over £15 to £20	17	7	7	15	10	12
Over £20	13	1	4	8	2	7

1. Paid job for thirty or more hours per week.
2. Housewife's estimate of the weekly income, net of direct taxes and national insurance contributions, of the member of the household with the largest gross annual income.

was 20 per cent, for private unfurnished tenancies 19 per cent). At the same time, the proportion with three or more people for every two rooms (8 per cent), though twice the national average, was not very high. In this sense of minimizing overcrowding and 'under-occupation', council houses are more 'efficiently' used than any other housing.

The small numbers of furnished tenancies appearing in these surveys make it difficult to discover what is happening in this sector of the market, but a report on the second survey drew attention to what appeared to be a considerable increase in the number of families with children who were living in this accommodation, adding that 'these developments may soon pose a serious problem'.

It is clear that a considerable advance in housing conditions had taken place during these years. People had more living space, because the average size of household continues, for the moment, to shrink more quickly than the average size of dwellings. They also had more of the essential amenities; between 1958 and 1962, the proportion of all households with a bath of their own rose from 63 to 71 per cent and the proportion with no access to a hot water supply fell from 28 to 20 per cent.

But despite this improvement many people remained dissatisfied with their housing; indeed, discontent – or the willingness to express it – appears to be growing. Table 15 shows the responses given to a question about this, and also the proportions in each sector of the market who say they would like to move house. The owner-occupiers were clearly the most satisfied group, private tenants the least satisfied. The opportunities for meeting these potential demands depend on the scope for change and movement the market provides.

MOVEMENT AND CHANGE

This analysis has been conducted so far in static terms, although comparisons have been made in the last few paragraphs between the situations at two different dates. It is time to attempt a more dynamic analysis, incorporating changes and their repercussions. Unfortunately the evidence for such an analysis is full of gaps and uncertainties. Reliable estimates of the numbers of dwellings in each tenure group are hard to come by. (In 1961 a question about tenure was included in the Census for the first time, but a post-enumeration survey revealed errors producing an underestimate in the numbers of households recorded as renting accommodation unfurnished from private landlords, and a small overestimate in virtually all the other groups.) Other factors to be considered cannot even be estimated. Thus although the logic of the analysis that follows is simple enough and the basis of the estimates and assumptions on which it is based can be explained, its outcome cannot be more reliable than the original estimates and assumptions themselves.

At the time of the Census taken in April 1961 there were 14,070,000 households in England. By the time of the sample Census taken in April 1966 there must have been about a million more. This estimate can be arrived at in the following way. During the intervening five years, 1,450,000 new dwellings were built. But 300,000 unfit houses were demolished or

TABLE 15

Tenure, Density and Satisfaction, 1962

	Household's Tenure of Accommodation					All house-holds
	Owns/ is buy-ing	Rents from coun-cil	Rents priv-ately unfur-nished	Rents furn-ished	Rent-free, etc.	
Number of households in sample	1,398	673	1,018	73	69	3,231
Persons per room	%	%	%	%	%	%
0·33 or less	20	5	19	7	12	16
0·34–1·49	80	87	76	81	86	80
1·50 or more	1	8	5	12	3	4
Average persons per room	0·6	0·9	0·7	0·8	0·7	0·67
Satisfaction with present accommodation						
	%	%	%	%	%	%
'Completely satisfied'	60	43	33	27	62	47
'Fairly satisfied'	32	39	39	48	29	36
'No feelings either way'	2	4	5	4	3	4
'Rather dissatisfied'	4	8	13	11	4	8
'Completely dissatisfied'	1	5	10	10	1	5
Percentage who would like to move	23	33	44	56	22	32

closed in the course of slum clearance, displacing about 270,000 households; about 50,000 temporary houses were demolished; and the gains from conversions, offset by changes in use, the abandonment of houses, and demolitions brought about by general redevelopment, produced another net loss of about

50,000. If empty houses continue to increase at the rate experienced in the previous decade, another 75,000 'household spaces' would be lost in this way. Decreases in households occurring when hitherto separate households share dwellings would be outweighed as others previously sharing secured a home to themselves by not replacing departing tenants and subtenants. But the outcome of these changes is peculiarly difficult to forecast: they might produce a net loss of 25,000 occupied 'household spaces'. Taken together, these estimates of gains and losses in dwellings, coupled with less reliable estimates of changes in the numbers of households they will accommodate, would produce an increase of about 950,000 households.

Thus, in round numbers, the building of a million and a half new houses in five years will provide for an increase of a million households. Slum clearance and other demolitions account for the bulk of the difference. But in future, as housing standards improve, there will be further increases in vacancies and in 'secondary dwellings' – country cottages and city flats, only occupied for parts of the year – and further reductions in sharing. There will also be an even larger programme of slum clearance. During the 1970s this country may have to build two houses for every additional household that comes into being. Thus although the housing requirements arising from population increases will be fairly modest, there is ample scope for further building, provided it caters for the right needs.

The gains and losses in this sum are not evenly distributed amongst the different tenures. During the last few years the owner-occupied sector has been growing, in England gaining between 200,000 and 250,000 households a year, mainly through new building but to a considerable extent by purchases from the rented sector. Council houses have been increasing, owing mainly to new building, at about 80,000 a year. The private rented sector has been shrinking, owing mainly to demolitions and purchases for owner occupation, by about 125,000 households a year. There are signs that the drift of rented property into owner occupation may now be slowing down. But these trends would produce a loss of at least half a million units of accommodation in privately rented housing over five years, half due to demolitions and most of the rest due to changes in tenure.

If these trends continue, more than half the households in England will own their own homes, or be buying them, before 1970.

Losses of privately rented housing are proceeding at a roughly similar pace from opposite ends of the quality range. Slum clearance and dereliction affect the older, smaller and more decrepit houses in the central parts of cities, while the drift to owner occupation affects the better houses in more attractive neighbourhoods. The process was traced for London in the Milner Holland Report which shows that the drift to owner occupation is running most strongly in the suburbs while slum clearance and redevelopment are concentrated in more central parts of the town. The housing that remains in this dwindling sector of the market is of diverse and special kinds: the better, purpose-built blocks of flats let at higher rents; larger houses in the central areas of the biggest cities, suitable (or unsuitably profitable) for subdivision into smaller units; and 'service tenancies' of various kinds, provided for farm workers, railwaymen, maintenance staff and others by their employers. The implications of these changes will become clearer when the formation and movement of households are examined.

Between 2 and 3 per cent of the households in England – over 300,000 of them – contain someone hoping to leave home and set up a new household. Two thirds of these people are under twenty-five and half of them give marriage as their principal reason for leaving home; many of them are already married. The households in which they now live are relatively large – nearly all of them being among the 'larger families' and 'larger adult households' (defined at the foot of Table 13) – and most of the potential new households intend to set up home with at least one other person: the average size of the households they intend to form is 2·2 persons.

In the Rowntree surveys of 1958 and 1962 special studies were made of those who had recently moved. The 'new households' among these constituted about a third of all movers. They were defined as those with housewives who had not been the housewife of their previous homes (about half the new households), those moving into houses from non-private accommodation such as hotels, hospitals and barracks (about a third) and those with housewives who were no longer living with the head of the previous household (the remainder).* Thus in addition to the young people who want to leave their parents and set up on their own, there are other, older people (not living in private households and therefore not revealed in surveys of this kind) who are waiting to establish new households. Between 1960 and 1962, two fifths of the new households bought, or started buying, homes of their own, and nearly a half went into private rented housing. The tenure destinations of those setting up new households are shown in Table 16 and in Figure 3 which accompanies it.

Meanwhile, among the households already formed, there is an even larger group wanting to move. We can examine three 'layers' of this potential demand for housing, each one bringing us closer to the 'effective demands' actually met: those who say they would like to move house; those among them who claim to have taken some action for this purpose, even if it was no more than asking the help of their friends; and those who actually move. It should not be assumed, however, that this measure of the 'effectiveness' of demand coincides precisely with the intensity of need or dissatisfaction: if a sample of households is reinterviewed after a year, some households will be found to have moved who expressed neither dissatisfaction nor a desire to move at their first interview.

Table 15 shows that one third of all households say they would like to move, with higher proportions among private tenants and lower proportions among owner-occupiers. Half of these potential movers had taken some practical step to achieve their objective – ranging from advertising or asking among friends to getting their names onto council waiting lists or actually buying a house. These potential movers are a representative cross section of all social classes, all age-groups except the very oldest, and all income groups except the very poorest. The oldest and poorest (generally speaking the same people) are less likely to seek a move, but an appreciable number of them, too, are 'in the

---

*There was also a very small group, not separately identified in the second survey, moving into England from elsewhere in the British Isles or from farther afield. These, too, are technically 'new households' so far as the English housing market is concerned.

market' for alternative accommodation. In London, the North and the Midlands there are more people (in every tenure group) wanting to move than in the south, and there are more in the cities who want to move than in rural areas. People in the area that used to be the County of London are more dissatisfied with their housing and more anxious to move, whatever their tenure, than people in any other part of the country.

The more active searchers who have taken practical steps to find a home are rather younger than the rest, but otherwise similar; two thirds of them want to rent and a third want to buy a house. When compared with the buyers, those who want to rent are rather older and are more likely to have manual jobs and lower incomes; their households are larger, their present housing conditions are worse and they are more dissatisfied with them. But despite their greater discontent and the larger size of their households their hopes are pitched lower: they say they require smaller and more modestly equipped houses than the buyers.

The desire for bigger and better housing and for a house in a better neighbourhood are the most common reasons for seeking a move, followed by personal reasons such as a change of job, marriage, a bereavement, or the need to move nearer to relatives. A few are looking for smaller or cheaper housing and others are compelled to move because their houses are being pulled down or the owner has told them they must go. Many want to find a house in a particular area, but for the prospective buyers this is often a distant part of the country, while the prospective renters are more likely to be tied to their present neighbourhoods, because they want to be near relatives or simply because they have always lived there.

Between 7 and 8 per cent of the households in England have moved in the past year, including new and existing households – less than a quarter of those who say they would like to move. Those who actually achieve a move are younger and more likely to have dependant children than the average run of potential movers, being drawn to a greater extent from the 'small adult households' and 'small families'; they also have higher incomes and are more likely to hold middle class jobs. In half these households the housewife is under thirty-five, while for England as a whole, half the housewives are under fifty. Those who move to private rented housing are the youngest, while those who move to council housing are the oldest – partly owing to council policies for rehousing old people and slum dwellers, and partly because the family on a council waiting list has to wait longer for a home than the family that can afford to buy. Personal reasons for movement, such as marriage and changes of job, figure more often among those given by the movers than the potential movers, and are obviously more compelling than the desire for better housing and housing in better neighbourhoods or of more appropriate size, all of which figure less often. The decision of landlords to get rid of their tenants constituted another compelling reason, affecting 7 per cent of recent movers in 1962. The largest, the oldest and the poorest households among the potential movers are less likely to achieve their aims – though many in the largest households must achieve some improvement in living space because it is from them that many of the new households split off.

At first sight it seems obvious that those with lower incomes would be fated to lose the race for better housing. But rent-paying capacity is certainly not the only explanation of this outcome. The maximum rents and house prices the potential movers said they were willing to pay were entirely realistic – appreciably higher, in fact, than those paid by the households who actually did move in the preceding two years. Restricted opportunities for borrowing money for house purchase, and the scarcity of good housing of the appropriate size in the appropriate districts for buyers and renters alike, must also play a part in the process. Current lending procedures virtually rule out borrowers over the age of forty-five unless they already have large incomes or considerable capital assets (generally a house they have bought or inherited). The policy, now adopted by many building societies, of reducing the borrowers' monthly payments by extending the period of repayment is of no help to older people with less than twenty years of working life ahead of them. Practically none of the houses now being built are suitable for the largest households, and few – outside the council building programme and a tiny group of luxury flats – are designed for the oldest or the smallest households. Private rented property that is still subject to rent controls (not the more recent 'rent regulation') now houses the older people whose tenancies began before 1957. Thus to the scarcity of appropriate housing there is added the sharp increase in rents which many older tenants would have to face on leaving controlled property, and this too must have deterred many from moving. Taken together, these points show there are unmet needs and a potential economic demand of considerable dimensions that might be satisfied in the coming years if houses of the right size and type were provided in the right places, and rent policies were rationalized. They also suggest that private builders and lenders may be underestimating the sums that people are willing to pay for housing.

The pattern of movement occurring in England in 1960 and 1961 is illustrated in Table 16 and the Figure on p. 208 which show, for a hypothetical population of 100,000 households:

(i) the original distribution of these households between different tenures (along line (a) in the Table);

(ii) the number of new households forming and the tenures they entered (line (b) in the Table);

(iii) the movement of existing households within and between the main tenure groups (at (c) in the Table); and

(iv) the dissolution and amalgamation of households (line (e) in the Table).

Property rented furnished and the miscellaneous category of 'rent free and other' tenancies have here been combined with the much larger amount of private property rented unfurnished (which also includes a negligible number of housing association dwellings). These constitute very different types of housing, often accommodating different types of household, but movement in the smaller groups cannot be reliably analysed with the data available. The original sample numbers on which the analysis is based have been included in brackets. This slightly confusing addition can be disregarded when reading the Table but the figures in brackets serve as a reminder that some of the findings are based on perilously small sub-samples, and the last two rows of figures – (d) and (e) beneath the double line in the Table – are not derived directly from field surveys.

TABLE 16

An Approximate Projection of the Formation, Movement and Dissolution of Households in England, During One Year

(Data from a survey dealing with the years 1960–62, applied to a hypothetical population of 100,000 households.)

	Household's Tenure of Accommodation			All households
	Owns /is buying	Council tenants	Other tenants	
(a) Total households (Original sample numbers)	43,000 (1,398)	21,000 (673)	36,000 (1,160)	100,000 (3,231)
(b) Formation of new households in one year (Original sample numbers)	890 (61)	280 (19)	1,010 (70)	2,180 (150)
(c) Movement of existing households in one year	The tenures to which they moved			
Previous tenures				
Owns /is buying	940	60	170	1,170
Council tenants	150	560	130	840
Other tenants	930	480	1,430	2,840
Total (Original sample numbers)	2,020 (139)	1,100 (76)	1,730 (120)	4,850 (335)
(d) Hypothetical change in occupied household spaces	+ 1,500	+ 500	− 1,000	+ 1,000
(e) Implied dissolution and amalgamation of households	240	40	900	1,180

Lines (a) to (c) in this Table show distributions of households
between the different tenures, followed by estimates of household formation and movement occurring in the course of a
year, which are derived from a survey carried out twelve months
after the Census of 1961. But the figures in the two rows at the
bottom of the Table, beneath the double line, are less reliable,
although as realistic as the available data permit. The first of
these – line (d) – shows an approximate estimate of the change in
occupied household spaces that would have occurred in a representative group of dwellings distributed among the tenures
shown. It is derived from official estimates of building, demolition, conversions, etc., from Rowntree and other estimates of
the drift to owner occupation in privately rented property, and
from certain assumptions about the growth of vacancies, the
decline in sharing and other factors. The figures, given in
deliberately round numbers, have been checked with official
statisticians and do not appear to be seriously misleading. The
last line of figures – at (e) in the Table – shows the amalgamation
and dissolution of households that the estimates in line (d) would
imply. If we know the number of households in a particular
tenure group at one point in time, if we have a good estimate of
the numbers of new households entering the group and the
numbers of existing households moving in and out of it during
the following year, and if we compare the net effect of all these
movements with an estimate of the growth of the total numbers
of households in this group during the year, then the discrep-
ancy between the total growth in the group of households and
the net effects of these movements must be accounted for by the
disappearance of households brought about by various forms of
amalgamation and dissolution.

This rather lengthy line of reasoning can be illustrated from
the column of figures for owner-occupiers. A representative
sample of 100,000 households would include about 43,000 of
them. In the course of a year, some 890 newly formed households would move into owner-occupied dwellings, another 2,020
previously existing households would also move into houses in
this group, and 1,170 would move out of such houses (940 to
buy another house, 60 to council houses and 170 to other
tenures). If no other changes occurred, then owner-occupiers

would require an additional 1,740 household spaces (890 + 2,020 — 1,170). But since an increase of only 1,500 occupied household spaces is assumed to have taken place in this sector during the year, it follows that 240 households must have disappeared (1,740 — 1,500). Some of the households that disappeared will have been people living by themselves who died or moved to non-private accommodation (hotels, hospitals, etc.). Others will have rejoined existing households (going to share with their relatives, for example). But an unknown proportion will have formed entirely new units, reappearing among the newly formed households at the top of the table. (Thus two people living separately in private rented accommodation who marry and buy a home to live in together would appear both as a 'newly formed household' among the owner-occupiers and as the 'amalgamation or dissolution' of two separate households among 'other tenants'.)

The figures in lines (a) to (c) of this Table provide a reasonably reliable guide to the movements taking place at this time. Those appearing in the last rows (d) and (e) have been inserted to complete an essential part of the picture; they are not unrealistic, but they should not be used as a basis for further detailed calculations.

Another limitation of this 'model' of the housing market should also be borne in mind. It is a 'closed' system, showing no movement of households into the country or out of it – or rather, it assumes that inward and outward movements exactly balanced each other within each tenure group. This is clearly unrealistic, but not drastically so, for England as a whole during one year only. The net movement of people in and out of England in a year is small, and the migration of households smaller still. Although the years covered by these figures were a peak period for immigration from overseas, most of the immigrants did not immediately form separate households; they started by joining friends or relatives already in the country, appearing subsequently in the figures for newly formed households when they set up home on their own. This omission means, however, that the figures for 100,000 households presented in Table 16 should not be applied to an individual town of that size without taking account of the movement of households between the town and other parts of the country. Such migration can make a crucial difference to the town's situation, as will be shown.

The movements recorded in Table 16 can be more clearly seen in Figure 3, where the three rectangles indicate the size

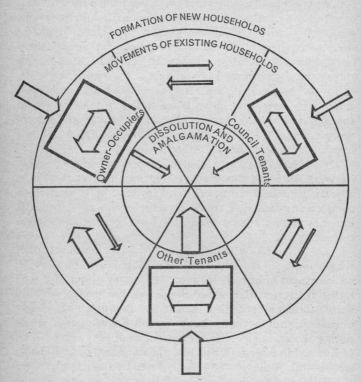

Figure 3. The movement of households in England

of the three tenure groups at the beginning of the period – equivalent to line (a) in the Table – and the arrows represent household movements. The areas of the arrows are proportional to the numbers of households involved in each type of movement, but to render them more visible they have been drawn to a scale five times larger than that employed for the rectangles representing the tenure groups. Four types of movement are shown. Starting from the outermost ring, there are newly formed households entering each of the three tenure groups – equivalent to line (b) in the Table. The next ring shows, within the rectangles, the movements taking place within each tenure group (owner-occupiers moving to buy another house, for example) and, between the rectangles, movements between one tenure and another – the lines at (c) in the Table. Arrows within the central ring – equivalent to line (e) in the Table – show the amalgamation and dissolution of households implied by the analysis that has been explained. Many of the amalgamated households reappear in the outer ring as newly formed households. How many, we do not know.

The main findings of this operation can now be presented. In England, in 1960–62, nearly half the newly formed (or reformed) households entered private rented property, and most of the rest started buying homes of their own. Very few went into council housing. In the few places where furnished accommodation was available, new households often began in furnished flats and rooms.

Subsequent moves among existing households followed a well-marked pattern repeatedly found in studies of this kind. More than half these movers went to property of the same tenure as that which they occupied before – about half the private tenants, the majority of council tenants and nearly all the owner-occupiers who moved stayed within the same sectors of the market. Most of those who changed their tenures came from private rented property and followed two well-marked routes leading to owner occupation and to council housing. These patterns of movement accounted for nine out of ten moves among existing households. The remaining tenth was fairly evenly distributed in very small numbers: very few moved back into private rented property from other tenures and very few moved in either direction between council and owner-occupied housing.

Which tenures enable or compel people to move most often? Comparisons between the rates of movement in each sector can be made on the basis of tenure before or after the move, with somewhat different results. If *all* forms of movement are analysed according to tenures *after* the move, the private rented sector is slightly more mobile than the others. But a large proportion of the movement in this sector occurs among new households and among the small group in furnished lettings, half of whom move in the course of a year. The large group of older private tenants is relatively immobile. If the analysis excludes newly formed households and is based on tenure *before* the move, then it is the owner-occupiers who are least mobile while private tenants are clearly the most mobile. Much of the movement among private tenants must be prompted by greater discontent over their housing conditions, but this is not the only factor involved. This tenure makes it easier for people to move and it accommodates more of the footloose households who need to move frequently. By contrast, people buying their own homes may find it harder to move and have less incentive to do so. People already in council houses move as often as the rest of the population – that is to say, a good deal more often than those who own their own homes but less often than private tenants. The 'administered market' in which they live has certain disadvantages: the people moving into council houses are mainly drawn from nearby and there are few long distance moves in this sector. But council housing appears to provide about as much opportunity for movement – and hence for choice – as the 'price market' in which the rest of the population lives, though a more detailed analysis of age groups, household types and the mobility of different social classes would be required to determine how far this outcome is due to the tenures involved, and how far it can be explained by the composition of the households concerned.

The amalgamation and dissolution of households is a more uncertain quantity and it would be a mistake to base too many conclusions on the scanty evidence available. The bulk of these losses come – from opposite ends of the age-range – among households in private rented property: from older people who die, join forces with their relatives, or move to hospitals and homes for the aged, and from younger people who marry or for other reasons join forces with households elsewhere. Nearly all the rest of the loss comes from owner-occupied property, probably from the older people in this group. Council tenants include relatively few of the youngest and oldest and very few single householders, and hence there is practically no loss of households from this sector. Thus local authorities secure negligible 'gains' from the normal processes of movement, amalgamation and dissolution of households. This is because very few council tenants move out to buy their own homes or return to privately rented housing, and because the age and family structure of these tenants' households minimize the chances of dissolution and amalgamation. As a result, many local authorities have to build an extra house for nearly every extra tenant they house.

These patterns of movement do not continue unaltered. It has been pointed out that in England the owner-occupied sector has been gaining between 200,000 and 250,000 households a year, and that council tenants have been increasing by about 80,000 a year, while the private rented sector has been shrinking by about 125,000 households a year. Thus the proportion of houses in each sector of the market is changing, and as the channels through which the flow of movement proceeds change in size, the flow itself must change too. Since the late 1950s there has been an increase in the proportion of new households buying their own houses, and a fall in the proportion going into private rented property. The local authorities, too, appear to have taken a slightly greater share of the new households, but their opportunity for increasing this share is inevitably restricted by the priority they are required to give to slum clearance and to old people – policies which cater mainly for households already established.

The pattern and implications of these movements will vary from place to place. Two contrasting examples may illustrate these variations. A city in Lancashire where employment opportunities change little from year to year may 'export' a large proportion of its new households to other more prosperous centres. Its private rented housing will probably be shrinking rapidly, but there is a continuous outflow of younger people. That outflow, coupled with continuing losses amongst older households, relieves pressure on this sector of the market. Council building will accommodate many of the poorer households from demolished property. The growing number and variety of owner-occupied houses, available at prices that reach down to very modest levels, will accommodate most of the remainder who do not want to rent private housing. The purchase of older property, badly needing repair and improvement, by owner-occupiers with low incomes may present new problems – briefly postponing and greatly complicating the task of clearance and replacement. But the great majority of people who wish to find a home will readily be able to do this.*

But the position may be very different in an expanding midlands city where a rapidly growing demand for labour draws young migrants from all over the country whose children subsequently increase the city's rate of demographic growth still further. The inflow of new households to private rented property will considerably exceed the losses due to dissolutions and amalgamations in this sector. Council building will relieve the pressure somewhat, but if the city is old and tightly packed, with a large slum clearance programme and no readily available building land within its boundaries, the relief will not be great because most of the property vacated by new council tenants will be torn down, to be rebuilt at lower densities. The other escape route, to owner occupation, will become increasingly difficult to negotiate as competition for houses drives up their prices, and as protection of the surrounding green belt and restriction of building densities compels developers to seek more distant sites. Many of those who cannot afford to buy will be forced to stay in privately rented housing. The demand for this property will drive up rents wherever they have been decontrolled. This could slightly reduce the losses occurring in this sector and encourage the improvement of rented property, but since landlords are concerned with the *comparative* gains to be secured from renting or sale to owner-occupiers, and the *comparative* rents to be secured from improved and unimproved property, rising demand in this sector is not likely to have much effect. Indeed, demand for houses to buy and demand for rented accommodation of the poorest quality may be rising even faster than the demand for good rented property. In that case, decontrol will not provide better or more plentiful housing for tenants. Those who cannot buy a house may find themselves

* See J. B. Cullingworth, *Housing in Transition*, Heinemann, 1963, for an account of a city showing many of these features.

in growing difficulties. For, once missed, the chance of buying may not come again. As families grow the household's income per head and its opportunities for saving fall, and as the head of the household grows older his hopes of borrowing money to buy a house will fade. The younger, growing households in this position will be paying decontrolled rents, driven upwards by competition from the continuing inflow of single people and childless households who can afford to pay more because they have no dependants to support. Too often, the housing in this decontrolled part of the market is quite unsuitable for a family; the kind of house they need – self-contained, with a garden or backyard – is the sort that is most likely to become owner-occupied or to be demolished, while tenement blocks and larger houses subdivided and shared by several households are more likely to remain privately rented. The average ratio of persons to rooms throughout the city will steadily improve, thanks to the plentiful space available to older shrinking households in owner-occupied property and in rented housing remaining under control. But such figures may conceal growing overcrowding and hardship among a considerable minority of families.

In such a city the stresses will be concentrated in older privately rented property in the central parts of the city, for it is in this property and in these areas that a large proportion of new households start life, subsequently moving outwards as opportunities arise for escape to owner-occupied or council estates in the suburbs. Until the gradual build-up of the postwar slum clearance programmes, these inner areas had been starved of every kind of investment, not only in the building and improvement of housing – for the improvements to older property have been mainly concentrated in suburban or more attractive neighbourhoods where owner-occupiers have taken over – but also for the provision of new shops, factories, schools, roads, hospitals and urban equipment of every sort. The resulting squalor and discontent have given a bad name to these neighbourhoods and to the owners of the houses in them, thus still further discouraging investment. But these difficulties are not the fault of landlords or their tenants; they are the outcome of the whole system and the patterns of movement it permits and frustrates. Just as delays and over-crowding on the railways may originate from dislocation of the traffic at other points far distant from the sectors of the line most affected, so hardship in particular sectors of the housing market may originate from a scarcity of appropriate housing in other sectors and failure to provide sufficient opportunities for people to move into it.

Thus the paradox of the increasing hardships found in parts of our richest cities may be partly resolved by opening up fresh escape routes to new towns and 'overspill housing' beyond their borders, and a great deal might be done to improve and redistribute the older rented property that cannot be demolished for many years to come. But steps must also be taken to provide escape routes for those who cannot get a council house or buy a home of their own – a diverse but large group, including many older people, single and childless people, migrants and newcomers. The growth of various forms of housing association now being fostered by the government could make a contribution to the solution of these problems, providing in time a fourth sector to add to those appearing in Figure 3 – an additional escape route from private rented housing, and a means of relieving pressure elsewhere by attracting a proportion of owner-occupiers and council tenants whose homes would then become available to others. But a fuller discussion of these questions must be postponed until the resources for investment in housing have been examined.

This survey of the housing conditions found in different sectors of the market, the types of household in each and the patterns of movement linking one sector to another, still gives no clear picture of the standards actually achieved by different kinds of people. The concluding section of this chapter provides a brief sketch of the position.

THE STANDARDS ACHIEVED

The size and security of people's incomes, now and for the future, go a long way to determine the housing standards they attain. The Rowntree survey of England made in 1962 showed that over 90 per cent of the households with heads in executive, managerial and professional jobs had baths, hot water and flush lavatories in their homes, over 80 per cent had a garden, and about a half had a garage. Among households with heads doing semi-skilled or unskilled manual work, the proportions were from 13 to 32 per cent lower – except for garages which were scarcely ever available. (As these households buy cars, the congestion arising from street parking in poorer neighbourhoods will become intolerable.) The differences emerging from a comparison of income groups were even greater: virtually all the households whose chief earners brought home more than £20 a week had a bath and hot water supply and nine out of ten had a garden, but only half of those with take-home pay (or pension) of up to £5 a week had these things. The reasons for this state of affairs are obvious enough; the upper income groups are more likely to move house when they wish to do so; they buy the more expensive houses, and those of them remaining in rented property pay higher rents and the increase in their rents since the 1957 Act has been greater.* While the rich remain richer than the poor, inequalities may be narrowed but such differences will persist. Even in centrally planned Poland, when households of any given size are compared, those with more children have lower incomes per head and fewer rooms per person.†

But a comparison of space standards reveals a more complex pattern: the central income groups (i.e., those with average incomes, not the middle classes) are the most crowded, while the poorest of all – being pensioners in the smallest households – have more space per person than anyone else. Housing varies greatly in its quality and equipment but much less in size, and its size cannot readily be changed: 83 per cent of the houses in England have two or three bedrooms. But the country's households are much more varied and their requirements continually change as time goes by.

Thus we require a method of analysis that tells more about people's housing needs than a simple contrast between income groups or social classes. Most people, it may be assumed, pass through five 'housing stages' in the course of their lives. (a) For the first twenty years or so they live in their parents' homes. (b)

* See J. B. Cullingworth, *English Housing Trends 1965.*
† See a paper by Wanda Litterer-Marwege in *Sprawy Mieszkanioke,* Volume 1, 1963. A study of urban areas throughout Poland.

Then a growing proportion of them spend a brief period on their own or with friends, after leaving home to study or to find work. The first year or two of marriage, when wives generally remain at work, may be regarded as a continuation of this phase: the household is small and mobile, and out all day; their home is not the centre of their lives. (c) As soon as their first baby is born the household's needs change again and become, during this expanding phase, increasingly extensive and demanding. (d) In time, all or most of their children leave home, and for those who do not have elderly relatives living with them there follows a fourth phase. The household is again small, and less dependent on its neighbours and the services afforded by the surrounding district, but a home has been established and filled with possessions, roots have been put down, and people are less likely to move than in earlier years. (e) Finally, in old age, households shrink still further; they become even less mobile, and their comfort and peace of mind depend increasingly upon security of tenure, upon the design and equipment of the home, the services available in the neighbourhood and the support of nearby relatives and friends.

The implications of this rough-and-ready outline of the five typical phases of people's 'housing history' will be pursued a little further in Chapter 8, where the design and building of houses is considered, and the following paragraphs are confined to a discussion of the housing standards achieved by people at each stage. But before embarking on this it must be made clear that the evidence available about each phase only records the outcome of the gains and losses people have achieved thus far in a search for housing that may continue, off and on, throughout their lives. It does not follow that the standards attained by each group are what that group wants, or that the younger people of today will in future find themselves in the same position as today's older generations.

Young people in the second stage of their housing history often live in small and ill-equipped flats and 'rooms', but although the numbers having exclusive use of a bath and other equipment are smaller than among other groups, many share these things with neighbouring households and, at least for the more fortunate, there is a prospect of better housing soon. Outside the bigger cities, many of them board with other people and do not set up separate households. Young people at this stage move house more often than any other group.

Standards of equipment – typified by the proportion of households with a bath in the home – rise steadily as people move into the third stage, attaining a peak among the 'larger families' (with three or more children under sixteen) and in households with housewives aged about forty. This group too, moves frequently in its early stages. It is then that the battle for housing is at its height and people make the crucial gains and losses of the campaign. Thereafter their opportunities depend increasingly on the standards achieved at that point. The council tenant can ask his local authority for another move and arrange exchanges with council tenants elsewhere; if he has repaid enough of his mortgage, the owner-occupier can buy another house, even if his income falls well below the level normally expected of house buyers. It is unlikely that the highest standards of equipment would now be found among people at this third stage had not the council building programmes of the first dozen years after the war catered mainly for young families with low incomes who could have secured good housing in no other way. But the subsequent reduction in council building threatened to sacrifice much of this achievement; the small increase in the numbers of young families occupying furnished rooms during the early sixties and the growing problem of homelessness in areas of shortage were the outcome.

Overcrowding is the most common problem confronting people at this stage of their lives. Nearly all the more crowded households – those with at least one and a half persons to every room – were found among the 'small' and 'larger families'. The Social Survey has prepared a better measure of space requirements, based on the bedrooms a household needs, on the assumption that a separate bedroom is required for every married couple, for every single person over the age of twenty-one, and for every two children below this age – separating the sexes over the age of ten. Applying this standard, the Rowntree survey of 1962 found that nearly half the 'larger families' – who constitute 12 per cent of the households in England – could not meet these requirements. (See Table 17.)

Although the rate of movement falls among the middle aged households with housewives in their forties and fifties and among the 'larger adult households' in which many of them are found, this is due partly to lack of opportunities. The pro-

TABLE 17

The Housing Conditions of Different Types of Household in England, 1962

	Number of house-holds in sample	Percentages of households having					
		Unshared use of		Persons per room ratio of		Bedroom space[1]	
		Bath	Gar-den[2]	0·33 or less	1·50 or more	above stan-dard	below stan-dard
		%	%	%	%	%	%
All households	3,231	71	69	16	4	52	12
Occupation of head of household[3]							
Professional, etc.	353	92	83	13	1	66	7
Small employers, etc.	172	90	80	14	0	64	6
Clerical, etc.	248	77	70	12	2	54	9
Foreman & skilled	1,119	72	68	5	5	43	15
Other manual	554	60	63	9	7	41	18
Retired & unoccupied	729	62	67	41	2	67	6
Age of housewife[3]							
Under 25	173	54	51	5	9	40	16
25–44	1,168	78	73	4	6	41	17
45–59	1,009	75	72	13	3	55	11
60 or over	881	60	65	38	1	69	4
Household type[4]							
Individuals under 60	110	52	53	85	0	72	0
Small adult h/hds.	498	69	60	13	1	77	1
Small families	693	75	72	0	4	46	9
Larger families	388	82	81	0	20	11	47
Larger adult h/hds.	753	79	76	0	2	37	17
Older small h/hds.	789	58	63	44	*	77	1

Footnotes: see p. 219.

portion who would like to move remains high, but the numbers who secure a mortage after the age of forty-five fall off sharply. Opportunities are already ebbing. This country is now achieving a reasonably high standard of privacy for the *household*, ill-equipped though many of its houses are. But it has far to go before a similar standard of privacy is assured to the *individual* in larger households, and this is not a problem that present building programmes will automatically resolve in the course of time: the proportion of houses built with four or more bedrooms has remained low for many years – at about 2 per cent for local authorities in England and Wales and about 4 per cent for private builders. Meanwhile forecasts prepared by the Ministry of Housing and Local Government show that the average size of household is expected to rise after 1971 in every region of Great Britain.

The fourth phase of this history, beginning when children leave home, is harder to define and the evidence about it is correspondingly weaker. It suggests that the equipment of the houses occupied by this group is slightly poorer, although the living space available for each person improves as the household shrinks in size. This does not mean that people move to worse housing as they grow older. They continue moving to better housing, but their moves become less frequent and their standards are therefore overhauled by those of younger households. Those now at this phase are less likely than the younger generation to have secured council houses after the war or to have benefited from the boom in private building that developed in the 1950s.

---

1. *Bedroom standards:* this standard, originally devised by the Social Survey, assumes that one bedroom is required for each of the following: each married couple, each single person aged twenty-one or more, and each pair of younger people – separating the sexes over the age of ten. Percentages in the table refer only to those households having more or less than the number of bedrooms this standard would provide.
2. A *garden* was defined as 'ground at the back of the house which can be cultivated (i.e. not paved or covered with ash, etc.) or space at the front of the house provided it is enclosed and the distance from the house to the garden wall or fence was more than five yards.'
3. *Occupation of head of household:* see Table 14 for fuller definition. Further details in J. B. Cullingworth, *English Housing Trends*.
4. *Household types:* see Table 13 for definitions.
*Less than 0·5 per cent.

Those in the final phase of their housing history are much worse off, being as ill-supplied with baths, hot water and other amenities as those in the youngest group, less likely to share such amenities with other households and far less likely to move to better housing in future. These are the people whose crucial housing decisions were made thirty or forty years earlier before the building boom of the 1930s. They are too old and too poor to raise a mortgage – the chief earners or pensioners of more than half the 'older small households' had a take-home pay of £5 a week or less – and until recently they could get little help with housing from the local authorities. Even now the building of new council flats and houses with one bedroom proceeds very slowly. Between 1956 and 1961 the population aged sixty-five and over in England and Wales rose from 5,173,000 to 5,520,000 – an increase of 70,000 a year. Very few one-bedroom dwellings were being built at that time, but the total has since risen, attaining 37,500 in 1964. The numbers needed cannot be calculated in this way: old people take some of the two-bedroom dwellings, younger people take some of those with one bedroom, and many old people live with others in larger households. But since the present output of these smaller houses is barely keeping pace with the growth in the numbers of older households it is unlikely to make an appreciable impact on the housing conditions of this section of the population for many years to come.

The older the household, the worse its housing conditions; more than a third of households with housewives in their seventies but more than half those with housewives over eighty had no bath or hot water supply – and those living alone in their old age were worse off than those living with other people. For many, space was the only plentiful thing their housing afforded; nearly half the housewives over seventy had at least three rooms per person. Many have drawn attention to this state of affairs, urging that old people be moved out of their relatively spacious houses to make room for younger families, but the scarcity of small dwellings (particularly in owner-occupied property where 37 per cent of the single-person households are found) generally renders this impossible.

Those who do not marry never pass through the middle phases of this housing history. 'Single housewives' are a varied group. Since the 'housewife', as defined in these surveys, is the person responsible for housekeeping, a large minority of the single ones are men. 'Single housewives' should not be confused with 'single-person households': many of them live with other people. More than half the single women in this group – well above the average for all households – are owner-occupiers, which may refute the widespread belief that building societies discriminate against the single woman, but also reflects the fact that very few of the single housewives (male or female) are council tenants. Although most of them have plenty of space, many have very poor housing conditions. The average standards of amenity and equipment achieved by the single are appreciably worse than those attained by married people in similar age groups – the men faring worse than the women, possibly because they give housing lower priority in their expenditure. The single are another group whose needs have never been effectively met by the local authorities or the private builders. But the measures of housing conditions used in this analysis probably exaggerate their deprivation for they take no account of location; single people may secure housing in more central or convenient districts, preferring this to the larger and better houses in the suburbs.

The classifications of households used in the census and in housing surveys, public and private, were not designed to distinguish the phases employed here. This analysis is therefore full of gaps, and the gains made during the last few years by households at different stages of their development cannot be traced with precision. Recent improvements in housing conditions have been fairly evenly distributed through most groups, but the 'older small households' appear to have made the slowest progress in raising the quality of their housing, although they have gained even more living space per head. People under the age of sixty who live alone have made the most rapid progress, because their higher incomes per head have enabled them to move more often and compete more successfully in the market.

A comparison of the social classes shows that the professional and managerial group, already the best housed, have made relatively small gains while the farmers, shopkeepers and small employers have achieved the greatest progress, but the differences are not large. Here again the evidence may be misleading: wealthier people may have sought better locations rather than better housing, or they may have invested in central heating, in country cottages or other things which the surveys do not reveal.

Some of the principal features of the picture described in the previous paragraphs are shown in Table 17, although the 'household types' used in this table do not coincide at all precisely with the housing 'stages' discussed. Perhaps the main conclusion to be drawn from this sketch is that the variety of human needs is not matched by a similar variety of housing. The vast majority of houses and flats built since 1919 have been designed for the young family to which lenders, and until recently the local authorities, have given priority. If they only have two or three children, these families will be well suited. Larger families cannot find sufficient well equipped living space unless they can afford to buy and improve the larger houses built for middle class households of an earlier generation. The young, the single and the old often have to accept, and if possible adapt, what is left: the conversions, the slums and 'rooms' in subdivided property – unless they choose to live in family houses built for larger households, and can afford to do so.

These problems will grow worse as time goes by, unless steps are taken to solve them: for the houses built since 1919 – throughout a period in which smaller households have rapidly grown in numbers – are peculiarly difficult to adapt or convert; the greater economy of their design means that halls and passages are smaller, ceilings lower and walls thinner than those provided in the more durable middle class housing built before the First World War. Inserting additional partitions and doors, and adding bathrooms, lavatories and central heating are all more difficult operations. The lateral conversions that can be made in Victorian and Georgian terraces are usually impossible in the modern semi-detached house. We have built houses of a peculiarly inflexible type that only suit households at particular stages of their existence. Like motor cars, they can be mass-produced, exchanged and scrapped, but they cannot be conveniently shared or subdivided, or radically modified.

If government in this country is to embark on a comprehensive attempt to meet housing needs and raise housing standards, then housing must increasingly be differentiated, not according to the income and social class of the head of household, but according to his needs and the needs of his family. We have already gone a considerable way towards this objective, but further progress will call for more systematic thought about the way in which the household's needs develop and change through its lifetime. It will also call for a reappraisal of the financial and administrative procedures that determine the flows of movement within and between the various sectors of the housing market. Our present system of private building was designed mainly to satisfy the demand for house purchase among younger households in the middle and upper income groups. To this a public sector was added, mainly to provide subsidized housing for similar households with lower incomes. Radical modifications will have to be made to this system if the new objectives now taking shape are to be realized. Some of the problems to be resolved will be discussed in the next chapters.

THE REST OF THE UNITED KINGDOM

A brief postscript should be added to this chapter, drawing attention to a few points at which England's housing situation differs from that of other countries in the United Kingdom. No attempt will be made to describe or compare these countries in detail. The different sections of Wales are too varied, and yet insufficiently different from England, to constitute a distinct region for housing purposes, though the large proportion of old houses in Wales should be noted: 32 per cent were over eighty years old in 1965, compared with 25 per cent in the whole United Kingdom,* and this means a large proportion lack baths and plumbing fixtures. Scotland and Northern Ireland differ more sharply, both from England and from each other.

At the time of the 1961 Census, Scotland's households included a much larger proportion of council tenants (42 per cent of all households – double the proportion found in England and Wales) and much smaller proportions of owner-occupiers (25

* *The National Plan*, Cmnd 2764, p. 175.

per cent, compared with 43 per cent south of the border). The average size of these households is the same as in England and Wales, but the houses they live in are much smaller and poorer: 58 per cent had less than four rooms (14 per cent south of the border) and the average number of persons per room was 0·93 (0·65 south of the border). The reasonably good conditions provided by the large proportion of council housing bring Scotland's average up to the national average for the equipment of houses, despite the large proportion (30 per cent) of houses over eighty years old.

Scottish averages are heavily weighted by the exceptionally bad conditions found in the remoter areas and in Glasgow. Very little building was done in Glasgow between the wars, and despite the large number of council houses recently built around its fringes and its rapidly growing slum clearance programme, Glasgow has changed less since 1914 than any other large city in Britain: the average number of persons per room is 1·09; a third of the population lives at over 1½ persons per room, and 39 per cent of households have no bath in their homes. But although the Scottish housing figures for crowding are depressed by the Glasgow situation they remain poorer than England's even when Glasgow is excluded: in Scotland as a whole, 13 per cent of households had more than 1½ persons per room, but in the United Kingdom as a whole only 4 per cent of households lived at this density.

Northern Ireland presents a different picture. The pattern of ownership is very similar to England's, and the average numbers of rooms per dwelling does not fall far short of English standards. Since households are slightly larger in Ulster, the average number of persons per room (0·8) is greater than in England, and 10 per cent of households live at more than 1½ persons per room.

Northern Ireland's main problem is the poor quality and equipment of her housing: in 1901 half her households did not have a bath in their homes and one in five did not have a cold water tap. Even among council tenants one in four had no bath. Many of the worst houses are found in rural districts, where housing – much of it owner-occupied – is appreciably poorer than in the towns. In Northern Ireland no less than 40 per cent of houses are more than eighty years old.

Regions which have had a slow rate of economic growth for two generations have gained relatively little new housing throughout the period in which we have been building to standards now accepted as a tolerable minimum. To reverse their continuing decline – or even to halve Scotland's annual loss of 40,000 people as the government hopes to do before long – will take more than the building of new factories and a redistribution of regional demands for labour. Scotland and Northern Ireland are in many respects a generation behind England and Wales, and it is in their housing conditions that the gap will be hardest to close.

CHAPTER 7

PAYING FOR HOUSING

THE last chapter described this country's housing market, the main currents in the tides of movement flowing through it, and the housing conditions achieved by households of different kinds. This chapter explains the situation it described, the changes now at work in the system and the directions these may take in future. It deals first with the pattern of new investment and with changes in the ownership of existing houses, which together account for the decline of the private rented sector and the growth of new sectors, and it explores the scope for arresting or modifying these trends.

The housing programme recently announced by the government provides a point of departure for a discussion of future investment in housing, the purposes this investment may serve and the impact it is likely to make on the market as a whole. But before speculating further about the future we must pause to consider how much people can be expected to pay for their housing, and what additional collective resources the government can bring to bear. Conclusions can then be reached about the financial implications of the goals to which government has committed itself. The next chapter examines the administrative and technical implications of this programme.

INVESTMENT IN HOUSING*

This country is now entering the later stages of a major revolution in its procedures for investment in housing – a revolution whose principal symptom is the replacement of private landlords by building societies and local authorities as the principal investors in this field. By the beginning of the last century a reasonably effective system of legal and financial instruments had been evolved for the provision and management of housing.

* This section, and much else in this chapter, is derived largely from A. A. Nevitt, *Housing, Taxation and Subsidies*, Nelson, 1966.

The owners of land, the lenders of money, the builders of houses and tenants who needed a home were brought together by 'landlords' who borrowed the money required to initiate and sustain the whole operation, commissioned the building of houses, managed the property and collected the rents – or formed the essential intermediary linking others who did these things. Much of the land they needed was held in large estates whose owners were unwilling to dispose of it entirely or were legally debarred from doing so, and in these areas the landlords bought leases entitling them to use land for long periods of time. Most of their capital came in modest sums from local businessmen, from trust funds administered for widows and children by local solicitors, and from others looking for a reasonable rate of return on their savings, combined with the safety conferred by mortgages secured on durable and saleable property. These lenders could withdraw their money if they needed it because they could generally find others willing to take their place and buy from them the income to be gained from mortgages of this kind. If the cost of building a terrace of houses was too high, the property could be divided among many owners and the burden of the lease could be shared among many people, entitling a succession of sublessors to draw an income in return for their contribution to the total costs of holding and developing the land. The landlord might also be the builder or the manager of the property and he might provide the land or part of the loans required, but his main contributions were to bring the parties to the transaction together, to bear most of the risks involved, and hence to take most of the profits or losses. As with all small-scale capitalism, the pattern was a local one, depending on trust in personal reputations for integrity and business acumen, and to the outside observer it appears exceedingly complicated and confusing. But it worked pretty well. It created whole suburbs and cities at a rate never before imagined, and it provided houses of all types and sizes at all sorts of prices for a diverse and rapidly growing population. Many of these houses were of poor quality – though they were much better when new than their survivors are today. By the standards of their times, however, they were not too bad: what are now the slums of Manchester and Liverpool were justly described in their day as 'the finest artisans' dwellings in Europe'.

That was a long time ago. Over the past sixty years private landlords have been turned into a stagnant and then a dying trade as a result of developments which can best be summarized by saying that the widespread increases in wealth which produced the local capitalism of which they were typical and successful representatives have now gone much further, creating a national and international capitalism that provides formidable competitors at every point of the landlords' operations. The same processes have brought about a massive growth in government, and correspondingly massive increases in taxation and subsidies which have been organized in a fashion that discriminates systematically against the private landlord while favouring his competitors. Rent restrictions, on which the whole blame for the landlord's difficulties has often been cast, furnished additional nails for his coffin – mainly important as a symbol of public discrimination against his trade and as a red herring diverting attention from more fundamental causes of his predicament.

The invention and rapid spread of building societies in their modern form furnished a means of raising money for house purchase from a much larger range of lenders, providing security – through mortgages, surveyors' valuations and cautiously systematic rules for the selection of borrowers – at least as good as the landlord could offer, and recouping from house buyers a continuing flow of repayments for reinvestment in housing. While landlords expected to retain the use of other people's capital as long as the interest on it was paid, the owner-occupier was willing to repay the money he borrowed as a means of securing an asset that could later be exchanged for another house or bequeathed to his heirs. Building societies learnt to vary the periods of repayment so that the burden of the buyer's debts could be adjusted to his capacity to pay, despite changes in building costs, house prices and interest rates. The buyer also gained in status and civic rights – becoming eligible for jury service perhaps – and the building societies' advertisements ('get rid of your rent man') did not hesitate to remind him of this.

War, inflation, town planning restrictions and the vagaries of rent control (first introduced in 1915) began to distort the private market for renting. The government's attempts to shed rent controls created a situation which encouraged landlords to get rid of tenants whenever a chance of selling houses 'with vacant possession' offered opportunities of greater profit. This made tenants anxious about their security of tenure. Those in new houses built between the wars and those in houses released from control had no security, while those remaining in controlled houses were repeatedly reminded by the government that the controls were only a temporary arrangement that would soon be eliminated. Thus security of tenure became one of the owner-occupiers' principal assets, encouraging people to buy homes of their own and to outbid private landlords who might contemplate building on the same sites.

Meanwhile the growth of building societies, trustee savings banks and borrowing by central and local government, and the development of stock exchanges through which people could buy shares that were much more readily saleable than privately negotiated mortgages, provided additional and formidable competitors for the funds the private landlord required.

Earlier, in the last quarter of the nineteenth century, by-laws imposing minimum standards had begun to make an appreciable impact on the quality and dimensions of new houses. They were coupled with increasingly severe restrictions on overcrowding, and standards for new development gradually moved upwards, taking another long step forward after the First World War – as can be seen in cities up and down the country at the point where the pre-1919 vistas of brick and tile suddenly give way to more open building, fronted by gates and hedges and backed by gardens. Figures 4 and 5 on page 252 illustrate these trends. The people who could afford higher standards were precisely those the building societies were beginning to serve on a massive scale. Those who could not afford them depended increasingly on the private landlord's other competitor, the public landlord, building with subsidies from central and local government. For a while (after 1921) the local authorities were not permitted to build unless they could show that private builders were incapable of meeting local needs, but this restriction was soon removed. Subsidies were offered to private builders for a time, but their distribution was difficult to control effectively – many people suspected that the houses built with this help went to people capable of paying their own way – and in any case the private landlords' reluctance to invest in this market was due to more fundamental causes than the subsidy disadvantage.

The country's fiscal system was weighted against landlords, owing to various accidents and necessities quite unconnected with housing policies. Houses built since the First World War have been valued for rating purposes according to a system that hinges on the rent-earning capacity of older property, much of which has always been subject to controls. New houses therefore tended to be under-valued for rating purposes, and hence under-taxed. This bias in favour of newer and predominantly owner-occupied property was reinforced by the fact that appeals against valuations came more frequently from owner-occupiers than from landlords or tenants.

Since the regulations of the Inland Revenue have always been based on the assumption that house property lasts for ever, private landlords in this country, unlike their counterparts in many others, cannot deduct the sums set aside to replace their capital assets in computing their taxable incomes. This imposes crippling restraints on new building and improvements. The owner of a factory and its warehouse, canteen, sports pavilion and associated buildings can deduct from his taxable profits the cost of depreciating this property; the owner of the adjoining row of houses cannot. The landlord who was offered a government grant under the Housing Act of 1961 in return for spending £100 of his own money on installing bath, lavatory and other improvements was permitted to raise his rents by 12½ per cent of his contribution. A gross profit of £12 10s. on an investment of £100 appears handsome at first sight, but if he paid £5 7s 6d. into a sinking fund each year (on the assumption that his house would last another fifteen years and that he must be capable of replacing his investment at the end of that period) then, when he had paid tax at the companies' rate of £6 14s. 4d. on his gross return of £12 10s., his *net* profit on an investment of £100 was only 8s. 2d. If his house had a longer life the improvement would be more profitable; but if its life was shorter than fifteen years, improvement financed on this basis would mean a loss for the owner. It is not surprising that 76 per cent of improvement grants have been going to owner-occupiers and local authorities; the grants offer less help to the private landlord, although his houses are in more urgent need of improvement. He can neither deduct the cost of improvements from his income, because they are treated as capital expenditure, nor deduct the cost of depreciating them because his capital is assumed to last for ever.

For many years the operation of the Schedule A tax did something to correct this handicap by incorporating standard deductions for repairs from the assessed value of houses before the tax was levied on them; this helped the owner of a house that was new, or newly converted and improved, because the cost of repairs would for a while remain below the level assumed in calculating the deduction. (Once the house grew old it encouraged people to postpone repairs because the deduction could be claimed whether they were done or not.) But when this tax was abolished in 1963 the owner-occupier secured another major advantage over the landlord because he was relieved of the tax while landlords continued to bear the same burden, or a greater one, under Schedule D. The cost of this concession to owner-occupiers was stated by the government to be £48 millions in a full year (equivalent to half the Exchequer subsidies on council housing, twice the cost of the Child Care Service, or about the price of a national system of nursery education that was legislated for twenty years earlier but has never been provided).

Owner-occupiers of the poorest property may secure another advantage over landlords if their houses are condemned as slums, for under certain circumstances they can be compensated on more generous terms – being paid something for their houses as well as for the sites on which they stand.

The building societies secured privileges in the nineteenth century which gave them more generous treatment than other forms of business in the taxation of profits, and this undoubtedly encouraged their later development, particularly during the 1920s; but these advantages were gradually whittled away, until in 1958 the societies were put on an equal footing with limited companies and other profit-making businesses.

But more important than any of these arrangements has been the tax treatment of ground rent, and interest payments made on borrowed money. When taxes were introduced under

Schedule A on income derived from property, the owners of houses generally let their property in return for rent and it was natural to deduct interest payments and payments to superior landlords as necessary expenses of their business before levying tax on the remaining income. Owner-occupiers, at first negligible in numbers, were given the same right to deduct these payments from their taxable incomes. But as their numbers grew, as house prices rose and interest payments with them, and as the rate at which income tax was levied also rose, so the government found itself helping owner-occupiers with increasing sums in tax foregone – amounting in 1960 to over £200 million.

This total includes another element not so far mentioned. The larger his income, the more profitable a house buyer finds it to purchase his home with the aid of a loan from an insurance company – a loan that does not have to be repaid until the insurance policy taken out in conjunction with it matures, perhaps twenty years later. Should he die, the policy matures automatically and his widow can repay the loan on the house. This enables him to pay a much higher tax-allowable total sum in interest, since the principal on which interest is levied is not reduced by regular instalments as it would be with a mortgage from a building society. It also enables him to claim a smaller but additional tax relief on the regular premiums he pays for his insurance policy. The owner-occupier's ground rent concession has recently been removed but, with further increases in incomes, tax rates, house prices and interest rates, the total relief to house buyers continues to mount. For the owner-occupier it is truly more blessed to borrow than to lend. Meanwhile the landlord can only set off such commitments against the income he derives from his property; to inflate his interest payments would only mean operating at a loss. Thus he cannot compete against owner-occupiers, and the richer they are the weaker his competitive position will be.

These arrangements mean that a man borrowing on mortgage at an interest rate of 6 per cent and paying income tax at only 4s. in the pound on earned income, pays an *effective* rate of interest, after allowing for tax relief on his interest payments, of 5·07 per cent. If his tax rate is 8s. 3d. in the pound his effective

interest rate will be less still – 3·6 per cent. The higher his
income, the fewer his dependants, and the larger the proportion
of his income falling in the 'unearned' categories, the larger the
concession will be and the lower will be his effective rate of
interest. As a result, the community contributes what amounts
in effect to a subsidy of well over £200 million a year to people
who are buying their own houses. The advantage this gives
them over landlords and tenants of privately rented property
can be seen in Table 18 which compares the position of two

TABLE 18

*Comparative Tax Position of Man, Wife and Two Children Under
Eleven, at Various Levels of Earned Income, 1965–6*

| Earned Income | Annual Income Tax Payments | | Subsidy to house buyers |
	Tenants	Buyers paying £100 a year in interest	
	£ s. d.	£ s. d.	£ s. d.
£800	10 12 0	Nil	10 12 0
£900	29 0 0	6 0 0	23 0 0
£1,000	52 6 6	22 6 6	30 0 0
£1,250	121 3 4	80 18 4	40 5 0

SOURCE: A.A.Nevitt, *Housing, Taxation and Subsidies.*

similar families, consisting of husband, wife and two children
under the age of eleven, depending entirely on earned income.
One family rents a house and the other is buying one, paying
£100 each year in interest to a building society. Their respective
income tax payments have been calculated for different levels
of earnings at the rates levied in 1965–6. The buyers would
secure a subsidy of £10 12s. if they earned £800 a year, and a
subsidy of £40 5s. if they earned £1,250 a year. At higher income
levels, or with fewer children to support, the buyers would
gain even more. When tax rates are increased the value of
these tax reliefs is of course greater still: under a progressive

tax system, a general reduction in the tax rate inevitably reduces the value of any privilege accorded to those who are more generously treated by the tax collector, while a general increase in the tax rate enhances the value of such privileges. The recent increase in the standard rate of income tax from 7s. 9d. to 8s 3d. in the pound increased by £10 2s. 3d. the tax advantage that the house buyer with an income of £1,250 had over tenants.

It has often been argued that this country should adopt a general system of reduced interest rates, as many other countries have done, to help the private house builder and those for whom he builds, but governments have resisted this pressure on the grounds that it would result in an extensive, costly and indiscriminate form of concealed subsidy. Yet in reality we already have just such a concealed subsidy: extensive, costly and worse than indiscriminate, for it discriminates in favour of one group of householders who are generally speaking richer and better housed than the rest, and within that group it confers greatest benefits upon those least in need of them. It has been distributed indiscriminately among all the buyers and sellers instead of being concentrated, as in some countries, on the promotion of new building. It has helped to eliminate the private landlord, particularly encouraging his richest tenants (who constitute one of the few corners of this market that might remain economically viable) to move out of rented housing and buy at high prices with the aid of the most generous tax privileges. There has also been no effective general control over the growth of the subsidy, arising as it did from an unperceived accident of tax laws. It has thus contributed quite unnecessarily to its own inflation by inflating house prices, conferring advantages not only upon buyers but also upon owner-occupiers and landlords who are in a position to sell houses to those taxed at a sufficiently high rate to gain most benefit from these privileges.

The taxation and subsidy of council housing present, in detail, an even more complicated picture; but their principal features are reasonably clear. In 1960 the total subsidy bill for all kinds of public housing in the United Kingdom – mainly the permanent houses of local authorities – amounted to £120 million, 75 per cent of which was contributed by the central government while the rest came from the rates. By 1964 this had risen to £134 million and the central government's share had fallen to 70 per cent.

But individual council tenants have been subsidized in various additional ways – particularly by drawing on the relatively high rents now charged for older houses, that were built more cheaply and with the aid of cheaper loans, in order to reduce the much higher rents that would otherwise have to be charged for houses built recently at higher prices with money borrowed at higher rates of interest. Thus, in general, the newer council houses are very heavily subsidized – particularly the high flats on costly central sites – while a large proportion of the tenants living in older houses pay a good deal more than the cost of maintaining and managing their homes and meeting the debt charges on them. The scale of the local authorities' operations and their capacity for redistributing resources among their tenants confers a further advantage upon them in competing with private landlords, the great majority of whom let fewer than six houses. It has enabled them to go on building and letting houses at rents which, in the cities at least, are not greatly in excess of the average rents charged by private landlords, despite the fact that subsidies have fallen drastically in relation to building costs. (In rural areas council rents are much higher than private rents, though here and in the towns the local authorities can give their tenants better value for money.) The average cost of a three-bedroom house rose from about £350 in 1930 to about £2,300 in 1964, excluding the price of land. In the course of these thirty-four years subsidies per house approximately doubled, while building costs were multiplied by more than six. The councils can only go on building for those in need because they are able to make tenants of their older houses subsidize those in the newer ones. Indeed it is their capacity for concentrating the subsidies accumulated over many years upon the most recently built houses – thus 'municipalizing' the capital gains on past building – which now makes the councils so powerful an instrument for meeting the needs of poorer families, providing them with resources far greater than the subsidies paid under the latest Acts for new building. The subsidies have primed a pump which now continues working with much less help from the taxpayer than was originally required.

Unfortunately the history of earlier building and borrowing by different local authorities under a rapidly changing succession of Housing Acts has produced some very odd patterns of subsidy which bear scant relation to the needs of the areas concerned. If housing authorities are to have the fullest opportunities for meeting these needs their burdens must be more equitably shared, and some means of 'nationalizing' and redistributing at least a large part of their debts will eventually have to be found. The more generous subsidy provisions announced at the time of writing will enable local authorities to keep pace with the rising costs of building and redevelopment, but have not led to any major redistribution of their debt burdens.

The other major development in housing finance that was being discussed as this book went to press would give a 2 per cent reduction in interest rates to poorer house buyers – roughly equivalent to the advantages already available, through tax relief on mortgage interest, to people paying the standard rate of income tax. It is encouraging that the impact of tax relief on house purchase is at last being explicitly recognized, but nothing has yet been done to reduce the greater privileges available to richer buyers. If this scheme has more than a marginal effect it may simply inflate the price of owner-occupied housing and draw into this sector of the market an even larger number of houses from the rented sector.

The main conclusions to be drawn from this brief survey of housing finance are simple but daunting. Private landlords still house about a third of the households in Britain. They appear to be holding their own in certain corners of the market: furnished tenancies, luxury flats in the centres of the bigger cities, tenement blocks not yet due for clearance, and houses for farm workers and others whose employers have to keep men close to their jobs – all these continue to be managed fairly successfully by private owners, a few of whom are even extending their investment in such housing. But the numbers of houses in these groups are not large. Meanwhile the traditional private landlord letting property unfurnished to ordinary families is becoming extinct. In some places, unattractive to building societies yet still beyond the reach of slum clearance, he is taking an unconscionable time in dying, and blighting in the process whole neighbourhoods which have been starved of investment for years.

The removal of rent controls which took place between 1957 and 1964 hastened the process of transfer to owner occupation, and did little to improve the condition of rented housing, except in a few areas where the character of a neighbourhood could be changed and a new and wealthier class of tenant could be attracted. The Act also brought about an increasingly inefficient and unfair distribution of house-room in the property that remained rented.* It was too readily assumed that the opportunity for higher rents would encourage landlords to invest afresh in this market; but such decisions depend on the *relative* returns to be secured from different courses of action, and the opportunity of selling to an owner-occupier remained far more attractive for most landlords and became more readily available to many of them. The advantages accorded for years to the landlord's competitors by taxation and subsidies have brought about a major redistribution of investment, not only between his sector of the market and others but between one neighbourhood and another. A change in rent restrictions, always capable of being reversed after the next election, was quite insufficient to turn the tide.

Landlords, moreover, are not an impersonal economic mechanism; they are people, whose character, abilities and habits go far to determine how they can be expected to behave. When an industry has been in decline for long enough those who remain in it include a high proportion of the less able and successful businessmen, together with others who entered the business for various rather accidental reasons – people who inherited property, for example, people who bought two houses because this was the only way to secure the one they wished to live in themselves, or bought the house next door to prevent it being put to uses that would disturb their peace and quiet, and others for whom the making of profits is not a principal motive.

*See Chapters 6 and 10.

Studies of London landlords carried out for the Milner Holland Committee revealed a considerable proportion who were not, in the normal sense, 'in business' at all; they let property to relatives, friends or employees – tenancies that would never be advertised on the market. Another study was made by John Greve, with the help of the British Market Research Bureau, of a sample of 269 landlords drawn from all parts of England. It suggests that three quarters of this country's private landlords are responsible for less than six tenancies, and the majority of them are individuals who have not established a limited company. It is among the larger landlords with a hundred or more tenancies that rent fixing and management policies appear to follow the most businesslike patterns – certainly it is among them that improvement grants have been most often used. But they own only a small proportion of the country's rented housing, and virtually none of these larger landlords are buying or building new housing for rent. Any new investment they make in property is now being switched to commercial and industrial sites.*

In Lancaster, where private landlords have been disappearing so fast that the species may be virtually extinct in a dozen years' time, Cullingworth found that over half of them were letting only one house, two thirds of them were aged sixty or more, and nearly half had incomes (including their rents) of under £7 per week. Most had inherited their property and nearly all intended to get rid of it as soon as a favourable opportunity appeared: 'In a strange way the problem of old housing in this city overlaps the problem of old people: both (the houses and their owners) are "living on low incomes" . . . private ownership of rented property in Lancaster is a dying institution.' 'A policy of modernization can hardly be expected to succeed with 853 individual landlords of whom the majority have no real interest in property ownership.'† This may be an extreme situation. At the other extreme, a study of landlords in the central London borough of St Marylebone revealed a larger number of big and businesslike landlords, more determined to hold onto their

* John Greve, *Private Landlords in England*, Occasional Papers on Social Administration, No. 16.
† J. B. Cullingworth, *Housing in Transition*, pp. 123–4 and 142, 1963.

property and more capable of managing it profitably.* Another study, made in a prosperous suburb on the fringe of Nottingham, found landlords whose characteristics fell somewhere between these extremes.† They too, however, were selling out whenever a profitable opportunity arose.

It is one thing for landlords to manage and maintain existing property, and quite another to build anew, to convert and improve, and to extend their investment in the housing market. The housing standards this country will require in future call for a programme of renewal and modernization that cannot be expected from this quarter.

The more puzzling question is not 'Why are private landlords disappearing?' but 'Why do any of them stay in business?' A few, indeed, have deserted their houses and left them ownerless. But 60 per cent of tenancies coming out of control in recent years appear to have been relet – an appreciable proportion being let to the owner's relatives and under other special arrangements. To make large profits by selling to owner-occupiers, landlords must sell their houses 'with vacant possession', which means they are compelled to wait until their tenants move or die and the house is empty. That may take a long time, particularly if the house is divided into several tenancies. Once empty, they must find a willing buyer who is capable of borrowing the money required. But since borrowers, subsidized by tax reliefs, demand more money than is available, the lenders must ration their mortgages somehow. They do this by insisting on a down-payment which for property in poorer areas may amount to at least 50 per cent of the price; and if the house and its surrounding neighbourhood are too decrepit they will not lend at all. Such houses may then have to remain rented until the bulldozers come, and that may take many years. There are signs that the drift of rented property into owner occupation has slowed down since the hectic years after the 1957 Rent Act. This, if it is true, should not be thought to presage a revival in the private rented market: it may only mean that the most

*Christine Cockburn, 'Rented Housing in Central London'. D. V. Donnison and others, *Essays on Housing*, Occasional Papers on Social Administration, No. 9.
†A study by A. J. Willcocks, to be published shortly.

attractive property has already been acquired, and buyers and lenders are wary of what remains.

The private landlord can still make a constructive contribution in restricted and rather specialized corners of the market where he is sheltered from the competition of owner occupation and council housing. In these fields he could be enabled to do more, particularly if taxation and subsidies were redistributed to give him some help, or at least to reduce the handicaps under which he has long laboured. But in the middle and cheaper ranges of the mass market the question confronting policy makers is not how to revive the private landlord, but who should assume his responsibilities, and how can the changeover be most quickly, efficiently and fairly brought about? The problem is not a new one; governments faced with a choice between paying to keep a failing industry in being and paying to close a large part of it down are generally compelled to adopt the latter course eventually – as witness the British cotton industry in the early 1960s, and small-scale farming and fishing in Britain and many other countries today. In such cases, the lives of large numbers of families can be blighted for years if the choice between these alternatives is postponed too long. The sooner a large part of this property is acquired by publicly accountable authorities of some kind, the larger the stock of cheaper accommodation that can be retained for the use of poorer households, and the more efficiently this stock can be maintained and managed during its remaining life.

Policies for future investment in new housing must depend on the channels of investment available and the needs that each can meet. Owner occupation is popular, rapidly expanding, and confers special benefits: the home owner has security of tenure, and as a result he generally invests far more than landlords or tenants in maintaining and improving his house. He is prepared to save large sums in order to get it, and willing to spend more, month by month, than he would spend on rent. He is less deterred from buying or improving his property by considerations of risk: the time and money he devotes to this task are not weighed against an expected increase in rents or capital values, but against the enhanced 'services' his improved home affords him – and some people enjoy the labour of improving a home

for its own sake. But owner occupation, as at present financed,
excludes large numbers of people who cannot meet the down-
payments and continuing expenditure it calls for, and some
people have no wish to own their own homes. Owner-occupied
property, as at present constituted, permits too narrow a range
of choices in the sizes and types of home it offers, and it may
render people unnecessarily immobile, as was shown in the
previous chapter. This immobility can become a serious
economic problem in areas where employment and property
values are declining. Owner occupation is also supported by
concealed, costly and inequitable subsidies of various kinds.

Council housing likewise offers special advantages: it is more
'efficiently' or fairly distributed than other property, minimizing overcrowding and wasted house room; it enables local
authorities, if they choose, to adjust rents and house room to
the needs and resources of the household, owing to the freedom
with which subsidies and the benefits of capital gains accruing
over the years can be redistributed among their tenants. Armed
with appropriate subsidies, the local authorities may be more
willing to build than the private developer: even if they cannot
let houses to those in the greatest need, they may still find tenants
further down the waiting lists. The private builder adds bigger
margins to cover his risks and, in some areas at least, appears
to be building well behind the demand.* But the public sector
has its disadvantages, too; for many years to come, its tenants
will be confined to an even narrower range of house sizes and
types than owner-occupiers; and they tend to be selected from
particular groups – mainly from slum dwellers and from
working class families with children, long established within
fairly restricted areas. It is uncertain whether local authorities
are politically and psychologically capable of extending their
recruitment to encompass the wider variety of people who must
be housed and rehoused in future. And as time goes by the
distribution of subsidies and debt charges among local authori-
ies has grown increasingly ill matched to their needs.

Thus alternative forms of investment and ownership may be
required to fill the gaps still left between the newer tenures
which now provide the growing points in the market. The

*See pages 203–4.

capacity of 'cost-rent' and 'co-ownership' schemes to fill these gaps will be considered later. But first the needs to be met and the resources available for meeting them must be examined in greater detail.

FUTURE REQUIREMENTS

No discussion of the sources and distribution of investment in housing can proceed far without some assumptions about the volume of building to be expected and the types of need to which priority must be given. In the past, the 'free market' furnished these assumptions and the interventions of government could be treated as a marginal addition to market mechanisms. Such an approach to forecasting housing demand is now obsolete. Even if the political tide should change, the foregoing pages have shown that the government is already playing so pervasive a role in the housing market – a role that is eliminating the private landlord and subsidizing owner-occupiers about as heavily as council tenants – that a 'free market' can no longer be said to exist. (Which is why the phrase carries a close escort of inverted commas throughout this book.) Thus government must itself decide the scale of the housing programme and the priorities for which it is to be designed.

What is the 'right' size of housing programme for this country and what are the 'appropriate' housing standards to attain? To ask such questions is rather like asking what would be the 'right' time for an athlete to take in running a mile: the answers given to all of them have had to be revised before long, for they depend not only on the resources and techniques available but also on judgement, morale and aspirations. Research cannot answer such questions and it will only mislead its readers if it purports to do so.

Therefore it will be more helpful to take the government's own estimates of the housing programme required and explore the implications of these commitments. The remainder of this book adopts the government's intended programme as the basis for its discussion of national requirements, fully recognizing that the past history of such commitments in this and other countries shows that they are likely before long to be revised, upwards or downwards – but more frequently upwards.

The government has announced its intention of increasing the building programme to attain a yearly output of half a million dwellings by 1969, and more thereafter. Whatever the rate of building to be achieved, it is vital, both for the successful development of the building industry and for the evolution of the economy as a whole, that a continuous and predictable long-term demand be assured for the future. This much is generally agreed. But it is doubtful whether the implications of such a programme have yet been publicly grasped. Where will all this building go, who will benefit from it, and how will it be paid for?

It was shown in the previous chapter that there has in recent years been a net increase of about two households for every three new houses built. One third of the houses built have been required for replacing demolished property and for making good many other smaller losses such as the increase in empty dwellings, the amalgamation of hitherto separate dwellings into larger units, the provision of extra houses for people who have two homes and so on. If this pattern continued unchanged there would have to be an increase of 333,000 households a year to sustain an output of 500,000 houses. But that is plainly impossible. The government expects only 150,000 new households to be formed each year between 1965 and 1970 as the generation produced by the post-war 'bulge' in births gets married. After that the rate of household formation will fall. No estimate has yet been given of the numbers of households that will die or amalgamate with others, but it is clear that the *net* rate of increase arising from demographic causes is likely to be well below this figure of 150,000. Past experience is therefore going to be a poor guide to the future and a new kind of programme will be required.

Estimates of future needs over a longer period of time have been prepared for Britain (not the United Kingdom) by the National Institute of Economic and Social Research.* These estimates show that there were approximately 16·31 million households in Britain in 1960. If headship rates remain unchanged – that is to say, if in future people of any given age, sex

*W. Beckerman and Associates, *The British Economy in 1975*, Cambridge University Press, 1965.

TABLE 19

The Numbers of Households in Britain, 1960 and 1990

Demographic group	Population (Millions)		Headship rates[1] (Percentages)			Households (Millions)		1990	
	1960 estimates (1)	1990 forecast (1)	1960 estimates (3)	1990 forecast lower (4)	1990 forecast upper (5)	1960 estimates (6)	at 1960 rates (7)	lower forecast (8)	upper forecast (9)
Married men:									
under 40	4·64	6·04	91	98	100	4·22	5·49	5·91	6·04
40–59	5·82	6·41	97	98	105	5·64	6·22	6·29	6·73
60 and over	2·60	3·46	98	98	100	2·55	3·39	3·39	3·46
Widowed and divorced:									
40–59 males	0·22	0·26	70	75	80	0·15	0·18	0·20	0·21
females	0·64	0·47	79	81	85	0·51	0·37	0·38	0·40
60 and over males	0·63	0·88	66	70	75	0·41	0·58	0·61	0·66
females	2·23	2·87	70	75	80	1·56	2·01	2·15	2·30
Single:[2]									
20–24	1·85	2·64	3	12	25	0·06	0·08	0·31	0·66
25–39	1·68	1·73	13	20	30	0·22	0·22	0·28	0·52
40–59 males	0·62	0·50	30	35	40	0·19	0·15	0·18	0·20
females	0·83	0·44	32	37	45	0·27	0·14	0·16	0·20
60 and over males	0·27	0·26	44	50	55	0·12	0·11	0·13	0·14
females	0·80	0·64	51	58	65	0·41	0·32	0·37	0·42
Totals	51·12[3]	64·65[3]	—	—	—	16·31	19·26	20·36	21·94

SOURCE: for all columns except 5 and 9, W. Beckerman and Associates, *The British Economy in 1975*.

and marital status have the same opportunity of establishing separate households as groups of the same type have today – then changes in the size and demographic structure of the population would by themselves create an extra 2·95 million households by 1990. (Although the births and international migration to be expected during the twenty-five years cannot be accurately predicted, the proportion of households with heads under the age of twenty-five and the net effects of migration are both small enough for the errors arising from these sources to be negligible.)

But people's opportunities for establishing separate households do not remain the same: they have been improving year by year and will continue to do so. The National Institute assumes that headship rates will rise in all groups, but henceforth at a slower rate than was achieved during the 1950s. On their assumptions, there would from this cause be a further increase of 1·10 million households between 1960 and 1990, producing, together with the effects of demographic growth and change, a total increase of 4·05 million households during these thirty years. (This can be seen in Table 19 by comparing the totals for columns 6 and 7 to find the increase due to demographic growth and change, and comparing those for columns 7 and 8 to find the increase due to a change in headship rates.) The Institute's forecast would therefore require an average output of only 135,000 dwellings a year over the whole period of thirty years – more in the first and last decades, and less in the middle one – to cater for the increase in households, leaving the rest of the programme to cater for all other requirements: slum clearance, redevelopment, an increase in vacancies and secondary dwellings, a reduction in the numbers of shared dwellings, and so on. Not unreasonably on these assumptions, the Institute concludes that the output of houses will fall well short of the government's plan, amounting to between 390,000 and 420,000 in 1970, rising to 420–520,000 in 1980, and falling again to 420,000–440,000 by 1990. The difference between their higher and lower estimates depends mainly on the different rates of replacement that might be achieved. Even their less ambitious estimate would call for the demolition of about 250,000 houses a year by the early 1970s and continuing clearance of about 270–280,000 dwellings thereafter, accounting after 1975 for nearly two thirds of the total programme. This rate of replacement would be more than three times the size of our present slum clearance programme.

Should these conclusions be accepted? The Institute describes its forecast of the rise in headship rates (compare columns 3 and 4 in the Table) as 'probably a maximum', arguing that the proportion of the adult population who were heads of households or the wives of heads rose from 66 per cent in 1931 to 79 per cent in 1961 and is most unlikely to go beyond the level of 84 per cent they assume for 1990. But the experience of other European countries shows that headship rates can rise to levels never before anticipated when the distribution of incomes and procedures for allocating and subsidizing housing change in favour of widows, students, single people and others whose opportunities of finding a separate home were previously restricted. The Institute's forecasts, although incorporating an increase in headship rates for every category of the population, appear to assume that the rates for particular groups of *people* may fall as these people grow older; many of the widowed and divorced (but not, for some reason, the single) are expected to move in with other households after they pass the age of sixty. But studies of old people suggest this does not happen to a great extent and very seldom happens willingly: if an improvement is made in the headship rates for younger people, they will want to sustain this improvement for the rest of their lives, and the great majority succeed in doing so. Meanwhile the growth of secondary dwellings among families that have two homes – in effect permitting husbands and wives to become heads of separate households for much of the working week or the school holidays – means that the ratio of houses to married couples may rise above the 'one to one' level usually assumed to be the absolute maximum attainable in this group.

Table 19 compares the Institute's forecasts with another set of assumptions – less 'realistic' perhaps, but undoubtedly realizable, to judge from the experience of other countries. Table 8 on page 154 shows the numbers of households already formed in various countries, expressing these as a percentage of the numbers they would have had if these countries had only attained the headship rates achieved in England and Wales by 1951. The numbers in England and Wales in 1961 were 6 per cent greater than our 1951 rates would have produced; the numbers in Denmark (in 1960) were 19 per cent greater than our own 1951 rates would have produced in that country. The more ambitious of the two hypothetical rates for 1990 proposed in column 5 of Table 19 would have only brought us to about the level already attained by the Danes – 20 per cent greater than our own 1951 rates would have achieved. The more cautious rates proposed by the National Institute are already surpassed by Switzerland and the Scandinavian countries quoted in Table 8.

If these more ambitious assumptions were realized, the total number of households would grow from 16·31 million to 21·94 million – an increase of 5·63 million. Over the whole thirty-year period that increase would take up an average of nearly 190,000 additional dwellings a year, in place of the Institute's assumed demand of 135,000. (The increase in households assumed by the Institute can be found by comparing columns 6 and 8; that derived from our more ambitious assumptions by comparing columns 6 and 9.)

The National Plan proposes an output of 12,000 houses a year for Northern Ireland by 1970 and intends that this should increase in the following years. It calls for a sufficient increase in the number of empty houses to produce a 3 per cent vacancy rate, saying this would require 300,000 extra houses – amounting to some 30,000 a year if the required level is to be attained in a decade. There is also a 'backlog' of shortage, mainly found among working class families in Glasgow and London, with smaller concentrations in Merseyside, the West Midlands and elsewhere. This backlog, it is said, could be met with 370,000 extra houses, but a considerable part of it has already been accounted for in our forecasts of the increase in headship rates; only where separate households have already been formed but are unwillingly sharing accommodation must an additional allowance be made. Assuming that the shortage will be made good in a decade, and about half of it will be catered for through an increase in headship rates, 20,000 houses a year might be allocated for the reduction of sharing. Net losses due to road

widening, conversions, private redevelopment and factors other
than slum clearance are expected to call for an extra 30,000
houses a year. (All these estimates include Northern Ireland,
but the proportions falling there are small enough to be disregarded for the purpose of these approximations.) On the
basis of these figures, a programme of the following type might
be envisaged for the future. The alternative figures proposed
for 'Replacing obsolete housing' are a balancing item designed
to match the alternatives proposed for 'Increasing headship
rates'.

A potential building programme of 500,000 houses a year	
Britain	
For demographic growth and change	100,000
Increasing headship rates	35–90,000
Reduction in sharing	20,000
Increasing vacancies	30,000
Replacing obsolete housing	215–270,000
Other demolitions, conversions, etc.	30,000
Total	485,000
Northern Ireland	15,000
United Kingdom	500,000

These figures have been calculated on a long-term basis,
and assume a continuing output of half a million houses a year.
The programme proposed by the government is smaller than
this in the first five years and larger subsequently; demographic
needs, the reduction of sharing and the advance of headship
rates are to be given priority to start with; slum clearance will
increase later. If the government intends to commit itself
to the continuing and predictable output of houses it has
repeatedly said the country and its builders must be assured of,
and if the programme is to be of the proposed size, these figures
provide an approximate indication of the purposes for which
the programme would have to be used during the next decade or
two. From time to time there would be considerable changes in
the distribution of building between the different subheads and
considerable changes in its regional distribution too, as will be

shown in the next chapter. But this is the pattern towards which the country must move during the next few years. It is a radically different pattern from the one we have been accustomed to, which was outlined in the previous chapter.

About half the programme will be required for the replacement of obsolete housing. Changes in the size and demographic structure of our population, which have hitherto been the dominant influence in the demand for public and private housing alike, will only account for about a third of the houses to be built. Of the total increase in households assumed by the National Institute, four-fifths will occur among married couples and most of the rest will be among the widowed and divorced. The average size of households would scarcely change but there would be rather more of the larger households (with five or more people) and considerably more of the oldest and smallest households. The more ambitious estimate presented here would still leave two-thirds of the increase among married couples (an appreciable part of it in the form of smaller secondary dwellings) but would divide the rest fairly equally between single people (particularly those in their twenties) and the widowed and divorced. The average size of household would fall, owing to the growing numbers of young people who would set up home on their own, but there would still be an increase in the numbers of larger households. Thus both forecasts assume there must be greater provision for families – including a number of fairly large families, many of whom will have modest incomes – and they give varying emphasis to the needs of the single and the previously married, and to the provision of country cottages and city *pieds-à-terre*.

The requirements of demographic growth are probably the most firmly predictable part of these forecasts. Building devoted to the reduction of sharing, the increase of vacancies, and the making good of losses due to causes other than the demolition of obsolete housing may vary considerably from time to time – the reduction of sharing may be given priority at first, while building to increase vacancies may come later in the programme, for example – but their total volume over a longer period should be reasonably predictable. It follows that most of the uncertainty about the longer term programme arises from the two remaining items: the replacement of obsolete houses, and the increase in headship rates. The outcome under both headings will depend mainly on government policies which determine who can secure a separate home and how much slum clearance will take place.

Turning next to consider how a programme of this kind can be financed, commentators typically proceed by forecasting the growth and future distribution of personal incomes, the progress of the building industry and the future costs of the housing it will provide. Arming themselves next with assumptions about the proportion of personal incomes that people can or 'should' devote to housing, they estimate the number of households who will need subsidies because their incomes are too low to pay the price required. But this procedure is liable to raise false hopes for the reduction of building costs, and omits crucial aspects of personal expenditure on housing. As a result it has sometimes inflicted real hardship. These two problems must therefore be briefly examined.

It was made clear in Chapter 2 that housing is not a standard commodity – like saucepans, or stockings – providing standard services for its users. It is the shelter, storage place, display case and environment for a large proportion of people's activities and possessions. Hence the consumption of housing and the share of personal expenditure devoted to it are likely to keep pace with changes in living standards; indeed their rate of growth may well exceed that of other forms of consumption. Reductions in building costs there may be, but not reductions in the cost of a house. However, the evolution of housing standards is not a smooth and continuous process; it has been shown that the flow of investment into this sector of the economy is directed and diverted, hastened and checked, by war and peace, by government policies on rents, taxation and other matters, and by the vagaries of the institutions through which the flow proceeds. Thus progress is likely to be uneven.

The size and quality of new housing move upwards after major wars and then decline and stagnate for a considerable time. (See Figures 4 and 5.) Fortunately we do not have to wait for another war before a new advance can be made; for war and the advancement of housing standards are linked by an intervening factor – the mobilization of the will to meet needs – and there is no reason why peace should be allowed for ever to emasculate this capacity for political mobilization. Figure 4, which shows changes in the average size of subsidized three-bedroom houses in England between 1920 and 1960 suggests the time has arrived for a new advance. Indeed there are signs that it is already beginning. Figure 5* shows the minimum standards prescribed for new working class housing in 'model' buildings erected in London before 1918 and in official handbooks since then. It shows the impact made by the two world wars. It shows, too, that larders, sinks, bathrooms, lavatories, passageways, storage space, and other extensions designed to accommodate a rising standard of living have expanded more quickly than the space provided in living rooms and bedrooms. The widening margin between living and floor areas provides an indication of the rising quality of these houses and the equipment incorporated in them. It would be very surprising if this century-old trend did not continue; the Parker Morris Report calls for more spacious housing, but it also calls for better design, more built-in storage space and a more generous provision of plumbing and other fittings, all of which would sustain the trend.

While it seems intuitively obvious that housing standards and costs will in the long run keep pace with the general advance in living standards and costs, reliable studies and international comparisons documenting this observation have run into difficulties over temporary and local factors (including subsidies, shortages, rent controls, building controls and changes in personal incomes) which interrupt and confuse the trends. Also there are differences in the definitions of housing costs used in each country – particularly in dealing with the owner-occupier who is regarded both as saving (in repaying his loan) and as spending (through his payments for interest, insurance, repairs and maintenance). As a normal rule, by endeavouring to

*Both these figures are based on data prepared by the Building Research Station. See Vera Hole, 'Housing Standards and Social Trends', *Urban Studies*, November 1965.

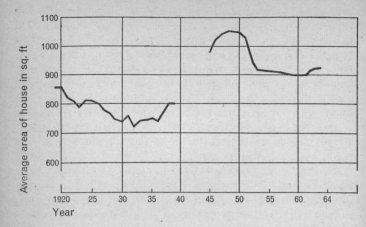

Figure 4. Average floor areas of three-bedroom houses built under subsidy in England

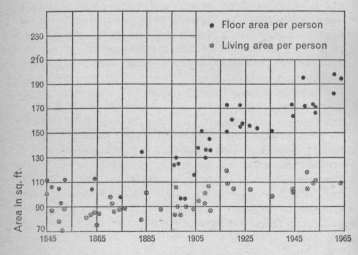

Figure 5. Recommended space standards for minimum family houses

exclude the element of saving, the definitions used in this and other countries greatly under-estimate the sums house buyers actually pay month by month for the right to occupy their houses. The issue is further confused by taxation on housing which is normally excluded from such comparisons – although, since it cannot be avoided, it should properly be regarded as a part of the price of shelter. The omission of tax and tax relief from estimates of housing expenditure can produce misconceptions and hardship. In this country rent controls have permitted the rates levied on poorer households to increase to levels that would otherwise have been politically intolerable. Thus a large share of the revenue of which landlords were deprived as a result of rent control coupled with inflation was not retained by tenants but diverted to local authorities. (It was no accident that the Allen Committee had to be established to study 'The Impact of Rates on Households'* six years after the 1957 Rent Act began breaking up the rent freeze. The Committee found the worst hardships in London where rents, house prices and rates had all risen fastest.) It would therefore be best to examine *all* the costs people have to meet if they are to occupy a house, pay the taxes on it, and heat, light and furnish it to the standard customary in their country and their social class.

One attempt to make such a comparison,† still bedevilled by the difficulties posed by house-buyers, shows that for countries in western Europe and north America the 'total costs of housing', including some of the costs directly associated with living in a house, took an approximately constant share of consumption expenditure as national incomes rose between 1950 and 1960. Comparisons *between* countries showed that the proportion of expenditure devoted to housing in this wider sense was generally higher in the richer countries than in the poorer countries. *Within* any given country, rent and rates generally take an appreciably larger share of expenditure from the poorest households than from the richest. In Britain, in 1961–63, 'housing

*Cmd 2582, 1965.
†Michel Baise, 'Comparaison internationale des dépenses d'habitation', Centre de Recherches et de Documentation sur la Consommation, Paris, *Annales*, 1964, No. 3.

costs', including rate payments, averaged 27 per cent of income for households with under £312 a year, and with rising income this proportion fell steadily to 6 per cent for households with £1,560 a year and over.* But a growing body of evidence, mainly from the United States, suggests that a lasting growth in incomes which is expected to continue for the foreseeable future generally leads, both for the nation and for groups within the population, to the spending of larger sums and a similar or larger proportion of income on housing.†

These conclusions are supported by the Rowntree Study findings reported in the previous chapter. People do not set up house or move simply because they can afford it or find a bargain – as they go off for the weekend on the proceeds of a premium bond prize, or buy detergent at '4d. off'. Housing decisions are taken at particular stages in their lives for more fundamental reasons such as marriage, a change of job, and the growth or decline of families. The price of housing may help to determine how soon they can make such moves, and then becomes important as a secondary factor, determining which of several houses people choose to go to. If the general development of the economy encourages people to expect a secure and rising income they are more likely to marry early, to have their children early, and to take risks in moving to new jobs; and those who lend them money or rent housing to them will be more confident of their ability to make continuing and higher payments in future. Thus housing expenditure will be related to longer-term future expectations about income.

Even the resources devoted to improving older housing – which are often expected to fall as the present campaigns for improvement and slum clearance extend to meet each other from opposite ends of the quality range – may in fact continue at a high or rising level. 'Improvement' now typically provides a bath, lavatory and hand basin, but people will soon become increasingly dissatisfied with more modern houses, thousands of which are still being built without central heating, garages or

* Cmd 2582, p. 77.

† For example, Margaret Reid, *Housing and Income*, University of Chicago Press, 1962; and various reports from Centre de Recherches et de Documentation sur la Consommation, Paris; e.g. *Annales*, 1964, No. 3.

proper storage space, and they may spend more on improvements, possibly with decreasing support from public funds.

It follows that this country will in future spend more, and probably spend a rather larger proportion of its income, on better and more expensive housing – provided that government policies for building, lending, subsidies, taxation and rents are designed to encourage this development. This process will make increasing demands on the building industry, but it may also help to increase savings if people are offered sufficiently attractive opportunities of setting aside money for their housing. Plainly it is among the richer households and among those with secure and rising incomes that there will be greatest scope for increasing payments without hardship. The two factors of current wealth and future expectations must be carefully distinguished: a household including four earners between the ages of eighteen and twenty-four has a high but exceedingly insecure income which is likely to fall before long to the level which these younger earners' parents can maintain unaided.

These conclusions prompt the question: 'What proportion of their income should people devote to the costs of their housing?' – a popular but ineptly posed conundrum for which some correspondingly inept solutions have been proposed. Its very phrasing overshadows any discussion with unspoken but weighty prejudices about the sanctity of the home and the virtues of paying rent which generate more heat than light. People seldom ask: 'What proportion of the family's income *should* be devoted to food? . . . to clothing? . . . to medical care?' although these commodities are at least as important as housing. They know very well that the needs of different families vary and no generally valid answer could be given to such a silly question. It makes better sense to ask what proportion of the *national* income should be devoted to capital investment in housing or to 'occupation costs' – provided the latter includes all the costs directly and unavoidably associated with the occupation of a house. But the outline given in the previous chapter of the way in which needs change at different phases of people's 'housing histories', makes it clear that the nation's expenditure on housing is likely to vary from time to time, for varying proportions of households will at different times be found in any

particular phase.* For individual households any reckoning
based on the income of the household or its principal earner is
likely to be misleading. A study of the household's income per
head throws more light on the problem.

Surveys of family expenditure carried out by the Ministry of
Labour show that the total income of the household is a poor
guide to housing expenditure but the head of household's
income is a better one, at least within any particular region and
tenure group. Likewise, within tenure groups, the households
with children spend more on housing than is spent by those
without children, but the number of children they have makes
little difference: indeed, married couples with four or more
children spend less in rent – though probably more on repairs
and maintenance – than families with fewer children: their
average income is lower, and their income per head much
lower. Yet local authorities which have introduced differential
rent and rebate schemes to ensure that such families do not have
to pay more than a modest proportion of *household* income in
rent have too often left them, when their rent is paid, with less
to live on than the National Assistance Board would have
provided before adding a rent allowance. Confronted with a
problem of budget balancing that would daunt the most skilled
housewife and economist, some of these families naturally have
difficulty in paying even a reduced rent. One of several studies
dealing with this problem shows that many council tenants in a
sample of unreliable rent payers in Southampton had incomes
falling below the Assistance Board's scales – well over half the
children in the sample must have been living below the standard
the National Assistance Board would have provided. The
author concluded that these families tend to be 'weak and
immature', and 'have poor powers of concentration and easily
turn to petty delinquency',† though he did not say whether these
characteristics were cause or effect of their poverty. This is not a
problem that afflicts only the most poverty-stricken. An extensive analysis of food consumption and nutritional standards in
this country, covering the period between 1950 and 1960, shows

---

*See Figure 1, pages 22–9.

† W. B. Harbert, 'Who Owes Rent?', p. 149. *Sociological Review*,
July 1965.

that despite a general improvement in every income group there had been an appreciable deterioration in the diet of families with three or more children – even among families well above any poverty line.* The general increase in housing expenditure which took place during this period, hastened and welcomed by people who think in terms of household incomes rather than incomes per head, must have contributed to this outcome. Old age pensioners, whose housing costs have been restricted to a much greater degree by rent controls, and whose rents are more frequently covered by allowances from the National Assistance Board, achieved a general improvement in diet over the same period despite their greater poverty.

SPECIFICATIONS FOR PROGRESS

Those who persist in asserting that people 'should' spend a particular proportion of their incomes on rent will either prevent the appreciable growth in housing expenditure and investment this country should now be capable of, by restricting rent–income ratios to a level designed to protect the poorer and larger families, or they will bring about a growth in housing costs that will inflict severe hardship on some people. They should instead be asking how to place the burden of an increase in housing expenditure upon those best able to bear it; and how best to help those who are already paying so much for their housing that they have difficulty in keeping all members of their family properly fed and clothed. The problem is not an easy one to solve, but we have not allowed it to defeat progress in the fields of education and medical care and it should not prove insoluble in the field of housing. If we cannot go a long way towards solving these problems in the housing field, then there is no hope of sustaining an output of 500,000 houses a year. For an output of this order, if it is to continue for long, must be directed to meeting the needs of many of the poorer families who are now worst housed, not out of any concern for social justice, but simply because the demand for so large a programme can be mobilized in no other way.

*R. Lambert, *Nutrition in Britain*, Occasional Papers on Social Administration, No. 6, Codicote Press, 1964.

The government already pays large sums, in subsidies, allowances and tax foregone, to help people meet the costs of their housing. If these sums were appropriately distributed, it should be possible to ensure that people can afford the housing they need without calling for an increase in government contributions that would outpace the general rate of growth in central and local government revenues. In 1960 the government was subsidizing housing in the following ways.

SUBSIDIES FOR HOUSING IN THE UNITED KINGDOM, 1960

	(Millions of pounds)
Approximate proportion of National Assistance allowances attributable to rent	£35m.
Exchequer subsidies on local authority housing	£89m.
Rate-borne subsidies on local authority housing	£31m.
Tax reliefs in respect of payments of mortgage interest, ground rent, and insurance premiums related to house purchase: approximately	£210– 220m.
Grants towards building of private houses, improvement grants, and other capital grants to private sector	£12m.

The first item in this table is a notional one, and some people would put it much higher. Since many people who drew National Assistance – old people who had moved to council bungalows, for example – were only compelled to seek assistance because of the rent increases they had to meet, it might seem appropriate to regard all their allowance as a housing subsidy. But it would be inappropriate to single out one item in their expenditure and say this had first call on their allowance; the proportion of assistance devoted to rent has therefore been assumed to be the same as the proportion of family expenditure devoted to housing costs among households in the lowest two income groups (all under £6 per week) identified in Ministry of Labour surveys of family expenditure. The actual proportion of assistance devoted to rent will almost certainly be higher than this.

In 1960 the government was spending money or foregoing revenue in ways that helped people meet their housing costs on a scale that amounted to between £350 and £400 millions a year. But the items listed in the table are of such different types that it would be a mistake to place too much weight on the precise total involved. (It could be argued, for example, that part of the benefit of tax relief is lost through the inflation of house prices.) Nevertheless the sums involved are very large, and they have since risen considerably, though later figures are not available.

To furnish an approximate notion of the scale of these transfers, they may be compared with government current expenditure at that date of about £800 million on health services, £650 million on education, and £1,600 million on defence. These resources were devoted to purchasing goods and services, whereas housing subsidies were a transfer of incomes from one group to another. More comparable, perhaps, are family allowances, national insurance benefits, national assistance and war pensions which together amounted to £850 million during the same year.

Government subsidies for housing should be contrasted with the other expenditures mentioned in another respect: whereas resources devoted to other purposes were distributed in a reasonably systematic fashion to attain prescribed objectives, those devoted to housing were the product of a variety of devices, practices and policies which were never conceived as a consistent or comprehensive programme. This is the outcome of Britain's failure to reappraise the objectives of housing policy and the resources deployed in this field during the wartime and immediately post-war years. If our health services and our social insurance and assistance systems had been allowed to grow piecemeal, without the reforms that took place between 1945 and 1948, they would now present a similarly incoherent picture.

Subsidies on council housing are often distributed in illogical ways, both between and within local authorities. The generous subsidies often given to the tenant of new council housing are financed partly by repeated rent increases levied on older council property. But it is the authorities with the largest stock of older houses built before and immediately after the last war who have been able to take advantage of this opportunity, and they are not necessarily the authorities with the greatest needs.

Yet within the confines of this imperfect system many authorities make an attempt – inadequate though it often is – to levy rents with some regard to their tenants' rent-paying capacity. The distribution of subsidies within the owner-occupied sector works in the opposite fashion, awarding greatest benefits to households with the highest incomes, the fewest dependants, the most expensive houses, and the largest proportions of 'unearned' income – and to those selling houses to such people.

This system is not well equipped for the period, now beginning, in which rapidly increasing proportions of a growing building programme must be devoted to the replacement of obsolete property and to providing houses for the oldest and youngest households, the single, the widowed and divorced, and for a small but growing number of larger families. The incomes of many of these people are bound to be low, unpredictable, or of brief duration. If houses are to be provided for them it follows that the security for the loans required for this purpose must be found in the property and its long term rent-earning capacity, not in the income expectations of the first households that live in it.

Local authorities will have to provide an increasing share of the new building, and must also acquire much of the older rented property if it is to be properly maintained and efficiently distributed for the remainder of its life. It is clear, however, that many authorities will have political and administrative difficulties in catering for some of the households that must be provided for: migrants from other parts of the country and from overseas, the young, the single – including rapidly growing numbers of students – and the middle class groups who must be attracted to the redeveloped and renewed central areas of bigger cities if such areas are to secure an adequate supply of teachers, doctors, administrators and social workers and have the kind of social diversity which ensures variety and a continued flow of private investment in new building and modernization. Even if local housing authorities were capable of housing all these people, and the people concerned were willing to become council tenants, there may be political objections to a trend that would give the authorities a monopoly of housing over large areas of our cities. Other forms of collective owner-

ship must therefore develop alongside council housing.

For the older parts of our towns that will require replacement and renewal over the next twenty years it may be found necessary to establish publicly accountable corporations capable of acquiring and improving property, and gradually redeveloping it. They could distribute leases among an appropriate mixture of local authorities, housing associations, and owner-occupiers. Such corporations, with members nominated by the Minister in consultation with municipal councils, could be set up within towns much as New Town Corporations were set up to build in the countryside. They could assume responsibility for the efficient management and redevelopment of particular areas, leaving local authorities or the central government to provide subsidies for individual households in need of them. This is what the Milner Holland Committee may have had in mind when it called for 'areas of special control' where

some authority might be set up, with responsibility for the whole area and armed with wide powers to control sales and lettings, to acquire property by agreement or compulsorily over the whole area or large parts of it, to demolish and rebuild as necessary, to require improvements to be carried out or undertake such improvements themselves, and to make grants on a more generous and flexible basis than under the existing law.*

Housing associations of various kinds building for 'cost rent' or 'co-ownership' schemes have now been freed from the tax handicaps which at first prevented them from competing effectively with owner occupation, and may in time secure from the new Housing Corporation and from the more friendly local authorities the leadership and recognition required to create and sustain a momentum of development. But the growth of these predominantly small bodies is bound to be slow and halting until a nationwide organization is available both at central and regional levels to provide the professional skills, the managerial talent and the capital they require.

Owner occupation can be developed to serve a much wider range of income groups if help equivalent to the tax privileges now available to wealthier buyers can be provided for

*Cmd 2605, pp. 122–3.

households with lower incomes. Various schemes for achieving this have recently been advanced.* Meanwhile, further steps will have to be taken, both to protect the poorer house-buyers from the risks of heavy repair bills to older property, and to eliminate the unnecessary costs and complications of house purchase. House purchase, said the *Economist* recently,

has become the bread and butter of the ordinary solicitors' business – with the butter spread pretty thick . . . Briefly, the case against (their) conveyancing monopoly, and particularly against the scale fees, rests on the utter simplicity of the majority of transactions, especially where the title is registered at the Land Registry. Any solicitor who is honest about it will admit that this is merely a matter of form filling normally left to his clerk.†

But although owner occupation can be extended, there are severe limits to its scope. Rowntree and Social Survey studies previously quoted show that the majority of those who want to move – and one fifth of those who actually buy houses – would prefer to rent if they could only find adequate housing in that way. Already, in order to reduce the annual costs of house purchase, some building societies are extending their borrowers' periods of repayment to twenty-five years, thirty years, or even longer. Purchase with the aid of such a loan does not differ greatly from tenancy; yet it is in practice even more severely restricted to the youngest households with secure income expectations than are purchases that take place over shorter periods. In these circumstances it would often be better to vest the ownership of houses in a housing association repaying its loans over forty years, and rent them to the wider variety of households who could then afford to occupy them. Such associations could in time make a valuable contribution towards housing the more mobile young and single people and the oldest households. Many in both groups will have reasonably adequate incomes but no hopes of securing – or no wish to secure – a council house or a home of their own.

The need for a rationalization and nationalization of housing subsidies has been repeatedly stressed. But how can this be

*See, for example, A. J. Merrett and Allen Sykes, *Housing Finance and Development*, Longmans, 1965.
†The *Economist*, 26 June 1965.

achieved? Della Nevitt, in her study *Housing, Taxation and Subsidies*, proposes that council houses should be rented at a price that would enable each authority to cover its debt charges and management costs without subsidy from the rates or the exchequer. Council tenants and private tenants would then be entitled to 'housing allowances' that would be designed to ensure that their gross incomes were still sufficient to pay an approved rent after deducting the cost of a defined level of consumption that would depend on the size of the family. These housing allowances could be subject to maxima of some kind that would incorporate regional variations. This would in effect turn local housing authorities into something more like public utility companies, responsible – like the gas boards and electricity boards – for providing the best service they can. They would impose some rational order of priorities in the selection of tenants, but leave the central government to determine, through its housing allowances, how much help each tenant had in paying his rent.

The owner-occupier's tax reliefs could not be drastically re-shuffled at short notice lest many people find their precariously balanced budgets upset by the unforeseen withdrawal of these privileges. But a maximum could at once be imposed on the tax relief allowed in respect of mortgage interest. (The Australians have always had such a maximum, though in their case tax relief is only available where house purchase is financed in conjunction with life assurance policies.) After a stated date the whole system could be revised in a way that eliminated the present tax reliefs for future house purchasers, and replaced them with tax reductions, and an annual grant for those too poor to pay tax, which would give greatest help to those with lower incomes and larger families, concentrating this help in the early years of repayment when it is usually most urgently needed. (West Germany has long had a system of this kind.) Help for house buyers should be organized on a basis that is comparable to that provided for tenants and members of housing associations – and publicly recognized as being comparable. Otherwise, as owner occupation spreads, governments will always be tempted to award additional benefits to owner occupiers while neglecting tenants – particularly if house buyers, and would-be

buyers, are more strongly represented in the marginal constituencies, as they appear to be.

If the total sum devoted by government to helping people
meet their housing costs (£350–400 million in 1960) could all be
redeployed to finance this scheme, and if part of the burden were
borne by a more general 'income guarantee' which raised the
incomes of the poorest households without regard to housing
costs, there would be no shortage of resources to finance these
proposals. But neither of these conditions is likely be to realized
in the near future. The introduction of the scheme would
therefore have to be more gradual, and resources for it would
have to be found in several quarters; the government's proposal
for converting the rating system into a more progressive tax,
the proposals made by Merrett and Sykes* for redistributing
mortgage repayments in a manner that would bear more heavily
in the later period of the loan, the redistribution of subsidies for
council tenants in a manner that would assist those in greatest
need – these are among the devices that could be used while a
more general reorganization of tax reliefs and the social security
system was taking shape.

Since the government already subsidizes house buyers generously, a return should be secured for this expenditure in the
form of better designed and better built housing, and hence in a
postponement of future replacement programmes. Now that
the extent of the subsidies provided for this form of building is
recognized it should be possible for government gradually to
insist upon a much wider acceptance of Parker Morris standards,
modular coordination, guarantees of quality, and other advances
that have been talked about for many years.

The exponents of a general system of housing allowances
that would help the private as well as the public tenant have not
always grasped that the corollary of their argument is a system
of rent regulation that must continue for as long as the private
landlord survives. Landlords must draw some benefit from
their tenants' allowances, since the purpose of such a scheme is
to enable poorer households to compete more effectively in the
housing market, and hence to make it more profitable than
hitherto to rent accommodation to them. But in areas of shortage

* A. J. Merrett and Allen Sykes, op. cit. p. 361.

landlords might be able to raise the rent of tenants entitled to an allowance and secure all the benefit conferred without providing anything in return, and that would not be a productive way of distributing public funds.

A general system of rent regulation is now being established but its objectives deserve some clarification. The regulation of rents imposed by Parts I and II of the 1965 Rent Act should be distinguished from Part III, which protects tenants' security of tenure and outlaws intimidation and other abuses by landlords. Part III applies to all tenants, public and private, furnished and unfurnished, controlled, regulated or decontrolled, and it should go far to establish responsible codes of behaviour in the management of rented housing.

Rent regulation is a more selective instrument, designed initially to deal with decontrolled unfurnished tenancies, other than the most expensive ones, and to restrain the more destructive effects of severe shortages. These shortages are created when the growth of employment and population outpace the growth of housing in centres where land scarcities and planning controls prevent a sufficient increase in the supply of housing. Discrimination, by private and public owners alike, against particular groups of the population – such as migrants and coloured people – may then impose hardships on such groups in the restricted corners of the market where they are able to secure a foothold. Complete decontrol of rents in face of such shortages inflicts entirely pointless hardships which produce no solution or improvement. In every other country this has been recognized by procedures which have varied the extent and pace of decontrol according to the degree of shortage in the areas concerned.

But regulating rents does not mean freezing them. Where good houses are plentiful and supply and demand are already in balance and in places within areas of shortage where there is such a balance – typically the most expensive property – rents must be freely determined. Regulation is only designed to ensure that other rents which are subject to special scarcities are rationally related to those that are freely determined. If a purpose-built, centrally heated flat, standing in an attractive London neighbourhood, commands an annual rent of fifteen shillings per square foot, then a self-contained house, without central heating or bath, standing in a clean but unfashionable street, should command a lower rent; and two rooms opening off a landing in a house that stands in a sleazy quarter should command a yet lower rent. The fact that rents per square foot in our bigger cities do not follow this orderly pattern, and may actually be higher in the worst property than the best, is a measure of the scarcities operating in particular sectors of the market, and of the continuing distortions imposed by old-style rent controls.

Unlike rent *control*, which was designed to freeze a market, thus eventually depriving its prices of any systematic or constructive meaning, rent *regulation* is designed to recreate a market in which the over-all pattern of prices responds to changes in supply and demand, while the local impact of severe and abnormal scarcities is kept within bounds. The general scarcity of housing throughout London being greater than the general scarcity throughout Birmingham, the whole pattern of rents should be higher in London than in Birmingham, just as Birmingham's rents will be generally higher than Oldham's, where the general level of scarcity is less severe still. But *within* each of these cities, differences in rents should represent differences in the value of the accommodation offered. The hardships such a change will inflict upon some tenants must be mitigated by government through housing allowances or other means, not by reductions in rent.

The first task of those responsible for regulating rents is to bring down some of the highest to a level that is rationally related to those that are freely determined in the open market. Their second task, when Parliament calls upon them to assume it, must be to help raise controlled rents to the same rational levels. It is this second phase which will be the most important numerically and the most difficult politically. In parts of the north of England and in other places where there is practically no shortage of housing, regulated rents may not differ greatly from controlled rents, for controlled rents of the older houses in these areas may not be far from the open market level for such property. But in areas of shortage, controlled rents will rise considerably. At the time the 1965 Rent Act was passed, few commentators grasped that it is in the longer run a measure for the raising rather than the lowering of rents. The second phase of its operation may never be brought into effect in areas of shortage unless a general system of housing allowances is first introduced to protect the poorer tenants involved.

It has been argued throughout this chapter that the new housing programme cannot succeed without a major redistribution of incomes that will enable poorer people to pay for the housing they need. How extensive this redistribution will have to be depends upon the general pattern of incomes throughout the population. Even if promptly put into force, the Labour Party's proposals for a radical reorganization of pensions and social insurance would not come into full effect for many years, since it takes many years for new and more generous pension schemes to mature. To cover the intervening period and fill the gaps such schemes would leave, the Party proposed a comprehensive scheme of redistribution that would adopt the principles and procedures of our progressive system of income tax but extend them downwards, below the tax-free level, to provide a progressively increasing annual grant for the poorest of households, just as a progressively increasing levy is now taken from the richest households. At the time of writing it appears that this scheme may have been abandoned. If it were introduced it would mainly benefit pensioners – particularly the oldest among them – together with smaller groups such as the widowed and physically handicapped. These are the poorest people in the country. Many of them already pay low rents. If a new and comprehensive system of housing allowances was subsequently added, this would mainly benefit families with several children, dependent on relatively low wages and requiring relatively large and well-equipped housing. Neither scheme would be sufficient without the other: housing costs vary so greatly from region to region and between houses of different age, size and tenure, that no 'minimum income guarantee' could enable everyone to pay the higher rents or prices that good housing standards demand. Likewise, no matter how generous a comprehensive system of housing allowances was, it could make no impact on the severe poverty found among older people and others paying very low rents.

In a rational world, the formulation of these two schemes

would be closely coordinated and a general redistribution of income would be introduced first, closely followed by a system of housing allowances that would 'top up' incomes for selected households during the, generally temporary, periods when their housing needs outpaced their capacity to pay. But in the world we actually inhabit, the defence of the pound is likely to be given priority over the needs of pensioners for many years. Ministers responsible for housing are likely to be regarded as senior to those responsible for pensions and may wield greater influence in the cabinet, and interdepartmental coordination of policies and legislative programmes is likely to remain difficult.

Redistributions of income designed for housing purposes may therefore take precedence over more general redistributions designed to eliminate poverty. In the longer run this may be a mistake – even for housing purposes. But recent proposals for a reform of the rating system, which would take account of the ratepayers' incomes and dependants and make rate payments a little more like income tax, hold out hopes of progress, not because the rates are a sensitive instrument for redistributing income – they are an exceedingly crude instrument – but because they exert an extensive influence on the incomes of households in all types of property, rented and owner-occupied, public and private. They also fall within the sphere of administration for which the Minister of Housing and Local Government is responsible. For these somewhat accidental reasons, further reforms of the rating system may offer the most effective means of enabling people to pay for the housing they need. But they will not achieve this unless tenants who pay their rates with their rent are as successful in securing reductions to which they are entitled as are other households who pay their rates separately.

The proposals made in the latter part of this chapter are frankly partisan. Their purpose is not to propagate particular views so much as to focus attention upon problems which will have to be resolved, in one way or another, if the ambitious objectives of the government's present policies are to be realized. This is why potential objections and obstacles to these proposals have not been considered in detail. Better proposals can doubtless be devised; but anyone tempted to dismiss plans of this general character as Utopian fantasies should bear in mind that he is also dismissing the government's housing programme. If this country cannot find ways of enabling many more slum dwellers, old people and poorer families to get good housing, while at the same time securing an appreciably larger contribution to housing costs from the many other households capable of paying more, there is no prospect whatever of sustaining a continuous and predictable building programme of the size to which the government is now publicly committed.

Even if the financial reorganization required for such a programme can be achieved, many other problems of administration, design and construction will remain to be solved before the houses can actually be built. These problems are examined in the next chapter.

THE HOUSING PROGRAMME

PREVIOUS chapters have traced the recent course of this country's housing policies, described the complex housing market over which the government now finds itself presiding, and discussed the forces that have created this system and the directions in which they are likely to lead in the future. This chapter deals in more concrete and practical terms with some of the problems that will have to be resolved by those administering housing policies. The government's intention of building half a million houses a year by 1970 was loosely described in the previous chapter as a 'housing programme'. But a great deal remains to be done before a sustained output of this order can be achieved, relied upon, distributed to those for whom it is intended – and properly described as a 'programme'. In a market economy, solutions for the financial problems considered in the previous chapter are the starting point for progress in other directions. But they are only a starting point. A continuing flow of land, appropriate for building and available in the right places throughout the country, is an essential requirement to be considered in the next chapter. This chapter deals briefly with other problems, each of which would merit a book on its own.

It begins by examining some of the implications of the government's objectives, dealing with the distribution of building for different purposes, in different regions and at different points in time. The discussion of the different phases of a household's history, already begun in Chapter 7, is taken a stage further in order to throw light on the problems posed by the attempt to provide housing that accords more closely with people's needs – problems of design and layout, and the problems that will arise in selecting tenants for the growing public sector of the housing market. The planning and management of new building operations and the replacement of obsolete housing are briefly considered. It is argued that new procedures will be required for identifying and distinguishing the hardships caused by slums, by overcrowding and mismanagement of housing, and by the decay of obsolete neighbourhoods. The final and longest section of the chapter deals with the evolution of the house building industry and the contribution that government can make to the industry's future development. A discussion of the research that will be required to plan and sustain progress in these fields might also have found a place here, but that has been postponed to Chapter 11 which deals more generally with inquiry and innovation.

To consider so wide a variety of questions in so short a space will inevitably prove frustrating to readers seeking a conclusive analysis of any one of them. The purpose of this discussion, however, is not to present a complete prescription for a housing programme but to identify the principal questions on the agenda of those who are called upon to plan such a programme, to show how these questions are related to each other – and here and there to press the discussion of these points a little further than has hitherto been attempted.

THE CHANGING NEEDS TO BE MET

It was argued in the previous chapter that about 100,000 houses a year would be required during the next few decades to cater for the growth in Britain's population and for changes in its demographic structure. About 50,000 a year might be required to reduce sharing and increase the number of empty houses. If this country is to build half a million houses a year, most of the rest must be devoted to increasing headship rates (35–90,000 a year) replacing obsolete housing (215–270,000 a year) and making good the effects of other demolitions and conversions (30,000 a year). It was pointed out that this programme differs radically from the pattern to which we have been accustomed – a pattern producing, during the past five years, an average of about 320,000 homes a year in Britain, of which some 70,000 a year have been devoted to slum clearance. But the implications of such a programme for those who will design and build the houses and manage the whole process and the distribution of the programme through time and space have yet to be considered.

Since the great majority of married couples now have a home of some kind, much of the increase in 'headship rates' must take place among the single, the widowed and divorced – particularly, that is, among the youngest and oldest people. During the next five years there will be a big increase in the number of marriages: the number of women in the United Kingdom getting married (for the first time) is expected to rise from 290,000 in 1963 to 328,000 in 1969, as the big generation born immediately after the war moves into the household-forming age groups. After that there will be a fall in the number of marriages until 1975, and then a new increase begins which will continue for the fore-seeable future.* Thus the best chance of replacing the slums and of improving the housing opportunities of younger and older people will occur in the mid 1970s. But the geographical distribution of both these parts of the programme will present complex problems.

Additional young households must be expected to form in the most rapidly growing centres of employment – particularly in the more central parts of the London and West Midland regions. The growing numbers of older households formed among the widowed and divorced will be more widely scattered – like building for older people in general. There are signs that the elderly tend to drift westwards and southwards to the warmer fringes of the country, but most of the houses built for older people must stand within reach of the areas where they now live. At present, large numbers are found in the more central urban areas where many will be rehoused in the course of slum clearance programmes. But in future the proportion of old people will rise in the middle ring of owner-occupied suburbs built around many cities during the 1930s.

The progress of the replacement programme prompts similar questions and different answers. The next fifteen years of clearance will have to be concentrated mainly in the north: particularly in Liverpool, Glasgow and the towns of Lancashire, the West Riding and Durham, with large patches elsewhere – in South Wales, the Potteries, London and the Birmingham conurbation – and lesser ones in every part of the country.

*Central Statistical Office, 'Projecting the Population of the United Kingdom', *Economic Trends*, No. 139 H.M.S.O., May 1965.

After 1980 the weight of the clearance programme will shift southwards, particularly to the Midlands and Greater London; for replacement must follow in the steps of history, starting with the cities created at the height of the industrial revolution and turning next to the areas built in the last quarter of the nineteenth century and the early years of the twentieth. Replacement brought about by road widening, conversions and general redevelopment will counterbalance these trends to some extent because it will proceed most rapidly in the areas where employment and wealth grow fastest. Although this enormous programme of replacement – larger than any country has contemplated hitherto – may rise to a sustained and predictable national level, local and regional rates of clearance are bound to fluctuate considerably over the years. Moreover the houses demolished in some areas must be replaced in others. Densely packed cities must export part of their population to new centres; and a few smaller towns and villages, originally created to work pits now closed or to serve industries which have moved or declined, will shrink or disappear entirely. Thus the instruments of government responsible for managing this programme must operate increasingly on a regional rather than a local scale.

Meanwhile the fluctuating output required for the new families coming into being, though it seems likely to account for a minority of the total programme over most of the next fifteen years, will cater for the most determined and politically persuasive competitors in the market – the people who *must* find a house if they are to lead a normal life, and those who will most rapidly appear on the television screens if they are evicted or homeless. They will make their needs felt all over the country, but it is in the West Midlands and in the area surrounding London that the influx of younger workers throughout the post-war years has already built in the most rapid rates of future demographic growth and family formation. Scotland, Ulster, the North West, Yorkshire and Humberside will experience slower rates of increase. Fortunately the distribution of these needs goes some way to counterbalance the distribution of building for replacement, helping to maintain a more stable rate of output at the regional level.

A continuing drive to improve older housing will be required alongside the demolition and rebuilding programmes. In 1961, 22 per cent of the households in England and Wales lived in homes without a bath. If the clearance programme were confined entirely to this housing (and was assumed to rise by uniform annual increments from its 1964 rate of 55,000 families rehoused to a rate of 220,000 in 1970, remaining unchanged thereafter) and if no other improvements were made, then it would take until 1981 to provide all these people with baths. But in recent years the number of houses in England and Wales which have had baths installed with the aid of improvement grants has risen, amounting to 41,000 by 1964, and there must be others which are improved without the aid of grants. If the baths installed with the aid of grants are added to these calculations and it is assumed that these improvements continue at the 1964 rate of progress, then the homes without baths would be eliminated by 1978 instead of 1981. These somewhat notional calculations show that a larger programme of improvement should be regarded, not as an alternative to demolition, but as a means of rendering older houses decently habitable during the long years before they are pulled down. If the greatly increased rate of clearance now proposed proves unattainable, the need for improvement will be even greater.

SOME IMPLICATIONS

Some implications of this glimpse of the future should already be clear. If the government's programme is to be realized, a large proportion of the houses built during the next decades must cater for people now living in obsolete property, and for the single, the young and the old. If such people do not get a large share of the new houses built, many of them must be rehoused in older property. Otherwise a building programme of this order cannot be sustained.

It was shown in the previous chapter that many of the houses in a programme of this size and type must be built for collective ownership of some kind – for local authorities and new town corporations, for example, or for companies undertaking mixed commercial and residential redevelopment, or for housing associations and other corporate bodies – because an increasing proportion of the additional households to be catered for are likely to be precluded from buying their own homes by poverty, age, mobility or taste. If a growing share of new building is done for institutions of these kinds, much of it on sites cleared for redevelopment in the older cities, this must affect the work of designers, builders, developers and lenders. Their efforts will be increasingly devoted to large-scale projects, to mixed residential and commercial development, and to complex, high-density projects, incorporating communications, shops, schools and other buildings besides houses. There are signs that these changes are already at work. In the local authorities' programmes the numbers of high flats are increasing, particularly in London and in cities further north where slum clearance and redevelopment are going ahead most rapidly. The density of persons per acre in new housing schemes is rising, and the size of contracts is growing: the proportion of council houses being built in contracts for over 250 rose from 18 to 26 per cent between 1960 and the first quarter of 1965.

As time goes by, the distinctions between architects, town planners, engineers and developers will become increasingly blurred; certainly these professions will have to work in closer collaboration. Despite the problems this may present, the opportunities could be challenging. While most housing is built in suburban, owner-occupied and council estates in which every inch of the site must be divided into separate and equal plots occupied by similar brick boxes, or in equally standardized blocks of flats fitted into any space that small-scale clearance permits, it is not surprising that the best designers and builders seek other work. But in future their attention should be devoted less exclusively to the individual dwelling and confined less closely by conventions imposed by building societies and the by-laws. They will increasingly have to consider the whole urban environment – the neighbourhood, the precinct, and the links to be fostered between people and the city around them. This growth in the scope of their operations need not result in an impersonal, concrete world; but spontaneity, individuality and human scale must be found less in the trappings of the individual dwelling, more in the design and layout of the whole development – particularly in its public places and the communications between them; in shops, schools, pubs and newspaper stalls, in coffee bars and strolling grounds, in the layout of open spaces and the arrangement of trees, lamps and street furniture. To be successful, such work must be based on systematic study and a sociologically sophisticated imagination. Since the war, some of the best designers and builders have been attracted to the cities where building of this scale and type has been done – notably in parts of London, Sheffield, Coventry and the new towns – and there are signs that more of them in future will be drawn into the housing field which need no longer be regarded as a professional backwater.

AGES, STAGES AND NEEDS

The people to be housed will include a growing variety of households, many of them very different from the young families for whom most of our building has hitherto been done. Just how different their needs may be deserves to be stressed, although so little research has been done on these questions that the sharp eye of the novelist still proves as revealing as more conventional instruments of research. The second of the five phases through which most people pass in the course of their 'housing history' (outlined in Chapter 6) begins as the young leave home to set up on their own for the first time. The increasing income and independence of the young, coupled with the growth of higher education and training schemes of many kinds, mean there will be many more small, young and mobile households of this sort. 'Home', to most of them, is still their parents' house. The rooms in which they live provide a place to sleep, to work, to fry an egg, to store belongings and talk with friends – a lair from which to raid the world. An undergraduate's rooms in an Oxford college may be the ideal version of such accommodation, but some of its virtues are found in surprising places. 'The room I inhabit in sunny Napoli', says one of Colin MacInnes's heroes, 'overlooks *both* railways (*and* the foulest row of backyards to be found outside the municipal compost heaps) . . .' And as for the landlord: '. . . if you make any complaint *whatever* – I mean even that the roof's falling in, and the water cut off . . . he does positively sweet b—r-all about it. On the other hand, you could invite every whore and cut-throat in

the city in for a pail of gin, or give a corpse accommodation for
the night on the spare bed, or even set the bloody place on fire,
and he wouldn't turn a hair – or turn one if anybody complained
to him about you. Not if you paid your rent, that is. In fact,
the perfect landlord.' And the neighbourhood? '. . . however
horrible the area is, you're *free* there! No one, I repeat it, no
one, has ever asked me there what I am, or what I do, or where
I came from, or what my social group is . . .'* The voice is
idiosyncratic, but the aspirations are familiar and must in future
be provided for. They are not the aspirations the spec. builders
and the local authorities are accustomed to, and they will call
for fresh thinking about the design, ownership and management
of housing in the years to come – particularly in redeveloped
inner areas which will often be especially suitable for young
people owing to their central locations and high densities.

But this phase does not last. 'Our life is lived between two
homes', as Captain Grimes reflected on the eve of his marriage.
'We emerge for a little into the light, and then the front door
closes. The chintz curtains shut out the sun, and the hearth
glows with the fire of home, while upstairs, above our heads,
are enacted again the awful accidents of adolescence. There's a
home and family waiting for every one of us . . . each of us
unconsciously pregnant with desirable villa residences.'† At the
third stage of this history, home becomes again the centre of
people's lives. Space, privacy and storage room – indoors and
outdoors – baths, hot water, properly equipped kitchens and a
parking space, become urgent necessities. The neighbourhood,
and the accessibility of its schools, doctors, shops, launderettes
and transport services, take on a new importance. If the roof
leaks you can no longer escape by moving; if the woman next
door bangs angrily on the wall you can no longer simply bang
back. You have to live with it – or your wife does – all day. The
security and privacy of this home and the right to go on living
peacefully in it are the foundation of the family's happiness.
It was the needs of such families that the Parker Morris Committee had particularly in mind when making their appeal for

* Colin MacInnes, *Absolute Beginners*, pp. 50–51. MacGibbon & Kee,
1959.
† Evelyn Waugh, *Decline and Fall*, p. 102. Penguin Books, 1960.

better, more spacious and more intelligently designed housing. Three years later, by 1965, only 20 per cent of new council houses fully incorporated these more generous standards; the proportion among private owners, though not precisely known, was also discouraging. If the enlarged building programme gets under way before these standards are generally adopted, the slum problem of the next century will loom larger and nearer than it should. And if the birth rate continues to rise, producing a growing number of larger families along with the growing number of small households, a continuing output of houses confined to the narrow range of sizes now provided will produce an increasingly ill-fitting stock of dwellings. It is not surprising that few of the more successful architects of the day live in houses built since 1918.

As children leave home and wives return to work, the family expands and disintegrates into phase four of its history. The home becomes a sort of hotel, and then an empty hotel, crammed to the roof from time to time in holiday seasons. These changes in the size and needs of the household are exceedingly difficult to accommodate conveniently and efficiently. Just as an airport is never finished – technological change overtaking the designer before the concrete sets – so a home too is never finished: fathers have scarcely completed a bunk for their youngest before starting on a motor cycle shed for their oldest, and before long they have no use for either.

In the fifth phase even greater changes in need occur, affecting not only the size of the house required but also its design, equipment and relation to the surrounding neighbourhood. Home becomes a refuge and the accessible world, inside and outside, shrinks drastically in size. A cupboard handle set too high, a drawer placed too low, mean whole storage spaces lost; a shop or a church too far away – or a change in the public transport routes leading to them – may cut people off from their friends as irrevocably as if they had emigrated to America. A leaking roof becomes a disaster; an unexpected increase in the rates worse still.

Peter Townsend's studies of old people show that supervised 'sheltered housing' is needed for at least 5 per cent of those over the age of sixty-five. It is now provided for 0·6 per cent of them, and by 1969 the government intends to raise this proportion to 2·0 per cent. 'Sheltered housing' consists of specially built flats, bungalows or bedsitting rooms with a warden or housekeeper living within reach, and the minimum 5 per cent assumed by Townsend to be in need of such accommodation were those who are moderately or severely incapacitated, live entirely alone, and have no children living within ten minutes' journey. There were about 300,000 of these people in Britain in 1962, and nearly half of them lived in houses lacking either a bath or a kitchen or an indoor lavatory.* Many more need modern and well-designed housing of a kind suitable for less handicapped elderly people. Meanwhile many of those living in residential institutions are reluctantly compelled to seek refuge there by the scarcity of sheltered housing of more independent kinds. 'I wanted a flat but I didn't stand a chance,' said an elderly spinster; 'Landladies don't like you when you're old and not at business in the day.' 'I can do everything for myself,' said an Irishman of eighty two. 'I've never had a day in bed except when I've taken bad after the beer,' but 'unless you've got relations an old fellow like me can't get lodgings.'†

To render our over-standardized – and increasingly standardized – housing better fitted to the variety of human needs, three solutions must be pursued. The first lies in providing a greater variety of house types and sizes. The greatest scarcities are of small housing of the 'lair' and 'refuge' types for the young and old, and for those who never marry; but there is also an urgent need for more larger houses with at least four adequately heated bedrooms.

The second solution is to enable people to move easily between one type of housing and another. If people are to move without abandoning jobs, schools and friends, different types of houses will be required within reasonable distances of each other, and new forms of tenure, payment and subsidy must be devised to encourage movement. Our present system might almost have

---

*Peter Townsend and Dorothy Wedderburn, *The Aged in the Welfare State*, Occasional Papers on Social Administration, No. 14, 1965.

† Peter Townsend, *The Last Refuge*, pp. 314 and 316. Routledge & Kegan Paul, 1962.

...en designed to prevent people moving as they grow older. If the proportion of English households moving each year was raised to a level nearer that experienced in the U.S.A., where mobility is about three times as great as our own, the scope for fitting houses to households would be greatly improved. Since the proportion of people in this country who say they want to move house is even larger, this may in time be possible. Townsend's studies suggest that 32 per cent of those over sixty-five and living in private housing would prefer to be in a different kind of dwelling if given the opportunity, and these are the least mobile households in the population.

Nevertheless there will always be many people who do not want to move as their families shrink in size; their accumulated friends and possessions and the pattern of life they have established in their neighbourhood make a move intolerable, and if they can afford to stay where they are no one is entitled to deny them the right to do so. Yet their immobility will waste an increasing amount of house room as the size of family dwellings increases in future, and may impose hardships on them and on others who are denied the use of this space.

A third approach to the problem is needed. If houses are built in a way that makes them easier to subdivide and combine as the needs of the household change, the family can secure additional space as it expands and contract out of it again as its numbers shrink. Long ago the 1944 *Housing Manual*, published by the government for the guidance of local authorities, showed designs for a house with separate but easily combined dwellings on each of two floors; and several countries deliberately encouraged the building of such houses in their post-war programmes – Norway and West Germany, in particular. Similar ideas have been incorporated in the design of flats. In Denmark, for example, blocks of flats have been built for a housing association to a design that permits each floor to be divided in eight different ways – providing two five-room units, or three units of one, two and five rooms, or a variety of other arrangements, by installing or removing plumbing and cooking fixtures and doors for which the necessary services and spaces are already incorporated. But although some thought has been given to these problems in Britain,* little progress has been made in this direction.

To local authorities building family housing to tight cost limits, the small increase in costs implied by such proposals is often unacceptable, and in any case they can move their tenants around more easily than other owners and achieve fuller use of their housing by other means. It is for the owner-occupier that more 'flexible' housing could offer greater advantages, enabling him to get some help with his mortgage payments by letting off a flat, expanding into it as his family grows, and relinquishing it again later to a married daughter, to elderly relatives or to others who need a good but small home. To such people a house in which space can be conveniently subdivided into separate dwellings offers real economies. Significantly, it has been in European countries where building for owner occupation has been most extensively developed that such arrangements appear to have been most popular. But they call for careful design, for more generous space standards and for the sympathetic support of lending institutions.

These proposals deal with new building, but for the vast stock of thinly spread and highly standardized suburban housing already in existence another form of 'flexibility' may be worth considering. It may particularly help the aged, without compelling them to move far from their relatives and take up more scarce land. Most of these suburban houses have reasonably large gardens in which it is now perfectly feasible to build small prefabricated additions of a room or two at modest cost – units that are quickly built, easily removed, yet of excellent quality. Where such additions are made, not to council estates but to owner-occupied property, the planning authority must impose some control on their future use lest they decay into unsightly sheds or garages when the people living in them move or die. But this need not present insuperable problems: ownership of these units might, for example, be vested in housing associations which were entitled to remove any that were no longer occupied and properly maintained. Indeed, local

*e.g. Ministry of Housing and Local Government, *The Adaptable House*, and C. Franck, 'Flexibility in the Planning of Flats', Society of Housing Managers *Quarterly Bulletin*, October 1960.

horities could promote the formation of such associations as a means of meeting the needs of old people. The costs involved would be less than those of providing council bungalows for the same people, and younger relatives would often be willing to bear the loan charges involved. With sufficient collaboration between designers, builders, lenders and planning authorities, these and similar schemes could help to solve the problems posed by the changing needs of individual households and the changing types of household to be housed.

It would be a mistake, however, to pursue the details of such proposals here. The principal problem to which they are addressed can be more simply posed. When Charles Booth and Seebohm Rowntree conducted their first social surveys towards the end of the last century they were able to classify the social composition of each neighbourhood largely by looking at its housing. Housing conditions were differentiated according to the economic and social class of the residents. The account of present housing conditions presented in Chapter 7 shows that this country has gone a long way towards breaking down these distinctions, particularly for the family with young children. But far more thought must be devoted to the problem before housing can be effectively matched to the size, character and needs of the household.

MANAGING THE PROGRAMME

The building programme now envisaged will call for a reappraisal of many aspects of administration and management, particularly at the local level. A large share of future building is likely to be carried out for local authorities and for corporate institutions of various kinds which cater for those who cannot be expected to buy their own housing through traditional forms of mortgage lending. These institutions will depend heavily on the policies and decisions of government. Thus it will become easier for the government to secure effective control of the size, character and distribution of the building programme, even without an increase in the general scope of economic planning. The national and regional output of new building can become increasingly predictable. If these powers are wisely used, there should be greater opportunities for reorganizing and re-equipping the building industry because the risks of investing in new machines and methods can be considerably reduced.

Schemes for the mass-production of a limited range of building components, made in factories and assembled on the site in the manner adopted over much of eastern Europe, offer the greatest economic advantages when long 'runs' can be achieved by building large numbers of houses to standard designs. It is ironical that this country is again trying to 'industrialize' the building of houses at the point when the needs to be met are becoming more diverse and the variety of house types and sizes required is greater than ever before. This by no means precludes the possibility of technical advance in house building, but it does give warning that the advances to be made must afford scope for diversity, and the routes to be followed may be different from those appropriate elsewhere.

Some of the administrative implications of the new housing targets should be explored before turning to the problems of the construction industry. There is little doubt that the industry can build the number of houses now to be asked of it and cope with the even greater problems of demolition and replacement: the total output envisaged is larger than ever before, but the rate of increase is slower than that achieved in recent years. It is much less certain, however, that the legal and administrative machinery of this country and the supply of people qualified to operate it are sufficient to cope with a rate of clearance and building that may rise to levels three times as great as their present ones.

The problem can be illustrated most vividly by examining the history of one project. This was a scheme for the building of 240 flats on less than four acres in a central part of London from which slums had first to be cleared; the architects were exceptionally experienced in work of this sort and well known to the officials concerned, and the buildings were completed without unusual delay at a cost appreciably within the original estimates.* This is how things work when all goes reasonably well.

*For a full account of this project see D. V. Donnison, Valerie Chapman and others, *Social Policy and Administration*, Chapter 9. Allen & Unwin, 1965.

Planning permission for redevelopment on this site was secured from the county planning authority in 1955 and a compulsory purchase order was submitted to the Ministry for approval in June that year; 159 houses and five other buildings were to be acquired. The owners objected for various reasons and a public local inquiry was held to deal with those objectors who could not be 'bought off' by concessions of one kind or another. Fortunately most of the houses belonged to the City of London which made no objection. The compulsory purchase order was confirmed and the site acquired in 1956. The architect's first plans for the site had already been prepared. Several more complete sets of plans were prepared and abandoned after repeated negotiations and disagreements between authorities at Borough, County and Ministry level. A plan was finally approved in July 1957. Since rights of way had to be extinguished under this plan and buildings over 100 feet were to be erected, people occupying neighbouring sites had to be informed and given an opportunity to object. Objections were duly made, another public inquiry was held, the objectors were overruled or bought off with further concessions and the council was given authority to go ahead in October 1958. By then a main contractor had already been chosen after competition among carefully selected builders, tenants of the old houses had already been rehoused, the site was being cleared, and the Ministry had approved the costs of the scheme and sanctioned the raising of the principal loans required.

Building began in January 1959, employing specially designed prefabricated units of a fairly advanced type. Tenants on a neighbouring site then objected to some concessions made to satisfy the leaseholder on another site and a third public inquiry took place –lasting three days and calling for the attendance of Town Clerk, Medical Officer of Health, Housing Manager, Borough Engineer, the architect, a Q.C. and others – resulting in the architect being censured for extending a six foot wall to a height of eight feet and only securing retrospective planning permission for this change. (The wall had been heightened to prevent the tenants' children climbing over into a space secured, in exchange for withdrawing objections about rights of way, by the adjoining leaseholder who hoped to use it as a car park. The space was not in fact used in this way, neither were the children deterred from scaling the wall.) Difficulties followed with the Metropolitan Water Board, which insisted that overflow pipes from storage tanks discharge over the 'head' end of baths because tenants could not be relied on to report defects in the stop cocks if cold water fell only on their feet. After weeks of discussion this requirement was waived. Then shortages of building labour developed, delaying work by some weeks. In March 1960 the Housing Manager asked for changes in the size distribution of the flats because the number of the smallest and largest households to be housed had both increased since the original schedule of accommodation was drawn up and approved in July 1957. Thanks – but only thanks – to the flexibility incorporated in the original design, these changes could be readily made. Tenants were selected before the end of that year and the flats were occupied in the first and second quarters of 1961 while playgrounds and landscaping were being completed.

This was a successful project, without exceptional delays or problems; yet it took six years from start to finish. In building schemes of this kind it is usually the administrative procedures, not the building operations, which constitute the 'critical path' of progress – the phases of the process which determine the minimum time the job requires. Other schemes have taken far longer than this, and some get so bogged down among legal and administrative obstacles that they are abandoned before they ever reach the building stage. The Banwell Committee later recommended many improvements of procedure in its Report on 'The Placing and Management of Contracts for Building and Civil Engineering Work'* (most of which were already adopted in the scheme described here). The Building Research Station and other official bodies are now making studies which may help to speed up the process while preserving necessary safeguards for individual liberty and the rights of property owners.

By-laws, regulations and conventions – about water storage, ventilation and fire-escapes, for example – which were designed for building materials and living patterns that may since have been superseded, are always easier to extend than to simplify.

*Ministry of Public Building and Works, H.M.S.O., 1964.

The cost of incorporating such extensions in buildings tends to increase, and the money available for providing living space and more urgently needed comforts may then be reduced. The by-laws are now being replaced by Building Regulations, framed by the Ministry of Public Building and Works under the Public Health Act of 1961.* These Regulations are designed to prevent hazards to health and safety while leaving builders as much freedom as possible. But many other problems remain to be resolved if a redevelopment programme on the scale now called for is to go ahead, if advances in building productivity are not to be frustrated by administrative delays, and if the energies of those who design and manage such projects are not to be exhausted in contending with the requirements of the planning authorities, the Ministry of Housing, the fire services, the gas board, the trade unions, neighbouring owners and leaseholders and many other bodies. Most of these interests are strongly entrenched and well represented, but the needs of future generations who will actually live in the housing to be built may too easily be forgotten.

When confronted with difficulties of this kind it is always tempting to call for a simplification of administrative procedures but, whatever steps are taken to eliminate unnecessary operations, local government will still have to secure the help of more trained administrators, lawyers, architects, engineers, surveyors and housing managers if it is to cope with a programme of the dimensions now proposed. And if local government cannot cope with the programme, central government may have to set up new agencies to help with the task. The recent creation of the National Building Agency to promote the development and application of industrialized building methods and the national Housing Corporation to promote building by housing associations shows the directions in which these pressures are already leading.

WHAT IS A SLUM?

An attempt to bring about a drastic increase in the rate of replacement must also make an impact on present definitions

* Ministry of Public Building and Works, *Guide to the Building Regulations 1965*, H.M.S.O., 1965.

of slum housing and present procedures for demolishing or closing slums. These definitions and procedures are still based on nineteenth-century legislation designed to control the menace to health presented by the slums of the industrial cities of that day. Although councils are buying an increasing number of technically 'fit' houses for clearance or improvement, the objectives and scale of their replacement programmes still depend mainly on the number of unfit houses they believe their areas contain; and the pace of their progress still depends on administrative, technical and judicial procedures designed to ensure that 'fitness' is justly and accurately defined and owners not unfairly dispossessed of property for which – if it is 'unfit' – they will be paid nothing but the value of the site.

These concepts and procedures are proving increasingly inadequate for several reasons. There is no longer any clear relationship between health, physical or mental, and housing conditions. Rising housing standards and the progress of curative medicine, resulting in the decline of some diseases (such as tuberculosis) and a relative growth in the importance of others (such as cancer and mental illness) have weakened and confused the always uncertain relationship between housing and health – as has been conclusively demonstrated in a recent study made by Dr Martin, Senior Medical Officer to the Ministries of Health, and Housing and Local Government.* In many parts of the country – and in more and more as standards rise in future – the relevant criteria for deciding on the replacement of houses will be those of the surveyor, the housing manager and the economist, not those of the medical officer of health. Public health inspectors already have increasing difficulty in reconciling the divergent objectives involved.

Meanwhile, despite repeated efforts made by the Ministry of Housing and Local Government to persuade local authorities to give more accurate estimates of the numbers of unfit houses in their areas, it is clear that the returns they send in are influenced by all kinds of diverse factors. The Ministry has probably been wise to give up publishing the results of this exercise. Many authorities are reluctant to look beyond the

* A. E. Martin, 'Environment, Housing and Health' (a forthcoming paper).

numbers of slums they are administratively and financially capable of dealing with during the next few years; some are more aggressive and ambitious and return very high figures; others are reluctant to give their cities a bad name, or deterred (in the most expensive areas) even by the site values of the property to be acquired. Their definitions of 'unfitness' follow a closely similar pattern when dealing with property actually acquired for immediate clearance: they have to, because the Ministry's nationwide inspectorate presides over the public inquiries involved and endeavours to make consistent decisions. But the local authorities' estimates of the total number of houses in their areas which are unfit vary without convincing justification. Although, when taken together, they furnish an approximate guide to the regional distribution of the problem, they provide neither a reliable measure of the long-term task confronting each authority nor a reliable measure of the national problem.

The increase in the supply of houses and the fall in the size of households mean that slum property, though damp and decrepit, often provides sufficient space for the people in it. In England it is seldom overcrowded. Meanwhile other property – the prison-like Victorian tenement blocks still found in many cities, and larger houses that have been crudely subdivided – may be structurally sound enough to escape condemnation yet be grossly overcrowded and mismanaged. Corridors, lavatories and bathrooms may be shared in intolerable fashion, and the surrounding district may be so blighted by decay, so overcast by pollution and so deprived of open space that it provides worse living conditions than the 'slums'. The working of the housing market described in Chapter 6, explains why some of the worst housing conditions are now found in subdivided decontrolled property, seldom technically 'unfit', that shelters people excluded from other sectors of the market.

As the general standard of housing improves, conditions that should be regarded as intolerable depend less on the structure and equipment of individual dwellings, more on the way in which housing is used and on the character of the environment in which it stands. The increasing scope of powers given to the local authorities for securing comprehensive redevelopment and for controlling ill-managed property show how the attack on bad conditions is gradually extending beyond the confines of traditional slum clearance procedures.

If the replacement programme is to be greatly enlarged, an increasing number of authorities will find they have cleared all the houses that could properly be described as 'unfit', yet they will not have eliminated bad housing conditions. Thus the extension of the campaign to new fronts will have to go further. If it does not, progress will be blocked. But if clearance continues without a recasting of the concepts and procedures involved, rational direction of the programme will become increasingly difficult, property may be confiscated from owners who deserve more than site value for it, and serious public opposition may follow, striking at the political support on which the whole programme depends.

If a larger replacement programme is to be mounted and sustained, different standards must be employed for different purposes, and information about the numbers of houses and households falling within the categories so defined should be published regularly.

The 'upper' standards should define the minimum housing conditions the nation aspires to achieve, and do this in the form of five separate assessments dealing with:

(a) The structure and condition of housing; its stability, freedom from damp, natural lighting etc.
(b) The equipment and services built into housing; water supply, baths, drainage, heating, artificial lighting, etc.
(c) The quality of the surrounding environment; air pollution, daylight, noise, traffic conditions, play space for children, etc.
(d) The indoor living space available to the household; the ratio of persons to rooms, the provision of adequate bedroom accommodation, etc.
(e) The privacy available to households sharing dwellings; the sharing of kitchens, bathrooms and lavatories, insulation from noise, etc.

Hardship can arise under one or more of these headings. The

formulation of criteria and procedures for assessing the extent
of these hardships is a difficult task, but not an impossible one:
assessments (a) and (b) deal with the dwelling, regardless of its
occupiers; (c) concerns the neighbourhood; (d) and (e) depend
on the relationship between the dwelling and its occupiers –
households of one or two people can without hardship share
dwellings that would be intolerable if shared by families with
several children, for example. How rapidly it will be possible to
eliminate bad conditions of these different kinds must depend on
the resources available, nationally and locally, and on the share of
these resources to be devoted to housing. Whether they be eliminated by demolition and rebuilding, by improvement of the
neighbourhood or its housing, or by redistribution of the people
living in the property, must depend on the character of the local
problem and the solutions preferred by the local authority.
Once these conditions have been distinguished and their
incidence and geographical distribution are known, it should be
possible to press for their elimination while leaving local
communities to choose whether they prefer to achieve this by
tearing down houses or by improving them and managing
them better.

A 'lower' standard, measuring the basic 'fitness for human
habitation' of dwellings, will still be required in some areas for
years to come. It should be a refined version of the present
standard rather than a more ambitious one, constituting the
minimum requirements under assessments (a) and (b) above. It
should clarify a number of points which now produce unnecessary appeals and litigation. Uncertainty about the present criteria
discourages local authorities from condemning houses whose
unfitness may be humanly speaking obvious, but legally speaking questionable. The purpose of the minimum standard would
be to provide as objective a measure as possible (perfection
cannot be achieved) for identifying houses which cannot provide
tolerable living quarters. It must provide clear and comprehensible justification for depriving owners of their property
without compensation (apart from site value) if they continue
to allow it to be so used. Since more and more of the owners
will in future be living in the property themselves, this standard
must be a justifiable minimum (humanly and legally speaking)

and it will provoke opposition and delay if it is fixed too high.

MEASURING NEEDS AND SELECTING TENANTS

Special attention has been given to the criteria to be employed when dealing with the worst housing conditions, but it should be remembered that building for 'general needs' must continue alongside the replacement programme, and much of this will have to be done by local authorities. There is no space here for a thorough discussion of council building programmes, but one aspect of this work must be briefly discussed: the procedures used by the local authorities for assessing the needs to be met and for selecting the tenants they rehouse.

Still relying mainly on 'points' systems of various kinds, most authorities measure the needs to be met by examining the people who happen to surmount the various barriers obstructing the climb to the top of their waiting lists. A period of residence within the authority's boundaries is generally required for entry to the list, but not always; the period may be anything from one to twenty years, or entry to the list may have been altogether closed some years before (by authorities which confuse the tasks of measuring needs and of selecting those who are actually to get houses, employing the same device for both purposes and hence concealing many of the most urgent needs from themselves). Scant attention is paid to the 'foreigners' living across the authorities' boundaries, although some of our largest cities are divided among many authorities and have relatively mobile populations who may be understandably incapable of distinguishing the territory of one authority from that of another. Few, even of the larger authorities, have yet made sufficiently systematic analyses of the changes in household structure to be expected within their own stock of dwellings, and the implications these changes will have for their future building programmes. With rare exceptions, they do not assume the comprehensive responsibility for assessing the needs of their areas which education authorities have assumed in their field. Neither has the central government expected them to do so. As a result, many households of the kinds that will have to be rehoused during the next twenty years do not appear on council waiting lists. The numbers and needs of the young, the single, the migrant and the aged are not at all precisely known. The national housing programme now envisaged cannot take shape until this state of affairs is remedied. If the local authorities prove incapable of doing this, regional bodies may eventually have to be created by government for the purpose.

The situation in Scotland was vividly portrayed in an extensive study, made by R. D. Cramond, of a sample of authorities covering 70 per cent of the Scottish population. He concluded that

many schemes . . . do not enjoy public confidence because allocations are not seen to be made in accordance with definite known rules. . . . People are least able to obtain a council house at the very stage in the household cycle when they most need one, and mobility is inhibited in some areas by discouragement of exchanges, most often between houses in different tenures, but even, in some areas, as between council houses. The answer to the original question – 'who get council houses?' – thus appears to be, 'those who can stay longest in one particular area and those who, by accident or intelligent anticipation, occupy a house which is high on the Council's list for closure or demolition'. Those who stand least chance in areas of shortage are young couples and other persons with small households, especially if they have moved recently from one area to another.*

South of the border the situation is much the same.

To go further in discussing these problems would call for a lengthier analysis of the structure, powers and procedures of local government than can be attempted here. But enough has been said to indicate some of the main questions now calling for exploration, and to show that reforms of the house building industry will be largely wasted if they are not preceded by equally ambitious reforms of the administrative organizations which will be the industry's principal clients.

*R. D. Cramond, *Allocation of Council Houses*, University of Glasgow, Department of Social and Economic Studies, Occasional Papers No. 1, Oliver & Boyd, 1964.

BUILDING HOUSES

Owing perhaps to its size, the high visibility of its operations, and the widespread practice of its simpler skills among a nation of 'do-it-yourselfers', there are few institutions that people generalize about more confidently than the building industry. The construction industry occupies a central place in the economy, employing 1·75 million workers – more than 7 per cent of the country's labour force,* responsible for nearly half the nation's investment. Nearly two-fifths of this investment is devoted to housing. This is not a stagnant industry, as is often alleged: its rate of growth in productivity, amounting for new work to an annual increase of nearly 5 per cent over the past decade, is better than the nation's average. But that advance has been greater in new work than in maintenance and repairs, and greater in industrial building and civil engineering than in house building. The construction industry's methods, organization and materials are changing continuously rather than radically. It includes a very large number of small firms, 70 per cent of them employing fewer than six workers. This is explained by the large amount of small jobs it has to do. No less than a third of its output is devoted to repairs and maintenance, and anyone familiar with life in places (such as the countries of eastern Europe) where small jobbing builders cannot be found knows how vital a contribution they make to a nation's living standards. Meanwhile a quarter of the industry's labour force works in firms employing 500 people or more, and the proportion in these large organizations is rising. The very smallest firms appear to be just about holding their own, despite the rapid turnover among them, and their costs are not unduly high. The larger firms (with over 250 workers) have the highest output per man, and it appears to be the middle sized firms, employing between ten and a hundred workers, whose productivity is lowest.†

Despite its reasonably good record of growth, the industry

*Ministry of Labour, *The Construction Industry*, Manpower Studies No. 3, H.M.S.O., 1965.
†Ministry of Public Building and Works.

makes wasteful use of manpower. Its recruits are found mainly among the young, and it offers apprenticeships of widely varying quality to two thirds of the boys who join, leaving the remainder, and its older recruits, without any systematic training. The industry then loses a great many workers early in life: losses considerably outweigh gains above the age of thirty – twenty years earlier than in most industries – and a large proportion of those who leave have no special qualification for other work. It has a high rate of turnover and far too high a rate of seasonal unemployment. There are big differences between the efficiency of individual building firms, which are due partly to geographical conditions but must be largely explained by differences in the quality of management. These differences are so great that many firms would go out of business (or raise their productivity) if they were not protected from effective competition by excessive demands for building work and by local monopolies of various kinds. A study of house building made by the Building Research Station in 1953 found that the labour expended on the worst contracts was nearly three times as great as that required for the best, and the pattern has not changed much since then. It is in house building that the growth in productivity has since then been slowest.

There has been much talk in recent years about the need for an industrial revolution in the construction industry, leading in some quarters to hopes of a spectacular 'break-through' producing major cost reductions, particularly on the housing front. Such hopes are likely to be disappointed, at least in their more extravagant form. Many countries have devoted years of effort and large sums of public money to this task. But in western Europe, where conditions are most nearly comparable to our own, no country has built houses at appreciably lower cost with the aid of radically new systems – with the possible exception of France where the evidence is not entirely convincing. Industrialized methods have often added to output by bringing additional resources to bear that would not otherwise have been employed in building, and under suitable conditions they have increased the speed at which houses are erected. But the case of Holland, which is well documented, shows the pattern most often experienced: the output of 'system built' dwellings rose steadily in number until the special subsidy paid for them was withdrawn in 1952; production then fell until a new boost was given to system building by offering 'continuous contracts' designed to assure a predictable demand; but as soon as this arrangement came to an end system building flagged once more. During most of this period the houses built under these systems were smaller than traditional houses, yet they always proved more expensive.*

In England and Wales (excluding London County) the proportion of council dwellings built by methods currently classified as 'industrialized' had by 1964 risen to 19 per cent of the total. For houses of all sizes and for low flats of two and three storeys the costs per square foot for industrialized construction were higher than those for traditional building methods; but in higher flats, which are in general more expensive, industrialized building was cheaper.† The new building methods, though classed as 'industrialized', did not necessarily constitute a radical departure from tradition. The Ministry's current definition, which may soon be revised, includes 'any method of construction which uses prefabricated or pre-cut components, or mechanized operations on-site, to a greater degree than is the current general practice'. It 'includes not only systems using mainly factory-made components, but also such things as "no-fines" concrete, on-site casting, and highly rationalized traditional methods of construction'. Many of these methods fall a long way short of technical revolution, but they may be none the less fruitful for that.

It must be remembered, too, that the scope for a reduction in house building costs is entirely different from that which was available in school building when the Ministry of Education's much-quoted development groups first set to work with 'consortia' of local authorities to produce improvements in design and spectacular savings in cost. 'The first post-war schools,' said the Ministry 'were very extravagant both of land and floor space.' Between 1950 and 1956 their area was reduced by about 40 per cent but teaching space was maintained or

*From an unpublished study made by Prof. Duccio Turin of University College, London.
† Ministry of Housing and Local Government.

slightly increased. Costs were reduced by about 20 per cent in money terms, and if allowance is made for the general inflation of building costs they were halved.* But in housing, costs have been pared down by every available means for years and the cost of building a house in this country is now probably lower, by comparison with the average wage, than the cost of building a house in any other European country. There is no 'fat' left on the designs and materials in this field. Indeed, most people agree with the Parker Morris Committee that there is now an urgent need for more spacious and better equipped housing. If greater efficiency is achieved in house building, its fruits are therefore likely to appear in the form of better housing rather than cheaper housing.

If these warnings are kept in mind, it should be possible to make a realistic assessment of the scope for progress in this field. The immediate reforms required are widely known and most of them have been repeatedly called for in studies made by professional associations and government committees – most recently in Sir Harold Emmerson's 'Survey of Problems Before the Construction Industries',† the Banwell Committee's Report on 'The Placing and Management of Contracts for Building and Civil Engineering Work'‡ and the N.E.D.C.'s study of 'The Construction Industry'.

There should be greater standardization of dimensions, products and methods. New methods have been devised in other countries to reduce, or altogether eliminate, seasonal variations in output and employment – even in the coldest climates – and there is no reason why similar progress should not be made here. Closer collaboration must be achieved between builders, architects, surveyors and their clients. The long-condemned practice of 'open tendering', leading automatically to the award of contracts to the lowest bidder, should be generally abandoned in favour of earlier and more systematic methods for the selection of contractors; builders can then be brought into the design team at a much earlier stage, at last correcting

*Ministry of Education, *The Story of Post-War School Building*. Pamphlet No. 33, 1957. See also Ministry of Education, *The Story of CLASP*, Building Bulletin No. 19, 1961.
†H.M.S.O., 1962. ‡H.M.S.O., 1964.

the anomaly, noted by Sir Harold Emmerson and repeated in the Banwell Report, that 'in no other important industry is the responsibility for design so far removed from the responsibility for production'. The professions involved should be better, and more often jointly, educated; the large number of ill-managed architects' offices should adopt more efficient procedures; barriers to the effective deployment of architects and surveyors, deriving from out-dated taboos restricting their participation in management, should be lifted. The engineer or clerk of works responsible for progress on the site should be recognized as a key member of the team and trained accordingly; the apprentice-ship system should be rationalized and its patterns and periods of training brought into line with modern needs. Building operations generally must be better planned and phased; and greater resources should be devoted to research, and particularly to the systematic application of tested research findings. Platitudinous as most of these proposals have become, progress in these directions is nevertheless urgent, and it is in fact being made – slow and uneven though it is in so vast and rambling an industry.

This is not the place to explore these reforms or to show in detail the part that government can play in bringing them about. But the bigger decisions to be taken by government must be outlined, for without them the conditions essential for success cannot be created. The main features of the policies required in the housing field are now reasonably clear from experience accumulated throughout Europe.

It is essential, but it is certainly not sufficient, to give the building industry a continuing high level of demand for housing. There has in fact *been* a high and generally rising volume of house building in most European countries through-out the post-war period, yet the industry's record in house building has generally proved disappointing. Builders must be assured, by genuinely convincing government commitments, that the demand for their work will be continuous and predic-table, regionally as well as nationally; for the industry is tied to local supplies of labour, and to heavy materials and components that cannot be readily transported about the country. The progress of industrialization makes this requirement even more important. To be efficiently used, a plant for producing large factory-made components of the kind employed on the continent must have a guaranteed market for 2,000 dwellings a year – eight every working day – within a radius of twenty miles, beyond which transport costs become excessive. A programme must therefore be prepared, incorporating regional as well as national demands; it should be published for five years or so in advance and revised year by year.

If technical advances are expected of the construction industry, then the technical continuity of this programme – the dimensions, performance standards and technical specifications it incorporates – will be as important as its financial and numerical continuity. The new Building Regulations may provide a sound framework within which these technical policies can develop, but any major advances in standards – resulting, perhaps, from the adoption of the Parker Morris Committee's recommendations – should be announced before the industry's plans develop too far and adhered to thereafter. Since the same building methods and materials are not best suited to different heights and styles of building – high flats, five-storey blocks, high density low buildings, and so on – decisions must also be taken about the regional distribution and 'mix' of the different types to be built.

These requirements for a numerically and technically predictable volume of building at regional and national levels can be fairly easily met in the public sector and in building for housing associations and other bodies that depend on government loans. They are harder to meet in the private sector. In future government may find itself compelled – as governments have been elsewhere in western Europe – to regulate the demand for new private housing, sustaining it when it falters or counterbalancing the decline with increased public building, and restricting it when it threatens to get out of hand. Without the assurance afforded by a programme of this kind, only the biggest and most progressive organizations will invest sufficient resources in new machinery and in the trained men required at all levels to operate it effectively.

If, despite these plans, the economic situation compels occasional cutbacks in spending, then housing – owing to the scale of investment going into this field and the relative ease with which it can be checked – has always been the most tempting target for those seeking economies, and the methods of control they employ have often been fiscal and financial. These are peculiarly inefficient means of control. Their effect is difficult to predict with any precision; they operate far too slowly – making their greatest impact after about two years, when a new expansion may already be required – and they tend not to restrain investment but to drive it into other forms of construction such as office building or luxury housing which may be less urgently needed than the standard forms of house building which are most easily reined in. The recent reintroduction of licensing to control industrial and commercial building will help to resolve these problems. But since the construction industry can fairly quickly divert resources from one form of building to another and from new work to repairs and conversions, it must always be treated as a whole for planning purposes. Ministries of Housing, being generally responsible for one sector of production and mainly for the public building programme within that sector, are ill-adapted to operate the comprehensive physical controls required. These controls, whether based on building licences or on informal but binding agreements with builders and their clients, must operate regionally as well as nationally and must be subject to continual adjustment based on up-to-date information, particularly about the supply of labour. A ministry responsible for all forms of construction, operating through a well developed system of regional offices and collaborating closely with the ministry responsible for labour supply, is generally best equipped for the task.

Through its central and local authorities the government now commissions so large a share of construction – nearly half the new work completed in the United Kingdom – that it can go far to establish efficient and uniform contract procedures, to coordinate dimensions and to control standards of work, because all the major builders depend to some extent on public contracts. But regulations and codes of this kind can become a rigid shell, restricting progress, if not kept continually abreast of technical development. Hence descriptive regulations specifying the materials and dimensions to be employed should give way increasingly to 'performance standards' specifying the loads to be carried, the insulation to be achieved, the stresses to be withstood, and so on. This cannot be done without a continuing programme of officially sponsored and well publicized research and testing. Once these conditions have been established, better progress should be possible in house building as in other sectors of the industry.

Little has been said about the introduction of radically new 'systems' of industrialized building and this possibility deserves to be briefly examined. The reduction of the man-hours of work to be done on the site, though it can be achieved in a variety of ways, is the essential requirement for progress in building methods. European experience shows that technical progress of all kinds, saving labour, simplifying manual operations and transferring production from the site to the covered and more easily controlled environment of the factory, only proceeds vigorously when builders are faced with severe shortages of labour that are expected to continue for a long time. West Germany's colossal output of housing was achieved by traditional methods, thanks largely to the continued inflow of refugees from the east and the recruitment of workers from Mediterranean countries. Switzerland also built ten houses per thousand population with traditional methods, thanks to immigrant labour. The recent introduction of more advanced methods in Germany followed the closure of escape routes from East Germany and the economic take-off in southern Europe which combined to produce growing labour shortages.

Britain's building industry is likely to face a similar predicament before long. Immigration has been severely restricted; the flow of school-leavers, upon whom this industry depends particularly heavily, will fall as the post-war 'bulge' moves on into higher age groups; and Ireland, the under-employed region of the British Isles' economy from which so much of our building labour has been drawn, has now embarked upon her own economic take-off and is achieving a rate of growth (considerably faster than the United Kingdom's) which is already producing a sharp fall in emigration. For all these reasons our building industry will shortly be faced with shortages of manpower that can only be surmounted by the adoption of more advanced methods replacing labour with machines and bringing factory resources to bear which would otherwise have been employed on other work. Painful though the next few years may be, they are likely to afford greater scope for technical progress than we have ever had before. The experience of other countries shows that technical progress is likely to remain slow until wage rates on building sites surpass those in factories. That may happen in this country before long.

But it does not follow that self-contained proprietary 'systems' of building, making use of large and highly standardized prefabricated components, will furnish the principal means of progress. In a country requiring a greater diversity of house types than ever before, and depending for the foreseeable future on many small and middle sized firms, more flexible and adaptable arrangements are likely to be required – methods capable of employing interchangeable components, made by a variety of producers to uniform dimensions and performance standards, and permitting builders of all sizes to select and assemble those they require. Lightweight, standardized, prefabricated components of interchangeable kinds have been developed with great success for American housing.* 'Closed systems', in which the builder has to work entirely with components produced to one pattern, have often attracted more attention, being more spectacular and more acceptable to some of the really large organizations which have taken the lead in prefabrication, but they may not be best suited to British needs and conditions.

CONCLUSION

The main conclusions of this chapter that deserve the attention of policy makers can be briefly summarized. Changes now envisaged in the scale of the housing programme must bring about changes in the distribution of house building, both among the types of households and between the regions to which priority will be given. These changes should be planned over longer forward periods of time on the basis of more refined and more regularly revised estimates of requirements. New types

* See, for example, Patricia Tindale, 'House Construction in the U.S.A.', *Architectural Association Journal*, March 1965.

of need will have to be met, calling for new forms of design and building, and a reappraisal of the methods of managing and financing housing. Local authorities and other publicly accountable corporate bodies will have to play a bigger part in the future building programme, and this development should make it easier for government to control and plan building operations. These changes will also call for closer collaboration between designers, builders and town planners. The large resources that will be required for repairs and improvements should be incorporated in the programme along with the new work to be done. To meet needs more effectively, there should be more frequent movement of households within the existing stock of dwellings. Steps should be taken to make this possible; if movement does not increase it will be impossible to sustain the demand for so large a supply of new building. Greater flexibility in the use of dwellings should be encouraged, both in the design of new housing and through the conversion or extension of existing property.

Unless the reform of administrative concepts and procedures, particularly at local levels, precedes the advances to be made in building technology, improvements in productivity are likely to be frustrated or wasted. Many more trained administrators and professional men will be required in local government. Existing procedures for acquiring and clearing sites and for new building may soon prove grossly inadequate. In particular, there should be a thorough reappraisal of procedures for identifying and eliminating the worst housing conditions, leading to the development of two standards of adequacy: an ambitious but systematic one designed to distinguish different forms of hardship, to appraise their incidence and geographical distribution, and to guide those planning the housing programme; and a minimum standard designed to eliminate the very worst houses and to ensure fair treatment for their owners – who will more often in future be their occupiers too. More comprehensive means must also be devised for the assessment of local housing requirements and for the selection of council tenants; otherwise local authorities cannot cater adequately for many types of household whose needs must be met, and other bodies may have to be created to do this.

There will soon be greater opportunities for technical progress in the construction industry, provided the government can first assure builders of a continuing and predictable demand within each region. House building must be planned within the context of a programme for the construction industry as a whole which is closely related to changes in the regional supply of labour. The industry's physical output should be more closely regulated; if financial devices have still to be used for this purpose they should operate more sensitively and directly than those employed hitherto. The government is now capable of establishing greater uniformity of building dimensions and quality, making less use of detailed descriptive regulations and greater use of performance standards, and opportunities for progress along these lines should not be missed. Industrialization can increase the resources available to the industry, its output, and the speed at which houses are built, but it is unlikely to achieve spectacular savings in cost. Readily adaptable building methods will be required, which are capable of being used by small firms and of meeting a wide variety of needs.

Some would argue that proposals for a major increase in house building, let alone the fixing of specific building targets, should wait until further progress has been made in preparing the groundwork for the housing programme discussed in this chapter. But the experience of other countries suggests, on the contrary, that effective procedures for planning and implementing such a programme, and the industrial advances required to achieve it, are generally fashioned under the heat and pressure brought to bear by ambitious political commitments. This order of events may be logically questionable, but it is politically normal.

CHAPTER 9

HOUSING, LAND AND PLANNING

LAND, its supply and price, and government's policies for regulating the uses to which it may be put, must be given a chapter to themselves. But a thorough treatment of these questions would extend far beyond the confines of this study and demand a book in its own right. This chapter therefore deals with land from the standpoint of those concerned with housing. It begins with a brief sketch of the means available to government for distributing the growth of population and regulating the demands people make on land in different parts of the country. The economic and social changes which the planners' decisions must accommodate and occasionally initiate now threaten to outpace the capacities of the system, and the problems these developments pose for housing policy and the impact they make on housing conditions are briefly explained. The chapter concludes with a discussion of objectives to be pursued in future. It must be stressed again, however, that this essay makes no survey or forecast of the nation's land requirements and attempts no general appraisal of the problems of town planning, land pricing and regional development. It is a 'houser's' comment on planning policies which omits many points that planners would want to consider.

THE PLANNING SYSTEM

Excellent descriptions of the history and workings of this country's town planning system are available elsewhere*; here it is only necessary to identify its principal elements and to show the relationship between this system and the general responsibilities of government for the development of the economy.

---

*e.g. J.B. Cullingworth, *Town and Country Planning in England and Wales*, Allen & Unwin, 1964. This book includes a useful bibliography. For a simple account of the citizen's dealings with the system, see Research Institute for Consumer Affairs, *Town Planning, The Consumer's Environment*, 1965.

An assessment of the land required for different purposes begins – but only begins – with an assessment of the population living in the country concerned, and the way in which this total and its continuing growth are distributed among different regions of the country. The growth and distribution of the population are influenced by policies of many kinds which help to determine the level and distribution of incomes, the supply of housing and the general aspirations and expectations of the people; but the first opportunity a government has to exert direct leverage on the regional distribution of population and the rate at which population grows in particular areas lies in the controls it exercises over the growth and distribution of employment. Since it is the younger workers who move most readily, a region in which employment has been steadily rising for some years tends thereafter to have a younger labour-force and a higher rate of natural increase than the areas from which its migrants were recruited. The London and West Midland regions have faster rates of economic growth and higher rates of natural increase than other regions. Of the increase of 2·9 million people expected in the South East region between 1965 and 1981, 2·2 millions will arise from natural increase and only 700,000 is expected to arise from further migration to the area. There are major differences within such regions, however. The central parts of the big conurbations are losing population, their fringes and the smaller towns surrounding them are growing most rapidly, and some rural areas in the most rapidly growing regions are losing population.

The government can exert both negative and positive leverage on the location of employment. It can refuse permission for industrial development by witholding the industrial development certificates required for all but the smallest industrial buildings and extensions. It has recently banned further office building in London and Birmingham and will shortly have to develop and refine these controls, since office building in such areas cannot simply be frozen for ever. It is reimposing a system of building licences which will provide a means of regulating most of the larger commercial and industrial building projects. These instruments exert a negative leverage on the larger and more rapidly expanding employers – often the most

efficient ones. They have little effect on small firms, on static
or stagnant firms with no intention of expanding, or on firms
whose operations are sufficiently profitable and adaptable to
expand by buying up existing buildings.

Positive leverage on the growth and distribution of employment can be exerted in a variety of ways. The Ministry of
Labour makes grants towards the lodging, removal and other
expenses of key workers transferred to selected development
districts, and it can make similar grants to help unemployed
workers move to places where they can find jobs. The Ministry
of Housing and Local Government offers special subsidies for
rehousing workers compelled to move by major industrial
changes such as pit closures. The Departments responsible for
Housing, Transport and Trade can contribute to the clearance
of derelict land, and the provision of roads, drainage systems
and other services, where these operations will help to attract
employment. In development districts the Board of Trade can
build factories for sale or lease – often at reduced rents – and
it can make grants and loans to firms building or installing
machinery in these areas or incurring exceptional expenses in
moving there. A new public agency, the Location of Offices
Bureau, has been established to stimulate and guide the dispersal
of office work from London. Special tax privileges in the treatment of depreciation funds are provided for manufacturers in
the development districts and these can amount to a major
subsidy. Government decisions about the placing of major
contracts, for liners or fighter aircraft for example, the investment policies of the nationalized industries, and the location
of major government offices such as those of the Ministry of
Social Security, also play a part in determining the distribution
of employment. Meanwhile long-standing general industrial
subsidies, particularly for agriculture, and new powers which
apply different tax rates to different industries likewise exert
some influence on the distribution of employment.

At the end of the Second World War the government was
determined to control the spread of great cities and to relieve
the congestion of the largest – particularly London. Within five
years, sites had been chosen and Development Corporations
appointed for fifteen new towns, eight of them surrounding

London. The general retreat from planning that occurred in the 1950s, coupled with Conservative suspicion of these communities – both in the central government and in the counties where they stood – prevented the starting of further new towns for a dozen years, apart from one in Scotland. But limited encouragement was given to the planned expansion of existing towns willing to accept people 'exported' from larger cities, and the London County Council succeeded, before its demise, in persuading a score of towns to take Londoners from the central third of the conurbation for which the Council was responsible. The Greater London Council is continuing this policy on an even larger scale. Belatedly, the government resumed the policy of creating new towns – sites for many more have recently been announced – and assumed a much more active role in planning and assisting town expansions in many parts of the country, now on a more ambitious scale and at greater ranges from the cities 'exporting' population. The planning and administration of new and expanded towns fall mainly to the Ministry of Housing and Local Government and the local authorities, but the principal decisions involved hinge on the capacity of these centres to attract investors capable of providing the necessary employment, and the people rehoused in this way are in effect selected by employers. Thus, unlike the building of conventional suburbs and municipal 'out-county estates', these schemes depend on the government's ability to forecast and control the location of employment.

The money and effort devoted to all these provisions has steadily increased in recent years, and the underlying philosophy of the system has been changing. For many years the main aims were to relieve congestion in London, and to mop up local pockets of unemployment by subsidizing employers to provide jobs in places where it exceeded specified proportions of insured workers. The government endeavoured to supplement or sustain the operations of the market without making any fundamental changes in the system. But the aims now taking shape are to build up strategically placed centres of continuing economic growth within regions where there is a surplus of labour, and to bring about a more balanced dispersal of growth among selected centres in the most rapidly developing regions. This calls for a more sustained investment in larger and more carefully chosen 'growth points'; it demands a regional rather than a local strategy, and much closer collaboration between the different departments of government at central, regional and local levels. The attempt to help the unemployed, from which these schemes originated thirty years earlier, is slowly developing into a more general policy for the development of the whole economy.

Thus government is securing increasing control over the location of employment. But such controls do not extend far beyond the major office and factory employments, and they could only be complete in an entirely static economy. Even in eastern Europe, where the state has a virtual monopoly of urban employment, urban land and building operations, and issues separate permits authorizing people to work and to live in specified places, the government is unable precisely to forecast or control the processes of economic growth which ultimately determine the distribution of the population – as was shown in Chapter 4. (Junior officials may confidently assert to the foreign visitor in Moscow that the city's population will not be allowed to grow, but immediately cast doubt on the assertion by telling him of the new schools, restaurants, shops, laundries and factories being built on every side. More senior officials may admit they do not even know what the city's population is.) The growing responsibilities assumed by our own government for the general development of the economy mean that projections of the growth and deployment of the labour force, though calling for constant revision, need no longer be a matter of pure guesswork. The responsibilities it had assumed for allocating to each housing authority its share of the housing programme compelled the Ministry of Housing and Local Government to prepare local forecasts of demographic growth – if only to demonstrate to the more ambitious authorities that an increase in population arising from a current increase in births would not immediately justify an increase in the number of dwellings (since the newly born would not be forming households for another twenty years). Since then the research officers of the Ministry, assisted by the Registrar General's department, have been devising more systematic and reliable forecasts of the size and demographic structure of the population in each region and in the areas of the larger local authorities. Like the future distribution of employment, the progress of migration, birth rates, marriage rates and death rates is impossible to forecast with precision; but there is an ascending order of predictability in that list, and the groundwork of regional and local information required for planning purposes is slowly being laid.

Armed with such information, the next steps towards an appraisal of land requirements should logically call for analyses and forecasts of the level and distribution of incomes. If enough were known about the elasticities of supply and demand for various goods and services in the public and private sectors of the economy, approximate projections could then be made of the nation's requirements for manufacturing, commercial and distributive industries of various kinds, and for schools, hospitals, parking spaces and other land-using services, including housing. How rapidly will wealth increase? Will a wealthier society prefer more pubs and bingo halls, or more and better furnished space around television sets in the home? Will its families prefer larger houses and small cars, or a small flat and a seaside cottage or caravan linked by larger cars? Will they prefer more restaurants and snack-bars, or more frozen and prepackaged goods retailed from a large number of local shops (with correspondingly extensive waste disposal systems for coping with discarded containers)? Will they prefer a few large universities providing residential accommodation for most of their students, or more numerous local universities whose students generally live at home or in flats and lodgings? In each case, people would probably like to have both; but where will the priorities of the market place, the hustings and the pressure groups lead?

Such forecasts are exceedingly difficult to prepare and must be constantly revised. The difficulties are greatly increased when estimates have to be broken down to the local levels where most decisions about land uses are actually made. The cars, the television sets and frozen foods required will seldom be produced in the area in question. But present trends in the economy are likely to make local analyses easier as time goes by. Computational methods are being mechanized and greatly improved. The rapid growth of 'service' industries means that an increasing proportion of consumption generates employment of two contrasting but roughly predictable and plannable kinds. There will be more jobs in the 'national' or 'metropolitan' services – insurance, central government, broadcasting, publishing, etc. – the main centres of which must be located in London while the more numerous routine jobs can be placed, with the aid of modern communications systems, wherever the workers concerned can be persuaded to live. There will also be more jobs in the 'local' or 'personal' services – teaching, retailing, catering, motor repairs, etc. – which must be located wherever people do live. The former make major demands on land in a small number of fairly easily identified places. The latter make much greater, but locally similar, demands on land everywhere. Meanwhile, the central component in most of these forecasts will be the demand for housing. This, and the land required to meet it, are falling increasingly within the government's control, as has been shown throughout this book.

The analysis outlined here starts with trends in employment, population and households. It then leads, through studies of the growth and distribution of incomes, to forecasts of the evolving patterns of demand for various commercial and public services. Reasoned estimates can then be made of the land uses required to meet these demands – the space required for housing, schools, shops, factories, and so on. The rate of household formation, and the size and character of the households to be catered for, play a central part at this stage of the analysis. Housing is an exceptionally greedy user of land, accounting, with its associated gardens and yards, for about one third of the total area of an average English town.* Moreover the number and size of many goods that a community demands (from refrigerators to doormats) depends on the number and size of its households rather than the number of its people.

When the distribution of various land uses upon the map has to be considered, the transport and communication patterns

*P. A. Stone, 'The Impact of Urban Development on the Use of Land and other Resources', *Journal of the Town Planning Institute*, May 1961.

linking their sites must also be incorporated in the 'model' of urban development. The forms of communication to be used go far to determine the practicability of different layouts, the amount of space required for moving and parking vehicles, and the share of public and private expenditure that must be devoted to meeting transport costs. Finally, via an examination of each industry's labour requirements and potential rate of growth, the analysis returns full circle to estimates of employment, population and households.

This is grossly to over-simplify the tasks confronting town planners. No one would propose that separate and detailed analyses of this kind could be made for the entire country, down to its smallest towns, or even that precise forecasts could be made for one town. But the principal elements in such a model should indeed be examined and related to each other, at least for a sample of towns, and the analysis should be repeated and revised from time to time to check its findings and take account of unforeseen economic and social changes. The findings of these studies would probably reveal patterns of urban growth that characterize communities of specified types: the old cotton towns of Lancashire, the south-coast resorts with high proportions of elderly people, and the first generation of post-war new towns might each be found to follow different but characteristic patterns of development. It would then be possible to foresee the principal adjustments called for and the principal stresses and 'bottle-necks' likely to be caused by specified changes, be they local (such as the establishment of a new university) or regional (such as the building of a new motorway linking one town to many others) or national (such as a major redistribution of income in favour of old people).

Parts of this analysis are already being carried out. Studies of transport systems, largely initiated by the Americans and since taken up by the Ministry of Transport, have attained a high degree of sophistication – though their application is a slower and more painful task. Plans for the distribution of school building have long been elaborated to the point required to ensure that every child can go to school, and the current reorganizations of secondary education are prompting further and more detailed studies by the local education authorities and the Department of Education and Science. The Ministry of Health has begun to prepare national plans for the hospital service; the Gas and Electricity Boards must be trying to improve their forecasts of consumers' demands; commercial organizations responsible for the investment of millions of pounds in manufacturing industries, or in restaurants, chain stores, filling stations or bowling alleys, cannot afford to make serious errors about the demand for their products. But where such research has been done it is often sketchy and generally isolated from knowledge of contiguous parts of the urban framework. Each ministry, industry or firm is responsible for its own immediate interests; none is responsible for preparing a more comprehensive, long-term 'model' of urban development – though a number of independent research groups are now exploring this field.

This account of an analysis, the central parts of which have not yet been attempted, leads on to a consideration of government responsibilities for regulating and planning land uses. At this stage, suspended over a gulf of ignorance, there is again a great deal of information and a well-developed administrative system at central and local levels – a system that regulates, initiates or frustrates land uses and investment decisions, ranging from the trivial (permission for a sign at a farm gate, saying 'Eggs for Sale') to the vast and irrevocable (the building of an urban ring road or a new town, for instance).

The principal responsibility for controlling new development and changes in the use of land or buildings rests with the local planning authorities: the Counties and County Boroughs in England and Wales – the Counties delegating many of their powers to the larger Boroughs and Districts within their boundaries. These authorities prepare, publish and from time to time revise 'development plans' which furnish a general framework for development showing, according to the Ministry's explanatory memorandum, 'which towns and villages are suitable for expansion and which can best be kept to their present size; the direction in which a city will expand; the area to be preserved as an agricultural Green Belt and the area to be allocated to industry and to housing'. Virtually all development must be approved by the planning authorities, and this includes 'the carrying out of building, engineering, mining or other operations in, on, over or under the land, or the making of any material change in the use of any buildings or other land'* – a very comprehensive definition.

The local planning authorities approve, modify or refuse applications for new development or changes in land use, or insist that certain conditions be observed in the course of such projects. They may 'designate' land that will be required by local authorities or government departments for specific purposes, thus strengthening powers for compulsory purchase of these sites; and they may acquire large blocks of land, termed 'comprehensive development areas', which are divided among many owners, call for wholesale development or redevelopment, and cannot be effectively handled unless brought into one ownership.

These formidable powers are subject at every point to rights of appeal to the Minister of Housing and Local Government – in effect to the Ministry, since the Minister himself can only see a tiny fraction of the appeals made to his department every year. The Minister has the duty of 'securing consistency and continuity in the framing of a national policy with respect to the use and development of land throughout England and Wales'. Subject to the approval of Parliament, he can make regulations for the administration of planning powers, he must approve development plans and revisions of these plans (every one of these plans has been modified to some extent by the Ministry), and he can approve, modify or revoke contested planning decisions. If adequately forewarned, he can 'call in' and re-appraise major planning applications (the redevelopment of Piccadilly Circus for example), or a whole class of applications (for ironstone workings, for example) which present special problems extending beyond the local context. Whenever people object to the planning authorities' decisions and appeal to the Minister, a public inquiry, or in some of the smaller cases a formal hearing, must be held at which a Ministry inspector presides,

---

* *Town and Country Planning Bill, 1947: Explanatory Memorandum,* Cmnd 7006, 1947, and *Town and Country Planning Act, 1962;* Section 12. Quoted in J.B. Cullingworth, *Town and Country Planning in England and Wales,* pp. 66 and 77.

later submitting a report for the guidance of the Minister.

This system of central supervision, from which there is no appeal except on points of law, can only work smoothly if the local planning authorities are given constant guidance about the general policies they are expected to follow. Personal contact and professional discussion among planning officers at central and local level, circulars and bulletins dealing with specific issues such as green belts or town centres, regular reports on the decisions made in leading cases, Ministerial statements, and major studies of the longer-term development of the country's principal regions – these are the means for shaping planning policies and maintaining a consistent evolution of ideas. At first the government gave little leadership in these matters, but in recent years it has begun to play an increasingly influential role. Nevertheless the application and interpretation of these policies in individual cases rests in the hands of the local authorities. Even if it had the knowledge and the manpower to give comprehensive national direction to the system, the Ministry feels compelled to play a fairly detached and uncommitted role if it is to arbitrate effectively between local authorities and the public, and between different public authorities which may come into conflict with each other. The local planning authorities vary greatly in the ways in which they interpret their powers and their obligation to consult the electorate. Some are well staffed and highly professional; many are not. Some make major decisions after a few private consultations with local developers and landowners, leaving the public to discover what is happening when demolition or building operations begin; a few take great trouble to inform people about planning proposals through publicity, open discussion, the display of maps and models, and so on.

SOME PROBLEMS

Briefly sketched in this way, the system appears rational and fair – though short of reliable predictive data – and a vast improvement on the clumsy and ineffective prewar planning system it replaced.* But town planning is today beset with

*See W. Ashworth, *The Genesis of Modern British Town Planning*, Routledge & Kegan Paul, 1954.

serious problems that may well assume disastrous proportions
during the next few years.

The present system was designed to secure public control of
all development rights, to establish procedures (radically
changed on several occasions since the war) for determining
land prices and for compensating the owners of property
acquired by public authorities, and to provide means for
regulating new building and industrial expansion, with the
intention of creating an orderly map of land uses and an orderly
distribution of employment, and preserving or extending the
amenities of town and country. But although the nationalization
of development rights was complete, the government regarded
the powers it had secured as being rather like those of the police:
designed to establish order by regulating, arbitrating and
occasionally exhorting – to control the traffic, rather than to
create it or decide its destinations. The traffic of development, it was assumed, would be reasonably well dispersed and
not too heavy. Once post-war reconstruction was completed,
the situation confronting government was expected to resemble
that of the 1930s, with a higher level of employment but a slow
rate of economic growth and a falling birth rate.

Today it is difficult for people to recall the social and economic
assumptions of those who created this system less than twenty
years ago. The prevailing opinion among experts at that time
is ably summarized in the Report of the Economics Committee
of the Royal Commission on Population,* published in 1950 but
prepared a few years earlier by some of the country's ablest and
most experienced economists. They calculated that the number
of 'families' in England and Wales (defined as the number of
married women, all widows under the age of sixty-five and 20
per cent of single women between twenty and forty-five) would
start to fall in the late fifties, slowly at first but faster before long.
They assumed that productivity per head would rise by only
$1\frac{1}{2}$ per cent a year, achieving, if there was a fall in the working
population, a growth in the total national income that 'would
only be one third of that on which we have hitherto been able
to rely'. '. . . we shall be faced within a measurable period with

*Papers of the Royal Commission on Population, Volume III,
H.M.S.O.

the task of effecting a transition from an economy adapted to a
very high level of real investment . . .' to an economy devoted
principally to consumption. After slum clearance had been
completed '. . . a large decline in the volume of house building
may sooner or later be well-nigh inevitable as a deferred
consequence of the altered population trend.' Fortunately,
they pointed out, it would be 'much easier to transfer work-
people from building, which is fairly evenly diffused throughout the country, than from a highly localized industry, such
as coalmining'. This trend, they said, 'makes it likely that
the rate of increase of the area of built-on land will be slowed
down. Secondly, the increase in the values of sites in the centres
of towns . . . must be expected to slow down. . . .' Meanwhile
'the course of land values may also be affected by a reversal of
the prolonged tendency towards concentration in large cities . . .
The net effect might well be to reduce land values in the aggre-
gate.' By the time the Report was published 'it was clear that
the economic position of the country was different in material
respects . . .', but the Committee saw no reason to amend its
principal conclusions about the trends of population and
economic growth, or the implications of these trends.

Five years later it was clear that an altogether different
world was taking shape. As post-war reconstruction drew
to a close, the rate of economic growth quickened to a faster pace
than ever before, bringing insatiable demands for housing,
motor cars and consumer goods. Social changes of many kinds
followed. The growth of wealth and population was not evenly
spread, but heavily concentrated around the capital and in a
broad belt stretching diagonally from the Thames estuary and
the Sussex coast up to the West Midlands. 'Service' industries,
particularly concentrated in the centres of the biggest cities,
grew most rapidly. Around these cities huge areas of closely
linked urban development continued to accumulate, making
city regions, which had begun to take shape in the inter-war
period, the urban form most typical of the later twentieth
century. After falling for several years, the numbers of births
began in the mid 1950s to climb steadily upwards; ten years
later they were back to their 1947 peak and still rising. Between
1951 and 1961 there was an increase of nearly 2 million in the

population of England and Wales, amounting almost to the figure forecast earlier by the Registrar General for the period between 1951 and 1971. The increase in wealth, coupled with the improvement in housing standards, was having – in every sense – a 'multiplier effect'. The replacement of obsolete housing, originally regarded as a once-for-all task of slum clearance, assumed growing proportions, and it is now becoming clear that the central third of many cities will soon have to be rebuilt. Meanwhile town planning policies and the emphasis accorded to different priorities among them have repeatedly changed: ten years ago green belts were the Minister's consuming interest; since then the emphasis has switched to roads and town centres, to the reappraisal of residential densities in the bigger cities, to hospitals and universities, and to housing and urban renewal, as the pressures of new crises, fashions and personal preferences succeeded each other at the Ministry. Town planning itself fell seriously out of favour for several years, and large numbers of trained staff were lost from the profession – particularly the economists and demographers, most readily employable elsewhere and now most urgently needed to fill the gaps in knowledge already mentioned.

Clinging to its detached, 'objective' role, the Ministry refused for many years to give a strong lead or take major initiatives. Overcrowded cities could negotiate for overspill agreements or traffic routes with neighbouring authorities, but if other authorities or private individuals objected to such arrangements the Minister would deal with appeals 'on their merits' without feeling obliged to ensure that alternative sites or routes were found to replace those that were vetoed. The Ministry of Transport, with more clearly defined responsibilities and much larger sums of money to spend, played a more forceful hand. But in the Ministry of Housing and Local Government senior officials long made a virtue of their reticence, asserting that policies could not be 'created' but could only emerge, like case law, from a mass of individual decisions. Since neither the planning authorities nor those who objected to their decisions could be sure what the Minister would decide, the Ministry had more than enough cases to handle. If final appeals over a large field must all be settled by the Minister, the on way of restricting his responsibilities is, paradoxically, to assume them – by explaining, publicizing and enforcing the major priorities. During the last few years the Ministry has begun to do this with increasing confidence.

Most of the objections made to planning authorities' decisions are settled locally; only about 3 per cent of them are pressed as far as an appeal. Yet appeals under Section 23 of the Act rose to about 9,000 in 1959, 12,000 in 1962 and 14,000 in 1965 – excluding appeals over advertisements, enforcement notices and other matters not covered by this Section. It takes about six months to arrange an inquiry into each, and about six more for a decision to be made. Proposals for several hundred town centre and redevelopment schemes are already awaiting decision in the Ministry. Meanwhile the calculations presented in Chapter 7 show that the rates of replacement and urban redevelopment are likely to rise sharply in the next few years, bringing a corresponding increase in the number of schemes to be dealt with. Rebuilding cities provokes far more conflict than extending them. The planning system is not geared to cope with the volume of work that will shortly be thrust upon it, and it lacks much of the information required to guide the major programme of investment to be handled. Already the reviews of development plans, originally intended to occur every five years, have been thrown hopelessly out of schedule: the great majority of the first plans had been approved by 1961, ten years after the date originally specified for their submission, but many authorities are still preparing the first reviews of these plans.

The local authorities responsible for this work are too numerous and too small; and their boundaries, drawn for quite different purposes a long time ago, often frustrate sane planning. Where administrative areas coincide with the built-up area of a town, the city's boundaries fall on the fringe – precisely in the zone of most active development, provoking dispute between neighbouring authorities and preventing effective long-term planning. But often the city has overflowed its boundaries and is subject to several different authorities: the Tyneside conurbation, to take one of the simpler examples, contains four County Boroughs and parts of two counties. One third of the planning authorities have populations of less than 100,000.

While general scarcities of trained people persist, the small size of these authorities means that many have no hope of securing the staff required for their work. In 1963 the great majority of counties had a chief planning officer with a separate planning department, and most of these chief officers had professional town planning qualifications; but of the eighty-three County Boroughs (in which the bulk of urban renewal will fall) only a dozen had chief planning officers, and half of the senior officials responsible for planning in the remainder lacked the appropriate technical qualifications.

The scarcity of town planners in the areas where they are most urgently needed is only part of a more general scarcity and maldistribution of professional staff: architects, public health inspectors, valuers and many others will be needed to rebuild the older cities. Moreover the task of rebuilding will be a shifting one, concentrated first in some areas and then moving on to others. Local government, by itself, is ill-equipped for this purpose. Greater use will therefore have to be made of private consultants in the fields where they exist, and central government redevelopment agencies may have to be established to serve local authorities throughout a region. A council's chief architect, for example, must often be prepared to become an entrepreneur – arranging contracts with any private architect who is capable of assisting in his programme – and abandon the idea that his own department should do all the council's work. The fiction that each local authority has an independent and equal status cannot be preserved; if resources are to be concentrated in selected centres of economic growth, other areas must be relatively starved of investment. Only central government is capable of planning and publicly justifying systematic discrimination of this kind. The first report of an interdepartmental Planning Advisory Group* makes proposals for coping with some of these problems which would give the local authorities greater freedom to deal with matters of detail and concentrate the Ministry's efforts on major questions of policy, but the weakness of the whole structure of local government and its over-numerous authorities restricted the scope of

*Planning Advisory Group, *The Future of Development Plans*, H.M.S.O., 1965.

their proposals. The announcement of a Royal Commission that seems likely to be given powers of reappraisal denied to the Local Government Commission it has superseded at last brings hope of radical reform. Meanwhile the Minister's role as protector of the citizen from arbitrary decisions of the local bureaucracy cannot be abandoned unless alternative procedures are devised for this purpose: the fact that many of these decisions are small ones does not make them trivial to the citizens concerned. Wherever these responsibilities are placed, they will demand skilled judgement and – if the pace of development is to increase – more trained staff to make such judgements.

Nothing has yet been said about the question of land prices, although this question has attracted more attention in recent years than any other in this field. The attention comes from different quarters and leads in diverse directions. Those whose main concern is social justice point out that the planning system concentrates upon particular sites, selected for development by the authorities, the general increase in land values that the growth of a community creates. It is unfair that the winners of this lottery should harvest rich gains (because their land happens to be chosen for a shopping centre, for instance), while the owners of neighbouring sites allocated to less profitable purposes should be deprived of these rewards. It would be equally unfair to the community at large if such profits were more widely distributed, for that would mean compensating landowners whose property is acquired for development at prices which assumed that each of them had won the lottery, when in fact the number of commercially profitable uses for land is limited – the site for a filling station or pub only retaining its value because the great majority of neighbouring sites are used for other purposes. It is even worse when people speculate in land without contributing anything to its development, devoting their efforts only to gaining planning permissions, subsequently securing revisions of the densities and other conditions attached to these permissions and selling and reselling at continually enhanced prices until the site finally reaches the hands of those who may actually do something with it – and then be blamed for the high prices they have to charge for the outcome of their development.

Other people are concerned mainly with devising new

methods of taxing land – methods that may be designed simply to raise revenue, or to provide built-in incentives for the development or redevelopment of land that is ripe for a change of use, or to secure for the community a share in the capital gains in land engendered by the growth of local population and wealth. Others, again, are mainly intent on bringing land into public ownership and gradually freeing the task of allocating it to different uses from the dictates of the price mechanism, subjecting it instead to more purely political and administrative criteria. Since there will always be keen competition to occupy land in city centres and other desirable places, and people will be prepared to pay for the privilege in some way or other, this can be interpreted as a proposal for subsidizing some people at the expense of others – though not unworthy of consideration for that reason.*

Several determined attempts have been made to resolve these problems during the past twenty years. In 1947 the state acquired all development rights and tried to acquire all the profits subsequently made from them; in 1954 it abandoned the attempt to acquire these profits if they accrued from private transactions rather than compulsory purchase; from 1959 compulsory purchases were based on the 'fair market price' for the use permitted by the planning authority – no compensation being paid to owners who failed to secure the right to develop. Now the government proposes to accept market prices, but to take a large and gradually increasing share of the profits of development; it is setting up a Land Commission with authority to acquire land that is ripe for development and redistribute it on terms that should in some cases secure a share in long term capital gains for the community.†

THE FUTURE

The issues at stake in this field touch on fundamental features of the economy, the fiscal system and the rights of the citizen, and they are far too complex to be resolved on the basis of

*See Peter Hall (ed.), *Land Values*, Sweet & Maxwell, 1965, for a summary of these debates and their implications.
† *The Land Commission*, Cmd 2771, 1965.

housing criteria alone. But these criteria may at least suggest some of the requirements to be looked for in any solutions proposed. The comments that follow deal first with the question of land prices and the conditions that must be realized if the housing programme now adopted by government is to succeed.

There must be a continuous flow of land available for development and redevelopment in the right places. In some centres – and Birmingham appears to be an example – the building sites so far available, inside and outside the city, are incapable of accommodating the population to be rehoused. Others must quickly be found. Since delays always occur in securing and developing sites, the pipelines must be considerably 'overcharged' so that alternative sites are always available when progress is blocked on those first selected for action.

Means must be found, particularly in redevelopment schemes, for the speedy collectivization of large blocks of property so that they may be replanned and redistributed in a comprehensive and efficient fashion. It does not follow that this collectivization must be permanent; indeed, if the resale of land or leases makes owners more willing to accept collectivization and secures financial resources needed for the acquisition of further land, temporary public ownership may be preferable. The small-scale rebuilding schemes now commonly found are wasteful of effort, since the time spent on many phases of the procedure bears little relation to the size of the project and the decisions made on small sites often frustrate more radical readjustments that a large-scale, long-term scheme would incorporate. The whole pipeline is too often throttled in this way: because one small block of flats can only accommodate a few people when it is completed, the next demolition scheme must be restricted to an equally small site. Redevelopment must proceed on a much larger scale.

Densities must be rapidly and authoritatively reappraised to permit increases where the severest scarcities are found, and to avoid unnecessary speculation and uncertainty. This, too, calls for large projects: tolerable living conditions can be provided at high densities, but only where designers can operate on a large enough scale to provide sheltered open space and appropriate commercial and public buildings in areas that are free of traffic.

It should not be assumed, however, that building at higher densities will achieve major savings in land costs per dwelling; experience shows that these costs do not fall greatly when houses are packed more densely on the land.* It follows that public acquisition should wherever possible precede an increase in permitted densities so that the capital gain in land values resulting from the increase may accrue to the community.

Means must be found to enable families with lower incomes to find decent housing in areas of shortage – particularly in London and Birmingham – otherwise they will be harried from one overcrowded slum to another or driven out altogether, depriving the great cities of much essential labour. Yet there must also be sufficient social diversity in redeveloped areas to ensure that middle class people, too – teachers and public health inspectors, for example – are not excluded altogether from large tracts of the city. A land pricing policy that amounted to a general and indiscriminate subsidy to all householders living in areas of shortage would sacrifice the advantages of the price mechanism : some people must be persuaded to move out if the shortage is not to grow worse. Thus selective forms of subsidy, whether operated through the Inland Revenue, the rating system or other instruments, will be required; an indiscriminate subsidy to large and arbitrarily selected groups, whether applied by municipal housing authorities or the Land Commission, will not help at all.

It has been shown in Chapter 7 that the larger housing authorities' capacity to acquire and redistribute the capital gains made on their property gives them greatly enhanced powers for meeting the needs of their areas. Similarly, the government should evolve means for securing a share in the general capital gains made on real property – both those made in the course of development, and those accruing from the continuing increase in land values that occurs in a growing community. Property owners expected to participate in development must nevertheless retain a part of the profits to be made from it, otherwise changes in land use and ownership will be brought to a halt.

Finally, it is essential that any solution adopted should

*See P. A. Stone, 'Prices of Building Sites in Britain', in Peter Hall (ed.), *Land Values*, 1965.

command the public acceptance required to give it permanence, unhampered by obstruction and speculation from those hoping for repeal and revision of the scheme.

If economic development is to proceed more rapidly in future, it must be distributed more widely between and within different regions; the local growth of housing can then more easily match the local growth of employment and land values will not be so heavily concentrated in the inner areas of a few large cities. Already there are signs that the government is realizing that massive public investment in the expansion of new centres is likely before long to prove a cheaper way of meeting needs than the increasingly heavy subsidies it has had to pay for costly high building on expensive central sites in older cities.

The volume of new building and redevelopment required during the next few years cannot be attained without a drastic increase in the speed at which land acquisition, planning and building operations proceed. The attempts now being made to clarify and publicize the policies to be followed should be extended, and this may help to reduce the number of objections and appeals. But many town planning decisions may have to be decentralized as soon as a local government framework sufficiently robust to bear the work is created.

The extent of the shortages of trained manpower, created in this and many other fields by current extensions of the responsibilities of government, has yet to be fully grasped. Determined attempts to recruit and train professional staff made in recent years by the Department of Education and Science (for teachers) and the Ministry of Health (for social workers) have already produced striking results, meeting a better response than was expected. But it was only in 1965 that the government first offered additional funds to universities prepared to establish or expand courses in town planning – and the offer was withdrawn before the year was out.

The structure and boundaries of local government are peculiarly inappropriate for town planning. The new regional bodies now being established can provide a base from which government makes its presence felt and its help more readily available. But the economic regions are far too large for the day-to-day work of planning and development: the major city regions with their immediately surrounding countryside would provide a more appropriate framework, with a lower tier of smaller authorities handling work that need not be done on so large a scale.

When training schemes are eventually launched to provide the professional staff required, the opportunity must be taken to re-examine their educational objectives. Town planners are still inadequately equipped for their responsibilities. They resemble in some ways the nineteenth-century medical officers of health: the social health of towns and the future opportunities of people in this country – opportunities for living space, movement, and a choice of occupations and recreations – depend very heavily upon them. They are gaining an increasingly authoritative voice in debates about that future, but it cannot be a wise and effective voice unless it is better informed. The respect in which the public holds its officials is fickle, as the medical officers found; when they fell temporarily out of favour the powers they retained in full lay in the one field – vaccination – in which the public was convinced they had proven and useful knowledge. An American observer shrewdly identifies the origins of the British town planning profession and some of its present weaknesses. The leader of the team that prepared the post-war plans for London 'was an architect and a landscape architect as well as a town planner. It is also significant that of the twelve other key staff members working on the two plans, nine were architect-planners (of whom three were also landscape architects), only one was an engineer-planner and one a surveyor-planner, and not one was a social scientist ... the end product was the spacial pattern of physical environment that was to be achieved ... neither the political economy in its broad operation nor the implementation measures and stages were dealt with or outlined with any thoroughness.' (The point was made more succinctly to the author by the chief planning official of a Continental country: 'Most of our town planners began as architects; architects are very good at dealing with *space*, but they do not understand *time*.') Turning to the education of town planners, the American says

taken as a whole, the volume and depth of research associated with the planning schools is not such as to spark the interest of able students or to bolster the profession's reputation for knowledge building. . . . Given the present state of affairs, it appears unlikely that new sources of dynamic intellectual leadership are likely to emerge from the profession's institutional structure.*

It may be salutary to conclude this essay with a few reminders of the problems already posed by the inadequacies of this system. The recent growth in the numbers of households – particularly the smallest households – was not clearly foreseen; in some areas this growth is placing severe strains upon a housing market in which new building has been devoted to other types of household. We still do not know how many households our population is capable of forming, or how small they may become. Many of the strains imposed on town plans and the general amenities of urban living by the rapid spread of the motor car could likewise have been foreseen had systematic projections of personal income and expenditure been attempted much earlier. Meanwhile within the larger cities the pace and pattern of replacement is being restricted and distorted by the difficulties and delays inherent in redevelopment procedures, the scarcity of people trained to operate the system and the lack of sites for the 'overspill' housing now required. Clearance is often confined to smaller sites where the population is not too densely concentrated; the rebuilding of the worst areas and the rehousing of those in greater need is in some places repeatedly postponed. Such problems will assume far more serious proportions in the future if the rates of building and redevelopment are to be sharply increased.

Equally threatening, in the long run, is the limited understanding of planning problems found among the population at large, and among many of those who select and present the news we read. Very few local authorities make the deliberate attempts that Coventry has made to consult, inform and educate their citizens about plans and prospects for redevelopment. The task is a time-consuming one, calling for imagination, patience and a fundamental confidence both in the capacity of town planners and in the ability of ordinary people to appreciate and share the planners' objectives when these are explained

*Donald L. Foley, *Controlling London's Growth*, pp. 171–2. University of California Press, 1963.

to them. People can easily be deprived of the opportunity of thinking boldly about the future development of the cities and neighbourhoods in which they live; but they cannot be deprived of their legal rights to object to planning proposals, and those who exercise these rights are liable to be the aggrieved, the preservationists, and the people who hope for concessions elsewhere in return for withdrawing their objections. Seldom will they be those in urgent need of housing. Town planners who prefer an ignorant or apathetic electorate may have to contend with greater obstruction in the long run, and their plans may be the poorer because they are not founded on an understanding of local needs and opinions.

CHAPTER 10

LONDON

WHEN the government set about shedding its responsibilities for housing during the mid 1950s, its critics naturally concentrated their fire upon particular steps in this process such as the abandonment of development charges, the curtailment of subsidies for local housing authorities, the ending of requisitioning, the relaxation of rent controls and the reintroduction of market values as the basis for transactions in land. While dispute centred on these measures the government's position remained strong, for although they might fail to achieve their objectives it was clear that changes of *some* kind were needed; the existing procedures for rent control, subsidies, requisitioning and development could not be preserved indefinitely. The weakness of the government's policies lay not in the attempt to abolish major features of an increasingly inadequate system but in the assumption that nothing need be put in their place. Underlying these policies was the belief that once the most urgent post-war shortages had been overcome, increasing affluence could in time be relied on to solve the nation's housing problems without further intervention by government. The time required might be long, but the belief was fundamental to the philosophy of government which produced the 'social 'pattern of housing policies described in Chapter 3. It was mistaken. Wealth, as earlier chapters of this book have shown, tends to grow fastest in particular regions and among particular types of households, and affluence that is allowed to accumulate uncontrolled does not automatically resolve housing problems. It often makes them worse. Thus it was no accident that the failure of the government's attempt to shed its housing responsibilities first broke surface in unmistakable form in the richest and most rapidly developing corner of the country.

A study of the housing situation in London is therefore particularly revealing. Besides bringing together and relating to each other the different policies – for planning, building, taxation, housing and so on – which have been examined separately in earlier chapters, it affords a preview of affluence that may furnish a glimpse of problems and a guide to solutions which will prove increasingly important in future. The problems have been described at length in the Milner Holland Report and elsewhere,* and no attempt will be made to cover all this ground again. But the legends created by some of the more dramatic features of London's situation and the myths fostered by ill-informed attempts to explain this situation show that the record must be set straight at a number of points before its implications can be usefully discussed.

This chapter therefore begins with a survey of the position in and around London, and of the main developments which brought about this state of affairs. The government's attempt to cope with the situation is then briefly examined and compared with policies adopted in the great cities of other countries. The chapter concludes with a set of proposals for the future. But its main purpose is to provide a case study of the impact made on housing conditions by economic growth during a period when government was ill-equipped to manage this aspect of the economy and unwilling, for much of the time, to attempt the task – a case study that draws together the lessons derived from earlier chapters of this book and poses problems to be considered in its final conclusions.

LONDON'S HOUSING PROBLEM

Reports of the more lurid aspects of housing conditions in London, many of them indisputably true, have created a picture of general deterioration and breakdown, enlivened by tales of abuse and intimidation – decked with rats in the stew and snakes in the bath – which may too easily distract attention from more widespread hardships once the more exaggerated features of the legend have been discredited. Popular explanations of the

*e.g. Ruth Glass and John Westergaard, *London's Housing Needs*, Centre for Urban Studies, Report No. 5, University College, London, 1965.
Pearl Jephcott, *A Troubled Area*, Faber & Faber, 1964.
Audrey Harvey, *Tenants in Danger*, Penguin Books, 1964.
Hilary Rose, *London's Housing* (forthcoming).

causes of this state of affairs often award central roles to a massive influx of population from the north and from overseas, and to the operations of ruthless landlords who prey upon defenceless tenants. Such explanations are liable to conceal more fundamental causes of trouble, and to encourage the belief that solutions will be found in the restriction of immigration and in the enlarged scope for criminal proceedings against landlords which recent legislation provides.

From the start, therefore, it must be recognized that in Greater London as a whole housing is generally better than the nation's average and housing conditions have for many years been continuously and rapidly improving. The overwhelming majority of landlords are responsible people, no less humane than their neighbours, and most of their tenants are well satisfied with their housing and the rents they pay. The population of Greater London has not been rising but falling steadily – by 2·7 per cent between 1951 and 1961, though there may have been a slight reversal of this trend after 1961. The average size of household and the average number of persons per room have been falling, and so have the percentages of households who are overcrowded, who share dwellings with others or lack baths and other essential equipment. London still has many more shared dwellings than the rest of the country, but it affords greater opportunities for people to form separate households; headship rates are higher here than elsewhere. In terms of broad averages, the housing situation in London is good, and getting steadily better.

But progress has been most rapid in parts of London where conditions are already good; elsewhere there has been less improvement or even a deterioration, and large numbers of people are living in conditions that no civilized community should tolerate. At the time of the Milner Holland Committee's study, relations between landlords and tenants had in some places deteriorated to the point of more or less open warfare. Although cases of persecution, intimidation, and deliberate trickery or abuse affected less than 1 per cent of private tenants, at least 3,000 households were involved, and possibly as many as 10,000 – every year.

Amongst the less lurid cases quoted in the report was that of

the 'deserted young wife with a child of 18 months (who) paid
£3 10s. a week for one room and shared w.c. "Room had to be
deloused by local authority before occupation and is said to be
permanently verminous owing to age and neglect. . . . Had to
take room after days and nights sleeping out with child, rather
than part with it to a Home. . . . Landlord has said he will throw
out any tenants who apply to rent tribunal. No rent book
supplied" . . .'* When the Milner Holland Report was published the *Estates Gazette* indignantly protested that such cases are
exceedingly rare and quite untypical of rented housing or its
owners; which is true. When the Royal Commission on the
Mines reported in 1842 that pregnant women were working
underground dragging trucks of coal through the muddy
darkness, it was likewise pointed out that such cases were
exceedingly rare. But there comes a point in the progress of
civilization when the *frequency* of certain conditions ceases to be
relevant; such conditions can no longer be tolerated *at all*. If
the Milner Holland Committee's muck-raking helps to bring
about a permanent change in the public 'shock-threshold' it will
have served its purpose. If it only assuages the guilts of an
affluent society by pillorying a few scapegoats without achieving
any lasting advance in public morality then the Committee's
efforts will have been largely wasted.

To discover how prosperity came to be mixed with such
squalor and injustice it is necessary to examine some of the
changes that have been going on in London since the war. The
capital has always attracted young people in search of training,
work and promotion. The flow has been hastened in recent years
by the rapid growth of 'service' industries in central London:
during the last few years, over four fifths of the additional jobs
created in the conurbation have been in 'service' employment
(including the construction industry) and a large proportion of
the increase has been concentrated in the small central area
lying within the circle of the main-line railway stations.

The growth in population throughout the region surrounding
London, resulting both from the growth of jobs and from the
enhanced rate of natural increase that followed, was not
catastrophic; but it was much greater than had been expected or

* Case 404, p. 284.

allowed for by policy makers. The land made available for
building by town planning policies and the housing densities
permitted on this land were therefore inadequate to keep pace
with the increase in the demand for houses. Employment in the
London conurbation was growing at the same rate as employment in England and Wales as a whole; but in the suburban
region immediately surrounding the built-up area employment
was growing three times as fast.* Meanwhile the number of
dwellings within the conurbation was growing more slowly – at
about three-quarters of the rate for England and Wales –
although others were being built further afield for Londoners
in new and expanded towns and for spontaneous private 'overspill'.

Though reliable evidence of the distribution of incomes is
hard to find, the jobs in central London include exceptionally
large proportions at opposite ends of the income range. This
is where the highest paid executives and those at the top of their
professions are found; but the country's industrial and
commercial headquarters and the great bureaucracies and professions require a supporting framework of transport, catering
and postal services, retailing, building, warehousing and other
industries, which together employ many of the country's
lowest paid workers. Thus while the average level of household
income is appreciably higher in London than elsewhere in the
country, the spread of incomes is greater, and in the inner parts
of the town the richest and poorest households compete with
each other for shelter in neighbouring streets – often, indeed,
in the same streets and the same houses. Both have to work in the
centre; the rich can afford to live there, and the poor cannot
afford to move out.

Young workers flow into the inner areas of London from their
homes in the suburbs and further afield, and the more fortunate
married couples escape outwards to council estates and to the
owner-occupied fringes of the town. Meanwhile growing numbers of older people, who were unable or unwilling to make their
escape in the past, remain in the inner parts of London; most of
them live by themselves or with other elderly people, and many

*Ministry of Housing and Local Government, *The South East
Study, 1961–1981*, H.M.S.O., 1964.

of them are poor. In the central third of London that used to be London County these population movements together produced a large outward migration of younger parents and children between 1951 and 1961, a smaller inflow of younger people, and a fairly high rate of natural increase. In the suburban fringe of Greater London and beyond, population was rising fast owing to the inflow of migrants (many of them from the centre) and a higher rate of natural increase. In the intervening zone, much of which was built between the wars, there was a larger proportion of middle-aged and shrinking households: natural increase here was slow, and the population was gradually falling through outward migration. But because death rates were still low in this demographically 'stagnant' zone, Londoners in search of family housing often had to go beyond it and deep into the surrounding green belt before they could find a home.

Despite the fall in inner London's population, the growing proportions of the youngest and oldest people living there produce an insatiable demand for smaller dwellings. While the *population* of London County fell by 5 per cent between 1951 and 1961, the number of *households* only fell by 1 per cent; and, since fewer people were sharing accommodation at the end of the period, the numbers of separate *dwellings* increased – by 14 per cent. The growth in households in the County was larger than changes in the size and demographic structure of the population would account for. In 1951, there were already about 60,000 more households in London County than would have been found there if headship rates had been the same as for England and Wales as a whole. If the estimate of headship rates made for England and Wales by the National Institute of Economic and Social Research in 1960 is correct, London County's lead over the rest of the country must by then have increased still further, producing about 100,000 more households than would have been expected on the basis of national rates. Thus headship rates had risen during the decade to a greater extent than in the rest of the country. But the growing proportion of the youngest and oldest households found in central London – those in the second and fifth phases of their 'housing history' – meant that there was a continuing increase in small households and in the demand for small dwellings.

If houses were fairly and efficiently distributed, these trends should have permitted an all-round improvement in housing conditions. The excess of households over dwellings in London County fell from 300,000 in 1951 to 169,000 in 1961, and the rest of Greater London made even better progress. To understand what went wrong it is necessary first to examine the changes going on in the stock of houses. The scarcity of land in this heavily built-up area meant that new building proceeded relatively slowly: nearly 34,000 new permanent houses were built in the London conurbation in 1948, but thereafter the numbers fell, fluctuating for the next fifteen years around an annual output of 25,000, augmented by continuing (but in recent years very small) net gains from conversion and redevelopment. A rising proportion of the houses built in the suburbs were for owner occupation, but in London County the great majority were for council tenants: among the metropolitan boroughs it was only in the West End – in St Marylebone, Westminster, Kensington and Chelsea – that an appreciable amount of private building took place (amounting to between 40 and 50 per cent of the housing completed in those boroughs between 1951 and 1961). Slum clearance got under way in earnest after 1956, demolishing annually about 5,000 houses, nearly all of which had been privately rented. During the early 1960s, clearance and acquisitions by local authorities were taking about 1 per cent of privately rented accommodation units each year, while other losses – due mainly to purchases for owner occupation in the area outside London County – were taking about another 2 per cent each year. For the reasons explained in Chapter 7 there was practically no private building of houses for rent. The housing most likely to remain in the dwindling privately rented sector consisted of older, purpose-built blocks of flats, and the larger houses that could be subdivided and rented to several families or let off in furnished rooms and flatlets. Self-contained rented houses of the kind most suitable for families with children were more likely to be lost, both to slum clearance and to owner occupation.

For the first five years after the war the local authorities provided increasing opportunities for the families on their waiting lists, and thereafter the growth of private building gave similar opportunities to those who could buy a home of their own. But council building fell off during the 1950s and, as slum clearance and redevelopment schemes gained momentum from 1955 onwards, priority for the houses in the reduced council programmes was switched from the waiting lists to the rehousing of those whose homes were to be pulled down. At its post-war peak, in 1950, the London County Council rehoused over 12,000 families, 84 per cent of whom were drawn from the waiting lists; but during the four years preceding the appointment of the Milner Holland Committee the annual total rehoused had fallen to about 7,500, less than a quarter of whom came from the waiting lists.

Thus opportunities for an improvement in housing conditions were restricted to particular groups: 1) to those whose homes were about to be demolished in clearance programmes; 2) to a small number of people, suffering from extreme but rather arbitrarily defined hardships, still being rehoused from waiting lists by the authorities whose land supply and financial history permitted further building for general needs; 3) to larger families, already fairly well housed, whose children were leaving home and releasing space for those remaining in the house; 4) to households, often consisting of earners with no dependants to support, whose incomes and personal contacts enabled them to secure the better rented property still available; 5) to those who could afford to buy a home of their own in London or travel the increasing distances covered by long-range commuters. These last were a group increasingly restricted by the prices that had to be paid for housing in the region. Those living or working in London had secured a disproportionately large share of the nation's recent increase in wealth, but a disproportionately small share of the nation's new houses had been built in the town. The prices of houses had therefore been driven higher in this region than anywhere else in the country, and they continue to rise.

Those most likely to lose the battle for housing space were the families with the lowest incomes and the largest numbers of dependants to support, particularly if they were compelled by shift work or social ties to live in central parts of the town, those

who had come more recently to London and lacked the supporting network of personal contacts through which many people
find their homes, and foreigners with lower incomes who were
excluded by their origin or colour from areas of the market
offering the best value for money. Research carried out by the
Centre for Urban Studies in North Kensington showed that

Rents seemed to be far less determined by relevant objective
criteria – such as the size and quality of the accommodation
provided – than by fortuitous . . . ones, such as the date of the
tenant's arrival at the landlord's doorstep, his origin and his
colour. There was apparently a 'newcomers' tax'; and on top of
that a 'foreigners' levy', high especially in the case of coloured
people. It is just these people on the move from places near and
far who are required to meet local labour shortages in service and
other industries; in all the unskilled and skilled occupations they
keep the metropolitan machine running. Indeed, the very people
who are not wanted on the local housing market are needed for the
local labour market.*

Slum clearance has transformed many of the oldest and
poorest quarters in the centre of the town – in Westminster, St
Pancras, Finsbury and Bethnal Green, for example. Private redevelopment and modernization, beginning after the war in
Westminster, St Marylebone and other west central boroughs
has spread further westwards through Chelsea, Kensington and
southern parts of Paddington – a continuing historical trend
which began farther east long ago in areas which have since
become the uninhabited commercial heart of the city. Fulham
and Hammersmith now lie in the path of this westward movement of investment. They, and other parts of London to the
north and south of the centre, are beginning to experience the
economic and social transformation which privately sponsored
renewal brings about: streets and squares are 'discovered',
'improved' and 'saved' – for the middle classes – but those who
cannot afford to pay the new prices resulting from this process
must find a home elsewhere.

As slum clearance and redevelopment, privately or publicly
sponsored, modernize many of the central parts of London,
those who cannot escape to the suburbs, or find a home in the

*Milner Holland Report, pp. 188–9.

council flats or the more expensive private housing left in the centre, are squeezed into the larger rented houses a little farther out. These houses are subdivided, overcrowded, sold at prices that reflect the high rents paid for such intensive use, and sub-divided yet again. Thus it is in Hackney, Hornsey, North Kensington, Willesden, Stoke Newington and Islington that overcrowding and the subdivision of houses without proper conversion have been increasing – boroughs on the fringes of the areas that have been most extensively improved in recent years. As the pressure rises in these districts, six-room and eight-room houses in seedy streets are sold for six or seven thousand pounds, and let at rents of £3 10s. or more per room. Converted to shillings per square foot, such rents are often twice those paid for good, purpose-built flats in the better parts of London. Such rents can only be charged because a large number of the tenants who pay them do not belong to the economic and social classes capable of securing council housing or good private accommodation. Once a landlord buys a house at a price that reflects these earnings he is compelled to go on using it in ways that enable him to make a profit from his investment. In first-class rented housing the boot is on the other foot: the landlord knows that most of his tenants could readily buy themselves a house or rent another flat elsewhere, and they will only remain in his property if he gives them value for their money.

THE SEARCH FOR SOLUTIONS

As it became clear that the Rent Act of 1957 was not achieving the results that had been hoped for, as the numbers of homeless families seeking shelter from the local Welfare Departments rose, as more and more children had to be cared for by the L.C.C. Children's Department simply because their parents could not find a home, and as the press and the television screens showed increasing signs of the unrest and scandal that resulted, the government was gradually compelled to intervene. In 1959 and 1961, and again in 1964, it offered increasingly generous improvement grants, but few landlords were persuaded to make use of them – for reasons which have been explained in

Chapter 7. In 1961 and 1964 local authorities were given greater powers to control houses that were let to several households without being converted into self-contained units, to enforce better standards of management, to reduce overcrowding, and to compel landlords to improve their property. In 1962 tenants were given more extensive rights to rent books and to information about the identity of their landlords. But while the spread of decontrol deprived growing numbers of tenants of security of tenure there was little they could do to enforce these rights, for they could be evicted at a month's notice if they showed any sign of giving trouble. For many this was no idle threat; the Milner Holland Committee found that each year 4 per cent of the decontrolled tenants in unfurnished property and between 9 and 10 per cent of the households with furnished tenancies were obliged to move against their will.

There was little the local authorities could do so long as they were unable to provide alternative housing. They reported to the Milner Holland Committee that 'tenants . . now run a very serious risk of eviction if they attempt to exercise any of their rights', that 'an increasing number . . . refrain from approaching the Public Health Department', and that the councils' attempts to regain control of the situation were only 'creating a battlefield where the local authority cannot provide the ambulance service to take off the wounded'. If a landlord was compelled to reduce the number of people living in a house he naturally evicted the largest families first, and could generally secure the same rent from smaller households of single or childless people who were less likely to make trouble with public authorities or the neighbours and (being out at work all day) inflicted less wear and tear on his property. These problems have not been resolved: the Protection from Eviction Act of 1964 and the Rent Act of the following year should in time create a more rational system of rents and assure tenants of the basic security of tenure without which no other rights can be exercised, but they will not provide an additional house, or distribute the existing stock of houses any more efficiently than hitherto and they are unlikely to slow down the drift of rented property into owner occupation.

As the severity of these problems became increasingly apparent, the government began to seek more fundamental remedies. There had, since the war, been close control over the growth of industrial employment; but a White Paper pointed out that about 80 per cent of the increase in jobs in the London conurbation 'was in service employment, particularly in office employment in central London'. The post-war growth of these jobs had not been foreseen and their distribution was much less effectively controlled. The problem was at first concealed because so little office building was permitted during the first years after the war. But the boom in this type of building that developed in the mid fifties and the strains it imposed – on traffic as well as housing – compelled the government to impose increasingly severe restrictions, to make increasing efforts to decentralize office work (including its own), and to establish the Location of Offices Bureau to ensure that larger firms 'are encouraged to consider the possibility of some dispersal to other areas'.* Then, in 1964, further building of this kind was simply banned. The increase in 'service' employment in the conurbation was then believed to have been running at about 32,000 jobs a year, about half of which were concentrated in the City and the West End. Meanwhile increasingly determined efforts were being made to expand selected towns throughout the South East Region – particularly those far enough away to constitute genuinely independent centres – and to create new industrial centres and rebuild old ones in Scotland and the North of England and attract employers to the 'development areas' where a surplus of labour could be found.

These policies will help, in time, to relieve pressures on the capital: but they will certainly not eliminate them – no country has achieved that – and they will take many years to exert an appreciable effect. The 'South East Study', which dealt with planning policies in the whole south-eastern corner of Britain for the period 1961–81, was welcomed as a major advance in government thinking. Yet it shows how much remains to be done before policies of this kind can make an impact on London's housing situation. This study constituted an important 'political' statement, publicizing the government's determination

* *London. Employment: Housing: Land.* Cmd 1952, 1963.

to bring about a dramatic expansion of several towns lying sixty miles or more from London, and justifying this decision with such evidence as was available. Since the need for expansion is urgent, and towns in this belt had not been led to expect anything of the kind, the study set in motion a long overdue reappraisal of development plans throughout the region and helped to mobilize the technical resources and the political support this task will require. The authors of the study examined trends in population, employment, and urban growth, they projected these trends forward twenty years on the basis of certain assumptions, they posed the problems implied by this exercise, and they outlined a framework for a solution. It was no fault of theirs that some readers interpreted their proposals as a blue-print for the future which had only to be published in order to be applied.

Closer examination shows that the elimination of the housing shortage identified in the study will be impossible if a building programme of the type assumed is carried out, for the bulk of that building will cater not for those whose needs constitute the 'shortage' but for other more fortunate people. No systematic attempt was made to convert population figures into estimates of households and the dwellings they would require, and the basis of the estimate of London's housing shortage was not explained. Its insecurity was soon revealed: when the study was published, early in 1964, London was assumed to have had a shortage of 150,000 dwellings in 1961; but within twelve months this figure was first increased to 185,000 for 1961, and then raised again, for 1964, to about 230,000.* This uncertainty was not surprising. The most valuable data from the Census were not available and there was no authority or committee responsible for assessing and meeting the housing needs of the capital. It was not until the Greater London Council came to power in 1965 that the metropolis was given a local government. Until then, responsibility for its housing was divided between the London County Council, whose area included only two fifths of Greater London's population, and about eighty-five other housing authorities; meanwhile responsibility for its town planning

*For a fuller discussion of these problems, see Milner Holland Report, pp. 105–7.

policies had been divided between the London County Council, three County Boroughs and five Counties.

Much of the groundwork has now been laid for an attack on London's housing problems. Long term plans are taking shape for the renewal and reinvigoration of industries and cities in more distant parts of the United Kingdom. Nearer to London there will be further expansion of the first generation of new towns, and a rapid development of selected centres such as Swindon, Ipswich and Southampton which should in time help to counterbalance London's drawing-power. Office building in London is slowly being brought to a halt, at least for the time being. Procedures have been devised for regulating private rents which should help to create saner price relationships, first by reducing some of the more exorbitant decontrolled rents, and then by raising controlled rents. London at last has a local government responsible for keeping track of its needs and organizing the resources to meet them. Local authorities have been given far more extensive powers for controlling the use of private rented housing and for compelling the less responsible landlords to improve their property and manage it more efficiently. Private tenants have been given security of tenure and anyone attempting to intimidate them or deprive them of their rights can henceforth be dealt with under the criminal law. More recently the Minister has encouraged local authorities to increase their building programmes and given them increased subsidies for this purpose. But the last of these measures is the only one that will make a direct and immediate contribution to housing those in greatest need, and much else will have to be done if the worst stresses and hardships are to be eased.

Before considering further action, London's experience should be compared with that of great cities in other industrial countries, for problems similar to London's have arisen in all of them. A comparative study of New York and the principal cities of north-western Europe, made for the Milner Holland Committee, showed that population has been rising faster than was originally expected in every metropolitan region, while fewer and fewer people live in the central parts of these cities. The growth of service industries has been proceeding apace everywhere, and controls on land uses and building densities have combined with other causes of scarcity to drive up rents and prices. Controls of some kind have been imposed on rents in all these cities.

London differs from the others in having a smaller proportion of private rented housing (34 per cent) and a larger proportion of owner-occupied (41 per cent). Flats form a smaller proportion of London's dwellings, and houses a larger proportion, particularly in private rented property; hence the purchase of rented housing for owner occupation is easier and more attractive in London and proceeds far more rapidly. Losses of private rented housing to slum clearance are also proceeding faster in London, owing to a larger clearance programme. London has more municipal dwellings (20 per cent) than most of these cities, but far fewer (1 per cent) belonging to housing associations, cooperatives and other non-profit-making bodies. Another contrast has been stressed more recently by Dr Peter Hall in his survey of 'world cities'.* London, like Paris, Copenhagen, Stockholm and other great cities, is at the same time the commercial, administrative, cultural and political capital of its nation. Countries such as Holland and West Germany, where the centres of these different aspects of the nation's life have come to rest in separate but closely related cities, have a less crowded urban pattern, better adapted for growth and for meeting housing needs.

Geneva was one of the cities examined by the Milner Holland Committee. It stands in the only European country in which there has been a large and continuous supply of capital for private building, on exceptionally easy terms, and its social composition (heavily influenced by the presence of international agencies and immigrant labour) provides a continuing demand for rented property. Thus private landlords have remained the principal instrument for the provision of housing in Geneva – as they once were in all these cities. In the other cities examined, greater use has been made of various newer forms of tenure, but the private landlord has generally continued to make an appreciable, though dwindling, contribution to new building. In London he makes practically no contribution at all.

This difference arises from the whole history of investment,

*Peter Hall, *The World Cities*, 1966.

housing policies and taxation in the countries concerned. In general, the private landlord in other countries has been given fairer treatment by the tax collector, and he or his tenants have more often been subsidized by government. At the same time he has been subjected to closer and more systematic controls dealing with the rents he may charge, the repair of his property, the number and character of the tenants he may house, their security of tenure, and the terms of their contracts. Though more comprehensive than our own controls, those imposed elsewhere have generally been more flexible and more carefully planned: controlled rents have been revised and raised more frequently, and some attempt has been made to discriminate between the needs of different areas so that restrictions can be relaxed or abolished in places where they are no longer required while continuing in the big cities where shortages persist.

The history of government intervention in this field shows that controls, even of the most severely distorting kind, can be maintained for many years without bringing about a complete breakdown of the market, because the stock of dwellings changes slowly and it is worth their owners' while to continue holding property in hopes of the profits that may follow a relaxation of restrictions. But this state of affairs cannot continue forever; eventually the houses deteriorate, and businesslike and responsible owners sell out, while new, and frequently undesirable, methods of securing profits are evolved. Before this point is reached government must either abandon direct controls and leave landlords and tenants to strike their own bargains – as it eventually did throughout the U.S.A. in cities other than New York – or it must take increasing responsibility for this sector of the market. Rent controls, originally introduced as a temporary wartime expedient, have always had to be coupled with security of tenure for the tenant if people are not to become homeless. But if controls are to continue, means must also be found for ensuring that houses are properly maintained and repaired, often by permitting rent increases only where repairs are done. Some countries – notably Holland, Norway and Denmark – have also compelled landlords in areas of shortage to seek municipal approval for their selection of tenants, thus ensuring that homes are found for poorer families with children and for other groups who might otherwise be neglected, and the space available is efficiently used. If rented housing is to remain in the market despite these controls, and not be demolished or sold for owner occupation and for non-residential uses, then government must eventually subsidize its owners or their tenants, or acquire the property and manage it for itself. Our own governments have consistently refused to face up to this dilemma. In the words of the Milner Holland Committee, they have

failed to take effective responsibility for this sector of the housing market, either subjecting it to severe restrictions (without the complementary support and the additional controls needed to offset and to mitigate the effects of such restrictions) or abandoning control altogether and leaving this sector to escape, haphazard and piecemeal, into a 'freedom' politically insecure and sometimes abused.

Since the Committee's report, new controls have again been imposed on the private landlord, and yet more advantages have been given to the local housing authorities and the owner-occupier – thus still further weighting the scales against the landlord and in favour of his competitors. These steps take the government nearer to the point at which it must decide what future, if any, the private landlord is to have.

THE FUTURE

Before embarking on a discussion of future policies, the essentials of London's problem must be briefly restated. It is not a simple question of scarcity. To the inner parts of the town there is a continuing migration of younger, single or childless people and, with the passage of time, growing numbers of old people are left in the same areas. Both need more and more small dwellings. The more fortunate young families find their way to better housing, generally in the suburbs. Meanwhile major changes are at work in these more central areas; housing is being demolished, subdivided and improved; people are squeezed out of some neighbourhoods and into others; living space is being redistributed, often in exceedingly inefficient and unfair ways; squalid and spacious conditions are found side by side. Those most likely to be stranded or submerged in these cross-currents are the families on low incomes with several children to support who cannot escape to the suburbs and are unable to get a council flat or good private accommodation in the inner parts of the town. Others suffer too: the aged, the migrant, and young couples compelled to share inadequate housing with their in-laws. Though the *hardship* may be worst among larger families it arises mainly from a maldistribution of the existing stock of houses. The *shortage* of housing is most severe among the smallest dwellings, and this is not a problem that can be resolved by redistribution; it can only be resolved by providing many more small units, both in new housing and through conversion of existing property. The pace of economic development and change in the capital is such that these problems can never be finally and completely resolved. But some means must be found to enable all who are to remain in London to benefit from the rapid improvement in housing and general living standards achieved here, so that minimum standards can be pushed continuously upwards and no one is permanently confined to the worst housing without hope of escape.

No simple remedies are available. Rent restrictions have helped to create the problem, but to abolish them now would not lead to a fairer or more efficient distribution of housing: indeed, it would make the situation worse. Council housing is already more fully and effectively used than other housing, and cannot shelter more people; some council tenants may be capable of paying higher rents, but few of them can afford to find a good home elsewhere in London. Restriction of immigration from overseas will not have a major effect; the immigrants' plight is the outcome, not the cause, of London's housing difficulties, and if the inflow of immigrants is stopped their places will be taken by people from other parts of the country – or a number of essential jobs will remain unfilled. There is no appreciable reserve of empty dwellings in London; indeed there are fewer here than in other parts of Britain.* London's difficulties have neither a single cause nor a single remedy.

*See Milner Holland Report, pp. 201–3, for a fuller argument of these points.

No attempt will be made to prescribe cut-and-dried solutions for these difficulties. Instead attention will be concentrated on problems that current policies will not resolve, and further steps that must be taken to complement and extend the measures already in force.

It is plain that greater and bolder use must be made of public ownership and investment, both in the building of new houses and in the management of existing property. Public enterprise, of which the local housing authorities are the principal example, has the advantage that it can give those with urgent needs and small incomes greater scope for choice and movement, and make more efficient use of scarce housing space; it provides security of tenure and protects tenants from abuses that have sometimes arisen in private property; and it enables the community to acquire capital gains that arise in the course of time and apply them in a constructive fashion. It must now be clear how disastrous was the restriction or closure of waiting lists which occurred in many places when slum clearance began. In future, slum clearance must not be regarded as an alternative to re-housing from the waiting lists but must be coupled with a continuing programme of building for general needs. Meanwhile, if public authorities acquire larger amounts of older rented housing they will have a wider variety of house types and sizes at their disposal and a wider range of rents to offer their tenants, and they can check the continuing loss of rented property to owner occupation which now deprives those with lower incomes of much housing that is suitable for family use. The authorities will in any case have to acquire most of the older rented houses in the course of the slum clearance programmes due over the next twenty-five years; and henceforth, when buying houses that are not technically 'unfit', they should be able to acquire them at the rather more modest prices that regulated rents and rigorous public health policies should produce.

But local authorities cannot make their most effective contribution unless the tangle of debt burdens imposed on them by the accidents of history is more rationally distributed. There is no valid reason for the major differences in subsidies and loan charges now to be found among London housing authorities, for these are determined not by present needs or resources but by the costs of past building and borrowing. This system rewards those who have built most extensively and borrowed most wisely during the period between ten and forty years ago, and discourages further building. For similar reasons the government must ensure that such reserves of land as remain in London – particularly the large 'windfall' sites, like disused airfields and goods yards – are employed as efficiently as possible to provide for those in greatest need, instead of being wastefully used, hoarded, or cornered for the benefit of the boroughs in which they happen to stand. Some boroughs have modest housing problems, large windfall sites within their boundaries, and a considerable population of skilled workers who will be capable of securing jobs in new and expanded towns. But others, with bigger and more urgent needs, very little building land or open space, and many unskilled or semi-skilled workers tied to trades in central areas of London, can only make progress with the help of neighbouring boroughs willing to accept some of their population. Since no borough can compel its neighbours to help it, the Greater London Council must be given overriding authority to ensure the best use of the resources available.

It would be a mistake, however, to rely solely on council housing to meet the needs of those who cannot fend for themselves. Their constitution renders democratically elected local authorities insensitive to many of these needs. Some London authorities exclude from their waiting list anyone without British nationality, others exclude childless couples, and many exclude single people; some accept anyone living in their areas while others demand seven years' residence or more; many require a minimum rent-paying capacity and refuse to house families deemed to be incapable of paying such rents (£2 10s. or £3 for example) even if they are currently paying larger sums for inadequate private accommodation. Despite the growing demand for small dwellings, few authorities are building appreciable numbers with less than two bedrooms. Current building programmes will increase the proportion of one-bedroom and bed-sitter council dwellings from 16 to 17 per cent of the total between 1963 and 1966; yet 37 per cent of those already on the waiting lists and 39 per cent of households coming from slum clearance areas require dwellings of this size.

Many of these smaller households must find small homes in private rented housing, and the considerable success with which they do this places an increasing strain on the larger families who must compete with them for space.

Although a good deal can be done to modify and diversify the selection policies of local authorities – particularly with the help of the Greater London Council which is less restricted by local loyalties and prejudices – other forms of public enterprise may be required alongside them, both for new building and for the management of older property. Otherwise the needs of those excluded from council housing may not be effectively met. It is not only the single, the childless and the migrant whose needs are at stake : all will suffer if social variety cannot be maintained. If slum clearance proceeds for some years at the pace now envisaged, vast areas of London may become municipal preserves, interspersed with small islands of expensive owner-occupied housing. It may then become increasingly difficult for such areas to secure teachers, social workers, public health inspectors, health visitors and many others without whose help these neighbourhoods will be severely impoverished. To secure the advantages of collective ownership and management without the social segregation arising from local government policies, it may be necessary to create and foster housing associations and co-ownership schemes and preserve a certain amount of private rented housing. Owner occupation, developed with the help of the Land Commission on the new 'crownhold' basis now proposed, will also have a contribution to make.

For relatively well-to-do households capable of paying the higher rents required for good rented housing, the private landlord can still provide an important service. But this contribution will not be an effective one unless the larger and more efficient landlords are freed from the present fiscal discrimination that prevents them from improving or replacing their property on terms similar to those available to investors in other industries. They must also be assured of rents that are a fair reflection of the value of the accommodation provided, without threats of new controls and rent-freezes. If the tax privileges now accorded to the wealthier owner-occupiers were curtailed, this too would strengthen the position of the larger landlord providing first-class accommodation, for it would reduce the wasteful and illogical incentives which now tempt his richest tenants to leave him and buy homes of their own.

To attract the resources required for redevelopment and modernization, to concentrate them in areas which have been starved of investment for years, and to achieve an appropriate blend of all the investors with a contribution to make – councils, housing associations, private landlords and the owner-occupier – it may be necessary to create new development agencies capable of acquiring large blocks of property that will become ripe for redevelopment during the next decade, and leasing appropriate sites to the investors concerned. The Greater London Council and the larger and better-staffed boroughs should already be capable of doing this, if given some additional powers. Elsewhere it may be necessary to set up specially constituted development corporations to undertake this task, on the lines suggested in a previous chapter.*

These proposals will not be effective unless the steps already being taken to check the growth of employment in the centre of London and to redistribute jobs and population to other parts of the country and to other centres in the region are pursued with vigour. This is not a question of preventing a southward drift of industry; for years the growth of employment in the south-eastern region has been self-generating, due to the capacity for expansion already built into local enterprises which include a high proportion of the country's most rapidly expanding industries. London's employers must in future be persuaded to establish new growing points farther from the capital. Meanwhile the tentative efforts already being made to move older people out of London, when they are no longer tied there by their work, should be extended. The objections of south coast towns, some of which have been reluctant to accept older emigrants from the metropolis, should not be allowed to frustrate this scheme. (They apparently fear these people may cast a burden on their, generally buoyant, rate income – though they welcome well-to-do commuters who then spend hours every day travelling to the city and back.) Once rents in London are effectively regulated and a larger proportion of rented housing

*See page 261.

is publicly owned, it should be possible to introduce a general system of housing allowances of the kind outlined in Chapter 7 that will enable larger and poorer families to secure housing of the sort they need. For those in slightly higher income groups it should soon be possible to offer loans at reduced interest rates so that they gain help in buying a house on a scale similar to that already available, through tax relief, to richer households. But in London's conditions of scarcity, this will only drive up the price of housing unless demand is kept in balance by simultaneously reducing the more generous fiscal privileges that now go to those least in need of them.

London constitutes a vast working model of the housing market described in Chapter 6, showing the stresses and hardships that arise when social change and increasing wealth make new demands on a stock of housing that cannot be readily expanded or adapted, and the flow of households from one sector of the market to another and from area to area within the town is checked and distorted. The solutions must be as extensive and far reaching as the problems themselves, and any government that tries to grapple with these problems will be compelled to assume increasingly comprehensive responsibilities, not only for the housing of Londoners but also for the distribution of incomes, for regulating rents and the rights of property owners, and for the regional distribution of industrial development, employment and urban growth.

But the daunting complexity of these problems should not conceal the essential simplicity of the issues at stake. They arise not from the quality of London's housing and civic design (people come from all over the world to see Roehampton and Golden Lane) nor from the shortage of living space (in terms of broad averages London is by no means ill-equipped) nor from the rate at which London's population is growing (for many other cities are growing as fast). The problem arises from the mixture of affluence and squalor, the persistence of bad housing conditions within a generally improving situation, and the degrading human conflicts fostered by these contrasts. It is a problem of justice.

CHAPTER II

RESEARCH AND POLICY

LESS than a decade ago the Ministry of Housing and Local Government did virtually no research on the questions discussed in this book (though a decade before that its record had been a good deal better). The statistics it published were scanty, being confined mainly to data on the building of new houses and other figures that recorded the extent of the government's efforts rather than clarifying the problems to be solved. Its annual reports were unrevealing – and still are. The only major public investment in research which had a direct bearing on housing was conducted through the Building Research Station, a large organization financed by the Department of Scientific and Industrial Research, producing work of the highest quality which was at that time confined to restricted physical and technical problems: its findings were not of great interest to the Ministry, and appeared to have little impact on the house building industry. Independent research workers outside government had little to say about housing, and academic studies in this field were fewer and poorer than those of the prewar period. Meanwhile senior administrators would modestly assert that they knew nothing about research and could not understand statistics, implying thereby that those with sufficient experience and ability need not encumber themselves with such knowledge.

Times have changed. The Ministry now has a small but competent statistical staff, a Sociological Survey Unit, and a consultant economist; its architects are conducting experimental work in several parts of the country and the outcome of their projects is being published and evaluated; town planners and others in the Ministry are collaborating with an expanding circle of research workers in universities and elsewhere, a growing number of whom are supported by government funds. Many more questions on housing have been squeezed into the Census. The Building Research Station has extended the scope of its work to include the economics of building, and various social, administrative and economic aspects of urban development. The Social Survey made its first published housing inquiry for the Ministry in 1958 and now seems likely to make regular inter-censal investigations of the housing situation. The initial reluctance to publish such studies appears to have been over-come (but the first two reports produced by the Survey – technically excellent though they were – were presented in a fashion that mystified journalists and others not accustomed to such material). Similar studies are being made in Scotland, although Northern Ireland is still left to its own devices. The Milner Holland Committee made the first comprehensive study of housing problems to be carried out by an independent com-mittee since the Royal Commission on the Housing of the Working Classes reported in 1885 – although, unlike the Royal Commission, it only dealt with London.

While a great deal remains to be done, these changes in the scale and influence of research on housing are so striking that the time for a general appeal for greater public investment in such inquiries has now passed. Attention should instead be given to the problems of a new phase in which the growing resources devoted to research may too easily be wasted on work that is badly done, on good work that answers the wrong questions, or on answers that nobody listens to.

Why did research make so little contribution to housing policies during the 1950s, and why is this state of affairs now changing? An understanding of the reasons for these changes will clarify the motives at work, the conditions fostering the growth of research, and the potential strengths and weaknesses of this development. The contribution that research can make to housing policies and the forms of organization required to make this contribution fruitful can then be explored. These questions and their implications are discussed in the pages that follow.

THE GROWTH OF RESEARCH

The housing problems confronting government at the end of the war were so obvious and urgent that little research was needed to identify them or to determine the first steps to be taken towards their solution. As the programme for building permanent houses got under way in 1947, the economic crisis of that year led to the imposition of controls which made it plain that resources for meeting housing needs would be severely restricted for a long time to come. Since government had assumed heavy responsibilities in this field, housing was bound to remain a politically sensitive topic. Research was likely to reveal yet more unmet needs and create further political problems.

These stresses meant that government was unenthusiastic about research on housing. To them was added in the early 1950s a more general suspicion of 'planning' and all that went with it: the word was dropped from the Ministry's title in 1951, and research and planning staffs were cut down – economists and statisticians, for whom there was keen demand elsewhere, usually being the first to leave. The Social Survey only survived in a shrunken form, losing nearly half its headquarters staff and many of its ablest young research workers.

Meanwhile the traditions of the civil service, somewhat disrupted during the war, reasserted a long-established pattern of organization, supported by a hierarchy of status relationships, which gave the general administrator a dominant position at every level of the administrative class. Professional staff were attached at each level in a fashion that gave the administrators control over the professionals' terms of reference and over their communications with higher levels of the organization. Since the upper reaches of the civil service are manned by some of the ablest and most devoted people in the country and provide as great an opportunity for ability (once recruited) to make its mark as any sphere in Britain, this system does not necessarily frustrate research. But when people trained to do research are very scarce, and are offered greater freedom, higher status and more opportunities for publication elsewhere, it is not surprising if those willing to remain in government have difficulty in securing an effective hearing. A Ministry gets the research staff it deserves.

In the academic world it is the administrators, by and large, who are subordinated to professional staff. But there, long-standing conventions awarded higher status to the 'pure' research worker than to the 'applied'. It was assumed that 'applied' research demands less intellectual rigour and must be parasitic upon the 'pure' research findings it 'applies'. This assumption and the pecking orders consequent upon it were unlikely to attract the best minds to study housing problems.

The first post-war census, like its predecessors, threw less light on housing than the censuses of many other countries. The United Kingdom's census still adheres to the traditions of an operation that was originally designed to count the population. Unlike some of our neighbours we have never had a census of housing. Meanwhile the Ministry of Housing and Local Government made practically no use of the government's other all-purpose mechanism for gathering information – the Social Survey. Although its responsibilities for housing, town planning and local government touch the public at innumerable points, this Ministry asked the Survey for fewer studies and spent less money on research conducted by the Survey between 1952 and 1963 than the Ministries of Agriculture, Labour, Health, and Transport, the Home Office, the G.P.O. or the Board of Trade.* The only comparable department with an equally economical record was the Ministry of Education which invested heavily in research conducted by independent workers, and had its own exceptionally well-developed procedures for inquiry, as its regular statistical publications and a series of famous studies (Crowther, Newsom, Plowden, etc.) clearly demonstrate.

The reasons for a slump in housing research, which formed part of a brief but more pervasive dark age on all social questions, are fairly clear: the future duration of the revival now taking place is less certain. As progress made between 1952 and 1956 relieved some of the more critical shortages, the totally insoluble problems passing across the Minister's desk each week declined in numbers. The relaxation of political pressures, coupled with an assured majority in Parliament, provided an opportunity for reappraising the situation, but the outcome of this reappraisal – as explained in Chapter 5 – was a determination to extricate

* Louis Moss, *The Social Survey in the Government Process*: unpublished evidence submitted by the Social Survey to the Heyworth Committee.

government as far as possible from its responsibilities in the housing field. Thus it was not in housing but in other fields – education, transport, criminology and agriculture, for example – that research and inquiry first began to revive.

Professionals of various kinds began to get a firmer foothold in the Ministry of Housing and Local Government. Architects, whom many had previously regarded simply as technicians to be consulted about the outside appearance of buildings, gained new leadership, grew in numbers, and introduced systematic procedures for the development and testing of designs and building methods – ideas which some of them had previously tried out under the London County Council and the Ministry of Education. The town planners were strengthened at the same time. Both professions, being more concerned at heart about the analysis of needs than the protection of the Minister, were avid for information, and their demands brought social scientists and statisticians in their wake.

Outside the Ministry there was growing concern about the stagnation of the British economy and about the unfinished business of the 'welfare state'. The creation of the N.E.D.C. which scoured the land for economists to man its secretariat, the rediscovery of poverty and homelessness in the midst of affluence, the substitution of radical for liberal definitions of 'equality of opportunity' in education (no longer 'equal opportunities for the intelligent' but 'equal opportunities for acquiring intelligence') were part of a gradual but general mobilization of interest in the responsibilities of government which made growing demands for research workers, encouraged social scientists to apply themselves seriously to problems of social and economic policy, and led in time to the Heyworth Committee's report* showing how ill-equipped the universities and the government were to promote social research and to recruit and train the staff required for it.

In housing, as in other fields, the crucial change in the climate for research arose from the acceptance by government of more comprehensive responsibilities for meeting the nation's needs – a commitment which compelled Ministers (sometimes in advance of their administrators) to call for more information

* *Report of the Committee on Social Studies*, Cmd 2660, 1965.

and advice, and encouraged them to shed inhibitions about inquiring into social problems and publishing the results. These commitments were themselves part of a more extensive mobilization of political pressures, and effective progress will not continue in the housing field if that broader tide loses its momentum.

For the time being the demand for research is in danger of outrunning the supply of trained workers, but as this bottle-neck is broken new dangers may arise. We are unlikely to find ourselves in the position of some of the east European countries where large and highly professional teams of engineers, architects, planners and scientists study the technical problems of building and urban layout, while inadequate resources are devoted to the analysis of broader social priorities and objectives. We are more likely to find ourselves in the American position where extensive research is constantly being done on urban growth and the housing market, but the findings make relatively little impact on the processes studied – tracing and predicting the spread of a forest fire, as it were, without doing anything to control it. Fascinatingly educative though such studies can be, our own resources (of land and research manpower alike) are too slender to be wasted in this way. But if research findings are to be considered by policy makers they must be assembled and organized more promptly and presented more readably than has been possible in universities where most research is done during vacations and publications may be designed principally for the eye of those who will determine the author's fitness for academic promotion. The remainder of this essay is designed to help in establishing a framework that will make it easier to resolve such problems.

THE ORGANIZATION OF RESEARCH AND RELATED ACTIVITIES

Research is designed to advance and communicate knowledge about specific problems or specific fields of inquiry. Those who secure knowledge of matters that are of great political interest and the right to communicate or withold such knowledge inevitably gain power of a kind. Therefore the organization of research on housing is a political matter, posing constitutional as well as technical problems. The politics involved may not be 'party politics', the power involved may in practice be negligible – and it usually is. But to disregard this feature of the issues at stake is a mark of amateurism which leads sooner or later to confusion and recrimination.

Those responsible for taking decisions about housing policies, whether at local or central levels of administration, continue to bear the full weight of these responsibilities whether research is done or not. If it is good enough, research can collect, codify and summarize past experience, it can subject the results to intellectual analysis and reveal things hitherto unknown, it can clarify problems, pose alternative solutions and calculate the probabilities of various outcomes. By doing these things it can free men's judgement to concentrate more effectively on the problems that only judgement can resolve. If the light thrown upon a problem is to be revealing, its beam must be concentrated, leaving large areas of darkness on either side: inevitably 'a way of seeing is also a way of not seeing'. Thus the more important decisions of policy makers and administrators can never be derived from research alone, for they demand an exercise of judgement, a balancing of risks, and consideration of many factors – legal, political, technical, personal – that must lie beyond the researchers' necessarily restricted terms of reference. By enlarging and clarifying the policy makers' or the public's understanding of a problem and by furnishing the government or its critics with ammunition for debate, research workers may influence the decisions to be taken or the public reception accorded to them. But the pressures exerted by supporters and opponents of government will continue, whether research takes place or not. Research itself is an essentially neutral instrument, contributing – if it is sufficiently well done – to a more rational resolution of these pressures. It can never shift the responsibility for decision from those who now bear it. Mutual understanding of these simple propositions is the starting point for any constructive relationship between research and policy making.

The account that follows outlines the activities that must be mounted and related to each other in the course of such a partnership, deliberately employing a simple formula that may

be generalized and modified to suit different contexts. The scale
of the activities involved will vary according to the size of the
organization concerned and the scope of its responsibilities:
work that may call for a well-staffed office within the Ministry of
Housing and Local Government may be done by one man in a
county borough, and take no more than occasional moments of
someone's time in a smaller urban district.

1. *Intelligence.* Before devoting resources to research, an organization should be equipped with effective means for mobilizing
the knowledge of its own staff, for summarizing the literature
already available and for communicating with research workers
elsewhere. Whether or not this task justifies a separate
'intelligence unit' – or several, or simply one or two people
alerted for the job – political leaders and their senior officials
need the help of staff who are equipped for this purpose.
Meanwhile those responsible for 'intelligence' need to be
sufficiently familiar with their own organization, its library, and
those who write the relevant literature to know where to go and
whom to ring up when help is needed. They must also be
sufficiently familiar with current developments in policy to
foresee some of the crises on which their help will be expected
during the coming months. 'Intelligence' is not 'research',
though it calls for communication with research workers. And
this communication should be a two-way affair, both seeking
information from research workers and prompting them to
study problems that will become increasingly important in
future.

2. *Information.* Closely linked to the task of intelligence, and
often performed by the same people, is the systematic collection,
analysis and publication of data derived from, and required for,
the organization's current activities. This again is a job that
must be done within the Ministry or department concerned
since much of the information needed can only be secured and
prepared in this way. The staff required will typically be larger
but, in the main, less highly trained than that required for
intelligence purposes. Computers will be needed in an
organization of sufficient size, as will the skills required to

operate them – whether on a resident or consultant basis. The Ministry and the larger local housing departments regularly collect far more, and far more useful, information than they publish. If their internal information services published fuller and more frequent data – on house prices and rents, for example, or on changes in the stock of dwellings and the anticipated growth of population and households – they would in time create a better informed and more rational public opinion.

3. *Specialist libraries.* For the proper functioning of information and intelligence services alike, as for the other activities to be discussed, a large organization requires a well-stocked library with sufficient staff to keep track of current research in their field and prepare properly catalogued abstracts from the journals. Expenditure on this service, which should be available to accredited scholars outside the department, will achieve considerable economies when grants for research are made to bodies that will otherwise have to begin by accumulating similar libraries, reading lists and summaries of their own.

4. *Applied 'project' research.* Research will be needed on particular issues, problems or questions of many types: for example, a comparison of the 'cost in use' of various kinds of building that fulfil the same functions, a study of the ownership and management of certain types of rented property, or a forecast of the effects exerted by migration from one region to another upon rates of demographic growth and household formation in each. Such studies can be done within government or in universities, research institutes and other outside bodies. If a prompt estimate is more urgently required than a systematic and refined analysis, if publication of the results is likely to prove difficult, or if the problem can be efficiently tackled in a 'self-contained' fashion that throws little light on neighbouring issues or disciplines, then such studies should generally be done within the organization requiring them. Otherwise the project should be handled by people, inside or outside government, who are most likely to secure a staff capable of doing the job well.

5. *Applied operational research.* Once objectives have been

chosen and decisions taken, problems arise in putting a policy into practice and improving the efficiency of a service. At this stage operational research may be required: for example, to hasten procedures for dealing with town planning applications and appeals, or to improve, simplify and standardize the design of building components such as doors and windows, or to discover an acceptable and efficient procedure for determining the incomes of tenants applying for rent rebates. Such work should be carried out by trained staff with a realistic grasp of the practical problems involved, working in close conjunction with the people who will be affected by the outcome or called upon to put recommendations into practice. A high degree of skill will often be required, and the specialists needed will vary from one project to another. Thus, although some of this work can be done within government service by Organization and Methods Departments and similar units, the help of commercial organizations and other outside bodies will often be required on a consultant basis.

6. '*Longer term*' research. This kind of work is sometimes, but misleadingly, described as 'basic' or 'fundamental' research. In fact it can only be approximately distinguished from 'project' research. Both draw on, and are capable of contributing to, the same academic disciplines. And in the social sciences distinctions between 'pure' and 'applied' research are always liable to become ridiculous; the great advances in thought and knowledge have always sprung from a mixture of the two. (Was Keynes a 'pure' theoretician? Was Marx, or Freud?) The distinctions between 'project' and 'longer term' research arise from the greater need of the latter to draw on a variety of academic disciplines, its greater potentiality for contributing to such disciplines, the greater likelihood that it will question policy objectives which may impinge on the responsibilities of several Ministries, the longer time-scale of the trends to be studied, and the longer period this research normally takes to complete. Examples of such research might include a study of the sources and distribution of investment in the housing market and their relationship to national trends in saving and expenditure, a study of the formation, movement and dissolution of households

in towns of various types and the implications of this process for the services their populations require, or a study of the technical evolution of the building industry and the impact likely to be made on building methods, productivity and the demand for labour by current changes in technology. Such research is likely to call for advanced scholarship, often drawn from several disciplines; and it must be capable of calling the current assumptions and policies of different government departments into question. Since the 'pay-off' from these studies is uncertain – they may prove fruitless, or their findings may be of more interest to neighbouring disciplines than to the bodies originally sponsoring them – since government departments may not be able to muster the skills required, and cannot publicly criticize the policies of their own leadership – let alone the policies being followed in neighbouring Ministries – such studies are often best conducted in universities or independent research institutes, though government may nevertheless provide the funds required for them.

7. '*Development work*'. Although it calls for many of the same skills, 'development work' is not research but systematically planned experiment and innovation, designed to reappraise knowledge and experience of specified problems, to devise new solutions that can be applied within normal staffing and cost limits, and to introduce these solutions in a fashion that can be further developed and widely applied. The character of development work was well summarized by those responsible for the development groups which revolutionized school designs and building methods.

Its underlying motive power might be called constructive scepticism: scepticism because it seeks first to question all accepted assumptions; constructive because it believes that, by analysis and experiment, a better solution can often be found than the best current answer.

It tries to tackle problems as a whole and not piecemeal. . . . Although this entails specialist investigations into general or specific aspects of design, structures, services, finishes, etc., these investigations are comprehended within the project as a whole and are not separate projects in themselves. . . .

Its objectives are controlled and finite. . . . The development team thus organize the time and brains available to give optimum results within the given terms of reference. . . .

Effective intercommunication . . . is assisted by means of the technique . . . of cost analysis and cost planning. These provide vocabulary, grammar and concepts which laymen and professionals can understand and use as a basis for collaboration. . . .

Developers are 'naturals', and comparatively rare. They tend to be what they are by reason of character and temperament. . . . Perhaps their most important characteristic, apart from professional skill, is a sustained spirit of curiosity and enquiry, coupled with a strong desire to see their work produce practical results.*

Development 'teams' (for a mixture of skills is required) have been organized in the engineering industry and for certain branches of architecture, and there is no reason why the method should not be more widely used. Operational research workers are applying a similar approach and similar techniques to problems of management and administration. Since such work must be done in close collaboration with those who will later have to use its results it must normally be organized by government.

8. *Spreading knowledge.* Those responsible for the more specialized forms of investigation that have been outlined can usually be relied on to communicate their findings to administrative and professional colleagues if authorized to do so. But normal methods of publication are inadequate when new methods and ideas have to be communicated to a large and widely scattered range of people – to builders or local authorities all over the country, for example – who must not only be informed but persuaded to adapt and modify their practices in the light of fresh knowledge. This task calls for careful selection and skilled presentation of the points to be put over: it is an educational task, and may indeed be carried out in conjunction with the preparation of pamphlets, and the running of regular courses and conferences. Those best equipped to discover new knowledge are often ill-suited for such work – it is the pursuit of truth that fascinates them, and truth itself, once discovered, often bores them. Thus in some countries the government has

*Quoted in the Zuckerman Report on *The Management and Control of Research and Development*, pp. 123–4. H.M.S.O., 1961.

set up special organizations, alongside building research stations and similar bodies but independent of them, which are responsible for getting new ideas put into practice. Our recently established National Building Agency does work of this kind within a limited field, but further institutions of this sort may be required. The placing of research contracts in colleges where training courses are given for administrators, town planners, builders and similar professions can also make it easier to disseminate knowledge of research findings.

9. *Training research workers.* Since research, particularly in the social sciences, is now one of this country's most rapidly growing industries, it is going to face serious labour shortages for a long time to come, and all the foregoing types of work will develop too slowly unless plans are made, well in advance, to recruit, train and support sufficient numbers of young people capable of doing the work required. There must therefore be a continuing flow of grants and research assistantships for graduate students, and of small-scale research projects that provide appropriate training for such people at this stage of their careers.

CONCLUSIONS

The purpose of this list of activities is to take the discussion beyond a simple appeal for 'more research'. Different forms of research with differing objectives will be needed. And the contribution they make – the influence they actually exert on policy and practice – will depend largely on the development of related activities without which research cannot be effectively linked to its environment: intelligence services capable of briefing decision makers and occasionally suggesting fruitful lines of inquiry to research workers; statistical and library services providing much of the research workers' basic data; development work, information and educational services capable of applying and disseminating the findings of research; and academic work of various kinds providing the manpower, the intellectual framework and much of the inspiration for research. Now that the necessity for research is generally accepted

there is little doubt that more of it will take place. But if they are
not closely linked to other organizations, research units – like
some benign but functionless growth in the body politic – will
be encapsulated in a membrane of indifference which effectively
isolates them from contact with points in the system at which
decisions are taken. The academic and commercial communities
generally recognize that about half their investment in research
must be devoted to the education of those who do it; the data
that emerge at the end are the other half of their dividend. Thus
the man in a market research or industrial consultancy firm who
'handles' the Cadburys' or Courtaulds' account will be brought
in later to discuss questions of marketing strategy or managerial
organization on which his studies have rendered him expert.
When government departments establish research units or
commission the Social Survey to make studies for them they
seldom seek their advice later when decisions have to be taken
that deal with the questions studied, thus wasting half the
investment made.

Most of the work that has been outlined must be conducted
by government agencies, central or local. Outside bodies such
as universities and research institutes can help with several
kinds of research, but their main contribution will be to longer-
term studies and the training of research workers. Longer-term
studies generally call for the use of data dealing with trends in
investment, consumption, demographic growth or other matters
which extend well beyond the confines of one government
department's sphere of interest. At the same time they pose
potentially critical questions about the policies of government.
Hence a delicate balance may be required to ensure they are
conducted in close collaboration with the departments that
possess the necessary data, without being distorted by the
interests of any particular branch of the administration. The
National Institute of Economic and Social Research provides a
useful base for such work, poised between government, the
universities and industry, and more centres of this kind may be
required in future. But until the supply of trained manpower
improves, the growth of such centres must be slow and selective,
otherwise resources will be wastefully scattered instead of being
concentrated to create viable teams.

Intelligence services and research will generally demand the scarcest and most advanced skills. But such work is relatively cheap: the annual costs of a trained research worker, together with supporting secretarial and technical services and the necessary overheads, are generally less than the capital cost of a house. The other activities demand rather fewer of the scarcest skills, but they are often more expensive. Development work must be particularly carefully planned because it calls for a wide variety of technical skills, the preparation of experimental designs, the fabrication of parts and the building of prototypes. Typically, therefore, it is more expensive than the rest of the programme put together.

Research of the kinds listed generally calls for inter-disciplinary teams and it cannot be completed efficiently unless a large proportion of their staff are full-timers. This means that a few major research centres will be required, capable of specializing in particular fields: one, for example, might deal with the economics of urban investment, the patterns of household formation and movement and the processes of urban growth and decay; another with the design and layout of residential developments and their relation to the rest of the urban environment and its transport network. Development work on the design of houses needs to be planned on a long-term basis. Czechoslovakian research, briefly described in Chapter 4, provides a useful model here: it proceeds through recurring cycles, from the first specification of performance requirements and cost limits, through the preparation and erection of experimental designs and the assessment of their inhabitants' experience and satisfaction, to the organization of mass production of buildings incorporating modifications required for technical or social reasons – the whole cycle taking nearly five years. As with the development of aircraft designs, the initial work on the next designs begins before the previous ones have gone into general production. The growing scale of publicly sponsored house building projects should in future make it possible to do work of this kind which is genuinely 'experimental' in the sense that the results are carefully studied and widely applied.

Unless there is continuing and competent work on central themes such as these, more specialized studies of specific problems (such as the design of shopping centres, the effects of rent control, or the insulation of buildings) will not be under-pinned by the broader framework of general knowledge and policy intentions required to furnish their basic assumptions and guiding strategy.

Further thought may have to be given to the careers and salaries appropriate for research workers in government. The best people available will often do their best work between the ages of twenty-five and thirty-five, when there is keen demand for their services elsewhere. Skilled administration, by contrast, calls for greater maturity and experience and the wider range of personal contacts which come later in life. Thus a salary structure appropriate for administrators may deprive govern-ment of research workers at the point when they can do their best work, and subsequently retain them in research posts when many would do better to move on to teaching or administration and make room for younger men.

Research of the kind discussed here is still too often conducted in an amateurish fashion; it must be managed more competently if it is to make the contribution it should. This is not the place to examine problems of research technique but a number of elementary precautions deserve to be stressed.*

Public authorities and charitable foundations financing inves-tigations should expect research workers to give them a non-technical explanation of their objectives, a brief summary of existing knowledge in the field concerned, a reasonably detailed estimate of the costs and timetable for the project, and an outline of their credentials and the qualifications of the principal workers who will be needed for the study; and, if this cannot be done and the project is nevertheless of sufficient importance, the sponsors should be prepared to finance a pilot study that will provide such information. That is to say, they should treat a research worker no less seriously than they would treat an architect or a builder who was contracting to serve them.

Government departments and local authorities asked to provide the facilities for research will need to know, in addition,

*For a fuller discussion of some of the points that follow, see National Council of Social Service, *Research in the Personal Social Services, Proposals for a Code of Practice*, 1965.

how much time their own staff will be expected to give to the study, what disruption it may cause to their work, what arrangements will be made to protect individuals among their staff and the public when the results are published, and what opportunities they will be given to correct, or reply to, research findings that might discredit them.

Despite the difficulties involved, anyone hoping that research findings will be applied in direct and practical fashion should endeavour whenever possible to secure a financial contribution towards the research from the organizations that should use the results. When practical applications of research findings are expected, it is important to remember that people find it much harder to disregard findings for which they have paid than those of a study that cost them nothing. Moreover, since authorization of such payments has often to be secured from senior officials or committees, the research worker who gains the payment has greater assurance that the existence of his study is known from the start to those who may be in a position to apply its results.

Research workers who have furnished appropriate information and assurances to their sponsors or employers and the organizations assisting them should expect in return the right to publish their results, except where it can be shown that these results may be erroneous, seriously misleading, or seriously injurious to individuals (not to organizations) or where some other convincing reason is explicitly given. It is to be hoped that government will no longer be prepared to spend large sums of public money on expertly conducted studies of important questions and then refrain from publishing its findings. Apart from its questionable ethics, such a practice casts doubts on the validity of the studies that *are* selected for publication, and deters self-respecting research workers from entering public service.

In a field as complex and extensive as housing, entangled as it must be with the neighbouring fields of building, town planning, local government, economic administration and so on, many of the people doing research will be but dimly aware of relevant work being done by their colleagues in other organizations and other disciplines. Thus the appropriate departments of government must assume some overall responsibility for assessing the quality of research and its relevance to current and future needs. Otherwise funds will be wasted on poor work, or good work will be done on problems that have been rendered irrelevant by the progress of events. In several European countries there are centres for research and development work in house building where vast resources are devoted to the perfection of techniques for the mass production of large blocks of flats. Meanwhile centres of economic and social research, responding to their governments' pleas for guidance on means for increasing personal investment in housing, are showing that people will spend a great deal more on securing and improving a home if they can buy separate owner-occupied dwellings. Elsewhere, studies of building technology are based on the assumption that houses will last for sixty or a hundred years, while simultaneous development work on the design of houses is intended to cater more and more precisely for current living standards and cultural patterns. In these cases, the more *successful* each study is within its own terms of reference and the more widely its findings are accepted, the more rapidly will new houses become obsolete. Governments may find themselves perfecting the techniques for building flats for letting while encouraging the demand for altogether different types of housing; and the more precisely and economically a house suits one way of life the more intolerable it is liable to become when patterns of living change. Extensive studies of building materials and methods that remain unsupported by the development and educational work required to put their findings into practice have been another common cause of wasted effort and talent – not least in Britain.

The coordination and management of research programmes calls for a difficult blend of freedom and control. Some overall strategy there must be if government is to invest heavily in research. But if a question is worthy of scientific study, the outcome of research upon it and the time required for the job cannot be precisely foreseen; and research workers of real ability will expect some freedom in selecting the questions they study and must be given it if their talents are to be fully used. These problems are easier to solve if the findings of research are promptly published and publicly discussed. Research workers can then more readily appreciate the needs of policy makers and

:he priorities these dictate, and can go far to plan and coordinate
:heir own efforts.

But the contribution made by research to this as to other
fields of social policy depends much less than might be supposed
on the technical quality of the research itself. It depends
primarily on the scope and character of the questions that
government and the public at large are prepared to ask, and on
whether anyone is 'listening' when the findings of research are
presented. Major advances in the scope and instruments of
government inquiry have always sprung from government's
assumption of new and greater responsibilities. The widespread
use of Royal Commissions after 1832, the creation of the Medical
Research Council and the Department of Scientific and Industrial Research during the First World War, and the creation of
the Social Survey, the Central Statistical Office and the Economic Section of the Cabinet Office during the Second World
War all illustrate the pattern. The neglect of the Haldane
Committee's ambitious recommendations for intelligence and
information services after the First World War and the
withering of economic and social research after 1951 illustrate
the converse effects that follow when government attempts to
disengage from its responsibilities. Research in housing has
been subject to the same influences – as can be seen in the few
studies made of rent restriction for example. Most countries in
western Europe have removed rent controls in various selective
ways during the past decade, but few seized this remarkable
opportunity for controlled experiment to study the effects of
decontrol; and on the rare occasions when these effects were
studied, politicians and administrators generally preserved
their beliefs about these matters unscathed by the findings of
research – unless political scandals and a more general mobilization of public concern compelled a reappraisal of the situation.

This is not to say that the quality of academic research is
irrelevant to government. Far from it: the advances made during
the great periods of public inquiry were rendered possible by
earlier academic work, such as the studies the Utilitarians made
before 1832, the poverty surveys made at the turn of the
century and between the World Wars, and the inter-war development of Keynesian economics and sampling methods. But the

scholar must be prepared to wait for a favourable political tide – or help to create one – if he wants his research to have an impact on the world at large.

Finally, it would be wrong to complete a discussion of research upon housing in Britain without a reminder that we already know enough to do a great deal more than has yet been attempted without waiting for further investigation.

CHAPTER 12

CONCLUSION

THE study of housing problems and housing policies presented
in this book has prompted a widely ranging discussion, touching
on many aspects of economic development and social change,
the response made by government to these processes and its
responsibility for them. Discussion of any other branch of social
policy would have revealed a similar cross-section of the nation's
affairs. This chapter neither summarizes the previous eleven
nor prescribes a housing programme for the future. To conclude
this case study of the functions of government, it seemed more
appropriate to make a general comment on the scope and
character of the housing responsibilities now assumed by
British governments and the directions in which these responsibilities are likely to evolve.

BRITAIN'S POSITION

Although the severity of hardship in the housing field varies
from one country to another, the more obvious symptoms of
trouble take broadly similar forms the world over. But the
nature of a country's housing problems and its opportunities for
resolving them depend on the stage of economic, social and
political development attained.

Britain's position is a distinctive one. This is a relatively
wealthy country; its most hectic phases of industrial and urban
growth are over, population is increasing at a modest rate, and
migration across frontiers produces a slow net outflow of people;
it builds houses more cheaply than its neighbours, it has a
long-established pattern of mortgage lending and municipal
building which together provide a restricted but reliable flow of
capital for investment in housing; and it has a stable and
relatively well-staffed system of central and local government.
In comparison with other European countries, these advantages provide reasonably spacious and comfortable housing

conditions, and the opportunity of making good progress in future.

But Britain's economy is exceptionally 'low geared'. It runs with low rates of saving and investment, at a generally sluggish pace of growth and change. The stock of houses is therefore relatively old and has been growing more slowly than our neighbours'. The replacement and modernization of these houses will not be brought about as a by-product of migration and urban growth as happens in some countries; most of it must take place in cities where people will continue to live, and it will prove an expensive and laborious process that can only be carried through effectively at the instigation of government. Private investment in housing proceeds on a sufficient scale to eliminate the more critical shortages and contain the more compelling political pressures, but it cannot meet the most urgent needs. Although the revenues of government are relatively large, they are heavily committed to obligations inherited from the past which restrict the government's capacity for investment and its room for manoeuvre. Thus the improvement of housing standards and the elimination of the worst conditions depend upon the capacity of government to devise ways of helping those in greatest need and to carry through large rebuilding schemes. Elsewhere, many governments were confronted with more urgent problems after the Second World War and had to rely more heavily on their own efforts for achieving solutions; here, the government has only recently accepted the massive responsibilities that a major attack upon the country's housing problems will lay upon it, and the full implications of these responsibilities have yet to be worked out.

HOW BIG A PROGRAMME?

If Britain's opportunities for progress in the housing field depend so heavily on the intentions and capacity of government, the scale and scope of the government's objectives should be examined before turning to the resources required to attain them. We are dealing, first and foremost, with a political problem.

Can the research worker furnish any guidance about the rate

of progress to be aimed at in this field? He can point out that by comparison with other countries in north western Europe, the British have rather poorer opportunities of establishing and maintaining separate households and achieving the independence and privacy to be secured in this way.* He can point out that houses in this country are older, and the stock of new dwellings is growing more slowly.† Although official slum clearance schemes are proceeding on a relatively impressive scale (until recently, little attention had been given to this problem elsewhere) the proportion of houses replaced in Britain each year may actually be lower than in other countries where conversions, private redevelopment and 'spontaneous losses' of various kinds exercise a greater though more indiscriminate influence.‡ The size and quality of the houses built in this country has risen and fallen through successive cycles, each peak attaining higher standards than its predecessors. After fifteen years of decline and stagnation, Britain now appears to be embarking on a renewed ascent that may keep pace with the rising standards achieved in other countries.§

This much has been made clear in previous chapters. But international comparisons, revealing though they may be, do not furnish a prescription of the priorities appropriate to any one country. What proportion of a rising national income do the British *want* to devote to their housing, and what proportions would they prefer to spend on other things? International comparisons, and national studies based on long-term income trends, suggest that countries which are getting richer generally devote larger proportions of personal incomes to housing costs. But although these relationships can be measured in economic terms they cannot be so simply explained. Housing forms so central a feature of people's aspirations, living standards and cultural patterns that the demand for it is a product of the whole process of economic and social development, and most of the causal relationships involved operate in more than one direction: wealthier people want better housing, and better housed people want to get wealthier; people want better housing when they get married and have children, and better housing encourages

*See pages 153–5. † See pages 54 and 156.
‡ See pages 36–7. § See page 252.

them to do both. The effective demand for housing depends not only on the incomes of the households concerned but also on their geographical and social mobility. The more educated people are, the more mobile they become, in both the geographical and the social sense. People who move from one part of the country to another, and people who readily adopt the aspirations of those more fortunate than themselves, are likely to split up into smaller and more numerous households and seek better housing. General advances in housing standards can only be achieved in a climate of social progress, but they can also contribute to the creation of such a climate. In future, the population movements provoked by large-scale slum clearance programmes may have effects similar to those arising from longer-range migrations, encouraging households to subdivide and seek better and more numerous dwellings.

The principal decisions about the scale and character of housing programmes must therefore depend on the pace and pattern of economic and social development which the country is capable of achieving. It is possible to show, in a general fashion, how housing problems are related to their economic and social context. It can be argued, in Britain, that progress in housing conditions has failed to keep pace with advances made in other sectors of the economy, or with the achievements of comparable countries. It can also be shown that the distribution of the housing available does not accord with any publicly defensible views about social justice and human rights. But to go further and prescribe the building programme 'appropriate' for this country would be to assume the politicians' responsibility.

TOWARDS A COMPREHENSIVE COMMITMENT

The government has now committed itself to a number of objectives in this field, among which the principal aim is a continuing increase in the rate of building, designed to produce 500,000 houses a year by 1969 and more thereafter. Given a firm and credible commitment of that kind, and sufficient building labour, the construction industry should be capable of achieving this output; faster rates of expansion have been achieved in recent years. But, as previous chapters in this book have argued, a continuing programme of this size would impose such severe strains on other branches of the economy and on government itself that it is unlikely to be achieved without major changes and bold improvizations in a number of quarters – 'structural' changes rather than a continuous series of marginal adjustments. 'The Housing Programme, 1965–70', is not, strictly speaking, a 'programme' at all; that would require an analysis of the demands to be met, a projection of investment flows, plans for the regional deployment of building resources, and much else besides. It is an outline of national building targets and a check list of the problems to be confronted on the route leading to them.

There is nothing surprising or abnormal about this state of affairs. Since the war, many countries in Europe have been compelled by threatened disaster and political pressures to bring about structural changes in their economic and administrative systems for the purpose of realizing more ambitious housing programmes. When a government adopts a new and sufficiently ambitious programme a succession of bottle necks and 'crises' can be expected to follow, and if these problems are tackled with sufficient determination and the continued support of the electorate the government will eventually emerge with a much more extensive and pervasive set of housing responsibilities. It will have adopted what was described in an earlier chapter as a 'comprehensive' system of housing policies.* Many of the difficulties to be expected on this route, and some of the developments in policy which they are likely to provoke, have been discussed in this book.

The character of the main requirements to be met will change from year to year. As the generation of babies born immediately after the war moves into the household-forming age groups during the next few years there will be growing demands for family housing. In England and Wales, reports Professor Parry Lewis, 'Marriages are likely to rise until 1968, in which year there will be about 35,000 more marriages than in 1964. The annual figure will then level out for a few years, before slowly dropping to reach a figure in 1975 equal to the estimate for 1965

*See pages 97–106.

of 369,000. Thereafter another boom begins. . . .' But 'between 1969 and 1976, when marriages will be constant or declining, the annual increases in the numbers of people in the age-group seventy to seventy-four will be at their peak', falling off again thereafter.* The replacement of obsolete houses on the enormous scale shown to be necessary if an output of 500,000 houses a year is to be sustained† could not be achieved until the 1970s. Until then, priority must be given to the newly-wed and to the 'backlog' of needs among people who are sharing other people's housing or overcrowded in their present homes. Later, priority must go to the replacement programme and to housing for the aged – needs which overlap to a considerable extent, since many old people live in houses due for replacement. It will be easier to sustain the momentum of the programme if these requirements are met in the right order, for there will be growing numbers of empty houses, and hence less resistance to demolitions, at the point when the rate of clearance has to be greatly increased. But from time to time there will have to be major redeployments of the building industry and the administrative and technical professions associated with it, for the slums to be cleared and the new young families to be housed are not concentrated in the same places. Meanwhile more homes will have to be provided for new kinds of households seldom deliberately catered for hitherto – particularly among young people and among the single of all ages. More ambitious programmes of modernization will also be required, as it is realized that the provision of a bath, a hand-basin and other 'standard improvements' will not long be sufficient to satisfy people's aspirations.

A government that sets its hand to implementing a programme of this kind will soon find that present channels for investment in housing, whether through building societies or local authorities, will have to be modified if they are to meet all these requirements. Surveys made by official and private investigators already show that the majority of those who want to move house wish to rent rather than buy. A good deal can be done, through amendment or extension of the present system of tax reliefs, to bring house purchase within the reach of lower

* From Chapter IV of a Report to the Civic Trust, 1965.
† See pages 247–50.

income groups. But many of the groups to be catered for –
including old people, single people, the young and footloose –
will never be found amongst the building societies' customers,
and many of them cannot be adequately housed in the types of
building the societies are accustomed to finance. Either the local
housing authorities will have to cater for many people whose
existence they scarcely recognize at the moment, or private
investment in rented housing will have to be revived, or other
bodies such as housing associations will have to be created and
expanded to meet these needs. None of these developments will
occur without determined leadership from government.

While the more ambitious programme now envisaged can be
based on the assumption that a wealthier society will be capable
of devoting a rather larger share of its income to housing, this
change will not come about unless deliberate steps are taken
to achieve it. It has already been shown* that government makes
major, though ill-assorted and contradictory, redistributions
of the costs of housing. More systematic and comprehensive
procedures will have to be devised to encourage saving for
house purchase and to increase the contribution to housing
costs made by those who can best afford it, laying the burden of
repayment upon households at a point in their development when
they are best able to bear it. The complex legacy of rent controls
and tax reliefs is peculiarly ill-suited to this purpose. The
government will likewise find itself compelled to exert greater
control over the flow of capital for house purchase. The increase
in building society funds over recent years has been allowed to
outpace the supply of new housing and inflate house prices:
since the Minister has recently promised the building societies a
secure and predictable share of the growing building programme, the government must in return secure closer control
over the flow of funds available to them – just as it already does
for the clearing banks and other lending institutions.

The points touched on so far deal mainly with the demand for
housing. They merit first attention because builders cannot be
expected to invest in the productive resources required to
achieve a much larger supply while any doubt remains about
the effective demand for their output. But it has been shown

*See page 258.

that builders are likely to face growing scarcities of labour during the next few years, even without the increase in demands on the construction industry to be expected for roads, schools, hospitals and industrial purposes.* The experience of other countries shows that government is likely to be drawn into deeper involvement on this front too, promoting new building methods, mobilizing productive resources not hitherto available for this industry, and matching supply and demand at local and regional as well as national levels.

But the greatest scarcities of productive resources are likely to be found among the professions responsible for planning and implementing building and redevelopment schemes – particularly among town planners, surveyors, architects, public health inspectors, and administrative staff at all levels of government. Already the unexpectedly rapid pace of economic and demographic development threatens to overwhelm the machinery for town and country planning. There will have to be greatly increased investment in the training of several of the professions involved and a thorough-going reorganization of the administrative machine they operate if the planning and implementation of the programme is to keep pace with the rate of building required. These developments are unlikely to leave the structure of local government intact. The experience of other countries suggests that administrative units dealing with 'city regions', or other areas intermediate in scale between municipal authorities and the larger economic regions, may have to assume many of the planning and administrative responsibilities now exercised at national or local levels of government.

A government that assumes increasing responsibilities for determining the size and distribution of new investment in housing and for regulating the flow of capital required for it will be led to exercise increasing control over the character and quality of new building. Recent ministerial statements, calling for the implementation of Parker Morris standards in new building and for guarantees of workmanship to which the buyers of new houses should be entitled, show that attention is already turning in this direction. These interventions deal with minimum standards, but many countries have also imposed

*See pages 300–301.

maximum standards, at least upon building to which government contributes any subsidy. Such controls have not been applied in this country since building licences for housing were abolished in 1954. They may never be reintroduced; but in that case there may be greater pressure for an upper limit to the tax reliefs available to purchasers of the most expensive houses.

Meanwhile, if government endeavours to match housing more closely to the needs of the household and brings about a re-distribution of incomes designed for this purpose, through housing allowances, tax reliefs or other means, it must also exercise some control over rents in areas of continuing shortage and ensure that tenants retain adequate security of tenure. The experience of other countries shows that legal regulation of the rights of private landlords and tenants tends to advance in step with the financial assistance given to either of them.

ALTERNATIVE ROUTES FORWARD

The foregoing paragraphs do not exhaust the list of responsibilities to which government is likely to be committed by a more ambitious housing programme, nor do they fully explain those mentioned. At this stage it is more important to identify the main problems on the agenda. Moreover the pattern of policies cannot be foreseen in detail, for the functions assumed by government and the manner in which they are interpreted must depend partly on the needs and pressures of the moment and on the political complexion of the party in power. The government will always retain considerable scope for choosing its priorities and the instruments for realizing them.

House purchase can be brought within the reach of many of the people to be housed, and this form of ownership is likely to be favoured by all parties. But although the local housing authorities must be responsible for housing many of the remainder, there will be a considerable number of intervening groups whose needs could be equally well met by councils, private landlords or housing associations.

Outside the worst slum areas, the greatly enlarged replacement programme implied by the latest targets would soon bite into property that is not technically 'unfit'. Much of this property is owner-occupied, and those living in it may be harder to dispossess than landlords and harder to rehouse than tenants. The comparative costs of modernizing and replacing such property are now being studied by the Ministry and they are not easily assessed; the political problems are even harder to weigh up. Thus there can be no hard and fast long-range programme in this field either: a considerable part of the replacement programme may have to be commuted to an improvement programme – possibly a compulsory one – and local authorities may have to be given a choice of weapons in their attack on obsolescence (just as they have been given a choice of routes towards comprehensive secondary education).

The redistribution of household incomes required to sustain the demand for a larger building programme and to ensure that it meets the most urgent needs can likewise be brought about in different ways. This country's original policy was to employ the authority that built and owned the houses – the municipal councils – as the principal instrument for this redistribution. But that arrangement is now increasingly criticized, principally because it tends to tie subsidies to houses rather than awarding them to the households thought to need them most, and also because the resources of different authorities are not well matched to their needs. Meanwhile it has been recognized that another redistribution, equally large in scale but contradictory in effect, has emerged in the tax reliefs available to house buyers. Fiscal procedures could in future be employed in a more deliberate fashion. Other instruments for redistributing incomes could be found in the social insurance and national assistance systems – the latter already making a major contribution to housing costs – or in the rating system which is beginning to take some account of the incomes and family responsibilities of ratepayers.

There are several advantages in any system that depends on public ownership of housing. If inflation continues, this arrangement enables the community to acquire the capital gains made on property built in earlier years and redistribute their benefits, restricting increases in the rents of newer houses by charging higher rents for older ones. The mobility of households in council housing is reasonably high – higher than amongst owner-occupiers, but more localized. The authorities with a sufficiently large stock of housing thus achieve a more 'efficient' distribution of living space than other forms of owner, minimizing overcrowding and under-occupation alike. To these means of redistribution, 'internal' to the council sector of the market, the public authority may add another advantage of a different kind. There are signs that private developers and lenders generally operate safely behind the demand for housing: several surveys suggest that people moving to new housing would be willing to pay more than the price actually charged for it, as would others who fail to secure such housing.* The public investor may therefore be less inhibited by anxieties about risk and the local housing authority may be a more willing and continuous builder, particularly if an enlarged programme increases the number of empty houses and frightens off the private builder and lender. But the councils only house a quarter of the country's households, and unless there is a wholesale municipalization of existing property their share of the market cannot be rapidly expanded. Their influence will therefore remain a restricted one.

Taxation and tax relief, whether operated by the Inland Revenue or the rating authorities, have the great advantage that they can make an impact on a much larger proportion of the population; indeed, they can be applied to all households whenever the authorities concerned choose to bring everyone into their net. This broader coverage gives the tax collector an opportunity of devising a comprehensive system of housing allowances that would apply to many who cannot secure any advantages from the privileges now available to owner-occupiers and council tenants. If they were coupled with a reform of the existing tax reliefs, these allowances could gradually eliminate the illogically generous benefits now given to richer house buyers – benefits which are partly swallowed up in the general inflation of house prices to which they contribute.

But the extent to which either of these general forms of tax-based redistribution would be required depends on the scale of the redistributions brought about through the social security system (including social insurance, assistance, family allowances

*See page 203.

and war pensions). A system that *completely* matched incomes to 'needs' could in principle eliminate all forms of subsidy and free service, provided the citizen, the authorities responsible for social security, and the authorities responsible for housing, health, education and other services all adopted similar priorities. Any system that goes some way towards that goal should reduce the housing subsidies required. But in practice this effect depends heavily on the groups who gain most from the social security system. More generous national assistance (which includes an allowance for housing costs and is subject to a means test) and more generous family allowances (which, being taxable, are subject to a mild form of means test, and go to households needing the largest houses) could both reduce housing subsidies. But more generous pensions would make much less impact on the need for housing subsidies because they would go to people whose housing needs are relatively modest and whose housing costs tend to be low. Moreover there are still so few good houses of a kind designed for old people that larger pensions could not, in the near future, bring about a major improvement in housing standards: by the 1980s things may be different, but for the next decade most of the pensioners' extra money would have to be spent on other things.

Thus an incomes policy which is designed mainly to benefit larger families and the poorest households will for the next few years reduce the income redistributions that would otherwise be required for housing purposes. But an incomes policy that excludes means tests and is designed mainly to redistribute income in favour of the retired at the expense of the working population will be of less help in resolving housing problems. If carried far enough it could actually frustrate progress in the housing field by pre-empting a large share of the resources that would otherwise be available for various forms of family or housing allowance, though it might have many other advantages unconnected with housing. Later on, if a major improvement is achieved in the housing conditions of the elderly and their housing costs rise correspondingly, the conflict between these objectives will become much less acute. (The Swedes have achieved a convenient compromise by demanding contributions for their pension scheme that will greatly exceed benefits for many years to come and investing much of the accumulating pension fund in housing, and by building more housing of the kind that suits their increasingly affluent pensioners.)

A major advance in housing standards can now be made if governments, regardless of party colouring are determined to achieve the general objectives of the new housing programme and do not abandon this resolve when confronted with balance of payments crises, bottlenecks of various kinds and other urgent claims upon their resources. There will still be plenty of scope for choice in their housing policies. It may be, for example, that the Labour Party will favour direct provision through council building and the municipalization and clearance of private rented property, while Conservatives lay greater stress on selective redistributions of income, on investment in rented housing by private landlords or housing associations, and on the improvement – rather than the replacement – of older property. Both are likely to encourage the spread of owner occupation which will soon provide for an unassailable majority of the electorate. Both may find the rating system an increasingly useful instrument for redistributing incomes in ways that help to attain housing objectives: it is in fact an exceedingly clumsy and unreliable instrument for the purpose, but it does bear directly on housing and happens to fall within the field of the Minister of Housing and Local Government.

CONCLUDING:

To those who hoped for a more rational route to Utopia this may seem a disappointingly shambling progress. Some have already criticized the government's latest proposals for offering no more than a destination, a list of problems to be encountered on the way and a few steps in the right direction. But if this chapter furnishes no other conclusion it should show how complex the task of planning will always be in such a field. The planner must take account of so many developments in neighbouring sectors of the economy that cannot be forecast with confidence; the level of defence expenditure, the demands to be made on the construction industry from all quarters, the policies to be adopted for pensions and family allowances, the outcome of the next election – these are only a few of the more obviously important and unpredictable factors confronting those responsible for housing policies.

The temptation in such a situation – a temptation to which British governments have often succumbed – is to improvise policies that make the best use of existing resources in the short run and leave the long run to take care of itself. By committing itself to a somewhat longer-term target of appreciably more ambitious dimensions than its predecessors' the present government has not produced a plan. But if these commitments are taken seriously they will concentrate the minds of many people in central and local government, the building industry and elsewhere, on the problems that must be resolved if there is ever to *be* a plan for housing.

The government has been criticized from the opposite quarter for announcing a programme that will strain the economy and the administrative system and demand structural changes in many fields. But while a more gradual and carefully balanced rate of growth might have been preferable from some points of view, the experience of other countries suggests that a government intent on achieving an appreciable improvement in housing conditions can seldom mobilize the material, technical and administrative resources required for this unless it raises its sights sufficiently sharply to compel a reappraisal of many accepted practices and assumptions. 'Planning' only begins when people are committed to objectives that *cannot* be attained under existing arrangements. Moreover a democratic government that seeks to narrow the gap dividing the best and the worst housed must get a great many houses built; since it cannot deprive the better housed of their homes, it must concentrate on rehousing those in the worst homes while producing sufficient to give more fortunate people some scope for advance too.

But the challenge of barely feasible objectives is no more than a beginning. As the predictable strains and the unforeseen accidents that ensue make their recurring impact, those reponsible for formulating and implementing the new policies must try to ensure that the true character of their enterprise is widely understood and accepted; otherwise its essentials will be lost in the compromises and adjustments that must be made from time to time. The evolution of this enterprise can be traced in many parts of Europe. Starting after the war with the intention of providing a 'separate home' for every 'family', governments have gradually extended the meaning of both these terms: it is no longer a separate home but good housing that they are committed to providing; and it is no longer the family that is entitled to this but every household that wants to set up on its own. Their increasingly ambitious and comprehensive objectives have compelled them to meet a growing variety of needs, ranging through all age groups and including all types of household, from large families to the growing numbers of people who live alone. They have gradually abandoned the narrower objectives of a 'social' housing policy, aimed like the poor law at restricted groups suffering particular hardships. Eventually the Ministers responsible for housing find they have embarked on a journey begun a generation earlier (though not yet completed) by those responsible for education, for medical care, and for the maintenance of full employment. This does not mean that housing must be indiscriminately subsidized; in the countries which have progressed furthest on this journey people generally pay handsomely for the privilege, government itself owns a smaller proportion of their houses than it does in Britain, and private enterprise has a major part to play.

It means that homeless families, overcrowding and the more squalid housing conditions have become as intolerable as untreated illness, hunger and lasting unemployment.

FURTHER READING

Books, papers and shorter articles have been quoted throughout this study. This note does not repeat all those references or catalogue the more extensive literature from which they were selected. It briefly describes a few books and periodicals that will help the reader to take his exploration of housing questions a stage farther. All the books mentioned are comprehensible to the layman, all were still in print at the time of writing, and all are good of their kind. They should be found in public libraries and in the libraries provided by good local authorities for their members and officials.

In *English Housing Trends* (Occasional Papers on Social Administration, No. 13, Bell & Sons, 1965, 10s. 6d.) J. B. Cullingworth describes housing conditions in England and the main changes taking place in this country. His book, *Housing and Local Government in England and Wales* (Allen & Unwin, 1966, 36s.), explains the recent development of housing policy and the work of the local housing authorities. Lionel Needleman's *The Economics of Housing* (Staples Press, 1965, 42s.) offers a descriptive economic analysis of many aspects of our housing situation, without advocating particular policies for the future. A shorter and more polemical discussion of this country's problems and policies can be found in Stanley Alderson's *Housing* (Penguin Special, 1962, 3s. 6d.). The plight of those in the worst housing and the attempts made by government to help them are critically examined, with comparisons between British and American experience, in Alvin L. Schorr's *Slums and Social Insecurity* (Nelson, 1964, 30s.).

Housing finance is examined by A. J. Merrett and Allen Sykes in *Housing Finance and Development* (Longmans, 1965, 15s.) which endeavours to show how the price of good housing may be brought within the reach of a larger proportion of people in this country. The same problems are placed in a broader historical context by Adela A. Nevitt in *Housing, Taxation and Subsidies* (Nelson, 1966, 35s.) which traces the impact made on investment in housing by our systems of taxation and subsidies and by the institutions of the market, and proposes new policies for the future.

The town planning system is well described and briefly discussed by J. B. Cullingworth in *Town and Country Planning in England and Wales* (Allen & Unwin, 1964, 36s.). The evolution of town planning ideas in this and other industrial countries is explained by John Tetlow and Anthony Goss in *Homes, Towns and Traffic* (Faber, 1965, 45s.) with the aid of plans, models and photographs. Peter Hall, in *The World Cities* (Weidenfeld & Nicolson, World University Library, 1966, 14s.), compares seven of the great city regions of the world and the policies for their development adopted by governments. His book has excellent maps. The citizen who wants to know and use his rights in town planning matters can find these briefly explained in *Town Planning: The Consumers' Environment*, a pamphlet prepared by David Woolley and John Bolt for the Research Institute for Consumer Affairs, (1965, 4s. 6d.).

Marian Bowley traces the history of the British building industry and discusses its failings and future prospects in *The British Building Industry* (Cambridge University Press, 1966, 70s.).

The United Nations has made a report on the housing problems and policies of European countries, supported with many descriptive statistics, in *Major Long Term Problems of Government Housing and Related Policies* (United Nations, New York, 1966, $2.95, obtainable through H.M. Stationery Office). A more critical, practical and forthright discussion of town planning, building and housing policies in the poorer but most rapidly developing parts of the world can be found in Charles Abrams's *Housing in the Modern World* (Faber, 1966, 42s.).

Those interested in the development of particular regions of this country should read the Regional Studies prepared by the Ministry of Housing and Local Government and published by the Stationery Office (*The South East Study*, 1964, 15s.; *The North West*, 1965, 18s.; *The West Midlands*, 1965, 12s. 6d.) which deal briefly with housing in the course of analysing the economic, demographic and urban development to be expected in each of these regions. Some more local studies of housing are available, of which J. B. Cullingworth's *Housing in Transition* (Heinemann, 1963, 42s.) dealing with the town of Lancaster, and the Milner Holland Report (*Report of the Committee on Housing in Greater London*, Cmd 2605, 1965, 22s. 6d.) are two of the best.

Any discussion of housing soon calls for some consideration of local government, its strengths, weaknesses and future development. There are many books on this subject; W. A. Robson's *Local Government in Crisis* (Allen & Unwin, 1966) presents a vivid analysis of current problems. J. A. G. Griffith's massive study of *Central Departments and Local Authorities* (University of Toronto Press for the Royal Institute of Public Administration, and Allen

& Unwin, 1966, 60s.) gives a revealing account of the relationships between central and local government. Both books will make an important contribution to the reforms now being considered in this field.

Housing problems and policies have so many ramifications that no single journal could adequately cover the subject. Useful articles can be found in a wide variety of journals, but the following are among the best sources: *Urban Studies* (published three times a year by Oliver & Boyd for the Department of Social and Economic Research of the University of Glasgow at 30s. a year), *The Housing Review* (published six times a year by the Housing Centre Trust, membership 60s.), *Town and Country Planning* (published monthly at 32s. 6d. a year), *The Architectural Review* (published monthly at 63s. a year), and *New Society* (published weekly at 1s. 6d. a copy). The United Nations publishes useful comparative statistics and occasional reports on specific issues which deserve to be more widely known: *The Annual Bulletin of Housing and Building Statistics* provides information year by year for European countries and the United States of America. The Ministry of Housing and Local Government publishes a quarterly, *Housing Statistics*, which provides some figures for Scotland and N. Ireland besides much information about England and Wales.

INDEX

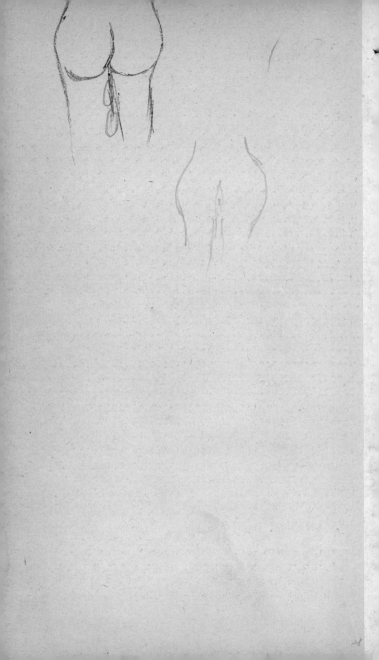